Connecting ICTs to D

Connecting ICTs to Development

The IDRC Experience

Edited by
Laurent Elder, Heloise Emdon,
Richard Fuchs and Ben Petrazzini

ANTHEM PRESS
LONDON · NEW YORK · DELHI

International Development Research Centre
Ottawa • Cairo • Montevideo • Nairobi • New Delhi

Anthem Press
An imprint of Wimbledon Publishing Company
www.anthempress.com

This edition first published in UK and USA 2014
by ANTHEM PRESS
75–76 Blackfriars Road, London SE1 8HA, UK
or PO Box 9779, London SW19 7ZG, UK
and
244 Madison Ave #116, New York, NY 10016, USA

A copublication with
International Development Research Centre
PO Box 8500
Ottawa, ON K1G 3H9
Canada
www.idrc.ca / info@idrc.ca
ISBN: 978 1 55250 563 4 (IDRC ebook)

First published in hardback by Anthem Press in 2013

© 2014 International Development Research Centre

British Library Cataloguing-in-Publication Data
A catalogue record for this book is available from the British Library.

Library of Congress Cataloging-in-Publication Data
The Library of Congress has catalogued the hardcover edition as follows:
Connecting ICTs to development : the IDRC experience / edited by Laurent Elder, Heloise
Emdon, Richard Fuchs and Ben Petrazzini.
pages cm
Includes bibliographical references and index.
ISBN 978-0-85728-124-1 (hardback : alk. paper)
1. Information technology–Economic aspects. 2. Economic development. 3. Economic
development–Developing countries. 4. International Development Research Centre (Canada)
I. Elder, Laurent.
HC79.I55C6698 2013
338.9–dc23
2013041530

ISBN-13: 978 1 78308 253 7 (Pbk)
ISBN-10: 1 78308 253 4 (Pbk)

Cover image © 2013 Raimundas/Shutterstock

This title is also available as an ebook.

CONTENTS

ACKNOWLEDGMENTS

This book, at times, seemed like a Herculean task. The incredible number of documents to sift through, authors and researchers to work with and myriad editorial opinions to mediate helps explain how the book – assumed to be a fairly quick and straightforward activity – became a complex two-year endeavor. Sifting through 15 years of documentation required a squad of young researchers, who trawled outputs, wrote précis of projects, compiled and analyzed data and assisted the editors and authors meet deadlines for "writeshops" and "editshops" that crystalized the chapters.

The result, however, is a much better piece of work than had originally been envisaged. For that we have to thank all those involved in the research for and writing of this book. The researchers, authors and editors played an obvious and essential role and are acknowledged accordingly; however, many others helped the book come to fruition. First and foremost, Silvia Caicedo ensured we were all rowing in the same direction and helped to deal with all the finicky details so essential to see the final product come to life. Ramata Thioune, Adel El Zaïm, Edith Adera, Phet Sayo and Fernando Perini reviewed and improved various chapters. Jennifer Vincent helped with data collection. Marcia Chandra and Silvia Caicedo transformed the book's material into a beautiful and comprehensive web collection. We also have to thank our previous IDRC ICT4D director, Michael Clarke, and the current director of Science and Innovation, Naser Faruqui, for the original idea for the book and also for guiding us through bureaucratic snags. Finally, we would like to thank Abigail Mulhall of the British Department for International Development who reinforced the idea that all these important findings and lessons should be compiled in a monograph.

Many hours of devotion to reproduce the lessons and knowledge that evolved in our programming have gone into developing this book. We thank everyone for dedication and hard work, but most of all for their patience and generosity of sharing such hard-earned wisdom.

Introduction Part I

FROM HERESY TO ORTHODOXY: ICT4D AT IDRC[1]

Richard Fuchs

Histories are written about people and events that are in the past. This book is not a history. Rather, it is a documentary or ethnography of a particular time in the business of foreign aid and of the ascendant role of Canada's International Development Research Centre (IDRC) in that time and space.

With the introduction of the first desktop computers in the mid-1980s, the postindustrial world was just awakening to the power and wonder of digital technologies. At the onset, the idea that digital technologies had something to do with social and economic development was a heretical notion. And it arose in unlikely locations in postindustrial North America and Europe – in places that were being bypassed by the first great wave of digital tools. In rural areas of Scandinavia,[2] in the ghetto that was East Harlem, in the Australian outback and in rural outposts of Canada's poorest province, Newfoundland, the first attempts to "leapfrog" past an industrial revolution that had already left them as outsiders were beginning.

Ideas of how computers, email and networks might advance the interests of the marginalized and the poor in the developing world were also beginning to percolate. In Brazil, South Africa, the Philippines and other developing places, early pioneers and heretics were introducing the digital idea into more commonplace notions of how "development" might occur.

It was the pre-Internet, early digital age and the first desktop computers were finding their way into workplaces. The early versions of this bulky rectangular device were first mistaken for a fast electronic typewriter – a supercharged IBM Selectric! New job descriptions for "Word Processor Equipment Operators" hit the employment boards in great numbers. In metropolitan places, very few understood how the invention of the personal computer and the introduction of Microsoft's Disk Operating System (DOS) would change organizational and professional capacity.

Among development activists, email lists, bulletin board services (BBS), CommunityNets and telecenters were introduced to help advance the prospects of underdeveloped places. The World Wide Web was still to be imagined. Gopher, file transfer protocol (FTP), FidoNet and WordPerfect signified modernity.

The "Great Transformation" (Polyani 1944) from agricultural to industrial economies had taken almost a century. The postindustrial society – based on the rise of knowledge, services and communications (Bell 1973) – would change the world in little more than ten years. The idea that digital tools might have something to do with the business of development was no longer heretical; digital tools and the Internet came to have *everything* to do with both business and development. What began as a heresy morphed into orthodoxy in a little more than a decade.

The IDRC Idea

Since its inception in 1970, IDRC had always understood that information and networks were essential elements in what the organization did. Relying on "outside" experts and knowledge did little to change the dependence that was underdevelopment. So, the architects of IDRC designed it so local knowledge might get produced to influence progressive policy formation. It was far better to have local evidence, produced by local knowledge producers, informing public policy. But, for this to occur, there first had to be systems for information management, knowledge sharing and cataloging for the social and economic development that IDRC hoped to support. As the IDRC Act states:

> IDRC shall [...] establish, maintain and operate information and data centres and facilities for research and other activities. (Government of Canada 2013)

A detailed description of early highlights of IDRC programming in the "information sciences" exists in the recently completed history of the organization (Muirhead and Harpelle 2010) so no further accounting of the early days is needed here. There is, however, unrecorded lore within IDRC of a continuing competition of ideas between those advocating research support in the natural sciences and others favoring support for the social sciences. Within this almost dialectical process, the position of information and communications technologies (ICTs) waxed and waned.

Reorganizational "fog"

The recent history of IDRC refers to the "fog of reorganization" (Muirhead and Harpelle 2010, 238) during the period from the late 1980s to the mid-1990s. In 1988, the principal responsibility for the modest funding of ICT in Development projects was transferred from headquarters to the East African regional office. It resurfaced again in 1994 with a new corporate-wide initiative, Bellanet. Bellanet – the name derived from a meeting of donors in the Rockefeller Foundation's Italian meeting site of Bellagio – was established to use ICTs to help donors cooperate and coordinate their programming and project development more successfully.

Continuing through the "fog," IDRC adopted its first region-specific ICT program, Pan Asia Networking (PAN), as one of seven new Asian initiatives in 1994 (Muirhead and Harpelle 2010, 256). A similar, but much smaller ICT project for the Americas, Pan Americas, would follow in 1997. The background and history to Acacia, the much larger regional ICT project, is substantially recorded in IDRC history (Muirhead and Harpelle 2010, 299–304). When it was first approved, IDRC "bet the farm" on the new project. With 15 percent of the overall IDRC program budget, Acacia was a flagship undertaking in Sub-Saharan Africa and provided a clear indication of the organization's willingness to innovate ahead of the curve. It sought to empower African communities with the ability to apply ICTs to their own social and economic development. The principal problem Acacia sought to address was the increasing digital divide between the continent and the rest of the developed world. With knowledge as the key commodity of the twenty-first century, many feared Africa would be left out of the knowledge revolution much like it had been left out of the industrial one.

By 1999, to clear away some of the "fog," IDRC adopted a new organizational framework that included program area directors. These directors assumed responsibility for existing and new initiatives within three thematic groupings, one of which came to be called "Information and Communications Technologies for Development" (ICT4D). The existing disparate regional ICT projects – Pan Asia, Pan Americas and Acacia – were subsumed under this new management and thematic leadership in January 2001. The author served as the first director for ICT4D from 2001 to 2006.

A New ICT Convergence

IDRC's approach to ICTs in development was pioneering, even in the developed world. As the impact of the first introduction to the desktop computer in 1984, the widespread diffusion of email and the Internet in the late 1980s and the introduction of the World Wide Web in 1994 were absorbed, many other institutions came to adopt the heresy of ICTs in development. The international and Canadian context for this is an important counterpoint and context for what happened at IDRC during this period as the new ICT4D program area came to take root.

There had always been a competition of thought-leadership between the Europeans and the Americans on what this new Internet technology might portend. The European Commissioner for information and communications technologies at the time, Martin Bangermann (1994–99), emphasized the social implications of these technologies and what they might mean for a new information society. Accordingly, European Commission programming in this area came to be called the "Information Society."

Not so in America. Al Gore (United States vice president from 1992–2000) became the American thought-leader and chief spokesperson about the information superhighway well before his Nobel Prize–winning campaign about climate change. The information superhighway – distinct from Europe's information society – was about private sector investment supplemented by smart public investment to improve productivity and build an information economy. Speaking at the Plenipotentiary Conference of the International Telecommunication Union in Buenos Aires, Argentina in 1994, Al Gore offered these comments:

> These highways – or, more accurately, networks of distributed intelligence – will allow us to share information, to connect, and to communicate as a global community.

From these connections, we will derive robust and sustainable economic progress, strong democracies, better solutions to global and local environmental challenges, improved health care, and – ultimately – a greater sense of shared stewardship of our small planet.

Among the G7 countries, Canada was no laggard in articulating its mission and mandate in the Internet Age. A new government under Prime Minister Jean Chrétien (elected in 1993) had a vision for Canada in this new world. Despite considerable budget constraints at the time, Canada's Connecting Canadians program began in 1994 and ran for almost a decade. It included accelerated access to the Internet for schools (SchoolNet), as well as for communities through community access and smart communities programs.

The Canadian government's minister for Industry Canada, not unlike his European and American counterparts, became the principal vision-and-thought-leader in the country for this. Industry Canada would launch its small-business-friendly website, Strategis, and, for several uninterrupted years, would win the top honors in global rankings for leadership in e-government. Having appointed a blue-ribbon information highway advisory panel that released its report in 1996, the government would pursue national initiatives to promote the diffusion of the technology in the hard-to-reach school, rural community and small business sectors well ahead of the market's reach to these slower-adopting markets:

> The now-defunct "Connecting Canadians" initiative supported programs to connect schools, voluntary organizations, and communities to each other and to the Internet. […] In 2001, the National Broadband Task Force recommended that high-speed Internet connectivity be made available to all Canadians by 2004 […] and programs were established to encourage the development of broadband infrastructure in underserved areas. (Middleton and Sorensen 2005, 463–83)

The rollout of computers, email and especially the Internet was fertile ground for political hyperbole. Few people knew about it, although growing numbers were becoming interested. Similar to the early political support for space exploration in the 1960s, a politician who wanted to be seen as farsighted and visionary could speak with uncontested and high-minded rhetoric about what the computer and the Internet might mean. In no way was this limited to political discourse in the US, Europe and Canada.

This lesson was not lost on politicians and officials in other parts of the developed world. By the late 1990s, the implications of the Internet for governments, businesses and communities were being widely considered and discussed. At the G7 meetings in Okinawa, Japan in 2000, the most powerful governments representing the largest economies in the world issued the Okinawa Charter. Among its many high-minded pronouncements was the following respecting the developing world:

> IT (information technology) represents a tremendous opportunity for emerging and developing economies. Countries that succeed in harnessing its potential can look forward to leapfrogging conventional obstacles of infrastructural development, to meeting more effectively their vital development goals, such as poverty reduction,

health, sanitation, and education, and to benefitting from the rapid growth of global e-commerce. Some developing countries have already made significant progress in these areas. (Okinawa Charter on Global Information Society 2000)

It is entirely coincidental that IDRC's new ICT4D program area was adopted by the board of governors in October 1999 and the G7 leaders' Okinawa Charter was promulgated nine months later in July 2000. The new program area had an unusual "perfect storm" of policy convergence in which to build the next generation of IDRC's programming in this area.

"Dancing on Someone Else's Stage": A Decade of Celebrity

As the ICT4D "storm" was building, there were major events that raised the priority of this new issue in development discourse. IDRC was affected by all of these and participated in many of them. As the new director of the ICT4D program area – beginning my tenure in early 2001 – I would describe the organization's approach to these as "dancing on someone else's stage." As the celebrity of the ICT and development issue increased, IDRC's role would be raised as well through its participation in these events.

In the 2001–2006 period, the IDRC budget for the ICT4D program area rose from $7 million a year to $33 million. This included more than $80 million in new external funding from new partners such as Industry Canada, the Swiss Agency for International Development, the UK Department for International Development, the International Fund for Agricultural Development and the Community Affairs Division of the world's largest software company, Microsoft. Three new program lines – the Institute for Connectivity in the Americas, Connectivity Africa and Telecentre.org (a global support network for telecenters) – were established alongside the pre-existing, internally financed IDRC ICT4D programming.

In this same 2001–2006 period, ICTs and development ranked first as the most frequently referenced subject in IDRC's annual environmental scan of international media for four out of these five years. For the first time in the organization's history, ICT4D's annual budget rose to the same level as that of the other major thematic groupings. "Dancing on someone else's stage" had everything to do with this growth, as did both IDRC's long-standing role in the area and the programming that grew out of this expanding social investment.

There were many "stages" and they all had something to do with the growing recognition of IDRC's history of programming in this area. The principal events included the following:

G7 Ministerial Conference on the Global Information Society

Brussels, 25–26 February 1995

Held in the European Union's main meeting halls in Brussels, this event featured the coming together of the competing European and American views of what the

Internet and the digital revolution meant for both society and the economy. Al Gore gave the keynote address. The conference was not about "development" except for one element of the programming. The keynote speech for the event was given by the South African deputy prime minister at the time, Thabo Mbeki. In his address,[3] Mbeki invited participants to attend an Information Society and Development (ISAD) conference in South Africa the following year. A report of Mbeki's speech referenced the following:

> The guest speaker was Thabo Mbeki, Executive Deputy President and heir apparent to Nelson Mandela, President of South Africa. Mr. Mbeki summarized the perspective of the developing world and, in the process, "fired a broadside" at all the delegates. He reminded us all that there were more phone lines in Manhattan than in all of Sub-Saharan Africa, and that half of humanity had yet to make a phone call. He spoke of the colossal challenges facing the developing world in this information revolution. "There are huge gaps of infrastructure, applications, and human resources that must be filled if we are to begin to build a Global Information Society, which incorporates presently disadvantaged communities." Mr. Mbeki challenged the G7 to establish a constructive dialogue with the developing world, which would result in concrete projects and collaborations to build a truly global information society. (Mbeki 1995)

The Information Society and Development Conference

Midrand, South Africa, 13–15 May 1996

This conference provided a platform for the early pre-inaugural launch of the Acacia program at IDRC. Chaired by Nelson Mandela, this was the first high-profile conference focusing on the issue of ICTs and development in the developing world. K. Y. Amoako, then secretary-general of the United Nations Economic Commission for Africa, gave one of the keynote speeches. He launched the African Information Society Initiative (AISI) – in which several IDRC staff and consultants played a principal role – and made the following comments:

> The truth of the statement that Africa will be further marginalized if it does not join the information and communications revolution, and that it will have new opportunities if it does, hits home more and more each day. The world is marginalizing Africa: the Internet Society in its annual meeting in Montreal next month has only one small item on connectivity in Africa on its agenda of some 300 presentations; and Africa is marginalizing itself: not thinking and acting globally means retention of local and parochial views, many of which lead to the conflicts which scar the Africa region. Information and communications are the prerequisites of global awareness; their use can help us maximize meager resources more effectively. The information revolution can make us more efficient in meeting basic needs. Leaders of developing countries must take responsibility to ensure that their countries are not left out of the information revolution. (Amoako 1996)

Global Knowledge Partnership: Knowledge for Development in the Information Age

Toronto, Ontario, 22–25 June 1997

This was the first of three Global Knowledge Partnership (GKP) major conferences. The others were held in Kuala Lumpur in 2000 and 2007, but this first GKP event was arguably the most important of the three. IDRC's Acacia program had more to show than it had at the ISAD event held in 1996 in Midrand. The event included many international development celebrities, including James Wolfensohn (president of the World Bank), Yoweri Museveni (president of Uganda), Maurice Strong (special advisor to the UN secretary-general), John Manley (minister of Industry Canada) and Kofi Annan (secretary-general of the United Nations). Private sector participation was also impressive with Michael Dell (founder of Dell Computers) and Jean Monty (CEO of Nortel) participating as speakers at the event.

This first GKP conference was co-sponsored by IDRC, the Canadian International Development Agency (CIDA) and the World Bank's *info*Dev, but this partnership did not endure much beyond the conference. IDRC went about its business and CIDA's programming in ICTs focused around the theme of "Knowledge for Development." The World Bank's *info*Dev went through several leadership and strategic changes. The GKP saw itself as inheriting the mantle and building on the events that had preceded it in Brussels and Midrand:

> It builds on what began at the 1995 G7 Global Information Society meeting in Brussels, and continued last year at the more broadly based Information Society and Development (ISAD) conference in South Africa, a process of collecting such questions and observations in order to nurture and guide the knowledge revolution. The sponsors intend Global Knowledge 97 to be only part of a much larger global learning process, open to all, and based on real partnerships, trust and transparency. (GKP – A Storyline)

Three years later, the Okinawa Charter would announce the establishment of the Digital Opportunities Taskforce (the Dot Force). Each of the G7 countries would appoint three co-chairs from government and the private and not-for-profit (NPO) sectors. Maureen O'Neil, IDRC's president, would serve as one of the co-chairs along with Peter Harder (deputy minister, Industry Canada) and Charles Sirois (CEO, Telesystems). The Dot Force co-chairs and their "sherpas"[4] would meet several times over the next two years to prepare a report for the G8 meetings to be held in Kananaskis, Alberta in June 2002.

Thabo Mbeki – at that time, South Africa's prime minister – was invited by Jean Chrétien to participate as an observer at the Kananaskis G8 meetings in 2002. At the conference, the Canadian prime minister announced three new major ICT4D funding programs for Africa. One of these was Connectivity Africa and included $12 million in new funding to IDRC. Connectivity Africa was designed to promote research, development and innovation in the use of ICTs for progress in Africa, focusing on the areas of education, health and the economy.

The other important "networking" outcome of the Dot Force was with the Department for International Development (DFID) and its "sherpa," David Woolnough. Three years after the 2002 Kananaskis meetings, DFID agreed to invest $10 million in ICT4D at IDRC for its programming in Africa and Asia. "Dancing" at the Dot Force provide to be propitious indeed!

The World Summit on the Information Society (WSIS)

Geneva (2003) and Tunis (2005)

It was never really clear how the two World Summits on the Information Society came to be. The former Tunisian leader, Ben Ali, claimed to have proposed the idea originally.[5] Legend has it that there was an early morning vote at the International Telecommunication Union (ITU) Plenipotentiary Meetings in Minneapolis in 1998 where sleepy delegates voted to approve the idea. The dotcom boom was in full stride. The G7 Dot Force and Okinawa Charter were brewing and the ITU had announced its Multi-Purpose Community Telecentre campaign four years earlier. There were apparently proposals from both Geneva and Tunis, among many others, to host the event. Geneva is where the ITU resides, so it is easy to have a major event there. But the summit was to focus on the information society in the developing world. Geneva didn't really fit that bill.

Tunisia had applied to host the event and put forward an aggressive lobbying effort. Faced with a choice between efficiency and geographic balance, the UN chose both. A decision was taken to have two summits: in Geneva from 10–12 December 2003 and in Tunis two years later, 16–18 November 2005.

IDRC's ICT4D program area invested considerably in participating at the ICT Pavilion at both these events. More than seventy-five partners and "recipients" were assisted to attend each summit. While IDRC was not materially involved in any of the discussions and deliberations by the national delegations to the summit,[6] it played a major convening role at the pavilion. Many private, public and NGO organizations involved with ICTs and development all over the world were in attendance. In light of this, IDRC was asked to host the Canada booth at the second summit in Tunis. Accordingly, it provided booth space to other, much larger Canadian agencies who participated in the summit, including CIDA and Industry Canada. The IDRC booth was commonly understood to be among the busiest at both events, especially in Tunis.

The profile generated for IDRC at both events was considerable. For example, in Geneva, as the director of the ICT4D program area, I was asked to meet Pamela Passman, the vice president of corporate affairs at Microsoft. We had a 20-minute chat on the busy floor of the pavilion – interrupted several times, beneficially, by passing IDRC partners and recipients. A year earlier, in 2002, I had been involved with helping Microsoft develop its business plan for a proposed new initiative with the unwieldy name of "The Community Technology Learning Center Global Support Network" at meetings in the software giant's Paris headquarters.

Once again, "dancing" on the WSIS stage proved fortuitous. Two years later, in 2005, at the Tunis summit, Pamela Passman, Maureen O'Neil and Walter Fust (director general of the Swiss Agency for International Development) made a major announcement of a new $22 million initiative to help network and share learning among telecenters all over the world. The new program, called Telecentre.org, would be among the very few "multi-stakeholder partnerships" involving the private sector that had been advocated at both summits. It survives as a stand-alone, not-for-profit global foundation – the Telecentre.org Foundation – with its headquarters in Manila, the Philippines.

Just as important, the two summits represented the first times that the ICT4D program area's three major regional programs and partners appeared "on the same page." African, Asian and South American ICT4D partners and collaborators were interacting without any particular geographic boundary or delineation. This had a major effect in raising some of the issues to a global frame of reference. All regions had lessons to learn from one another in areas such as telecoms policy, ICTs in health and e-government. The ideas, strategic directions and programming requirements would find their way into all three sets of prospectuses that would be submitted and adopted by the IDRC board of governors the very next year, in March 2006.

> After 5 years of the Dot Force, UNICT Task Force and World Summits on the Information Society, the developing world seems to have gotten the point. In relatively rapid order, many developing countries have come to understand that information and communications technologies have something directly to do with the wealth of nations. (Fuchs 2005a, 3)

There were, of course, many other events, or "stages," where ICTs for development at IDRC were prominently profiled. For example, at the 2001 Summit of the Americas in Quebec City, the prime minister announced the establishment of an Institute for Connectivity in the Americas (valued at $20 million) at IDRC. IDRC's ICT4D programs also created their own "stages" to help network the researchers and activists who participated in its programming. Important among these were the Pan All Partners conference in Vientiane, Laos in June 2003 and the Acacia/Connectivity Africare launch conference, "Networking Africa's Future," in Kwa Maritane, Pilanesberg, South Africa in April of the same year.

These were important mid-term, mid-prospectus reality checks for how IDRC's ICT4D programming was going. In an area where rapid technological change affected the research questions, designs and priorities, they were fundamentally important mechanisms for assessing and retooling the strategic directions of ICT4D programming at IDRC.

Regional Roots

From its inception in 1994, the ICT4D programming at IDRC was based on a regional approach to research for development. The Pan Asia program had begun in 1994 and was followed by a much smaller Pan Americas and a much larger Acacia[7] program in Africa in 1997.

Decentralized and regional

While management responsibility for programming was centralized at headquarters, the original regional orientation of the ICT4D programming would be reinforced and strengthened. In the annual report to the board of governors, the strategic directions of the ICT4D program area were described as follows:

> IDRC's programs in this area include a recognition that special measures need to be taken to ensure developing world participation in the social, cultural and economic opportunities which these technologies portend. At the same time, a regional approach is used to ensure that the globalizing impacts of these technologies engender and build diversity, rather than fortify cultural and economic hegemony. (IDRC 2001, i)

The renewed regional approach was not just a matter of management convenience. It was understood to be an approach that built upon regional strengths, opportunities and challenges that were distinct in each of the three regions.

Africa was considered to be in a "pre-market" situation where there was very little penetration of ICTs and the Internet. This called for particular programming that continued to demonstrate the relevance of ICTs in social and economic development sectors. South Africa at the time was – and continues to be – a technology engine on the continent. Retaining a satellite office in that country was a key mechanism for linking research institutions involved with the sector there with those in the later-adopting regions of the continent.

The situation in the Americas was very different. South America had already gone through the demographic shift to become a predominantly urban place with more than 80 percent of its population living in cities. The Americas were understood to represent a "dual" e-market: ICT markets and Internet access were already available in most cities, yet the smaller populations in the rural areas made it uneconomic for the private sector to develop there. Programming in the Americas would seek to connect the rural with the urban ICT sectors while also supporting the demonstration effect of ICTs in the rural areas.

Lastly, Asia was considered to have a "split" e-market. Some of the world's most advanced technology engines existed in the region beside some of the latest adopting nations on the planet. Singapore, Japan and Korea were already ICT leaders while places like Laos, Vietnam, Indonesia and the Philippines were just beginning to adopt ICTs. The strategy in Asia would be to link advanced research institutions with those in the later-adopting countries, a strategy that has worked remarkably well and that continues to this day.

While the programming approach was customized to the particular circumstances in each region, there was a clear, overall common purpose for ICT4D programming:

> The information economy could conceivably bypass all but a slim segment of people in the developing world. We intend for our applied research and demonstration projects to help forestall this eventuality. (IDRC 2001, 2)

While there was a common vision and purpose to the programming, the regional orientation was seen as fundamental. ICTs were understood to have the potential to centralize and homogenize systems in government, health, education and other key development sectors. If local institutions were not given the time and space to develop their own approaches, skills and networks, they might easily be overwhelmed and forestalled by mature systems from the developed world.[8] So, while the new ICT4D programming had common themes, it was conscious of the need to avoid these hegemonic types of outcomes, as is referenced in the director's report to the board:

> Yet the world is an increasingly global place, a place where people, communities and institutions know about one another sooner, rather than later. We now live in a world where virtual networks often extend much further than interpersonal ones and where network interests have real meaning in social and economic life. As information and communications technologies accelerate the "miniaturization" of the world, where we come from, the geography with which we identify, have even more importance. [...] In a world that is virtually "shrinking," globalization need not be synonymous with homogeneity. Worldliness need not disrespect local wisdom. Knowledge development can mean diversity. The ICT4D program area and the prospectuses that we submit are organized upon these values. (IDRC 2001, 1)

Given the regional emphasis, decision making for development projects was highly decentralized. Individual program officers, mostly located in the regional offices, had considerable authority to develop project ideas in discussion with their regional team managers. They had the principal responsibility for ensuring fidelity with the prospectuses that had been approved by the board of governors.

The headquarters' role in this context was strategic rather than transactional. Indeed, the director for ICT4D had no direct budgetary capacity at all. All the budgets were regionalized and under the authority of the regional managers.

This presented particular challenges with the infrequent global initiatives that were pursued, such as the participation in the two WSIS events and the short-lived headquarters demonstration project called the "sand box." In these types of circumstances, the ICT4D program area adopted a system referred to as "tithing," whereby each of the regional programs would contribute to a common pot of funds to support a global initiative.

This approach did not translate into regional fragmentation as might otherwise have been the case. The board of governors had approved overarching objectives for the ICT4D program area. As such, all programming supported at the regional level had to have some relevance to the five research themes that had been authorized within the program area, including:

- Poverty reduction
- People development
- Partnerships

- Opportunities
- Networks and learning and development

Two rounds of independent external evaluations were conducted on these research themes and objectives over the decade 2001–11. The evaluators noted the fidelity of the project development to both themes and objectives. They were equally positive about the importance of the regional approach within the ICT4D programming, as the following indicates:

> Without exception, all of the programs reviewed were judged to have either met, exceeded or were in the process of meeting their objectives. In every case, in the sample projects considered by each evaluation team, there were clear examples of real policy influence leading to implementation. Additionally, demonstrated capacity building, successful networking-partnership formation and generally acceptable, but uneven, integration of gender considerations into programming outputs were identified in the programs reviewed. (Fuchs 2005b, 2)

From country to region to network

In each of the regional approaches, at different times and in different ways, the ICT4D programming generally began within a country focus and gradually moved to support intraregional initiatives, including regional demonstration projects and research networks. The demonstration effect at the national level was generally understood to be an important starting point. Once national demonstration was accomplished, it took little effort to build regional awareness and involve regional research institutions in both collaborative demonstration projects and applied regional research. Strengthening and helping to sustain the regional research networks was a considerable challenge and one that continues to this day.

By 2011, most of the programming in each region had moved to supporting applied research networks in eHealth, e-learning, ICT policy, gender analysis and e-government. This would not have been possible at the outset in 2001. Over the decade 2001–11, the ICT4D program area matured, as did its research partners. It had major and lasting impacts in many of the areas where it supported applied research for development.

Building the Field: A Decade of Achievement

IDRC has long been committed to the idea of capacity building with its partners in the developing world. The investments in support of research were never just about completing a useful, accurate and timely piece of research that might beneficially influence a progressive policy outcome. Other organizations support applied research for development in the developing world without a priority being placed on the local self-directed capacity that will remain once a particular research project is complete.

IDRC is just as concerned that its investments in policy-related research strengthen the ability of researchers and research institutions to complete high-quality, policy-related research as it is with the actual results of the research itself. Equally, the organization wants its investments in research to help build the level of interest among policymakers in using applied research in their public policy decision making. Being committed to capacity building in research for development often means taking more time and effort with the understanding that, in the long run, it is really the most efficient route to actual policy change.

The quicker "fix" of having outside consultants and experts complete relevant research on policy-related development issues may translate into a particular report being completed more quickly or by more prestigious institutions. It seldom, if ever, translates into faster or more relevant policy influence and change on important policies in the developing world. The ICT4D program area director's report to the board of governors speaks to this issue:

> In many respects, policy change is very much an outcome of "sequential causation." It is very seldom one factor alone that determines a change in policy and practice. This underscores the need to be locally rooted in order to assist when the opportunity for policy transformation arises. (IDRC 2005, 21)

Capacity building is difficult enough in established fields such as social and economic policy or policies respecting the environment or natural resource management. Investing in "field building" is orders of magnitude more challenging, time consuming and expensive. The ICT4D field had to be "made" for researchers and research institutions to come to understand why it was important in development and how it might be approached. Unlike more traditional disciplines in, for example, agriculture, forestry, energy and economics, the ICT4D field was a hybrid. At the same time that capacity was being built, awareness and understanding of the importance of the actual field had to be established. IDRC's director of evaluation, Fred Carden, describes the process:

> This goes beyond training and capacity building to embracing all the elements a field of practice will have: training, research, curriculum development for academic as well as technical education, executive training, a professional association that considers standards, advocates on […] policy, brings innovation to its members, and so on. Building the field […] involves enabling citizens, researchers, and […] professionals to build indigenous […] cultures and capabilities to contribute to improved decision making. (Carden 2010, 220)

The Research ICT Africa network – supported by Acacia over three generations of funding – could not begin with ready-made institutions and researchers who were already working on the issue of ICTs in development. Yet, informed choices and policy on how access to telecoms and the Internet might best be approached in a specialized African context were essential as Africa entered the Information Age.

There were almost no researchers or research institutions focused on the building of Unicode in local languages in Asia when Pan Asia began its programming in this area in 2002. Almost seven years later, the field for this has been established to a great degree.

Software can now be written in local and indigenous languages – which poor people most often speak – making access to the Information Age available to them.

When IDRC's ICT4D program began working with the UN's Economic Commission for Latin America and the Caribbean, the commission had never developed statistical tools to help track and measure progress toward participation in the information economy in the region. Most of the national offices with responsibility for official statistics in the countries with whom they regularly worked had never addressed these issues either. Working with ECLAC to develop a methodology to approach this and testing it with several national statistical offices took patience and practical testing of systems and methods.

These are but three examples where IDRC's ICT4D programming engaged in significant and successful field building. There are, of course, many others. The field building also went beyond IDRC's partners and clients. The program staff and managers who worked in IDRC's ICT4D program at its peak also had to be "built." There were few, if any, universities specializing in this area and, therefore, few people with "paper" qualifications in the sector. The result of this was a staff with specializations as varied as the social sciences, engineering, computer science, journalism and even divinity – a multidisciplinary team of dedicated professionals!

Field building requires a different kind of approach from the conventional donor-recipient "fund-a-project" interaction. Rather than funding projects, the field building methodology used by ICT4D involves funding partners. This is most often done within custom-designed, multi-country and interdisciplinary research networks over several generations of social investment. This both builds and shares excellence in research and, over time, helps a field of expertise to develop roots and enduring engagement within both new and existing research institutions.

As the earlier quote from Carden indicated, field building also involves support for activities beyond just the research exercise. Providing assistance with communications, improving research to policy linkages, training in resource expansion and building a strategy for partnership development are all part of the field building approach. The "dancing on someone else's stage" approach referenced earlier is also part of the field building strategy as well. For example, the 75+ research partners that participated in both World Summits on the Information Society had an opportunity to increase their contacts and networks in a global forum to which they would not otherwise have had access. They also built new alliances and partnerships with research institutions from other parts of the world as the field of ICT4D research became established and gained more recognition.

Field building necessarily involves longer-term commitments to lines of research than might otherwise be the case. It is, however, important to remain open to new ideas and new partners who may be outside the existing research institutions that participate in the supported networks. Accordingly, IDRC's ICT4D program integrated "small grants" programming modality that broadened the reach to new partners and new ideas. Perhaps the best example of how this approach can pay dividends is the case of the Pan Localization research network.

Along with multi-phase support to research networks and remaining open to new ideas and new partners through small grants competitions, the field building approach used by the ICT4D program at IDRC includes several other elements, some of which are the following:

- Supporting the formation of ICT4D journals
- Hosting and supporting conferences on important ICT4D research themes
- Providing mentoring, training and applied research opportunities for young researchers

The field building approach is not without its perils. Once a research network has received several phases of support, it can be challenging to disengage if no successor or institutional sponsor has been found. Beginning the work of partnership development in the early phases of a network's life is therefore mission critical. As well, while small grants programs can be important sources of innovation and outreach, they are time consuming and administratively burdensome. In recent years, IDRC's ICT4D program has outsourced this role to partner organizations wishing to become more involved in business of ICT4D research.

It is clear that IDRC's ICT4D program has contributed to building new fields of research and policy relating to how the digital economy and society can be of service to the poor. Additionally, it has helped to advance the social and economic prospects within developing countries. This is true in sectors that have already been referenced. It is also the case that, more generally, IDRC has helped to build the general field of applied research in ICT itself over the last decade. New specialist research institutes in this area have arisen and researchers with this as their specialization are now much more likely to be included in think tanks, universities and other research organizations.

A Good Time, Not a Long Time

The celebrity of ICTs and development began to fade almost as quickly as it arose. By 2005, it was becoming clear that other international development agencies were beginning to withdraw from the field. The 2005 ICT4D report to the IDRC board of governors referenced this fact, quoting from an OECD report (OECD Development Assistance Committee 2005):

> The % share of aid flows relating to ICTs fell from 4.5% in 1990 to 0.6% in 2002! This decline, the report indicates, has been partially offset by several special initiatives within OECD countries.[9] But the bottom line is ICTs for Development have not been mainstreamed despite Dot Force, UNICT Task Force and WSIS in 2 episodes. (IDRC 2005, 5)

There had been signs even earlier that this was happening. In July 2003, IDRC's ICT4D team hosted a major partnership meeting with the United Nations Development Programme (UNDP) in Ottawa. July in Ottawa is a time when most Canadians want to be on vacation. More than eighty staff from UNDP's worldwide "practice" of ICTs and development met with IDRC staff and discussed collaboration into the future.

Unbeknownst to IDRC, this was a last-ditch effort by the director general for the ICT for development "practice" at UNDP to avoid having the program discontinued. But this is exactly what happened. The ICT for development "practice" was dropped – some would say cynically – right before the first World Summit on the Information Society in Geneva in December of the same year.

Other withdrawals would soon follow. With Walter Fust's retirement from the Swiss Agency for Development Cooperation (SDC) right after the GK III conference in 2007, SDC announced that it would discontinue its dedicated programming in support of ICTs and development. Both Denmark's DANIDA and Sweden's SIDA would follow with similar announcements shortly thereafter, although SIDA subsequently reengaged in the field.

It is difficult to ascertain what may have prompted these decisions. Donors are notoriously fickle when it comes to programming priorities. But anecdotal evidence points to questions about the role of aid – in contrast to private investment – in reducing the digital divide (especially with the growth in mobile telephony) and a perception that the ICT4D field was littered with technologically driven, unsustainable pilot projects.

The Dot Force and the two summits served as powerful magnets to generate great interest in the ICT4D sector throughout the developing world – an interest that continues to this day. Many new activists, researchers and institutes entered the new field that had been created. In late 2010, IDRC moved from a dedicated ICT4D program area to mainstreaming thematic issues into other programs such as health, agriculture and governance, among others. In addition, IDRC maintained a more focused effort in this area through the Information and Networks (I&N) program, now a part of the Innovation Policy and Science program strategy. I&N's work touches on cross-cutting issues such as intellectual property, privacy and rights around information networks; the program's work is described in more detail in the epilogue.

A Great Transformation

The first decade of the twenty-first century saw a major transformation in how the developing world uses the tools of ICTs. In many ways, while the shift has yet to be named, the changes in access to communications and computing in development in the past decade have been at least as transformative as the Green Revolution was in agriculture two decades earlier.

Human, organizational and business output has been dramatically increased through telecommunications. Networks of knowledge and information sharing that never could have existed without these ICT tools have become commonplace. The emerging-market countries that were early adopters of these new tools now account for increasing shares of world output and productivity. There are now more than 6 billion mobile phone subscriber accounts – most of them in the developing world. The social networking tools of the Internet have helped to bring despots and dictators to their knees. Mobile telephony and the Internet are now part of the everyday elements of business and organizational life in the developing world.

The ICT for Development program at IDRC was a pre-market enabler and facilitator for this process in Africa, Asia and the Americas. While the chapters that follow serve as a further testament to this, IDRC's work helped to foster pro-poor ICT policies, build an understanding of why these issues were important in development and underscore the need for major investments in new infrastructure. It also helped to establish cadres of knowledgeable researchers and sustainable institutions that continue this important work in the developing world into the future.

This is no mean feat for a hastily assembled, rapidly grown, multidisciplinary team of development professionals. It is time that this be chronicled, understood and shared.

References

Amoako, K. Y. 1996. Keynote speech at the Information Society and Development Conference, Midrand, South Africa, 13 May.

Bell, D. 1973. *The Coming of Post-Industrial Society*. New York: Basic Books.

Carden, F. 2010. *Knowledge to Policy: Making the Most of Development Research*. New York: Sage Publications.

Fuchs, R. 2005a. *Information and Communication Technologies for Development (ICT4D) Program Area Report to Board of Governors*. Ottawa: IDRC.

_____. 2005b. "Evaluation Memorandum to IDRC Board of Governors." Ottawa: IDRC, 31 August.

Global Knowledge Partnership Foundation. "GKP – A Storyline." Online: http://gkpfoundation.org/page/gkpf-conferences (accessed 12 August 2012).

Government of Canada. 2013. "International Development Research Centre Act." Published by the Minister of Justice. Online: http://laws-lois.justice.gc.ca/PDF/I-19.pdf (accessed 14 March 2013).

IDRC. 2001. *DPA Report to IDRC Board of Governors*. Ottawa: IDRC.

_____. 2005. *ICT for Development DPA Report to Board of Governors*. Ottawa: IDRC.

Mbeki, Thabo. 1995. Banquet speech at the G7 Ministerial Conference on the Global Information Society, Brussels, 26 February.

Middleton, C. A. and C. Sorensen. 2005. "How Connected are Canadians? Inequities in Canadian Households' Internet Access." *Canadian Journal of Communication* 30, no. 4: 463–83.

Muirhead, B. and R. Harpelle. 2010. *IDRC: 40 Years of Ideas, Innovation, and Impact*. Waterloo: Wilfred Laurier Press.

OECD Development Assistance Committee. 2005. *Financing ICTs for Development Efforts: Review of Recent Trends of ODA and Its Contribution*. Paris: OECD. Online: http://www.oecd.org/dataoecd/41/45/34410597.pdf (accessed 11 September 2012).

Okinawa Charter on Global Information Society. 2000. Kyushu-Okinawa Summit, Okinawa, 22 July. Online: www.g8.utoronto.ca/summit/2000okinawa/gis.htm (accessed 15 January 2013).

Polyani, K. 1944. *The Great Transformation*. Boston: Beacon Press.

Introduction Part II

FROM BEGINNING TO END
TO BEGINNING AGAIN

Katie Bryant, Laurent Elder,
Heloise Emdon and Richard Fuchs

Digital technologies today are indispensable tools used in almost every facet of our daily lives. Especially in the developing world, mobile phones have transformed the lives and livelihoods of average citizens. Yet, two decades ago, when there were more phone lines in Manhattan than in most of Sub-Saharan Africa, only a few visionary institutions could have imagined that computers, the Internet and mobiles would be so prominent in poverty-stricken environments. Information and communications technologies (ICTs) began to emerge as an issue in the field of development at a time when the concepts of sustainable development, biodiversity, economic growth and services for all dominated the landscape. These discourses did not consider the introduction of technology to address development issues, as technology was perceived as a luxury item rather than an indispensable building block for social and economic development. The rhetorical question, *"Which is more important, hospital beds or computers?"* was a common dismissive response to the suggestion that digital tools had a place in international development programming.

Despite this early skepticism, a few institutions and players in the world of development were prepared to argue that, like implementing basic needs infrastructure, access to ICTs was also needed. These early advocates for exploring the use of technology in the global south assumed that, by supporting and researching the ways in which ICTs could be used for development purposes, they would be able to overcome a range of developmental barriers such as access and performance in the education, health, political and community sectors of life.

As discussed in the first introductory section of this book, the International Development Research Centre (IDRC) was one of these early advocates. It recognized that ICTs could play an important and complex role in fostering human development and reducing poverty. As a Canadian Crown corporation, IDRC supported developing country researchers to conduct in situ research on social, economic and environmental issues related to growth and development.

From its inception in 1970, IDRC had understood that information technologies were an indispensable element in this mission. Not only did developing countries require these technologies to reach out to the best sources of knowledge about health, agriculture, the environment and other socioeconomic development essentials, they needed the same tools to become knowledge producers in these areas themselves. Information technologies – and, later, communications technologies as well – were essential ingredients to accomplish this.

IDRC's special remit to support development research for progressive public policy in the developing world necessitated that it understand the context of research institutions and researchers in the global south. This relative autonomy and focus on the needs of the developing world helped to form IDRC's approach to its work. Accordingly, the organization's programming was more patient than fickle and focused on the skills and capacities of its partners in the developing world just as much as it did on the results of this or that project.

IDRC as a donor believed that capacity building was the most important mission of its work. The process and the skills acquired in the process of research for development by southern researchers and institutions were at least as important as the results of the research itself. Rather than relying on "quick fix" approaches to "flavor of the month" thematic priorities, IDRC was able to work over the long term with partners and to commit to development issues before many other agencies did. It also remained with them over the long term.

ICT for Development at IDRC is a good example of this. IDRC understood that the pre-market circumstance of most developing countries meant that computers, the Internet and telephony were unlikely to be of benefit beyond the minority elites who could afford them. The approach taken by IDRC in this case was to make pre-market investments in pre-market circumstances in support of pro-poor sectors like healthcare, agriculture, rural development and education. This helped to create an awareness of the usefulness of these tools and it built local demand for these services. This accelerated the formation of local markets and helped to build the first generation of local entrepreneurs that would sustain the sector in the long run.

But IDRC's remit is research for development, so demonstration projects in pre-market environment, while important, do not provide the kind of evidence that can change, shape and form public policy. For example, the ICT for Development program at IDRC supported the formation of an important research network, Research ICT Africa (RIA). What began in just a few places now includes most countries in Africa. RIA researchers review evidence on how public policy is affecting the use, penetration and price of ICTs in Africa. Telecoms regulators and policy leaders learn how well or how poorly their jurisdictions are faring based on solid, comparative evidence. Accordingly, the pressure for progressive reform mounts and policies change.

Along with the significant financial investments IDRC makes in support of development research, the programming staff at IDRC are more than just administrators. They are specialists in their respective fields and have real world experience in doing development research and working in the developing regions of the world. IDRC doesn't just provide financial support; staff are also peers, mentors and advisors. They engage with grantees in framing research problems, improving research designs and choosing methodologies.

In the early going, IDRC's approach to ICTs included "old media" – in particular, radio and television – but quickly grew to include the exploration of interactive digital technologies to investigate their role in developing countries and communities, as well as to facilitate various opportunities and services.

The work of IDRC in this emerging multidisciplinary field of research came to be known as "Information and Communications Technologies for Development" or "ICT4D."[10] Its interdisciplinary nature stemmed from the composition of researchers from various disciplines of study, i.e., engineering, computer programming, economics, sociology, linguistics and so on. Moreover, it tended to include an important contingent of ICT practitioners – NGO activists, software engineers, physicians, epidemiologists, linguists, political scientists and lawyers, all with their own interest in being hackers (not to mention a few connectivity rebel activists) – who straddled the worlds of research, advocacy and practice. These multidisciplinarians led the charge in piloting innovative solutions to challenging information and communications problems. New policy dialogues led to more affordable mobile phones and better access to information in remote areas improved agricultural markets. The solutions would also make for better management of drugs for chronic diseases in remote clinics, improved access to educational materials and more secure communications to tackle issues of domestic abuse or even dialogue over tabooed cultural practices.[11]

These individuals continue to work together to (i) engage in research that studies the complex relationship between a development phenomenon and ICTs; (ii) demonstrate and research the innovative use of ICTs in pro-poor social and economic segments as a research for development laboratory prior to wide-scale adoption; (iii) develop university-level courses at institutions throughout the world to train a new generation of ICT4D researchers; (iv) create and contribute to venues for new research such as international journals and conferences on ICT4D; and (v) share their findings with the wider public – particularly developing country and international development institutions – to influence national and international policies. It was the specific interest of IDRC's ICT4D program to support research that not only investigated the relationship between development issues and ICTs, but also built the capacity of developing country researchers to take up related research questions in their own regions. This research would contribute to debates in this emerging academic field, as well as influence global and local policy dialogues.

In a relatively short time period – a little more than a decade – an incredible amount of work has emerged in the field of ICT4D, which can be seen in publications such as Unwin's edited collection entitled *ICT4D: Information and Communication Technology for Development* (2009); Pannuand Tomar's *ICT4D Information Communication Technology for Development* (2010); and Weigeland Waldburger's edited publication *ICT4D – Connecting People for a Better World: Lessons, Innovations and Perspectives of Information and Communication Technologies for Development* (2004). This book is an attempt to contribute to this body of literature by synthesizing the work of IDRC-supported researchers in the global south over the last decade. Much of this knowledge is tacit, buried in technical reports or in siloed project outputs. This book is an opportunity to consolidate lessons learned from across regions and projects and to bring gray-area literature to light.

At the same time, this text acts as a legacy of IDRC's ICT4D program area. Research related to ICTs and development is now being mainstreamed into IDRC's other research themes, although a program that focuses on issues such as openness, privacy, intellectual property and censorship still exists. Therefore, as the program area was in a process of transition, the idea of writing a book to share both our partners' research, as well as our own lessons in supporting the decade and a half of research in the field of ICTs for development emerged. This book is, therefore, a foundational building block in what will continue to be a space – both inside and outside IDRC – to build an understanding of how to achieve equitable, sustainable and inclusive development outcomes using ICTs.

This book is especially relevant to the many researchers, practitioners and policy activists who participated in the area of ICTs for development over the past two decades. It is also a practical documentary for more recent entrants into the business of social and economic development in the global south, whether they live and work in the postindustrial and the developing world. To achieve this book's dual purpose, we have had input from all levels within the former ICT4D program of IDRC, including management, long-term program professionals, research officers, interns and students. In putting these chapters together, we have drawn on our partners' research publications and gray literature such as final technical reports, policy briefs and IDRC's own internal documents. The book attempts to capture the most relevant research findings and achievements from hundreds of ICT4D-supported projects. The result is the chapters that follow; each discusses a key research area and its relationship to ICTs.

Synthesizing research that had, until the creation of this book, often been divided regionally[12] proved quite difficult at times. The different situations and issues in these regions meant that each program initiative within ICT4D had its own individual perspective and, at times, more than one theory of change.[13] For the purpose of synthesizing work in this field, however, we were able to see that all three of these programs shared one underlying assumption or theory of change: that supporting applied and action research on ICTs in pro-poor social and economic circumstances could accelerate the information, knowledge and productivity impacts of digital technologies in these domains.

Specifically, these programs assumed that ICTs could act as vehicles to help address the most pressing development challenges in the global south such as providing or improving people's access to quality healthcare, improving developing countries' governance, improving people's educational outcomes, enabling people to be food secure, as well as improving people's livelihoods, ensuring vulnerable communities' resilience to environmental shocks, disasters and pandemics and supporting the development of new employment opportunities for people. These were enormous challenges, but the ICT4D team believed that ICTs could play an important role in addressing them; the key question was how to make it happen.

This book has been loosely structured on the evolution of IDRC's ICT4D programming approach. At the inception of the program, there was heavy focus on the issue of access. The book's first section, Catalyzing Access, is composed of five different chapters and explores how IDRC-supported researchers investigated this issue from many different angles. For example, in Chapter 1 ("Catalyzing Access through Social and Technical Innovation"), Valk et al. examine the ways in which ICT4D researchers attempted to address issues of access through technical innovation. The early days of the ICT4D program saw researchers and innovators using various technical innovations to address the digital divide between the developed and developing world. They were particularly interested in trying to help populations living in rural and poor areas to gain access to information and communications tools such as computers, the Internet and mobile phones. As researchers attempted to address the digital divide with innovative technical solutions such as local wireless networks, Internet connections in schools and telecenters, the IDRC ICT4D team and its partners began to realize that the system was incredibly complex; as one problem appeared to be addressed, many others began to emerge.

These emerging problems provided the topics for the next four chapters: the ways in which IDRC's ICT4D program supported research to investigate the problems and the findings from these studies. In Chapter 2 ("Catalyzing Access via Telecommunications Policy and Regulatory Research"), Valk and Fourati explore how, as technical solutions were developed and implemented in various developing countries to address the digital divide, the problems inherent in developing countries' communications policies and regulatory environments came to light. In response to these problems, IDRC's ICT4D program supported research that looked at the limitations to expanding access to communications in developing countries – particularly, studies that contributed to the construction of sound policies to address the digital divides in developing countries. Access to connectivity and tools is only the first step. The next challenge is to ensure access to the content or knowledge conveyed by those tools.

In Chapter 3 ("Access to Knowledge as a New Paradigm for Research on ICTs and Intellectual Property Rights"), de Beer and Bannerman discuss the ways in which intellectual property rights (IPRs) in developing countries continued to be a significant issue as people's access to the Internet and online materials began to increase. IPR research also began to investigate the other side: access. For example, what types of policies and laws need to be in place or relinquished to allow individuals living in the global south to access digital materials? Also, how do we ensure that these people have the opportunity to contribute to the creation of such materials?

In Chapter 4 ("ICTs and Social Inclusion"), Sinha and Hyma take up another significant issue that emerged as access to communications tools began to increase in the developing world: questions such as whether communications tools are accessed equally by all social groups such as women, youth and members of different linguistic groups – particularly groups that traditionally did not have a written language – and how these tools are being used.

In the last chapter of this section, Chapter 5 ("Access and Use of ICTs by the Poor"), Diga focuses on findings from household survey data on ways in which the poor in the global south access and use ICTs, as well as describing broader relationships between ICT access and economic indicators. The role of ICTs in either reducing poverty or further marginalizing the poor is one of the least understood topics in ICT4D, which is why IDRC made it a priority to support projects that explored the subject. The chapter therefore ends by presenting lessons learned from that research.

While access remains an important issue throughout, the second section of the book focuses on the IDRC-supported research on sectoral issues in the developing world. Work was done around specific development or disciplinary sectors to potentially address specific development problems such as access to employment, education, healthcare and governance. In Chapter 6 ("Local Economic Opportunities and ICTs: How ICTs Affect Livelihoods"), Diga explores ICT use in improving livelihoods. Specifically, the chapter investigates those members of society working in small and medium enterprises (SMEs) and agriculture.

In Chapter 7 ("Research on eHealth Across Health Systems: Contributions to Strengthen a Field"), Sinha and Garro-Strauss shift the focus to the healthcare sector and examine research on the relationship between the use of ICTs and the healthcare context of developing countries. The chapter looks at the ways in which developing countries can use ICTs to improve the healthcare they provide for their citizens, particularly in light of significant health pandemics such as HIV/AIDS and tuberculosis.

In Chapter 8 ("Making the Grade: The Role of ICTs in Providing Access to Knowledge"), Rashid et al. examine another key sector of the developing world: education. This chapter discusses the IDRC partners' research on how ICTs could be used to address access to education as well as access to educational materials – two significant issues in many developing countries. Many children and adults are unable to go to school or to gain access to materials such as textbooks once they are at school. This chapter also investigates how ICTs can improve the educational experience for students once at school; for example, by helping students to engage with the learning material and raising students' grades.

In the final chapter of this section (Chapter 9: "E-Government for Development"), Fischer et al. discuss research on yet another key issue in many developing country contexts: the issue of governance. This chapter looks at studies that investigated how developing countries can potentially use ICTs to strengthen government administration and services and expand citizen engagement in governance. It also examines the tensions between realizing the benefits of e-government and the threats to democratic rights and freedoms that emerge as ICTs become more prevalent throughout government and society.

The last section of this book is composed of two chapters that are significant for both the ICT4D researcher and the development practitioner working in this area. In Chapter 10 ("Innovations in Evaluating ICT4D Research"), Earl et al. examine the work that IDRC's ICT4D program has done to support innovative ways of evaluating ICT4D research and projects. It explores methods such as outcome mapping (OM) and gender evaluation methodology (GEM), impact evaluation and utilization-focused evaluation (UFE). IDRC, through its ICT4D program and its evaluation unit, played a crucial role in supporting researchers and practitioners in this field who developed, refined and assessed the appropriateness of particular methodologies and approaches of evaluation for ICT4D research projects.

In the final chapter of the book, Chapter 11 ("Conclusions: A Decade of Innovation That Matters"), Fuchs and Elder draw conclusions about the over a decade of work that the ICT4D program has dedicated to this field. The book ends with an epilogue that discusses key emerging issues and research questions in the field and addresses how IDRC will engage in this area in the future.

Notes

1 Appreciation to David Balson and Mike Jensen who offered helpful comments on an earlier draft of this chapter. As well, thanks to Maureen O'Neil and Caroline Pestieau – respectively, the former president and vice president (programs) at IDRC – for helpful interviews on historical issues relevant to the chapter.

2 There is no recorded history of the first attempts to introduce ICTs into the business of social and economic development. The examples here refer to the Velmdalen Telecottage (1985) in Sweden, the Playing to Win Computer Center in East Harlem (1983), the Walcha Telecottage in New South Wales, Australia (circa 1986) and the Enterprise Network telecenters launched by the author in Newfoundland and Labrador (1988).

3 The speaking notes for Mbeki's address were drafted by Mike Jensen, a contributor to this volume and a long-time IDRC ICT for Development staffer, partner and consultant.

4 The two Industry Canada "sherpas," Richard Simpson and Richard Bourassa and the IDRC ICT for Development director, Rich Fuchs, came to be known as "les trios Richards." An informal alliance formed among them that endured until they had all retired by the end of the decade.

5 Little did he realize that information society technologies would be a decisive factor in his ouster several years later.

6 The ICT for Development director sat in on the deliberations for less than half a day.

7 The Acacia name is not an acronym as many have tried to decode. It was named after the acacia trees that are prevalent there.

8 The rise of mobile telephony and its unique rollout in the developing world is perhaps the best example of a local approach that is very different from what preceded it in the "North."

9 These would include post–Dot Force special initiatives such as Connectivity Africa, USAID's Doc Com Initiative and DFID's CATIA, along with several others.

10 Indeed, the first director of the ICT4D program at IDRC easily secured the domain names ICT4D.org, ICT4D.net and ICT4D.ca in early 2001 – a clear indication that the field had yet to get "crowded."

11 At its peak in 2006, the 30+ professional staff in IDRC's ICT4D program included specializations in sociology, engineering, economics, linguistics, computer science, journalism and even theology!

12 As mentioned in the preface to this text, IDRC's ICT4D program area was organized along regional lines of programming: Pan Asia Networking focused in Asia; Acacia focused in Africa; and Connectivity and Equity in the Americas focused in Latin America and the Caribbean.

13 This refers to the hypothesis for expected outcomes to result from the particular interventions.

References

Pannu, P. and Y. A. Tomar, eds. 2010. *ICT4D Information Communication Technology for Development*. New Delhi: International Publishing House.

Unwin, T., ed. 2009. *ICT4D: Information and Communication Technology for Development*. New York: Cambridge University Press.

Weigel, G. and D. Waldburger, eds. 2004. *ICT4D – Connecting People for a Better World: Lessons, Innovations and Perspectives of Information and Communication Technologies for Development*. Geneva: Swiss Agency for Development and Cooperation (SDC) and Global Knowledge Partnership.

Chapter 1

CATALYZING ACCESS THROUGH SOCIAL AND TECHNICAL INNOVATION

John-Harmen Valk, Frank Tulus, Raymond Hyma and Florencio Ceballos[1]

The main goal of the International Development Research Centre's (IDRC's) "Information and Communications Technologies for Development" (ICT4D) program was to harness information and communications technologies (ICTs) for the benefit of all citizens of developing countries. Increased access to ICTs was recognized as a means to a greater end – building an inclusive knowledge society and economy in the developing world. Yet it was also recognized that a non-uniform spread of ICTs was contributing to a persisting and, in some cases, widening gap between the information "haves" in more developed countries and the information "have nots" in less developed regions of the world (Sciadas 2005).

IDRC's ICT4D program aimed to mitigate the persisting inequality in access to ICTs. It first addressed connectivity to ICTs, or the so-called "first order digital divide" (Riggins and Dewan 2005). Second, it tackled access from the standpoint of the ability to use ICTs and to contribute content, the so-called "second order digital divide" (Brotcorne et al. 2010; Hargittai 2002). (See Box 1.1.) This chapter describes the work of IDRC and its partners in overcoming the first order digital divide by way of social and technical innovation.

For the first order digital divide, the driving idea behind the program was to demonstrate how social and technical innovations could be adopted and adapted in the developing world so as to catalyze access and therefore bring about socioeconomic dividends for disadvantaged populations. Throughout its history, IDRC's ICT4D program sponsored an extensive range of research on numerous ways to increase access to ICTs in the less developed regions of the world. Action research projects focused on Internet service providers (ISPs), Internet exchange points (IXPs), very small aperture terminal (VSAT) satellite connectivity, bandwidth consortiums, as well as telecenters and community wireless networks.

IDRC's funding related to overcoming first order digital divide issues generally evolved from a main focus on social and technical innovation to a focus on policy and regulatory environments. However, this shift in thinking does not mean that it eventually ignored

Box 1.1. Dimensions of catalyzing access

1. Catalyzing access via social and technical innovation to address the first order digital divide: demonstrating the feasibility of establishing backbone Internet infrastructure, bandwidth consortiums and community-level connectivity for the purpose of stimulating demand. This is the subject of the current chapter.
2. Catalyzing access via policy and regulatory research and interventions to address the first order digital divide: researching the status of policy and regulatory frameworks and demonstrating how policy changes can lead to increased access. This is the subject of the following chapter.
3. Catalyzing access via social and technical innovation to address the second order digital divide: increasing the ability to use ICTs by, for example, working on issues related to the graphical user interface, e.g., localization. This is the subject of subsequent chapters in this book.
4. Catalyzing access via bolstering interactivity and production of information to address the second order digital divide: increasing the ability to contribute to the continual transformation of content and information by addressing issues such as literacy, government regulations on access to information or government controls of the Internet. This is addressed in subsequent chapters in this book.

the former focus in favor of the latter in working toward increased access. The research findings and lessons learned through partners funded by IDRC reveal that concurrent attention to social and technical innovation and to policy and regulatory environments is needed to increase access to ICTs. This chapter and the following provide a two-part story about how IDRC sought to catalyze access to overcome the first order digital divide in two distinct, but interrelated ways.

Part I: Demonstrating the Feasibility of and Demand for ICTs (ISPs, IXPs, VSATs and Bandwidth Consortiums)

IDRC recognized that it had to direct its programming toward implementing basic Internet backbone connectivity infrastructure before the benefits of ICTs as a driver of socioeconomic development could be realized. In certain regions, this meant showing that establishing national-level connectivity infrastructure was feasible. In other regions, it meant extending connectivity infrastructure to rural or underserved areas. These latter areas are often referred to as the "last mile" because governments and telecommunication companies often delay or avoid rollout in these areas due to the high cost and challenge of managing those parts of a network.

IDRC's early programming focused on supporting partners in a limited number of countries that were chosen because they had little or no connectivity infrastructure. Later programming expanded beyond these target countries to focus on underserved populations in the developing world generally. IDRC funded research on the creation of ISPs, on the effectiveness of local peering points such as IXPs and on the possibilities for overcoming the high cost of international satellite services by using VSATs. It also supported bandwidth consortiums to reduce connectivity costs. Most notable was the interaction with African universities – key research recipients of IDRC grants – to initiate discussions about more effective and efficient access to Internet connectivity.

Internet service providers (ISPs)

Early ICT4D programming at IDRC, begun in the late 1990s, funded a series of partners in Asia that sought to establish national Internet connectivity via the creation of ISPs to try to determine how developing countries in Asia could best achieve national and local connectivity. IDRC took on the high-risk role of investor for the establishment of ISPs when no other investors existed in order to demonstrate the utility of Internet connectivity and to stimulate demand. In four of the countries targeted, IDRC-funded ISPs were the first to provide stable Internet connectivity. In those countries that already enjoyed stable, albeit limited connectivity, IDRC-funded ISPs expanded networks and initiated significant reductions in connectivity prices (Graham and Harfoush 1999, 9).[2] This funding of ISPs in Asia was highly significant, as it showed that creating national Internet connectivity in countries with poor Internet infrastructure was possible. The "demonstration effect" became apparent as a private ICT sector quickly emerged in those countries where IDRC had helped to establish ISPs – countries that continue to experience sustainable Internet services today.

IDRC pursued ISP implementation in a variety of ways, exploring different technological alternatives and organizational models that would be sustainable and provide reliable performance and services at a reasonable cost. Pan Mongolia, the first IDRC-funded ISP project in Asia, involved Datacom, an already-existing electronic networking company in Mongolia. The project supported Datacom so it could follow through on plans for network expansion that required capital investment on a scale unaffordable at the time. In Laos, IDRC teamed up with the government's Science, Technology and Environment Organization (STENO) to connect the country to the Internet for the first time.[3] Similarly, in Vietnam, IDRC worked in conjunction with a government agency called the Institute of Information Technology (IOIT) to establish a full Internet link and an Internet backbone as well as an ISP. IDRC also initiated ISP projects in several other Asian countries: Bhutan, Bangladesh, Cambodia, the Maldives and Sri Lanka.

For most of its projects, IDRC's ICT4D program provided loans that it would recover several years after the ISPs had been firmly established. IDRC also tried a special approach of acquiring equity in an ISP company, forming public–private partnership models as a way of creating sustainable ISPs. This was the case with its ISP project in Sri Lanka, called Pan Lanka. Here, IDRC teamed up with the Norwegian Agency for Development Cooperation to form a joint venture, for-profit company called Pan Lanka Networking (PLN) (Afonso 1999, 44). The first model (recoverable loans) required much less time and fewer resources than the second model (forming a joint venture company). The second model posed significant challenges with regard to both the time and the skills needed on the part of IDRC to operate such a venture. While this second model should not be excluded outright, its challenges would have to be considered in any future attempt to pursue such an approach. In both models, however, IDRC was able to influence the private sector and to build development objectives into commercially sustainable operations.

The rationale for public–private partnerships in the establishment of ISPs in several Asian countries was based on two assumptions, both of which proved to be well founded. First, IDRC recognized that establishing ISPs is a costly affair in the initial years with recovery of initial investments not seen until a few years into the endeavor. It was for this reason that few private investors at the time were interested in creating and expanding services, particularly to rural regions or to regions where awareness and demand were low. Second, IDRC assumed that, if well marketed and well managed financially, ISPs could potentially operate at a break-even or even a profitable point. In other words, IDRC could create self-sufficient ISPs that would, in turn, contribute to development in their respective countries. Project sustainability was key to IDRC's ICT4D programming and was built into the structure of the ISPs from the outset. By 1999, the various ISP projects funded by IDRC were financially viable. While some ISPs would later become uncompetitive with the emergence of other private ISPs – particularly given the transition in the telecommunications industry worldwide to increased international investment – the rationale for establishing ISPs still held. IDRC achieved its objective: providing quality service at lower cost by creating ISPs in regions where connectivity was lacking (Afonso 1999, 47).

While IDRC hoped to ultimately start extending access to Asian populations broadly through the creation of ISPs, it came to realize that the ISPs it funded would necessarily have to target government, NGOs, private businesses, universities and research institutions as primary clients. It focused on these groups for several reasons. First, as the ISP needed to recover costs and operate at a sustainable level, it had to target groups that were able to pay for the services. Second, IDRC concentrated on these groups because they could create further demand for ICT service provision, resulting in the emergence of and growth in a private ICT sector to cater to that demand. In other words, by initially aiming at these groups, IDRC could realize its objective of establishing national-level Internet connectivity infrastructure. The resulting demand for ICT services would stimulate an ICT market that, as it developed and expanded, would lead to service provision at more affordable prices and greater accessibility to the population at large (Graham and Harfoush 1999, 12).

IDRC operated with the assumption that attention to such groups would lead to expanded service for all. It also recognized that, because the demand for ICT access could grow tremendously, it had to target its interventions in feasible and effective ways. In this regard, IDRC learned that it had to be conscious about focusing its social and technical interventions (in the case of ISP creation, toward limited groups) in order to work toward increased access and broad social and economic development (Afonso 1999, 20).[4]

Box 1.2. Pioneering adoption of Internet services in Bhutan

IDRC's ICT4D program support in establishing ISPs facilitated the emergence of "digital pioneers" who, in turn, paved the way for later adopters. Developments stemming from work in Bhutan provide one example. Due to low technical capacity and awareness about the Internet, Bhutan's Ministry of Communication was reluctant to develop a national Internet infrastructure. It preferred to opt for a national Intranet with only email connected internationally. However, the development of a web-based Intranet system – which mostly targeted government workers – quickly revealed the benefits of connectivity. Therefore, with the support of IDRC, the first ISP (DrukNet) was created to facilitate wider access to the Internet. While initial demand for the service was low, an education campaign undertaken by the Royal Institute of Management in Bhutan expanded the number of clients.

One of the early adopters of the Internet service was Dago Beda, the managing director of Etho Metho Tours & Trek. Beda quickly experienced the benefits of the Internet for advertising and for communicating with clients: "Once we advertised our address, we got a lot of people with enquiries, so we spend more time on the email than ever before and it has been a big help – it makes everything so quick." Today, Etho Metho Tours & Trek remains one of the leading licensed tour operators in Bhutan. Their early adoption of the Internet prompted the growth of the Bhutanese tourism industry in the early 2000s as other companies such as Bhutan's national airline also began to advertise their services online (IDRC 2002b).

In short, IDRC's job was to help stimulate demand within its principal client base – universities, public policy research institutes, NGOs and international agencies – and to withdraw once the private sector emerged to provide the services.

Internet exchange points (IXPs)

In the early 2000s, developing countries wanting to access the Internet needed to connect with hubs in North America and Europe and pay for the associated costs of up and downward linkages to these hubs. More than 90 percent of international Internet traffic at that time passed through the United States. The IDRC-sponsored map "The Internet: Out of Africa" provides a striking picture of this reality with regards to Africa (see Figure 1.1). Intra-African Internet traffic in 2002 was sparse, paling in comparison with the traffic routed via North America, Europe and Asia. The global Internet infrastructure at the time resulted in a net outflow of funds from developing countries to the United States, with the cost of the international links borne by customers in developing countries. The high cost of international bandwidth was the key bottleneck constraining access to the Internet in developing regions.

Figure 1.1. The Internet: Out of Africa

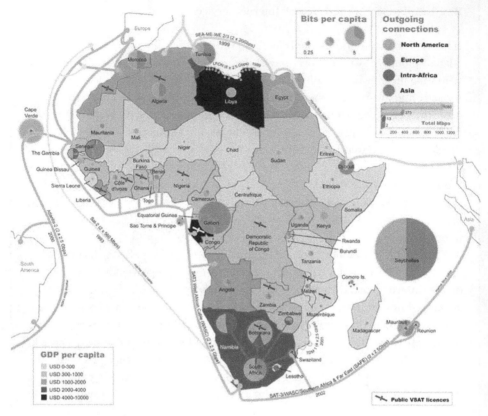

Source: IDRC (2002a).

In an effort to overcome this cost challenge, IDRC's ICT4D program and the ITU commissioned a paper on establishing local and regional IXPs written by the African Regional ISP Association (AfriSPA) for the 2004 Global Symposium for Regulators (IDRC and ITU 2005). The paper showed that the use of international bandwidth for the routing of national or regional African data cost African users an estimated US$400 million per year (IDRC and ITU 2005, 4). AfriSPA, with support from IDRC, developed technical guidelines for establishing IXPs that were applied in six countries – Nigeria, Tanzania, Uganda, Mozambique, Ghana and Kenya. These IXPs made it possible for local Internet traffic between ISPs to be routed within a country, bypassing the need for an upstream service that was likely outside the country or even the continent. The IXPs resulted in routing efficiency by cutting the latency (i.e., the delay in data packets being sent through the Internet) of interconnection between ISPs and by preserving international bandwidth capacity for international Internet traffic. IXPs also reduced the costs of interconnection, thus enabling more affordable access to the Internet.

Data regarding the impact of IXPs on national, regional and continental African Internet flow showed positive developments (UNGANA n.d., 4–5). For example, data

Box 1.3. A map initiates a tidal wave

"The Internet: Out of Africa" map, sponsored by ICT4D, was the first easy-to-understand and publicly available visualization of Internet traffic patterns within Africa and between Africa and other regions. Such information had previously been available from private companies doing market research for telecommunications companies, but the data had to be purchased and it was expensive. The map publicized the concept "bits per capita" as a useful measure of Internet uptake in a country, a concept proposed by Mike Jensen (who was part of IDRC's ICT4D team) and later taken up by the International Telecommunication Union (ITU) and many other organizations.

The Canadian government included this map in approximately 5,000 press kits at the G8 meetings in Kananaskis, Alberta in 2002. The map also spread rapidly throughout the development community. Partly as a result of the map, attention was given to resolving the lack of submarine Internet cables to East Africa. This attention ultimately led to landing the East Africa Marine Systems (TEAMS) submarine cable at Mombasa in 2009.

The success of this map spurred IDRC to commission many other visualizations of telecommunications sector data. One such example is *The Acacia Atlas* (IDRC 2005).

on Internet flow in Kenya demonstrated a significant improvement in the performance of local infrastructure. Data from Rwanda revealed a great increase in connectivity speed, making local ICT applications such as e-learning, telemedicine, e-commerce and e-government that had been previously hindered because of the high cost of satellite links possible (Longwe and Rulinda 2005). These projects showed the importance of IXPs to interconnect ISPs within the countries and regions of Africa so Internet users could exchange domestic and regional Internet traffic on the African continent without having to route Internet traffic via Europe or the United States.

With regard to regional IXPs, research funded by IDRC's ICT4D program showed that two factors in particular affect the feasibility of creating a regional IXP. The first is the percentage of Internet traffic directed toward another country; a low percentage makes it less worthwhile. The second is the price of international bandwidth; falling international bandwidth prices erode the economic imperative of establishing a regional IXP. That said, for landlocked countries with no access to submarine Internet cables or for countries further removed from main international Internet hubs in Europe or the United States, the utility of a regional IXP is substantial (IDRC and ITU 2005, 17). To establish a regional IXP, IDRC-supported research also learned that it would be important to open up competition for the operation of the international Internet gateway in those countries where a monopoly existed – or at least to make it a regulatory priority to reduce the costs of purchasing bandwidth through the monopoly operator controlling the international gateway (IDRC and ITU 2005, 19, 23).

Without such measures, those holding the monopoly for the international gateway enjoyed a substantially more privileged position because they could control pricing of all Internet traffic routed in and out of the country. IDRC-supported research findings regarding IXPs at both the national and regional levels show that, due to their importance, they should be included as part of national ICT development strategies and regulation (Longwe and Rulinda 2005).

Very small aperture terminals (VSATs)

As mentioned above, the cost of Internet access in Africa remained extremely high at the turn of the millennium. Rates were more expensive than in other regions of the world, ranging from 10 to 100 times those in North America and Europe (GVF 2004, 8); compared with the average African's purchasing power, they were astronomical. In light of this cost, IDRC explored satellite technologies – specifically, VSAT – as a potential mode by which to roll out cheaper, wider-scale Internet access. VSATs were a potential solution for overcoming the nonexistent or inadequate Internet backbone infrastructure, as well as a way of avoiding the high costs of installing fiber connectivity to remote regions. Installation of VSATs was possible because satellite coverage spanned nearly all regions of Africa, as shown in the map "Open and closed skies: Satellite access in Africa" produced in 2005 (see Figure 1.2).

This map shows Ku-band satellite coverage and VSAT licensing in Africa as of 2005. The extensive satellite coverage and availability of more inexpensive VSAT technology presented an opportunity for more affordable rollout of Internet connectivity, although regulatory issues presented certain hurdles.

IDRC's ICT4D program funded the Global VSAT Forum – a partnership with a business association – to investigate access to satellites for development purposes. Research revealed that changes in satellite technology and the resulting reductions in the cost of installing satellite equipment made satellite access a feasible option to explore as an alternate solution for Internet access in Africa. Older satellite technology (using the C-band spectrum) needed large, costly land stations; new satellites over Africa (on the Ku-band spectrum, which emitted more high-powered beams) enabled the use of smaller transponders and more remote terminal locations. In addition, VSATs could potentially provide access to more bandwidth with less energy required (GVF 2004, 23). Furthermore, because of increases in global production of VSAT hardware, prices had dropped from upwards of US$16,000 in 1990 to less than US$1,000 by 2005 (GVF 2005, 5). The reduced cost of VSATs therefore made them accessible to small and medium-sized organizations and to the general public via cyber cafés and telecenters (GVF 2004, 23). In addition, falling prices meant that VSATs could serve as cost-effective platforms for the provision of various ICT applications such as e-learning, telemedicine and rural telecenters, examples of which were already springing up at the time.

A prime example of the potential offered by VSATs was a project spearheaded by the Songhai Centre in Benin. The Songhai Centre set up VSAT-equipped telecenters in three towns – Porto Novo, Savalou and Parakou – as a way of overcoming challenging geography and inadequate infrastructure. VSAT connections reduced transportation

Figure 1.2. Open and closed skies: Satellite access in Africa

Ku-band Satellite Coverage & VSAT Licensing

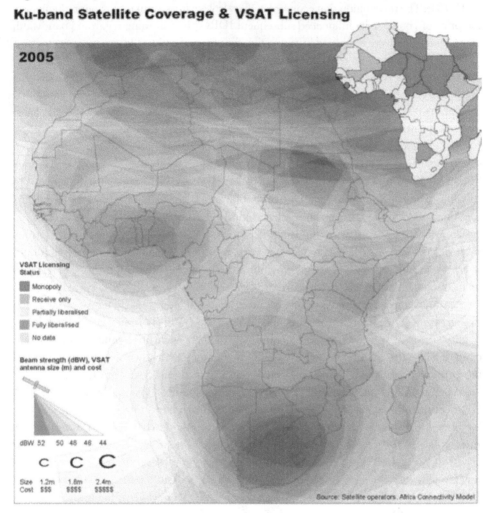

Source: IDRC (2005), adapted from the original in GVF (2004, 2).

and communication costs for the Songhai Centre itself and the telecenters provided social and economic benefits for the surrounding communities. Farmers could use the telecenters to research new equipment and entrepreneurs could search for new business opportunities. The telecenters charged a small fee to cover operating costs, but it was generally lower than that charged by private telecenters. With over 1,500 people visiting the telecenters each week, the Songhai Centre was able to cover the expenses related to the telecenters (Ladikpo 2005, 130–33).

Research, however, provided several lessons regarding the feasibility of VSATs for Internet access in Africa. First, despite significant drops in prices, VSATs remain an expensive option for Internet access. The Songhai telecenters proved financially viable because sufficient funds could be collected from the large number of users to cover the cost of VSAT access. Without these cost recovery structures, organizations face financial challenges with VSAT (Ladikpo 2005, 134). The recognition that economies of scale were important for further reductions in the price of connectivity influenced subsequent IDRC programming regarding bandwidth consortiums that were interested in optimizing the cost/use ratio of Internet connectivity, as well as IDRC's work with telecenters and community WiFi networks.

Through its research on VSATs, IDRC's ICT4D program also realized the importance of policy and regulatory regimes for cost reductions. Studies revealed that regulation played a major role in preventing further reductions in VSAT costs. Most notably, licensing schemes for VSAT remained out of date in many African countries. Up to 35 percent of ISP expenditures at the time could be directed toward VSAT regulatory charges and licensing fees per terminal for a 128 kbps connection could range from US$5,000 to US$10,000 (GVF 2005, 6). Such license regimes might have been suitable in an era when the high cost of technology and bandwidth meant that VSATs remained the purview of post and telecommunication organizations and transnational corporations. However, with reduced costs for both VSAT technology and monthly subscriptions, elevated licensing fees hindered uptake of VSAT by small and medium-sized organizations (GVF 2004, 8). Such findings confirmed the importance of IDRC's focus on policy and regulatory research.

Research ultimately revealed that VSATs remained an intermediary, temporary solution to increasing connectivity in rural regions. The costs of VSATs remained high while the quality of service provided by them could not compete with fiber connectivity where it existed. Since the VSAT research was undertaken, major advances in fiber connectivity infrastructure occurred in Africa, making the choice to adopt VSAT less attractive.

When the "The Internet: Out of Africa" map (see Figure 1.1) was released at the 2002 G8 meetings in Kananaskis, Alberta, the debate in Africa had shifted to seeking solutions for fiber broadband access along the East Coast to provide cheaper and more reliable Internet access for the coastal countries from Mozambique to Djibouti. Fiber broadband access in Africa has since increased with the completion of several new undersea cables that provide high-speed connectivity and link African coastal countries with each other and with Europe, North America and Asia. Prior to 2009, only two of the undersea cables shown on the "African undersea cables" map (see Figure 1.3) were in operation – the SAT3 and SEA-MW-WE4 cables, completed in 2001 and 2005 respectively. Since that time, the number and capacity of undersea cables have increased significantly, as has demand for Internet services. The rapidly falling prices and technical advantages of fiber networks may reduce the demand for expensive VSAT connections in those countries that have the choice, particularly in urban areas. This is not to say, however, that the utility of VSAT will disappear in the near future. National fiber backbones must become much more extensive before VSATs in remote regions are no longer necessary. Where such fiber networks are not in place, VSATs remain a viable and attractive option (GVF 2004, 12).

Consortiums for the bulk purchase of broadband connectivity

IDRC's ICT4D program also supported bandwidth consortiums to spur social and technical innovations to address the high cost of Internet connectivity in the developing world.

Figure 1.3. African undersea cables

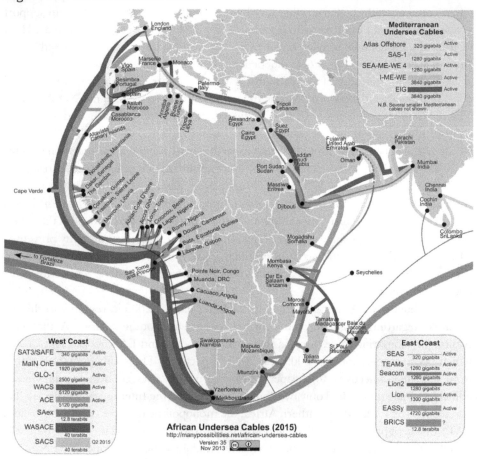

Source: Song (2011).

These consortiums leveraged economies of scale to achieve reduced connectivity costs for individual users. IDRC supported consortiums in both Africa and Latin America.

African research and education networking

IDRC, as part of its "Promoting African Research and Education Networking in Africa" (PAREN) project, released a study at the 2005 annual general meeting of the Association of African Universities (AAU) that mapped out activities on the continent related to higher education institutions and research networking. Results of the study spurred the AAU leadership to identify bandwidth as a key item going forward. While the initial aim of this project had been to facilitate collaboration among the many donors who were working on African university networking in an uncoordinated fashion, IDRC soon moved to supporting emerging and new African research and education networking organizations. This included support for the newly established Southern African Regional University

Association (SARUA) to explore high-speed network alternatives in the region. IDRC also teamed up with the Partnership for Higher Education in Africa (PHEA) to support a research and education networking unit at the AAU. In addition, it assisted PHEA in transitioning its own satellite-based university bandwidth consortium, based at the African Virtual University, into an independent entity.

A significant outcome of the early discussions that were promoted on research and education bandwidth consortiums was the establishment of the Ubuntu Net Alliance.[5] The Ubuntu Net Alliance has shown the effectiveness of research and education consortiums in confronting the problems of low bandwidth and weak capacity of African research and educational institutions that make it harder to realize the potential benefits of ICTs. The alliance represents a social innovation that has achieved solid results in catalyzing access to ICTs. When the Ubuntu Net Alliance was created, the average African university had the same aggregate bandwidth as a single home user in North America and African universities paid hundreds of times more for bandwidth than their counterparts in Europe and North America. Inadequate Internet connectivity prevented African educational institutions from producing and disseminating knowledge. Greater access would enable African researchers to better exchange ideas and work with peers elsewhere in the world.

The Ubuntu Net Alliance emerged in the latter half of 2005 in response to shifting dynamics regarding broadband connectivity in eastern and southern Africa. At that time, two major submarine cables were in the works – Seacom and EASSy (see Figure 1.3) – which became operational in 2009 and 2010 respectively. These cables enabled a shift from satellite connectivity to cheaper and better-quality fiber connectivity. Previously, educational institutions had only two choices for access to the Internet: expensive satellite connections or, for those in southern Africa, the monopolistic undersea cable consortium SAT3 that kept prices artificially high. Universities were also coming together around the middle of the decade to form national research and education networks (NRENs). The Ubuntu Net Alliance sought to connect NRENs in eastern and southern Africa at the regional level to achieve national and intraregional high-speed broadband connectivity for higher learning institutions and to link African universities and research institutions with global research networks.

The principle behind the Ubuntu Net Alliance was that NRENs could band together to form economies of scale that would give them the clout to negotiate better rates for broadband connectivity. Most NRENs on their own did not have the critical mass of institutions needed to negotiate better prices, as has happened in other regions of the world. The Ubuntu Net Alliance has been quite successful in this regard, arranging deals with Seacom, among others, for privileged access. NRENs have managed to negotiate with submarine cable providers for considerable quantities of bandwidth at prices between 20 and 25 percent below commercial rates (*Balancing Act* 2009).

Of course, cheaper access to increased bandwidth via submarine cables is useful only if national governments establish backbone infrastructure that can link to the submarine cable landing points and that holds greater bandwidth capacity. Ubuntu Net Alliance has been involved in pushing for policy changes to ensure reform in those countries without adequate backbone infrastructure. It has also lobbied for reforms to regulations that prevent educational institutions in some countries from owning and operating broadband fiber and wireless networks or from establishing cross-border connections.

The Ubuntu Net Alliance has also been successful in connecting African NRENs with those around the world. In May 2011, the European Commission pledged just under €15 million via the European research network operator DANTE to enable the development of high-capacity Internet networking infrastructure that will facilitate intraregional connectivity between research and educational institutions in Sub-Saharan Africa. And it selected the Ubuntu Net Alliance as a key partner in the initiative. The Ubuntu Net Alliance also established a connection between African NRENs and the Pan European research network GEANT in 2009 (Ubuntu Net Alliance 2011).

Building on an earlier IDRC-funded project to support training for optimization of university bandwidth in Africa, a key aspect of the Ubuntu Net Alliance's mission has also been to enable NREN members to collaborate in capacity building and learning. The result has been greater awareness and understanding of Internet network management and utilization among the NREN members. In addition, the Ubuntu Net Alliance has produced a variety of instructional materials, including a guide that details how to establish and finance NRENs (Ubuntu Net Alliance 2009).

E-Link Americas

IDRC's ICT4D program supported another attempt at social and technical innovation, called E-Link Americas, to catalyze affordable access to the Internet in Latin America and the Caribbean (LAC). E-Link Americas was a not-for-profit corporation launched in 2004 that sought to purchase broadband satellite and terrestrial wireless-based Internet connectivity and support services and resell them on a fee-for-service basis. By so doing, it could facilitate access for small communities at a rate much more affordable than the rate charged by commercial service providers. It could also stimulate demand that would provide a return on the initial investment and lead to it becoming a self-sustaining organization. However, shortly after it became operational, E-Link Americas began to experience difficulties, including technical challenges, start-up delays, cost overruns and problems in procuring anticipated seed funding. The project ceased operation at the beginning of 2006.

Lack of demand was not the reason for the failure of E-Link Americas. Market research had demonstrated significant demand for the services that it was supposed to offer. The organization could perhaps have benefitted from a more bottom-up, demand-driven approach. This could have included developing the necessary local expertise and technical infrastructure in a smaller number of communities so as to drive demand. More private–public partnerships aimed at collaboration and sharing of costs might also have helped. But the lack of adaptation to local demand did not ultimately cause the demise of the project. Based on much advanced planning and assessment, E-Link Americas had ensured that it avoided competition with existing companies by providing value-added services.

Failure was also not due to the choice of technology. The operational structure of the organization was a central hub in Canada that would manage sub-networks in LAC. It would leverage existing infrastructure in hospitals, schools and other community organizations by providing satellite and WiFi technology and nonproprietary software to extend services. It would also lease excess capacity on the network to other service providers. This structure worked reasonably well. However, the project did fall victim to an unfortunate technological mishap. An accident during shipment irreparably damaged the main hub that caused a delay of several months in launching service provision, as well as causing quality of service issues for some time. However, the resulting cost overruns could have been overcome had other seed funding sources fallen into place in a timely manner.

The most significant factor in the demise of E-Link Americas was perhaps its business and funding model. First, the project's business plan in many ways resembled a venture capital undertaking, but the funding structure of the project made such an approach more difficult. Seed funding was earmarked with the assumption that E-Link Americas would become self-sufficient three years after its incorporation. This timeline pressured E-Link Americas to risk bigger initiatives – rather than multiple smaller initiatives – to meet the objective of self-sufficiency in a timely manner. Second, E-Link Americas was started with the assumption, based upon concrete indications, that other donors would grant future funding. It was decided to proceed without fully secured funding because there was a small window of opportunity to get the project off the ground. But these funds did not materialize, which effectively brought the project to an early end.

Despite the project's demise, E-Link Americas did raise awareness among many groups – including the private telecommunications sector – that its low-cost approach to providing connectivity to underserved communities was a feasible one. Anecdotal evidence indicated that commercial service providers came to recognize possible areas for new commercial activity. E-Link Americas thus represented a response to an apparent need, albeit a poorly implemented response. It provided a host of important lessons regarding project management, the most notable of which were the lessons related to funding models for such innovative and risky projects: the need for appropriate funding to reflect the risks of venture capital-type projects, the importance of securing seed funding from the outset and the potential relevance of public–private partnerships as an avenue toward self-sustainability.

Part II: Demonstrating the Feasibility of and Demand for ICTs (Telecenters and Community WiFi Networks)

Implementing Internet backbone infrastructure represented one level of technical and social innovation for catalyzing access. However, IDRC's ICT4D program also supported technical and social innovation at the community level to improve access to ICTs at the "last mile." IDRC helped spur innovations related to both telecenters and community WiFi networks to demonstrate their usefulness in catalyzing access. Two parallel stories of support and investment are relevant here; both assumed that connection to backbone Internet infrastructure was feasible or available.

Telecenters

In an effort to mitigate the growing digital divide in the late 1990s, IDRC's ICT4D program sponsored telecenters in rural and remote regions of the developing world where telecommunications companies and governments were unwilling or unable to extend connectivity. It was envisioned that telecenters could provide places where specific groups and members of the general public could learn about the advantages of digital tools and access computers, the Internet and other digital technologies. Digital awareness could be expanded among those who were unfamiliar with ICTs and the Internet and demand could be bolstered.

Some telecenter projects demonstrated positive social outcomes. For example, in India, ICT4D partnered with the M. S. Swaminathan Research Foundation (MSSRF) in a pilot project to explore the potential of leveraging telecenter impact. The project employed wireless technology in a hub-and-spoke model where a central telecenter served as the communication point from which to relay connectivity to other telecenters in surrounding communities. While the project did not represent the ideal model of sustainability, it did have significant social impact on the lives of people in the poor rural villages of Pondicherry, India.

For example, in one fishing village, the telecenter – known locally as a village knowledge center – prevented the loss of local fishermen's lives by providing timely weather information. Among other information, the knowledge center provided 36-hour advance notice of weather forecasts for the Bay of Bengal, including wave height and direction of currents. These forecasts were derived from information downloaded from the US Naval Observatory in Rota, Spain.

Although the forecasts were general and not specific to the local area, they greatly reduced the loss of lives among fishermen. Before this service was established, up to half a dozen fishermen would die each year after being caught in rough weather far offshore. In the 10 years following the establishment of the service, no fishermen from the local village lost their lives while fishing (Nanda and Arunachalam 2009, 40).

In the LAC region, research showed that the establishment of telecenters had a great impact on the organizations that hosted them, as their members received technical and managerial training plus an expanded network of contacts. It also showed that both men and women used telecenters in equal numbers. Schoolwork, job searches and communication with family members abroad represented the main reasons for using Internet connections at the telecenters.

However, for the most part, the telecenter approach to extending connectivity took much more time and cost more than originally anticipated. Telecenter pilot projects brought rural underserved populations into contact with ICTs, but scaling up remained a persistent problem. As well, reliable connectivity to the Internet took longer to achieve for many telecenters. For example, a telecenter in Timbuktu had a significantly low number of users, while an evaluation of telecenters in South Africa revealed that only three of the six telecenters remained open not long after they were established. In Uganda, the poor state of Internet backbone infrastructure and irregular power supply led to severe connectivity problems (Etta and Parvyn-Wamahiu 2003, xxii, 90–91, 119, 167).

The problems in Uganda also occurred in Asia. Two telecenters in the Philippines struggled to maintain an Internet connection. In India, the effect of frequently occurring power outages on rural telecenters was minimized by using solar-powered backup systems, but unreliable power still plagued them (Shore 1999). Additionally, many of the telecenters were built in areas that did not have people trained for technical support or general management. It became apparent from the pilot projects that cost, space constraints, location, management, hours of operation, lack of awareness and literacy and language barriers were all factors that hindered the assumed potential of individual telecenters to bring people in rural regions in contact with ICTs (Etta and Parvyn-Wamahiu 2003, xxiii).

With this knowledge, IDRC's ICT4D programming shifted from promoting the setup of telecenters to promoting their sustainability. IDRC still saw telecenters as a necessary service in certain regions but sought to fund only those that would actually add value. This was a big change from the original "build it and they will come" mentality. With this aim, IDRC funded telecenter projects that would involve technology with minimal recurring costs. In Africa, IDRC directed funds to telecenters that employed wireless networks, assuming that these networks could be managed locally and sustained through business models that shared the high cost of connectivity with other users.[6] In the LAC region, IDRC came to recognize the need for collective processes for fostering the capacity and sustainability of telecenters (Gómez and Reilly 2001). Collaboration and exchange of information regarding problems faced by telecenters in the region – management, training, financial sustainability, community relevance and policy engagement – thus became a key component in the regional strategy to improve public access to ICTs.

IDRC's thinking regarding telecenters shifted further in subsequent years, moving away from involvement in starting up telecenters toward strengthening existing telecenter initiatives. This was driven by the realization that, by the year 2004, a seeming paradox marked the telecenter landscape. Despite the evident sustainability issues facing telecenters, the number of initiatives in the developing world kept growing. New national pilot programs were launched and some ambitious statements were made about scaling up telecenters as a national policy by which to achieve access in urban and rural communities (Proenza et al. 2001).

At the same time, the international development community was questioning the effectiveness of telecenter investments more vigorously given the rapidly changing context for access to technologies. Mobile telephony was becoming widespread; residential Internet penetration and public–private access initiatives, namely cyber cafés, had increased (Finquelievich and Prince 2007). Also questioned was telecenters' effectiveness because of some centers' inability to demonstrate and communicate impacts to ensure a return on investment and to increase the variety of services provided to communities (McNamara 2003).

Telecentre.org

Motivated by its previous findings in the field, IDRC entered into a strategic partnership with the Swiss Agency for Development and Cooperation (SDC) and Microsoft to shift the debate and modify the international development community's approach to public access efforts. This initiative, named Telecentre.org, was launched at the 2005 World Summit on the Information Society (WSIS) in Tunis and represented an innovative and well-funded five-year program hosted by IDRC. Telecentre.org shifted the focus from piloting telecenter activities to addressing the most obvious difficulties that telecenter initiatives were experiencing: implementing innovative sustainability models, developing effective and low-cost training methodologies and contents and increasing the quality and range of services offered to the local community. It also recognized that, just as there were similar types of challenges among telecenters worldwide, there were also opportunities to share knowledge and resources in a networked modality so as to leverage learning and results. Social innovation principles were thus central to the way that Telecentre.org addressed telecenter challenges. It identified telecenters as a nascent "movement," as well as a part of a broader "ecosystem" of interdependent innovators, suppliers, brands, delivery channels and financing mechanisms.

Early research on telecenter networks in three very different locations (Uganda, Sri Lanka and Chile) allowed progress on the sustainability aspect of Telecentre.org's mission. Research provided evidence in two critical respects. First, it identified successful emergent "social enterprise" models being tested in the field that could inform a revenue-generating strategy for telecenters. Second, it revealed the pitfalls and challenges that social enterprise models may face when adapted to local contexts. Those at Telecentre. org thus realized that no "one size fits all" approach was conceivable and that successful programming first needed research to assess the social enterprise readiness of local organizations as well as local business environments. For instance, in Uganda, the main impediment seemed to be associated with the lack of local services to be offered, while in Chile, an overcrowded field of service providers made it difficult to identify specific areas where telecenters could have a comparative advantage. As for Sri Lanka, the key challenge appeared to be the capacity to unify diverse telecenter networks in order to offer similar scaled-up packages of services (Comolli 2008).

Around the same time in India, other research looked at the potential for relatively dense rural telecenter networks to engage in business process outsourcing (BPO) activities. The research outlined the benefits and challenges associated with extending major urban telecenter-based BPO enterprises into rural areas. It was shown that telecenter-based BPO models could provide ownership to partners, which leads to greater motivation, faster learning, improved work efficiencies, absence of attrition and higher individual earnings. Furthermore, the BPO model was a low cost, flexible and scalable solution with the potential to enhance income generation opportunities for rural educated youth and village entrepreneurs. It also worked as an incentive to strengthen the telecenter movement in rural India (Datta 2009).

Another research project investigated an alternative business model in Brazil, Colombia and Chile. It explored the feasibility of using existing and already networked telecenter initiatives to channel services to the base of the pyramid by generating economies of scale and capturing multiple services providers interested in reaching a large number of small, relatively isolated and underserved communities. The research provided key information on how to adapt standard social enterprise implementation processes such as pre-feasibility studies, market assessment, organizational readiness studies and long-planning strategies to the specific needs of telecenters.

With regard to fostering collaboration among telecenters, research in LAC from 1999 to 2004 showed the potential of regional networking for providing more visibility, sense of purpose and capacity for policy advocacy. The creation of Somos@Telecentros[7] – a Latin American network of telecenter practitioners – was a result of this early phase. However, research also revealed some pitfalls that Telecentre.org should avoid – namely, overregulated, centralized and closed networks that excluded other key players in the broader ecosystem in which telecenters were embedded. Therefore, Telecentre.org did not establish a regional entity that developed national chapters based on a membership model. Rather, it provided human, technical and financial resources to increase organizational capacity among and to develop partnerships with a large range of potential stakeholders on a project-by-project basis.

"Networking by doing" instead of "networking for doing" was a wise initial approach. It allowed partners to generate a culture of collaboration that helped them later to move naturally into creating national networks (e.g., Chile, Colombia, Peru, Sri Lanka, Uganda, the Philippines and Bangladesh) and later on regional networks (e.g., Latin America, the Caribbean, the Middle East and North Africa, Asia and Europe). Systematic work on the part of Telecentre.org in facilitating knowledge exchange was instrumental in this approach. Telecentre.org organized periodic face-to-face "Telecenter Leaders' Forums" at the national, regional and global levels, as well as a collaborative, multilingual online platform of 6,000 members. Both of these initiatives became innovative and participatory ways of exchanging practices, building confidence and strengthening relationships among the growing number of Telecentre.org partners. When Telecentre.org incorporated as an independent foundation in 2010,[8] the regional networks formed a part of the governance structure of the organization.[9]

Telecentre.org identified the building of skills among practitioners, leaders and supporting staff as a starting point to generate socioeconomic innovation and effectiveness in telecenters. This was the case because previous ICT4D research had clearly shown that the lack of appropriate, continuous and rewarding training to telecenter operators and infomediaries made it virtually impossible to generate any significant change within telecenters. Nevertheless, generating locally adapted and educationally sound training materials was a challenge that not even the best-prepared telecenter networks could undertake by themselves. Thus, a bottom-up, collaborative approach led to the creation of the Telecentre.org Academy,[10] a complex of content creation, repositories, e-learning platforms and certification where local networks, universities, business partners and training organizations had the common objective of bringing training for grassroots telecenter operators to the next level.

Community WiFi networks

Advances in wireless technologies presented another potential alternative for extending connectivity to underserved regions that lacked viable infrastructure or faced high costs of access. Wireless technologies could enable significant reductions in deployment costs, particularly for "last mile" connectivity in low income and rural areas; WiFi is relatively low-cost once the backbone connectivity infrastructure is in place. WiFi technologies also made it possible for an infrastructure development model based on community demand and resources, small-scale investments and user experimentation (Purbo 2004a).

IDRC's ICT4D investment in wireless pilot projects in Africa, Asia and LAC demonstrated that WiFi can expand access to the Internet at a low cost, even in regions marked by challenging physical terrain and restrictive regulatory policy frameworks. It also demonstrated that low cost WiFi connectivity stimulates demand for ICT access among targeted populations. Furthermore, it showed that wireless technologies can lead to considerable cost savings for social services and business enterprises. As an example, a 24 percent reduction in costs between 2004 and 2009 was precipitated by the Uganda Health Information Network (UHIN) wireless model (discussed below). This model replaced the traditional paper-based approach to collecting health information.

Mesh networks

IDRC's ICT4D program funded a large number of wireless pilot projects that explored a variety of social and technological models. A pilot project in Peebles Valley – one of a collection of projects in southern Africa known collectively as the "First Mile First Inch" project – implemented a successful mesh wireless network. Peebles Valley is located just outside White River in Mpumalanga province, South Africa. An NGO-run clinic that distributed anti-retrovirals before there was a national public health program in place was linked to the supporting health service in Johannesburg via an expensive satellite link. The clinic had to keep contact with its hospice, which was across the national road in an adjoining valley with no direct line of sight communication. The project linked the clinic with the hospice using a mesh network: each connection point or node was connected to more than one other point. The network bounced a WiFi signal from one router to the next to reach homes of rich farmers, the home of a community health worker, a local school and, eventually, the hospice. This configuration involved eight connection points.

This configuration avoided the need for a costly central tower to provide connectivity to the various nodes and also offered redundancy to ensure that connectivity was maintained even when one node in the mesh was not operating. A particularly innovative part of the network was the deployment of a "cantenna" – a modified coffee can that served as a substitute for an antenna. This cantenna managed to establish connections at distances over 2 km, demonstrating that such low-cost, low-tech solutions are reliable for establishing community WiFi networks. The mesh network successfully provided Internet and, with the possibility of voice-over-Internet protocol (VoIP), reduced the cost of calls between the clinic and hospice (Morris and Makan 2008, 25, 48).

The mesh network functioned on a business model whereby the central clinic took responsibility for the VSAT connectivity bill of approximately 3,000 rand (US$500) per month for three gigabytes (3G) of download capacity. The Internet connectivity would satisfy the needs of the clinic and distribution to other users could lower the costs for all parties involved. The pilot was originally free for users and, as a result, users did not warmly receive the implementation of a payment model once the pilot phase came to an end. With the expansion of 3G mobile networks in the area, some of the farmers opted for 3G connectivity instead of joining the network. In addition, the establishment of a mesh network in White River – about 20 km from the clinic – that was based on an ADSL fiber backbone created the opportunity for a wireless link from White River to the Peebles clinic and mesh network at an even lower rate than that afforded by the VSAT connection in Peebles (Morris and Makan 2008, 52).

Despite the changes to the mesh network following the end of the pilot phase, the project demonstrated the feasibility of establishing low-cost connectivity in a challenging physical environment. It confirmed the claims of IDRC sabbaticant Onno Purbo, on whose ideas the project was based. Self-financed, bottom-up and community-based ICT infrastructure represents a viable, demand-driven process to overcome telecommunication companies' failure to address the last mile.[11]

Star typology networks

Another IDRC-funded pilot project, run by the Fantsuam Foundation in Kafanchan, Nigeria, successfully established a star typology WiFi network. Kafanchan, a community of roughly 83,000 people, is located 200 km northeast of Abujain central Nigeria. At the time of the project, it was poorly connected both in terms of fixed telephony and Internet; even mobile service was notoriously unreliable. The community also faced significant problems with power due to a poor electrical grid in the area.

The Fantsuam Foundation thus established the first not-for-profit wireless ISP in Nigeria called Zittnet, meaning "our network" in the Fantsuam language. Fantsuam used its satellite connection – which had a monthly subscription cost of US$1,250 – as the backbone connection for the network. A mesh network was not a feasible option in Kafanchan because of the low density of users and their geographical distribution. The project therefore deployed the network in a star typology, meaning a centralized wireless network using a communication mast to interconnect the various network nodes. The project also secured reliable power by setting up a hybrid system consisting of a deep-cycle battery pack that could be charged by the local power grid when functioning, from solar panels when possible and from a generator when the other two sources of power were not feasible (Berthilson et al. 2009, 76–8, 81–2, 86).

According to the business model for Zittnet, the Fantsuam Foundation shared bandwidth with external clients. Fantsuam charged each of its departments on a usage basis, while also charging the external clients a fixed monthly fee for predetermined usage rates. Income from the clients covered almost 80 percent of total bandwidth costs. Including the fees internal to Fantsuam, total money raised resulted in a surplus of US$430 a month that was used to pay Zittnet staff and maintenance costs. Challenges experienced during the project included difficulties accessing appropriate hardware (securing wireless equipment was not an issue in Nigeria, but securing the equipment for the power backup system was difficult), various technological issues, maintaining trained staff and securing an upstream Internet provider that was open to establishing business with Fantsuam given the size of the organization and the business model of its wireless network (Berthilson et al. 2009, 90, 97).

Relay devices

An IDRC-funded project jointly run by SATELLIFE, Uganda Chartered Health Net and the Makerere University's Faculty of Medicine demonstrated the viability and cost-effectiveness of integrating handheld computers, wireless relay devices and low bandwidth mobile networks into an affordable and sustainable wireless network capable of supporting two-way health information dissemination, data collection and email in under-resourced areas. Key to this wireless network was a relay device called a "wide ray jack." This adapted, SIM card-based, point-of-sale device served as a relay station between handheld computers and a central server housed at Uganda Chartered Health Net in Kampala. With the infrared beam of the handheld computers, users synchronized with the jack. The jack then communicated with the central server by way of the mobile network, enabling transmission of email, data and documents (see Figure 1.4).

Changes to the mobile networks in Uganda greatly enhanced the affordability, functionality and scalability of the network. Upgrades from a GSM to a GPRS network meant that users were no longer charged usage per minute, which had required UHIN users to transmit data during off-peak times to reduce costs. Costs dropped from approximately US$150 a month for each jack to US$15. The GPRS protocol also enabled much faster rates of data transmission (SATELLIFE and UCH 2006, 11).

To further enhance scalability, the UHIN project developed another relay device called the African Access Point (AAP) in later phases of the project to replace the

Figure 1.4. Components of the Uganda Health Information Network (UHIN)

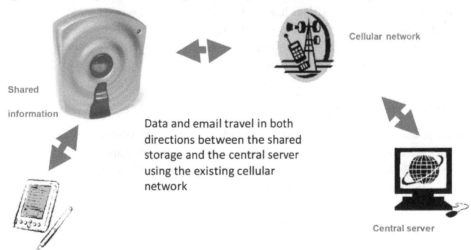

Source: Adaptation of the original in SATELLIFE and UCH (2004, 6).

commercially produced wide ray jack. The AAP offered additional features, used open-source applications and was significantly cheaper – US$600 compared with US$1,500 for the wide ray jack (SATELLIFE and UCH 2006, 42). A continual challenge to further scalability throughout the project's lifespan was reliable power to run the jacks. As a result, the project developed solar power units connected to batteries to power those jacks not attached to the national electricity grid. It implemented rechargeable battery packs for the jacks that were attached to the grid, but experienced regular power interruptions. Charging the handheld computers proved to be a challenge, requiring distribution of solar chargers (SATELLIFE and UCH 2006, 12).

The UHIN project achieved considerable success. The Uganda Ministry of Health was originally skeptical about using the wide ray jacks in the first stage of the pilot project that had established the UHIN in the Mbale and Rafiki districts of Uganda. However, it eventually realized the importance and utility of this wireless network. Studies revealed that, compared with the traditional paper-based method of data collection and transmission, the UHIN network reduced the cost over 24 percent from 2004 to 2009. The Uganda Chartered Health Net even received the 2006 Public Sector Excellence Award from the World Information Technology and Services Alliance (WITSA) in recognition of its innovative efforts to improve healthcare service delivery through the UHIN.

Long-range WiFi networks

The promise of WiFi technology prompted IDRC to explore the deployment of long-range WiFi networks in the LAC region. In this sense, the project was significantly different from the other WiFi projects IDRC sponsored that had demonstrated the feasibility of short-range, local WiFi community networks. This project succeeded in creating "EwiLD," an improved Media Access Control (MAC) protocol of the IEEE802.11 to allow for longer-than-usual WiFi links (300 km or more) at both 2.4 and 5 GHz. This project demonstrated the feasibility of WiFi networks (using low-cost, consumer-grade equipment) over very long distances and as a lower cost alternative to the more expensive WiMAX technology (Pietrosemoli 2008).

Financial sustainability

Many lessons emerged from the IDRC-funded community wireless network projects. Besides various technological challenges pertaining to both hardware and software, these include lessons regarding financial sustainability, necessity of human capacity for sustainability and regulatory frameworks. As for financial sustainability, various wireless projects revealed the importance of user-centric approaches to identifying and developing the products and services to be offered in community wireless networks. For example, a community wireless project in the Cambodian villages of Kep and Kamchai Mear created, among other services, a "family linkup" via Skype that enabled villagers to talk to and even video conference with family in Cambodian cities and abroad. The project applied a small fee to this service, recognizing that villagers would be attracted by the major cost saving compared with the alternative, mobile networks. This service proved popular among the community and generated income to cover costs of connectivity. Yet the project still faced the challenge of developing a model for longer-term sustainability and had to reduce staff costs and other expenditures (iREACH 2010, 17).

One service alone is often not enough to sustain community wireless networks financially. Increasing the basket of services is crucial to creating economies of scales. For example, VoIP services can be important but ideally should be combined with other products and services of relevance to users to maximize the added value of connectivity in remote and underserviced areas. This also means that demand has to be created by providing user-relevant content and applications and demonstrating their utility. In regions where technological literacy is low, users may not be aware of the opportunities afforded them. The sustainability of wireless network projects thus entails training and community empowerment to ensure the required user base (Berthilson et al. 2009, 68).

Also vital to financial sustainability is the ability to expand the payer base. A project in Huambo, Angola (AngoNet) was able to achieve a sustainable business model by expanding WiFi connections to other aid agencies and NGOs. This allowed AngoNet to recover the costs for a very expensive VSAT backbone connection. In fact, the success of the project led to a push to commercialize AngoNet as an ISP. Furthermore, the AngoNet project was replicated in every province to help the Angolan government meet its mandate to provide communities with access to ICTs (Morris and Makan 2008, 3). Another project in Kabale, Uganda also succeeded in establishing a business model whereby partners connecting to the network paid for the services; the network was therefore able to sustain its business model well beyond the donor funding stage (Berthilson et al. 2009, 10). However, achieving successful models is not always easy, as was discussed previously with regard to the Peebles Valley project.

Human resources

Human resource capacity is also vital to the sustainability of community wireless networks. This includes the use of technology that is easily manageable given the human resources available. In an IDRC-funded project in Uganda, ensuring adequate human resources entailed partnerships with third party organizations that could advise and train so the appropriate skills were developed for effective deployment and maintenance of the network. The project also institutionalized the required technical knowledge by placing the project under the auspices of the Uganda Community Wireless Resource Centre (CWRC), which was housed in the Department of Electrical Engineering at Makerere University (Berthilson et al. 2009, 10). But building adequate capacity is difficult. One IDRC-funded action research project in the LAC region resulted in the successful deployment of WiFi networks. However, sustainability of the networks remained a challenge, due mainly to a lack of technical knowledge in the communities where the networks were built. While WiFi technology helped to overcome the barriers of cost in this case, there remained other capacity-related obstacles – network management, maintenance and upgrades.

Regulatory framework

The regulatory framework is also vital to the feasibility and sustainability of community wireless networks. Several action research projects revealed that the successful implementation of community wireless networks requires significant regulatory overhaul because there often exists a gap between ICT policy and the reality on the ground. This is the case both because many existing regulatory regimes do not take wireless networks into account as positive catalysts for increased access and because wireless networks often cross various regulatory boundaries. Frequency spectrum, infrastructure and service provision are all areas requiring licensing. And, given that community wireless networks employ payment models but on a not-for-profit basis, they exist in a gray area between for-profit networks and networks that employ no payment models.

In the case of South Africa, for example, the regulatory structure was not conducive to the establishment of community wireless networks at the time IDRC funded a project in that country. For community-run wireless networks to be legally pursued, projects had to obtain both a private telecommunications network (PTN) license (operating on the 2.4 GHz band outside of one's own property was illegal), as well as a value-added network service (VANS) license should such community networks be connected to the Internet. The regulator further stipulated that the networks must be interconnected with those belonging to the mobile operators in the country. In addition, legislation indicated that the project would require a class license to cover use of necessary infrastructure (Morris and Makan 2008, 62).[12]

South African regulatory officials also were less than helpful regarding the establishment of community wireless networks due to an apparent lack of interest in the promise of community WiFi networks. Leaders of the Tsilitwa wireless project funded by ICT4D had difficulties gaining access to government and regulatory officials. Applications for permission to construct rural networks were fed through the slow, formal application process – further slowed by staff changeover – instead of being prioritized because of the benefits for rural inhabitants.

For example, it took one year before the South African regulator granted a three-month temporary license to conduct long-range transmission as part of the wireless network. It subsequently granted a further six-month license, but then indicated that additional extensions would require a telecommunications license. For this reason, the project leaders decided to proceed until challenged by regulatory officials, meaning that the project always operated with the threat that it could be closed down at any moment. The project thus operated illegally on two accounts: transmitting connectivity internally within the community without a license and adding a pay-for-service component without the appropriate license (Morris and Makan 2008, 7, 52).

The experience in Uganda was the complete opposite of that in South Africa and contributed to the success of efforts there to establish community wireless networks. The regulatory framework in Uganda allowed for community-owned networks. It also made the band between 2.4 and 2.4835 GHz unlicensed as long as the maximum power output did not exceed a specific amount. Because the equipment used by the CWRC did not exceed the maximum amount, it did not need a license. It did, however, need to secure a different license because the Uganda Communications Commission (UCC) required all

ISPs to obtain a license for operating public networks in this frequency range. However, the project could avoid most of the processing time because the network was non-profit and in a rural area, which meant no problems with interference. Furthermore, the UCC charged no fees for such a license.

Similarly, SchoolNet – a wireless network project in Mozambique – was able to operate in a more conducive regulatory environment. In Mozambique, commercial applications required a license, while not-for-profit applications merely required registration. The regulator indicated that SchoolNet required a license to operate the wireless infrastructure, but needed only to register (not get a license) as a service provider. Given that the project involved a cost-sharing mechanism, project leaders had to explain the details of the network deployment to the regulator – that the use of WiFi was in support of increased access and not commercial gain. Regulatory policy indicated that not-for-profit health and education service provision was eligible for license exemption provided that the relevant ministry signed off on the project (Morris and Makan 2008, 62).

Conclusion

This chapter explores examples of IDRC's programming directed toward catalyzing access through social and technical innovations to address first order digital divide issues. IDRC recognized that socioeconomic inequalities between the developed and the developing world, as well as between regions in the developing world, persisted and even increased with the emergence of ICTs. This was in part the case because of the non-uniform spread of ICTs and the resulting benefits that they accord. IDRC's ICT4D program therefore supported a variety of socially and technologically innovative connectivity projects that sought to demonstrate feasibility, to stimulate demand for ICTs and to develop the capacity needed to appropriate them. This programming revealed many important lessons and also raised further questions for future investigation.

A tension that emerged through IDRC's social and technical innovation funding was the viability of private versus public access to ICTs. This tension was particularly evident with regard to telecenters. This arose in part because most research on telecenters did not actually demonstrate that their impact was linked to the "public" aspect of using ICTs; the impact of telecenters could just as easily be identified with the impact from other modes of using ICTs. Tension also developed because of the growing spread of mobile phones (discussed further below), another access platform that did not need expensive public subsidies. Such developments raised questions about continuing to fund public access initiatives. For IDRC, however, dropping public access programming completely would come at the cost of losing past investments that still had social and economic relevance. It is for this reason that IDRC continued to support existing telecenter initiatives – most notably through Telecentre.org – by fostering sustainability and collaborative networking while also moving into research on other modes of access to ICTs such as community WiFi networks and, later, mobile applications.

Findings from partners supported by IDRC also reinforced the notion of a second order digital divide. Strict connectivity alone would not be enough to overcome inequalities in access and, as a result, socioeconomic divides more generally. Research revealed that simultaneous attention had to be paid to bolstering the ability to use ICTs and to creating relevant content. Programming related to catalyzing access would therefore also need to address issues such as education, standards, quality of service, censorship and intellectual property, many of which are policy and regulatory issues.

While IDRC's pioneering investments – establishment of and research concerning ISPs, IXPs, VSATs, bandwidth consortiums, telecenters and community WiFi networks – were expensive and risky, many of the social and technical innovations it sponsored managed to reduce the cost of access to a more affordable and sustainable level. Thus, IDRC and its partners paved the way for governments and other donors to commit resources, greatly increasing the spread of ICTs in less developed regions of the world as a result.

It also spurred a demand for ICT services that, in many cases, could then be taken up by the private sector. In this regard, there was a continual tension between public versus private provision of access throughout the duration of IDRC's ICT4D programming. In many cases – for example, in the early days of establishing national connectivity in Asia or in last mile regions throughout Africa, Asia and LAC – public investment was required to kick-start ICT services and IDRC often played a role in doing so. However, IDRC also recognized that private sector involvement was important. Hence, it increasingly sought to establish self-financing initiatives such as with ISPs, telecenters and community WiFi networks. Recognizing the importance of private sector involvement also spurred IDRC's increased attention to policy and regulatory environments.

It should be noted that the mobile revolution contributed greatly to IDRC's recognition of the importance of private sector involvement. Mobile phone penetration increased rapidly in the developing world in the early 2000s and its growth far surpassed any other form of ICT. What was significant about the growth of mobile telephony was that it occurred by way of market innovations like prepaid plans rather than through public subsidy. The mobile revolution therefore caused IDRC to look again at whether public subsidies were the best way to increase and broaden access to ICTs.

Furthermore, the ubiquity of mobiles also raised the question for IDRC as to whether fixed broadband connectivity was the best way to increase connectivity to the Internet in the developing world or if mobiles presented a more viable route. IDRC had supported action research pertaining to the development of fixed broadband Internet infrastructure and public access venues where users could access ICTs. The issue of fixed broadband versus mobiles, of course, remains a hotly debated one. However, given the spread of mobile telephony, IDRC subsequently gave greater attention to funding research on mobile applications. The fact that the mobile revolution came about through private investment spurred IDRC's interest in further exploring telecommunications policy and regulatory environments as the way to encourage increased ICT access. It did so with a focus not only on policy and regulation pertaining to fixed broadband connectivity, but also on mobile telephony.

IDRC's social and technical innovation programming geared toward increasing access to ICTs to address the first order digital divide combined with lessons from the mobile revolution raises important issues for future research. One issue is net neutrality with regard to mobiles. In the developing world, most people will increasingly access the Internet through mobiles. Openness of the Internet (because an IP address treats all bits the same way) has been a key element helping to ensure incredible amounts of innovation by all types of institutions, not just the telecommunications companies that own the network infrastructure. But the openness of the Internet does not apply to mobiles. Therefore, the implications of mobile-enabled Internet access for spurring innovation remain to be seen.

The role played by ICT4D at IDRC in catalyzing access to ICTs in Africa, Asia and the Americas was broad and diverse. It moved just ahead of the market and resulted in new public and private sector investments and opportunities.

As we sit in front of our Facebook and Twitter accounts now, it is easy to forget that the first Internet services in North America were not launched by the private sector. Rather, they were mostly public sector and university initiatives (e.g., the Advanced Research Projects Agency Network, or ARPANET, launched in 1969) to help link researchers with databases and with one another and it would take 25 years for them to be "commercialized."

Notes

1 The authors thank Katie Bryant and Kathleen Diga for their research assistance.
2 IDRC's rationale for funding additional ISPs in countries where ISPs already existed was that the existing ISPs either provided services only to select groups or the costs were so prohibitive that funding another ISP was warranted. Such was the case, for example, with IDRC's support for an alternative ISP in Sri Lanka, where service quality was poor and the average Sri Lankan could not access the Internet because prices were extremely high.
3 Also interesting about these ISP projects was the trajectory of the people who led them. The individual who spearheaded the Laos project moved on to lead the Science, Technology and Environment Agency (formerly STENO), the country's principal ICT agency. The leader of the project in Mongolia proceeded to run a successful IT company and was elected to parliament in 2010.
4 IDRC also learned that its ISP funding in Asia would have to first focus on national capitals and larger regional circles before moving to rural and remote regions. The rationale for this approach was much the same as the rationale for focusing on the initial target groups: service provision in urban cores would facilitate eventual expansion of services to rural regions.
5 For further information, see the Ubuntu Net Alliance website at http://www.ubuntunet.net/node/1 (accessed 17 June 2011).
6 Examples of these projects are discussed in the WiFi section that follows.
7 For further information, see the Somos@Telecentros website at http://telecentros.org/paginas/inicio.php (accessed 22 April 2011).
8 For further information, see the Telecentre.org Foundation website at http://www.telecentre.org/.
9 Several members of the Telecentre.org community collected and synthesized the lessons learned through Telecentre.org's network-building process into a collaborative and still-evolving wiki-book. See http://en.wikibooks.org/wiki/A_Guidebook_for_Managing_Telecentre_Networks (accessed 15 June 2011).

10 For further information, see the Telecentre.org Academy and content repository website at http://telecentreacademy.org.
11 For more on Onno Purbo's emphasis on community-based WiFi networks, see Purbo (2004b).
12 It should be noted that, as of 2008, these restrictions are no longer in effect in South Africa.

References

Afonso, C. A. 1999. "A Report on PAN-Supported Internet Service Providers." Online: https://idl-bnc.idrc.ca/dspace/handle/10625/23182 (accessed 11 October 2011).

Balancing Act. 2009. "African Universities Will Buy 60 GB of Bandwidth and Set Up a Continental Network." *Balancing Act* 475 (9 October). Online: http://www.balancingact-africa.com/news/en/issue-no-475/top-story/african-universities/en (accessed 4 November 2011).

Berthilson, L. et al. 2009. *Internet in Africa?(A)bort,(R)etry,(F)ail: A Compilation of Three Years' Experience Working with Wireless Networks in Africa.* Åkersberga: IT46. Online: http://idl-bnc.idrc.ca/dspace/handle/10625/42143 (accessed 17 June 2011).

Brotcorne, P. et al. 2010. *The Second Order Digital Divide: Synthesis of the Research Report.* Namur: Fondation Travail-Université. Online: http://www.ftu-namur.org/fichiers/FTU-Second_order_digital_divide-Synthesis.pdf (accessed 17 June 2011).

Comolli, L. 2008. "Increasing Telecentre Network Sustainability through Social Enterprise." *Telecentre Magazine* (December): 18–22. Online: http://telecentre.eletsonline.com/2012/04/increasing-telecentre-network-sustainability-through-social-enterprise/ (accessed 19 June 19).

Datta, R. 2009. *Rural BPO through Telecentres.* Final technical report prepared for IDRC. Ottawa: IDRC. Online: http://idl-bnc.idrc.ca/dspace/handle/10625/44633 (accessed 19 July 2012).

Etta, F. E. and S. Parvyn-Wamahiu. 2003. *Information and Communication Technologies for Development in Africa: Volume 2 – The Experience with Community Telecentres.* Ottawa: IDRC. Online: http://www.idrc.ca/EN/Resources/Publications/Pages/IDRCBookDetails.aspx?PublicationID=195 (accessed 22 March 2012).

Finquelievich, S. and A. Prince. 2007. "El (involuntario) rol social de los cibercafés." Online: http://www.oei.es/noticias/spip.php?article905 (accessed 23 April 2012).

Gómez, R. and K. Reilly. 2001. "Comparing Approaches: Telecentre Evaluation Experiences in Asia and Latin America." *Electronic Journal of Information Systems in Developing Countries* 4, no. 3: 1–17.

Graham, M. and N. Harfoush. 1999. "PAN: An External Review." Online: http://idl-bnc.idrc.ca/dspace/handle/10625/29595 (accessed 19 March 2012).

GVF (Global VSAT Forum). 2004. *Open and Closed Skies: Satellite Access in Africa.* Horsham: DS Air Ltd. Online: http://idl-bnc.idrc.ca/dspace/handle/10625/4903 (accessed 12 March 2012).

_____. 2005. *African VSAT Regulatory Regimes Study.* Final technical report prepared for IDRC. Ottawa: IDRC. Online: http://idl-bnc.idrc.ca/dspace/handle/10625/33461 (accessed 12 March 2012).

Hargittai, E. 2002. "Second-Level Digital Divide: Differences in People's Online Skills." *First Monday* 7, no. 4.

IDRC. 2002a. "The Internet: Out of Africa." Online: http://web.idrc.ca/en/ev-6568-201-1-DO_TOPIC.html (accessed 29 January 2012).

_____. 2002b. "The Travel Agent – Dago Beda." Online: http://www.idrc.ca/cp/ev-10136-201-1-DO_TOPIC.html (website discontinued).

_____. 2004. "Open and Closed Skies: Satellite Access in Africa." Online: http://web.idrc.ca/uploads/user-S/11247501711openskiesAfricaReport1.pdf (accessed 26 September 2011).

_____. 2005. "The Acacia Atlas: Mapping African ICT Growth." Online: http://www.idrc.ca/EN/Resources/Publications/Pages/ArticleDetails.aspx?PublicationID=445 (accessed 2 October 2011).

IDRC and ITU. 2005. "Via Africa: Creating Local and Regional IXPs to Save Money and Bandwidth." Discussion paper prepared for IDRC and ITU for the 2004 Global Symposium for Regulators. Online: www.itu.int/ITU-D/treg/publications/AfricaIXPRep.pdf (accessed 25 January 2012).

iREACH (Informatics for Rural Empowerment and Community Health). 2010. *Final Technical Report iREACH May 1, 2006 – August 31, 2010.* Ottawa: IDRC. Online: http://idl-bnc.idrc.ca/dspace/handle/10625/45274 (accessed 2 October 2011).

Ladikpo, M. 2005. "The Songhai Network of Telecentres." In *Connected for Development: Information Kiosks and Sustainability*, edited by A. Badshah, S. Khan and M. Garrido, 129–35. New York: United Nations. Online: http://idl-bnc.idrc.ca/dspace/handle/10625/28182 (accessed 4 November 2011).

Longwe, B. and C. Rulinda. 2005. "Of Gateways and Gatekeepers: The History of Internet Exchange Points in Kenya and Rwanda." In *At the Crossroads: ICT Policy Making in East Africa*, edited by F. E. Etta and L. Elder, 199–212. Nairobi and Ottawa: East African Educational Publishers and IDRC. Online: http://idl-bnc.idrc.ca/dspace/handle/10625/30363 (accessed 19 March 2012).

McNamara, K. S. 2003. "Information and Communication Technologies, Poverty and Development: Learning from Experience." Background paper for the *info*Dev Annual Symposium, Geneva, 9–10 December.

Morris, C. and A. Makan. 2008. *Comparative Study of "First-Mile" and "First-Inch" Technology in Different Low-Density Contexts.* Final technical report prepared for IDRC. Ottawa: IDRC. Online: http://idl-bnc.idrc.ca/dspace/handle/10625/42074 (accessed 12 March 2012).

Nanda, S. and S. Arunachalam. 2009. *Reaching the Unreached: Community-Based Village Knowledge Centres & Village Resource Centres.* Chennai: M. S. Swaminathan Research Foundation. Online: http://www.suchit.net/books/Reaching-the-Unreached.pdf (accessed 4 November 2011).

Pietrosemoli, E. 2008. "Setting Long Distance WiFi Records: Proofing Solutions for Rural Connectivity." *Journal of Community Informatics* 4, no. 1.

Proenza, F. et al. 2001. "Telecentros para eldes arrollo socioecómico y rural en América Latina y el Caribe: Oportunidades de inversión y recomendaciones de diseño con especial referencia a Centroamérica." FAO, ITU and IDB working document. Online: http://www.eamericas.org/contenido.asp?idcontenido=9 (accessed 29 September 2011).

Purbo, O. 2004a. "Motivating Community-Based ICT Infrastructure Development Using Wireless Technology." Online: http://onno.vlsm.org/onno/some-http://www.choike.org/documentos/community_ict_infrastructure.pdf (accessed 14 March 2012).

_____. 2004b. "Self-Finance Sustainable ICT for Development: Strengthening the Grassroots." Online: http://idl-bnc.idrc.ca/dspace/handle/10625/35785 (accessed 2 October 2011).

Riggins, F. and S. Dewan. 2005. "The Digital Divide: Current and Future Research Directions." *Journal of the Association for Information Systems* 6, no. 12. Online: http://aisel.aisnet.org/jais/vol6/iss12/13 (accessed 12 March 2012).

SATELLIFE and UCH (Uganda Chartered Health Net). 2004. *Uganda Health Information Network September 2003 – October 2004.* Final technical report prepared for IDRC. Ottawa: IDRC. Online: http://idl-bnc.idrc.ca/dspace/handle/10625/28191 (accessed 16 September 2012).

_____. 2006. *Uganda Health Information Network January 2005 – March 2006.* Final technical report prepared for IDRC. Ottawa: IDRC. Online: http://idl-bnc.idrc.ca/dspace/handle/10625/44121 (accessed 16 September 2012).

Sciadas, G., ed. 2005. *From Digital Divide to Digital Opportunities: Measuring Infostates for Development.* Montreal: Orbicom, ITU and NRC Press. Online: http://www.itu.int/ITU-D/ict/publications/dd/material/index_ict_opp.pdf (accessed 27 February 2012).

Shore, K. 1999. *The Internet Comes to Rural India.* Ottawa: IDRC. Online: http://idl-bnc.idrc.ca/dspace/handle/10625/25123 (accessed 12 March 2012).

Song, S. 2011. "African Undersea Cables (2013)." *Many Possibilities* (blog). Online: http://manypossibilities.net/african-undersea-cables/ (accessed 29 January 2012).

Ubuntu Net Alliance. 2009. "How to Set Up and Finance National Research and Education Networks." Document UA151. Online: http://www.ubuntunet.net/how-to (accessed 13 March 2012).

_____. 2011. "Africa–Europe Research Collaboration to be Transformed by EC-Funded Research Infrastructure." Press release. Online: http://www.ubuntunet.net/africaconnect_press_release (accessed 13 March 2012).

UNGANA. n.d. *The Immediate and Medium-Term Impact of African Internet Exchange Points*. Final technical report prepared for IDRC. Ottawa: IDRC.

Chapter 2

CATALYZING ACCESS VIA TELECOMMUNICATIONS POLICY AND REGULATORY RESEARCH

John-Harmen Valk and Khaled Fourati[1]

The International Development Research Centre's (IDRC's) "Information and Communications Technologies for Development" (ICT4D) program realized in the early days of its programming that a key part of catalyzing access to information and communications technologies (ICTs) involved attention to policy and regulatory environments. This was needed to understand the policy bottlenecks that hindered access to and use of ICTs. On its own, catalyzing access through demonstrating social and technical innovations is not enough to build an inclusive knowledge society and economy in the developing world.[2] ICT policy and regulation play a key role in determining market and pricing conditions that influence the extent to which people can access ICTs. A key element of IDRC's ICT4D program was funding research on policy and regulatory frameworks, their effectiveness or lack thereof and policy interventions that would lead to increased access.

Two IDRC-funded projects show how social and technical innovations depend heavily on appropriate policies and regulation for increased access. Beginning in 2003, IDRC funded a project that explored the potential of low-cost WiFi technology to overcome the high cost of Internet connectivity in Africa. However, the project soon found that existing regulatory frameworks hindered the deployment of community wireless networks on the continent (Morris and Makan 2008, 3). In some countries, regulatory frameworks slowed the implementation of wireless technology. In others, like South Africa, community wireless networks were actually illegal. So, to use wireless technology as an effective and low-cost method to extend connectivity to underserved populations, changes to the telecommunications regulatory framework were needed in many countries.

Research in Africa on implementing very small aperture terminals (VSATs) – a technology used to connect to the Internet via satellite – also revealed that, despite rapidly falling costs for VSAT technology, regulatory regimes prevented further reductions in VSAT connectivity costs. At the time of the VSAT research, up to 35 percent of Internet service provider (ISP) expenditures were spent on VSAT regulatory charges; licensing fees per terminal for a 128 kbps connection ranged from US$5,000 to US$10,000 (GVF 2005, 6). These regulatory regimes had been created when the high cost of technology and bandwidth meant that VSAT was used only by post and telecommunications organizations and transnational corporations. However, with reduced costs for both VSAT technology and monthly subscriptions, high licensing fees hindered the uptake of VSATs by small and medium-sized organizations (GVF 2004, 8).

These examples show that attention to policy and regulatory frameworks is vital for catalyzing access. Identifying the policy and market bottlenecks that made these connectivity projects expensive, difficult or even illegal furthered IDRC's resolve to support data collection and to foster the knowledge and capacity of actors in the field to carry on what an IDRC research partner called "policy entrepreneurship" (Samarajiva 2012). It also became evident to IDRC that, if ICT applications were to be useful and sustainable in fields such as health, agriculture or education, focus was needed on impediments to rolling out ICTs and this was generally the high costs. It realized that the main way to tackle these high costs was to try to reform telecommunications policies and regulations, particularly with regard to facilitating greater competition. The mobile revolution played a large part in influencing this thinking.

The mobile revolution initiated a shift in thinking because it occurred without public subsidy, thus challenging IDRC's earlier understanding of how policy and regulation could lead to increased access. Before the mobile revolution, IDRC funded partners had been promoting public subsidies via universal service funds (USFs) as a way to increase access. The effectiveness of this approach was put to the test by the success of the innovative prepaid mobile plans that lowered the price of services and equipment and provided affordable access to vast numbers of people. This transformation motivated IDRC to fund research that explored how policy and regulation – along with introducing competition in the telecommunications sector – could achieve increased access.

The mobile revolution also tested IDRC and its partners' previous assumption that fixed broadband connectivity to the Internet was the most appropriate model by which to achieve increased access. The rapid spread of mobile telephony showed that mobiles might in fact provide alternative Internet access. So IDRC-funded partners to explore mobile access and usage patterns, as well as policy and regulation geared toward mobile telephony. This research looked for the most appropriate policies and regulations for increasing access for marginalized and underserved populations.

IDRC funded three networks that conducted research to provide the data and analysis necessary for sound evidence-based policy and regulation. Research ICT Africa (RIA) conducted research in 20 African countries, LIRNE*asia* in Asian countries and the Regional Dialogue on the Information Society (DIRSI) in Latin America and the Caribbean (LAC). This research suggested that the best way of increasing access for underserved and disadvantaged populations was by having the appropriate price entry points. And these could be achieved through policy and regulation that was attuned to the desired socioeconomic development targets and that was based on sound data and analysis, as well as through increased competition in the telecommunications sector.

The networks undertook a two-pronged research approach. First, using the data from household and individual user surveys, they compiled and measured a variety of ICT access indicators (i.e., the uptake of ICTs) and usage indicators (i.e., the frequency of ICT use). These indicators gave a solid picture of ICT access and usage in Asia,

Africa and LAC. Second, they investigated the current state of policy and regulatory environments by looking at sector performance reviews (SPRs) and telecommunications regulatory environment (TRE) surveys. The methodological instruments developed by these organizations – access and usage surveys, SPRs and TRE surveys – are extremely valuable contributions to improving ICT policy and regulation in developing countries.[3] These instruments equip researchers with the capacity to put critical information in the public realm to help government officials and regulators establish evidence-based frameworks. The chapter explores this two-pronged approach in the sections that follow.

Tracking ICT Access and Usage Indicators

By tracking relevant indicators, research revealed the extent to which households and individual users in the developing world can access and use ICT services. These indicators provide valuable information about the level of success of ICT technological advances, markets and regulations in improving access and usage. They also point to the policy and regulatory changes required to support more affordable mobile and Internet penetration.

LAC

Regional Dialogue on the Information Society (DIRSI) conducted research into access to and usage of mobile telephony in LAC. Average mobile tariff rates in LAC were substantially higher than in other regions of the world – almost twice the average in OECD countries and over three times the average in South Asia (DIRSI 2010, 1). But DIRSI did not simply investigate tariff rates. It also researched the affordability of mobile tariffs to get a better perspective on the access situation in LAC, measuring affordability by using two indicators. First, it looked at prepaid mobile service rates as a percentage of the average income in the lowest third of the income bracket. Second, it looked at the difference between prepaid rates and 5 percent of the income of potential users in each income decile. The benchmark of 5 percent of income was used because this number is generally accepted as the ability-to-pay threshold for users of telecommunications services.

Research findings on the affordability of mobile services in LAC provided valuable evidence to guide policy and regulation. They showed, for example, that Costa Rica was the only LAC country to have affordable rates for mobile services. In Brazil, 90 percent of the population spent more than 5 percent of its income to buy mobile services (DIRSI 2010, 3). Overall, LAC countries could be divided into three categories: an adequate affordability gap (e.g., Costa Rica) because of low tariffs and low levels of income equality; a moderate affordability gap (e.g., Ecuador, Jamaica and Paraguay) because of somewhat higher tariffs and levels of income inequality; and a large or very large affordability gap because of high tariffs (e.g., Brazil) and high levels of inequality in income (e.g., Honduras, Nicaragua and Peru) (Galperin 2010, 5).

The research produced two other important findings. First, low-income subscribers normally paid additional money to ensure greater control over mobile spending patterns. This extra money was not usually significant, which was why the poor were willing to pay it. Second, mobile operators were not employing innovative business models that would attract low-income subscribers (Barrantes and Galperin 2008, 6). Because of these two issues, the subscriber base in the LAC region was growing very slowly despite widespread availability of mobile infrastructure. In addition, while LAC had a high penetration of mobiles, levels of use remained low. For example, mobiles in LAC were used on average 116 minutes per month, quite low when compared with 129 minutes in Africa and 290 minutes in Asia (DIRSI 2010, 3). As for reasons for use, DIRSI research indicated that the poor viewed mobile telephony as a valuable tool for strengthening social ties and for increased personal security. Mobile telephony was also beginning to prove useful for enhancing business and employment opportunities. So, the benefits of using mobiles were largely related to social capital – increased trust networks and coordination of informal job markets (Galperin and Mariscal 2007, 2).

There have been some positive developments that benefit low-income subscribers in the LAC region. These include dropping the cost of handsets, prepaid subscription plans, favorable policies such as calling party pays and high fixed-to-mobile interconnection rates, as well as policies that encourage investment. Yet prepaid tariffs still remain above affordable levels for low-income brackets. Policies and regulations in place encourage cost-saving measures like beeping or the use of payphones for outgoing calls, not regular and sustained use of services. Therefore, according to the research, these policy frameworks do not provide a solid basis for a sustainable market in the long term (Barrantes and Galperin 2008, 25). DIRSI suggested that lower tariff rates would improve subscription and usage. Studies revealed that the poor were willing to invest significant amounts into buying a handset, which ranged in price from US$53 in Peru to US$68 in Argentina (Galperin and Mariscal 2007, 6). DIRSI's research findings supported these claims, showing that innovative policies geared toward low-income subscribers have led to positive results both for subscribers and operators. In Paraguay, Bolivia and Guatemala, for example, TIGO – the new entrant in the mobile market – employed a low-cost model similar to the ones implemented in South Asia. This approach has led to tariff reductions to levels more affordable for low-income brackets. This, in turn, led to significant gains in market share for the new operator (Galperin 2010, 6).

Building on these access and usage findings, DIRSI made several recommendations for improved mobile policy and regulation in LAC. These included increasing competition by allocating more spectrum, introducing regulatory incentives to encourage innovative models like per-second billing and micro-prepayment, and the restructuring of other mobile policies that were mistakenly premised on the assumption that mobile telephony is a luxury good. With regard to the last recommendation, DIRSI particularly emphasized that taxation schemes must be revamped so they do not burden a method of communication on which the low-income bracket has a greater dependence – due to the high cost and lack of fixed-line telephony – than those with higher incomes (Galperin 2010, 6).

A key development emerging from DIRSI's work was the creation of the Support Mechanism for Telecommunications Regulation in Latin America, known as MARTA (Mecanismo de Asistencia Para la Regulación de las Telecomunicaciones en América Latina). Regulatory agencies and other organizations, whether affiliated with government, civil society or academia, can request assistance from this program for short research projects and policy reports in key areas of the Latin American regulatory agenda.

Box 2.1. Policy interventions and outcomes in Brazil and Mexico resulting from DIRSI research

With IDRC support through the DIRSI project, the Study Group on Telecommunication Law (GETEL) at the University of Brasília researched the issue of universal service and spectrum policy for rural, low-income and low-density areas. This study group organized the first seminar on that topic at the Secretariat of Strategic Affairs of the Presidency of the Republic of Brazil. At this seminar, the head of the Executive Office of President Lula presented the guidelines of the presidential broadband plan to be announced in the first half of 2010. After the seminar, one of the researchers from GETEL accepted a position as coordinator for the Broadband National Plan (at the Executive Office of President Lula). The group also contributed to the public consultation 24/2009, which dealt with the assignment of the 450 MHz frequency to fixed and mobile networks in rural and underserved areas in Brazil.

In October 2009, the government of Mexico proposed an amendment to the law on special tax on goods and services (IEPS), intending to include telecommunications in this special arrangement. A 2009 report by Flores Rouxet et al. from DIRSI argued that the tax would adversely affect economic growth, job creation and productivity. According to the report, the measures proposed by the government would increase the tax burden on telecommunications from 15 to 21 percent and result in the following: a reduction in mobile penetration of between 2.2 and 4.3 percent, a negative economic impact between 20 billion and 80 billion pesos, and a reduction in economic growth of between 1.7 and 6.8 percent over the next 10 years. CIDE Mexico sent the report to key stakeholders, telecommunications operators, senators and civil society organizations. The report's main conclusions were also publicized through various online forums. A microblogging campaign called #internetnecesario reached the second highest topic on Twitter at the national level and captured national and international media attention. These campaigns resulted in a reduction of the proposed telecommunications services tax from 4 to 3 percent with no additional tax for Internet access.

This program has contributed to a wide range of debates and regulatory reforms across LAC, such as the role of the 450 MHz frequency band in increasing access to mobile networks in rural and underserved areas in Brazil and Mexico's ICT taxation policy. (See Box 2.1 for further details on DIRSI's involvement with these two policy issues.)

Africa

IDRC-funded research in Africa undertaken by RIA revealed the challenges to increased affordability of ICTs for low-income brackets. Mobile telephony, RIA suggested, had addressed the access gap but had not solved the usage gap. Additionally, it had not yet helped to address the gap between those who could access the Internet and enhanced services and those who could not.

Mobile telephony had proven so important for addressing the access gap because fixed-line telephony was mainly available only in urban centers. Furthermore, fixed-line telephony tended to serve the more well-to-do as fixed-line expenditures were double those of monthly mobile expenditures. This is most likely the reason why at least forty percent of respondents in all countries surveyed (with seventy percent in over half of the countries) said they did not want a fixed-line telephone. Yet significant mobile uptake remained concentrated in urban areas. As penetration rates matured, uptake expanded to rural areas, meaning that those countries with high penetration rates exhibited a smaller urban-rural divide. Affordability of mobile services in Africa remained substantially less than in other regions of the world. The lowest percentage of income spent on mobile services was in South Africa at 7.4 percent and the highest percentages were in Kenya (16.7 percent), Tanzania (15.4 percent) and Senegal (14.2 percent). If percentage of income was calculated solely with respect to the bottom 75 percent of households, the figures jumped to 26.6 percent for Kenya, 23 percent for Ethiopia and 22 percent for Tanzania (Gillwald and Stork 2008, 7, 10, 15).

Surveys of willingness to pay for mobile services showed that minor reductions in the cost of equipment and services would result in a significant increase in subscriptions and in revenue for operators. In the meantime, payphones remained important in regions where they were reasonably accessible. 97 percent of respondents in Tanzania, 90 percent in Zambia and 73 percent in Rwanda indicated that they had used a payphone in the month preceding the interview. Owners of mobiles in those countries still used payphones to a significant extent.

As for the Internet, surveys found that, at the time, a low number of people were aware of it. Fewer than five percent of households in all the countries surveyed had a working connection with the percentage dropping to less than one percent in most countries surveyed. With the low penetration rate for home PCs across the continent, private access remained very limited, very expensive and far below the critical mass needed for it to have a significant impact on the economy and society (Gillwald and Stork 2008, 17–18, 25).

The research findings in Africa led RIA to make a variety of policy recommendations. With regard to fixed-line telephony, recommendations included encouraging increased competition to reduce access charges (i.e., monthly line rental) – even if that would result in higher usage charges – to enable new consumers to enter the fixed-line telephony market. RIA also suggested increasing competition in the mobile telephony market and reducing taxes on communications services to increase usage rates of mobile telephony. In addition, RIA suggested removing existing customs, excise or VAT taxes on handsets costing below US$50 to reduce access barriers. To improve Internet access and use, RIA recommended extending services at public access points, introducing Internet training at educational institutions and reducing the costs of Internet-enabled mobile services (Gillwald and Stork 2008, 35).

The RIA research findings were the first information of that nature to be available in the public domain and the ICT policy community made considerable use of the information on access and usage. Organizations that have employed these data include the International Telecommunication Union (ITU), UNCTAD and the Organisation for Economic Co-operation and Development (OECD), as well as many African governments (IDRC 2010). (See Box 2.2 for further details.)

Box 2.2. Groundbreaking baseline data

The household and individual user surveys conducted by DIRSI, RIA and LIRNE*asia* provided groundbreaking and extremely valuable information for the creation of evidence-based telecommunications policy and regulation. The data were important to better understand whether the poor and marginalized were benefitting from telecommunications policies that had been put in place. The data also provided insights into where private sector rollout was succeeding and where public sector intervention was needed.

The most important aspect of the surveys is that they brought comprehensive baseline access and usage data into the public domain for the first time. Private telecommunications companies had been commissioning research on access and usage but these data were either kept secret or were extremely expensive to obtain. As a result, many policymakers and regulators were working without the data and analysis necessary for informed decision-making.

Access and usage data could be triangulated with the sector performance data, which were more comprehensive and relevant than the data with which governments and international organizations had been working. The household and individual user surveys thus allowed greater understanding of the linkages between policy and regulation, market structure and services and users of services as well as non-users who were marginalized from ICT services. The fact that key international organizations have taken up the data that RIA collected shows the importance of the household and individual user surveys. In 2007, the ITU – and, later, UNCTAD – began to draw on RIA research findings. These proved instrumental in identifying policy outcomes and points of intervention, given that reporting by African countries to the ITU had been intermittent. Likewise, the OECD also incorporated RIA research findings into its analysis of ICT developments in Africa. The OECD benefitted greatly from the wealth of demand-side data provided by the household and individual surveys; previously, it had been working just with supply-side data from the ITU. OECD datasets now include the independent, public domain research conducted by RIA, rather than just the limited data provided by multilateral organizations and governments. RIA research was extensively referenced in the 2009 issue of *African Economic Outlook*, which explored issues related to ICTs and innovation in Africa (OECD 2009).

Asia

IDRC-funded research in Asia, conducted by LIRNE*asia*, found that access to a phone was high in the countries surveyed. Of those contacted for the survey, over 90 percent had used a phone in the past three months. However, ownership was low, implying a high reliance on shared access modes, whether private or public. Low ownership rates also revealed that space exists for a large increase in mobile ownership. Use of public phones decreased substantially between 2006 and 2008 among individuals at the base of the pyramid in South Asia, due in large part to a rise in ownership of mobile phones as the price of subscriptions and handsets fell. However, public phones still played an important role even among phone owners when, for example, mobile credit was low or the cost was cheaper (Sivapragasam 2010, 18).

More recent research in Asia revealed that mobile telephony had the characteristic of a necessity at the base of the pyramid. Those in the lowest income brackets spent a significant amount of their income on mobile services while those in high-income brackets spent only a little. In each of the six countries studied, the lowest quintile spent 24 percent or more on mobile services while the second lowest quintile spent at least 11 percent. In contrast, the highest quintile spent between 3 and 6 percent of income. As a result, flat taxes affected the poor disproportionately (Agüero and de Silva 2009, 10–11, 15). The main perceived benefits of owning a mobile, according to survey respondents, were the ability to act in case of an emergency, maintaining personal relationships and a greater ability to earn and save. LIRNE*asia* found that income did not play a significant role in explaining whether usage among low-income households was responsive to a price decrease, although it did play a factor in mobile ownership (Ramachander 2010).

LIRNE*asia*'s access and usage research led to one particularly significant policy-related outcome. LIRNE*asia* used results from its survey on telephony use at the base of the pyramid to convince the Sri Lankan government to amend a proposed flat monthly tax on mobile services. LIRNE*asia* argued that such a regressive tax would negatively target users at the base of the pyramid. Subsequently, the government adopted a tax framework that reduced the tax burden on those spending less than US$20 per month (LIRNE*asia* 2008, 84–5).

Investigating Policy and Regulatory Environments

In addition to tracking access and usage patterns, IDRC's ICT4D-funded research (in the form of SPRs and TRE surveys) investigated the effectiveness of policy and regulatory environments. This research produced valuable findings that explain why access and usage trends have developed in particular ways. It also has revealed which policy and regulatory changes are required to enhance access and usage.

The SPRs and TRE surveys revealed that effective policy and regulation is necessary to make ICTs affordable and to meet the pent-up demand for ICTs, demonstrated by the access and usage research. Furthermore, the research found that increased competition in the telecommunications sector was generally the most appropriate way of achieving affordability. LIRNE*asia* discovered that the movement toward promoting increased competition has greatly benefitted the telecommunications sector in Asia, leading to the growth of the sector and greater efficiencies. Results in India, for example, have been impressive. Teledensity increased from 2 percent in 1999 to 26 percent in 2008 with approximately six million subscribers being added every month in 2008. Mobile telephony has been the principle engine of telecommunications growth, with a jump from just under 1 million subscribers in 1999 to just over 162 million in 2008 (Malik 2008, 6). Pakistan provides another example of the benefits of increased competition. The awarding of licenses to two mobile operators in 2001 brought prices down and the subsequent rapid growth in the subscriber base reveals that such actions made mobile telephony more affordable (Wilson 2009, 8).

RIA research revealed that competitiveness trends in the telecommunications sector in Africa were troublesome because they were negatively affecting greater ICT uptake. RIA found that market entry of new telecommunications companies was efficient in fewer than half the countries studied. Only Nigeria[4] and Côte d'Ivoire scored positively for having a regulatory environment conducive to competition (Esselaar et al. 2007, 43). The research also called into question prevailing approaches to privatization in the telecommunications sector in Africa. In South Africa, RIA found that privatization of the state-owned fixed-line operator was carried out in such a way so as to maximize the return on the state asset. This approach to privatization – involving market share guarantees for the buyer – came at the cost of developing a competitive sector. Thus, while the rollout of fixed-line telephony increased, ironically, subscribers were unable to afford the service (Gillwald 2010). RIA therefore pointed to the need for regulation to ensure that monopolies, duopolies and oligopolies do not negatively affect affordability of telecommunications services. Increased competition, RIA emphasized, can both enhance rollout and, importantly, better meet pent-up demand for ICT services by addressing the greatest hindrance to increased uptake – the high cost of services.

Research findings point to several regulatory practices that can increase access to ICTs by fostering increased competition. One area of primary importance is regulating interconnection fees to curb anticompetitive practices on the part of telecommunications operators. Contrary to conventional wisdom on termination rate theory, RIA argued that termination rate benchmarking – the process whereby the regulator sets termination rates according to the cost of an efficient operator, a cost based on comparison with other similar jurisdictions – can lead to greater competition, lower end-user prices, more subscribers, higher investment and increased profitability for the incumbent mobile operator. It pointed to Namibia as an excellent example: regulators cut interconnection rates by almost fifty percent after implementing termination rate benchmarking (Stork 2010). (See Box 2.3 on RIA's termination rate benchmarking research.)

Managing scarce resources is another key function of telecommunications regulators. Spectrum regulation, for example, is an important tool for promoting technological advances considered integral to socioeconomic development. RIA investigated whether wireless frequencies in South Africa, Kenya and Uganda were optimized for rapid and cost-

---

Box 2.3. Policy outcomes from RIA's termination rate benchmarking research

In 2009, the Namibian ICT regulator sought to reduce the costs associated with interconnection, the cost customers on one network pay when phoning customers on another network. The Namibian government commissioned RIA on the basis of their indicator research to undertake a termination rate benchmarking study. The government wanted to avoid undertaking a best-practices methodology that would require an expensive international consultant to do long-range incremental pricing; benchmarking represented a much cheaper regulatory tool. Drawing on studies recently conducted in a number of African and international jurisdictions, the RIA research demonstrated that termination rates on mobile networks in Namibia were way above cost. This finding provided the regulators with the information and analysis to cut interconnection rates by almost fifty percent.

The Namibian study also led to changes in the South African telecommunications sector. South Africa noted the reductions in costs in Namibia as a result of termination rate benchmarking. Parliament put together hearings on the issue, during which RIA gave presentations. Following the hearings, pressure from the South African government and media convinced the mobile operators to agree to a reduction in interconnection rates. The South African changes in turn led the Kenyan regulatory authority to further reduce the mobile termination rates in that country beyond a recent cost-based reduction that followed consumer pressure on the regulator. The story of reduced interconnection rates in Namibia following RIA's termination rate benchmarking study was also recently included by the Information for Development Program (*info*Dev) and ITU in their 2012 *ICT Regulation Toolkit*. This web-based toolkit serves as a resource for policymakers and regulators worldwide.

---

effective rollout of wireless broadband services in rural areas. Research findings showed that the administrative allocation and assignment mechanisms of technology-neutral licensing regimes created competitive advantages for operators already holding premium frequencies. This led to spectrum scarcity and represented a major bottleneck for new licensees to enter the market. In Kenya and Uganda, where an increased number of wireless licenses were awarded, spectrum scarcity hindered the new licensees from operating. The results of this research pointed to a much more productive policy and regulatory approach to achieve increased wireless broadband rollout: liberalization and refarming (reallocation of frequency for new purposes and users) of premium bands necessary for wireless broadband (Calandro 2011). The story of Onno Purbo's work, which sought to catalyze access via no-cost wireless transmission, further demonstrates that spectrum regulation can serve as an effective, direct tool to achieve development outcomes. (See Box 2.4.)

The research findings, while identifying the countering of anticompetitive practices and monitoring of scarce resources as areas in which regulators should be actively involved, also suggest areas in which regulators should minimize involvement. One such

Box 2.4. Onno Purbo and spectrum regulation

The story of Onno Purbo is an example of how spectrum regulation can greatly increase access to the Internet. Purbo, with IDRC support, managed to convince the Indonesian government to allow unlicensed use of the 2.4 GHz spectrum because it provides wireless access to data and voice communications important in those "last mile" areas that lack adequate fixed connections. The regulatory changes to the 2.4 GHz spectrum enabled affordable access to the Internet because it provided the possibility of no-cost wireless transmission for a radius of 6 kilometers. The only associated cost was that of Internet access points, which had decreased due to continued technical innovations. The great impact of this spectrum regulation change on access and usage was shown by the fact that, shortly after the Indonesian government passed the legislation freeing the 2.4 GHz spectrum, more than a thousand Internet points of presence sprang up on a monthly basis.

Source: Fuchs (2005).

area is quality of service. LIRNE*asia* suggests that Thailand provides an example of how service quality can be achieved despite the failure of regulation. Improvement in quality of service has been attributable to market forces because the regulator has not established a system to collect and monitor service quality (Nikomborirak and Cheevasittiyanon 2008, 26).

Tariff regulation is another area in which regulators should minimize involvement. Findings reveal that indirect regulatory approaches are often most effective for reducing tariffs. Developments in East Africa provide perhaps the foremost example of how tariff rates can drop because of market forces rather than direct regulation mandating tariff rates. Mobile operator Celtel (now Bharti Airtel) was losing market share. It took advantage of its presence in three countries – Kenya, Uganda and Tanzania – to launch the One Network that abolished roaming charges in those three countries and allowed users to maintain their number and use the same SIM card. Competitors quickly moved to adopt similar networks in response. The result of this network was reduced costs for subscribers and an increase in number of subscribers across all networks. The main drivers for this innovation, suggests RIA, were loss of market share on the part of operators; high cross-border traffic in the region; an infrastructure system established prior to 1977 by the then East African postal and telecom operators network; and an enabling regulatory framework, particularly with regard to the international gateway (Mureithi 2009). This example shows how tariffs were reduced by market competition combined with the conducive, indirect regulation of the international gateway.

Successful indirect regulatory strategies to reduce mobile tariffs in the countries studied include calling-party-pays systems, fixed interconnection rates, prepaid cards and reduced roaming rates. However, LIRNE*asia* did find that Bangladesh was an example of an instance in which more direct regulation served to reduce tariffs. In this country, the regulator set a price band for mobile services and mobile prices in the country have been some of the lowest in the world (Khaled 2008, 20).

As for reducing Internet tariffs, LIRNE*asia*'s research revealed that leased-line[5] costs in Indonesia were a key input in the overall cost of Internet in the country. LIRNE*asia*'s research convinced the Indonesian government to undertake regulatory changes that would lead to reduced leased-line costs. LIRNE*asia* pointed out that international bandwidth prices were roughly twenty-one times the price in India and argued for the complete liberalization of the international gateway instead of simply licensing one more international operator. The government soon amended its regulatory framework so that domestic leased-line providers could connect directly to international cable or set up their own international landing stations. The result was a drastic drop in the price of domestic leased-line prices (Samarajiva 2012).

RIA research found that opening the market to competition in Africa has done more to meet demand for connectivity than have universal service efforts (Esselaar et al. 2007). LIRNE*asia* also confirmed this finding in its discovery of problematic implementation and management of USFs, funds established to finance expansion of telecommunications services to rural and underserved populations. In Asia, research revealed USFs to be moderately beneficial at best and to be vehicles of corruption at worst. In the case of Indonesia, LIRNE*asia* found that money existed in the USF, given that operators were required to contribute a portion of profits as outlined in the universal service obligation (USO) master plan of 2005. However, the government had not dispersed the money to universal service applications, thus failing to meet targets for universal service rollout in the country. Such developments raised questions about the effectiveness of USFs in Indonesia to bridge the urban-rural connectivity divide. In fact, LIRNE*asia* suggested that, since Indonesia had experimented with multiple models of USO provision with no success, the country should revisit the idea of having any USO plan at all. Other regulatory measures, such as establishing a competitive market or stimulating investment, might bring the same or better results (Wattegama et al. 2008, 25–6, 28).

The response in Thailand is an example of other challenges with USFs. There, stakeholders complained of unclear rules and selective implementation through incumbent state operators only. Interestingly, while state operators complained about having to implement USOs without financial subsidy, private operators resented having to contribute to the USF when they would prefer to deliver the services themselves (Nikomborirak and Cheevasittiyanon 2008, 24). The USF in Sri Lanka was even more troublesome. Levies on international calls had been applied to the fund since 2003 and it was estimated to be in the billions of rupees. However, LIRNE*asia* found that the fund had not yet been dispersed and industry stakeholders expressed concern that the money was being used for other purposes (Knight-John 2008, 28). The negative findings with regard to USFs thus suggest a better alternative – effective policy and regulation that prioritizes increased access by fostering fair competition – as the way to ensure the private sector delivers on the overall goal of spreading connectivity to marginalized populations.

While substantive regulatory reforms are important to encourage the competition that leads to lower prices and greater access for marginalized groups, the institutional aspects of the regulator and its practices are also important. For example, a regulator – legally and financially autonomous – is key to the effective functioning of the communications sector. An autonomous regulator, free of political interference, can ensure certainty and stability in the market. Furthermore, research findings reveal that adequate capacity on the part of the regulator is crucial for an effective regulatory environment. Regulators' lack of capacity to collect the information needed for sound and effective regulation was characteristic of several countries studied. In Thailand, the regulator lacked a comprehensive database on regulatory variables such as cost, capital expenditure, price levels and quality of service. Without such information, the regulatory body in Thailand did not have the adequate capacity to structure complicated regulatory rules that require significant knowledge of the issues at hand. LIRNE*asia* therefore recommended that the Thai regulatory body work toward creating a database on the telecommunications sector that included detailed data about service providers, their revenues, output, prices and quality of service (Nikomborirak and Cheevasittiyanon 2008, 6, 8). Lack of adequate knowledge and skill on the part of personnel working for regulatory bodies was also a notable research finding. Thus strategies on the part of regulators to attract high-caliber staff are vital for effective regulation in competitive telecommunications environments.

Research findings also point to the importance of transparency on the part of the regulator. Regulatory bodies should operate with clarity by, for example, being consistent in defining anticompetitive pricing or making the terms and conditions for the granting of operators' licenses publicly available. This is because unpredictable and subjective rules lead to market instability and negatively affect the functioning of telecommunications operators. More consultation in the regulatory process is also important. LIRNE*asia* found that the national regulator of the Maldives would benefit the telecommunications sector by creating channels for industry stakeholders to provide input on proposed rules. Also of benefit to the sector would be drafting standard procedures to govern areas under the purview of the regulator. These include establishing rules for issuance and renewal of licenses, allocation of frequencies, quality of service regulations, as well as creating rules defining anticompetitive behavior (Galpaya 2008, 8, 32–3). A study conducted by RIA found that national regulatory bodies in Africa did not use websites to communicate with consumers, citizens, the private sector, media and researchers. Only ten regulators had websites with content adequate enough to inform stakeholders and to enable their participation in regulatory processes with Egypt scoring the highest among all countries surveyed (Kerretts-Makau 2008).

The three networks (DIRSI, RIA and LIRNE*asia*), in addition to influencing governments directly through policy entrepreneurship, also motivated other organizations to lobby for policy and regulatory change. A prime example is how collaboration between RIA and the educational bandwidth consortium Ubuntu Net Alliance[6] – a collaboration enabled by IDRC – led to a greater recognition on the part of the alliance of the importance of policy and regulation for improving connectivity for higher education institutions in Africa. The Ubuntu Net Alliance had been involved in negotiating preferential rates with submarine cable operators for its national research and education network (NREN) members. However, it began to lobby more concertedly for changes to national telecommunications policies to improve connectivity infrastructure, for changes to the regulation stipulating that its members must purchase bandwidth from existing network operators rather than owning and operating their own networks and for changes to the regulation that prevented the implementation of cross-border connections.

Conclusion

IDRC's ICT4D program recognized early that policy and regulation play an extremely important role in increasing access to ICTs. Improvements to policy and regulation would help boost ICT access and usage significantly. This realization was further confirmed by the research it supported on social and technical innovations, which often ran into policy and regulatory bottlenecks that hindered the feasibility, scalability and effectiveness of these projects. IDRC funded research that would provide the information needed for informed, evidence-based ICT policy and regulation. It supported and developed the capacity among researchers to question and critique inefficiency and laxity in achieving increased access to ICTs. The three research networks IDRC supported – RIA, LIRNE*asia* and DIRSI – compiled great amounts of extremely valuable information in this regard. Of particular note were the methodological tools they developed to assess the state of the telecommunications sector in the developing world: SPRs and TRE surveys, as well as household and individual access and usage surveys. These methodologies enabled the compilation of information to be used in creating informed policy.

The research that explored access and usage as well as ICT policy and regulatory environments in Asia, Africa and the LAC region showed that increased access can generally be best achieved through a threefold process: gradually introducing competition in the telecommunications sector, creating an independent and capable regulator and streamlining regulatory mechanisms. Market competition combined with innovative regulatory policies suited to the contexts of developing countries can ensure that marginalized populations enjoy the benefit of the information society.

These findings led to a transformation in IDRC's thinking regarding how policy and regulation would achieve increased access to ICTs. The research undertaken by RIA, LIRNE*asia* and DIRSI revealed that evidence-based policy and regulation that prioritized equitable access while introducing competition into the telecommunications sector achieved greater results than the universal service policies espoused by governments and managed by regulators. Furthermore, the findings also confirmed initial interpretations of the mobile revolution – namely, that mobile telephony represented a socioeconomic development platform that needed research attention, attention previously concentrated on fixed broadband Internet connectivity. IDRC's policy and regulatory research investments focused increasingly on the likely impact of mobile telephony on the affordability of ICT services for the poor.

The quality and scope of the research carried out by the three networks not only informed and supported policies and regulation benefitting millions in developing countries, but also built capacity among talented young researchers in the developing world. This new generation of policy entrepreneurs now has the tools and the skills to continue to support the important and valuable work of their national ICT policy and regulatory bodies from within each country. IDRC's ICT4D program therefore implemented one of its most valued mandates – building capacity and expertise of local researchers to provide local solutions to the most challenging development problems faced by their countries.

IDRC's niche in international development is to support local research that constructively influences pro-poor policy reforms by governments and other institutional actors. IDRC's support for the work of these three networks clearly fulfilled this mandate and did so within time frames that were quicker and more focused than might have been expected. In the business of international development, it is seldom the case that major transformations can be observed in less than a generation.

Notes

1 The authors thank Kathleen Diga and Raymond Hyma for their research assistance.
2 This chapter represents the second in a two-part story of IDRC's efforts to catalyze access to ICTs in order to address issues related to the first order digital divide and thus socioeconomic development more broadly. For the other half of this story and for an explanation of various dimensions of catalyzing access to ICTs to address the first and second order digital divides, see the previous chapter in this book.
3 For further information on these methodological instruments, see Samarajiva et al. (2007), Calandro et al. (2010) and Stork and Stork (2008).
4 It should be noted that Nigeria data were not nationally representative.
5 A leased line is a two-way link between two or more points that is reserved for exclusive use, usually on a subscription basis. A leased line differs from a traditional public switched telephone network (PSTN) in that it is always permanently connected. For further information on LIRNE*asia*'s leased-line research methodology, see LIRNE*asia* (2005).
6 For further information on the Ubuntu Net Alliance, see Chapter 1 in this book. See also the organization's website at http://www.ubuntunet.net/node/1 (accessed 23 July 2012).

References

Agüero, A. and H. de Silva. 2009. "Bottom of the Pyramid Expenditure Patterns on Mobile Phone Services in Selected Emerging Asian Countries." LIRNE*asia* working paper.

Barrantes, R. and H. Galperin. 2008. "Can the Poor Afford Mobile Telephony? Evidence from Latin America." *Telecommunications Policy* 32, no. 8: 521–30.

Calandro, E. 2011. "Refarming Frequencies in Rural Areas: A Regulatory Perspective." Presentation given in Lima, Peru. Online: http://www.researchictafrica.net/publications.php (accessed 3 August 2012).

Calandro, E. et al. 2010. "Comparative ICT Sector Performance Review 2009/2010." Research ICT Africa Network, Policy Paper Series Towards Evidence-based ICT Policy and Regulation 2, paper no. 5. Online: http://www.researchictafrica.net/publications/Policy_Paper_Series_Towards_Evidence-based_ICT_Policy_and_Regulation_-_Volume_2/Vol_2_Paper_5_-_Comparative_ICT_Sector_Performance_Review_2009_2010.pdf (accessed 3 August 2012).

DIRSI. 2010. "Mobile Telephony: Are Services in Latin America Affordable? Policy Brief no. 1." Online:http://www.dirsi.net/sites/default/files/PB1-MobileTelephony-Galperin_0.pdf (accessed 23 July 2012).

Esselaar, S. et al. 2007. "Telecommunication Sector Performance in 16 African Countries – A Supply-Side Analysis of Policy Outcomes." Research ICT Africa Network, Research ICT Africa e-Index Series. Online: http://www.researchictafrica.net/publications/Research_ICT_Africa_e-Index_Series/Telecommunication Sector Performance in 16 African Countries - a supply-side analysis of policy outcomes.pdf (accessed 2 August 2012).

Flores, R. et al. 2009. "Telecomunicaciones: Servicios con efectos positivos para enfrentar la crisis: los impactos de la nueva propuesta de IEPS a los servicios de telecomunicaciones." DIRSI working paper. Online: http://dirsi.net/sites/default/files/DIRSI_09_MARTA_MEX_01_0.pdf (accessed 14 June 2012).

Fuchs, R. 2005. "Onno the Liberator! A Very True, Very Short Story." Online: http://idl-bnc.idrc.ca/dspace/bitstream/10625/34704/1/126212.pdf (accessed 5 August 2012).

Galpaya, H. 2008. *Telecom Regulatory and Policy Environment in Maldives: Results of the 2008 TRESurvey.* Colombo: LIRNE*asia*.

Galperin, H. 2010. "Tariffs and the Affordability Gap in Mobile Telephone Services in Latin America and the Caribbean." DIRSI working paper. Online: http://www.dirsi.net/sites/default/files/DIRSI-ITIC-10-affordability-EN.pdf (accessed 9 July 2012).

Galperin, H. and J. Mariscal. 2007. "Mobile Opportunities: Poverty and Mobile Telephony in Latin America and the Caribbean." DIRSI working paper. Online: http://www.dirsi.net/sites/default/files/dirsi_07_MO_reg_en.pdf (accessed 10 July 2012).

Gillwald, A. 2010. "Economy of Infrastructure: ICT." Presentation to the National Planning Commission in Johannesburg, South Africa, 23 September. Online: http://www.researchictafrica.net/publications.php (accessed 2 August 2012).

Gillwald, A. and C. Stork. 2008. "ICT Access and Usage in Africa." Research ICT Africa Network, Towards Evidence-based ICT Policy and Regulation 1, paper no. 2. Online: http://www.researchictafrica.net/publications/Towards_Evidence-based_ICT_Policy_and_Regulation_-_Volume_1/RIA Policy Paper Vol 1 Paper 2 - ICT Access and Usage in Africa 2008.pdf (accessed 3 August 2012).

GVF (Global VSAT Forum). 2004. *Open and Closed Skies: Satellite Access in Africa.* Horsham: DS Air Ltd. Online: http://idl-bnc.idrc.ca/dspace/handle/10625/4903 (accessed 22 July 2012).

_____. 2005. *African VSAT Regulatory Regimes Study.* Final technical report prepared for IDRC. Ottawa: IDRC. Online: http://idl-bnc.idrc.ca/dspace/handle/10625/33461 (accessed 29 July 2012).

Information for Development Program (*info*Dev) and ITU. 2012. "Interconnection." In *ICT Regulation Toolkit.* Online: http://www.ictregulationtoolkit.org/en/Section.3585.html (accessed 8 August 2012).

Kerretts-Makau, M. 2008. "African National Regulatory Authority Benchmarking." *Southern African Journal of Information and Communication* 9.

Khaled, M. 2008. *Telecom Regulatory and Policy Environment in Bangladesh: Results of the 2008 TRE Survey.* Colombo: LIRNE*asia*.

Knight-John, M. 2008. *Telecom Regulatory and Policy Environment in Sri Lanka: Results of the 2008 TRE Survey.* Colombo: LIRNE*asia*. Online: http://lirneasia.net/wp-content/uploads/2009/07/TRE_SriLanka_Final_2008Nov28.pdf (accessed 23 July 2012).

LIRNE*asia*. 2005. "A Preliminary Methodology for the Comparative Analysis of Domestic Leased Lines Tariffs in the South Asian Region." Online: http://lirneasia.net/wp-content/uploads/2005/08/leased-line-tariffs-v1.pdf (accessed 14 July 2012).

_____. 2008. "Final Technical Report on Research Program of LIRNEasia in Its Second Year." Final technical report prepared for IDRC.

Malik, P. 2008. *Telecom Regulatory and Policy Environment in India: Results and Analysis of the 2008 TRE Survey.* Colombo: LIRNE*asia*. Online: http://lirneasia.net/wp-content/uploads/2009/07/TRE_India_Final_Nov16.pdf (accessed 10 May 2012).

Morris, C. and A. Makan. 2008. *Comparative Study of "First-Mile" and "First-Inch" Technology in Different Low-Density Contexts.* Final technical report prepared for IDRC. Ottawa: IDRC. Online: http://idl-bnc.idrc.ca/dspace/handle/10625/42074 (accessed 13 July 2012).

Mureithi, M. 2009. "One Network: Pioneering the End of Roaming Charges in Africa." Presentation at the Africa Parliamentary Knowledge Network's "Development of an Equitable Information Society: The Role of African Parliament" conference in Kigali, Rwanda, 4–5 March. Online: http://idl-bnc.idrc.ca/dspace/handle/10625/40890 (accessed 13 July 2012).

Nikomborirak, D. and S. Cheevasittiyanon. 2008. *Telecom Regulatory and Policy Environment in Thailand: Results of the 2008 TRE Survey.* Colombo: LIRNE*asia*. Online: http://lirneasia.net/wp-content/uploads/2009/07/TRE_Thailand_Final_2008Nov11.pdf (accessed 9 July 2012).

OECD. 2009. *African Economic Outlook 2009.* Paris: OECD.

Ramachander, S. 2010. "The Price Sensitivity of Mobile Use among Low Income Households in Six Countries of Asia." LIRNE*asia* paper.

Samarajiva, R. 2012. "Policy Entrepreneurship through Research." Presentation at IDRC "Workshop on Innovation for Inclusive Development" in Negombo, 2–3 February. Online: http://lirneasia.net/wp-content/uploads/2012/02/Samarajiva_IIDworkshop_negombo12.pdf (accessed 10 May 2012).

Samarajiva, R. et al. 2007. "Telecom Regulatory Environment (TRE) Assessment: Methodology and Implementation Results from Five Emerging Economies." Presentation at the 35th Telecom Policy Research Conference in Fairfax, 28–30 September. Online: http://papers.ssrn.com/sol3/papers.cfm?abstract_id=1562424 (accessed 12 May 2012).

Sivapragasam, N. 2010. "Mobile Phone Ownership among Low-Income Earners: Substitutes or Complements to Traditional Public Phones?" LIRNE*asia* paper.

Stork, C. 2010. "Mobile Termination Benchmarking: The Case of Namibia." Research ICT Africa Network, Policy Paper Series Towards Evidence-based ICT Policy and Regulation 2, paper no. 3 Online: http://www.researchictafrica.net/publications/Policy_Paper_Series_Towards_Evidencebased_ICT_Policy_and_Regulation_-_Volume_2/Vol 2 Paper 3 - Mobile Termination Benchmarking - the case of Namibia.pdf (accessed 10 June 2012).

Stork, C. and M. Stork. 2008. "ICT Household Survey Methodology and Fieldwork." Research ICT Africa Network, Towards Evidence-based ICT Policy and Regulation 1, paper no. 1. Online: http://www.researchictafrica.net/publications/Towards_Evidence-based_ICT_Policy_and_Regulation_-_Volume_1/RIA Policy Paper Vol 1 Paper 1 - Household Survey Methodology and Fieldwork 2008.pdf (accessed 10 June 2012).

Wattegama, C. et al. 2008. *Telecom Regulatory and Policy Environment in Indonesia: Results of the 2008 TRE Survey.* Colombo: LIRNE*asia*. Online: http://lirneasia.net/wp-content/uploads/2009/07/TRE_Indonesia_2009Mar18.pdf (accessed 9 September 2012).

Wilson, J. 2009. *Telecom Regulatory and Policy Environment in Pakistan: Results of the 2008 TRE Survey.* Colombo: LIRNE*asia*. Online: http://lirneasia.net/wp-content/uploads/2009/07/TRE_Pakistan-Final_2009Jan22.pdf (accessed 10 May 2012).

Chapter 3

ACCESS TO KNOWLEDGE AS A NEW PARADIGM FOR RESEARCH ON ICTs AND INTELLECTUAL PROPERTY

Jeremy de Beer and Sara Bannerman

Why is an authorized copy of a Hollywood film worth $15 in the United States offered for sale at the same price in a much poorer country like India? Factoring in purchasing power parity, is it really surprising that consumers refuse to pay the roughly $641 price tag and turn instead to piracy to satisfy their understandable demand for access to foreign culture? What is being done in developing countries, effectively or ineffectively, to enforce laws designed to deal with such dilemmas? Maybe more importantly, if enforcement efforts succeeded in stamping out piracy, what would happen to the jobs, income and gray market spinoffs generated in the informal sectors where this activity mostly takes place? Could these losses be offset by net social or economic gains through innovation or formalization in low-income countries that better comply with the legal standards set by the world's most developed nations?

And might this debate be different if we were talking about *education* instead of *entertainment*? For example, how do students in Senegal behave when confronted with conflicting information about acceptable practices for photocopying textbooks and other educational materials? How should they behave? They're explicitly asked to photocopy books instead of taking them home or tearing out the pages but, at the same time, by so doing, they learn that most copy shops around post-secondary campuses, not to mention their own libraries, operate illegally. Do students at the wealthiest South African universities or researchers at renowned institutions like the Bibliotheca Alexandrina in Egypt face similar challenges? What can we learn from comparisons across the African continent or through similar studies in Asia or South America?

Looking at such issues from another perspective – from that of the producer instead of the consumer or the student – what incentives would exist to create textbooks, films or cultural products if they could be freely copied without compensation? Can publishers in developing countries effectively use creative licensing techniques established in European and American software industries for broader distribution? In Brazil, there are hints that it is possible to build alternative business models for producing music or other cultural content. But are these models scalable beyond the informal sectors in which they emerged? Can they be replicated in other regions of the world?

All these questions share at least three common threads: (i) their answers depend partly on the contentious topic of intellectual property rights (IPRs); (ii) the problems are complicated by the rapid proliferation of information communications technologies (ICTs) in developing countries; and, for these two reasons, (iii) these issues are the kind that interconnected communities of researchers have explored through collaborations established during the past decade.

On a somewhat deeper level, all of these questions concern an issue of increasing relevance to anyone interested in development: access to knowledge. Effective participation in the "knowledge society" requires, rather obviously, access to its most important commodity, knowledge. Knowledge is a prerequisite to – or, at least, a component of – poverty reduction, population health, food security, universal education and most other human development goals.

Access to and control over knowledge is influenced by many factors. Some are technological, like the now well-documented "digital divide" between rich and poor or between urban and rural populations. Some are social. A good example includes gender biases embedded in cultural practices that tend to impoverish women more than men by creating access barriers or by devaluing certain kinds of knowledge. There are also economic and legal factors, like IPRs, that affect access to knowledge for better or for worse. IPRs do not just operate as a key trading currency of firms doing business in the global information economy. IPRs also control the extent to which individuals can create and access knowledge-embedded cultural works, acquire new knowledge through learning materials, communicate knowledge with others using new technologies and exploit knowledge to build their own entrepreneurial businesses.

To address this issue, IDRC's ICT4D program has supported partners' work throughout the developing world to better understand the relationship between IPRs and ICTs and to use new understandings to create positive changes in policy environments and grassroots practices in these fields (Bannerman 2007). This chapter reviews and synthesizes some of that work to enable deeper reflection on earlier research results, integrate this learning into answers to broader questions and inform the strategic direction of future research.

The chapter has four parts. Following this introduction, the second part sets the legal, economic, technological, social and geopolitical context in which debates about IPRs and ICTs have unfolded. The third section describes select research activities addressing the connections among IPRs and ICTs. The strategy here is to perform grounded theoretical research – that is, to glean new insights and develop overarching concepts from evidence already gathered "on the ground" by researchers closely connected to real world problems and potential solutions. Notably, the underlying empirical research was gathered using mixed quantitative and qualitative methods that included statistical analyses, legal reviews, survey questionnaires, interviews, focus groups and other kinds of fieldwork. This hybrid methodological approach facilitates the fourth and final section of the chapter, which contains conclusions and recommendations.

Linking Theory and Practice among
IPRs, ICTs and Development

Standard economic theory suggests that exclusive IPRs provide an incentive for firms to invest time, effort and money into the creation and dissemination of new ideas (WIPO 1997). Without IPRs, the theory suggests, fewer firms would be interested in innovation in these fields and society would be worse off as a result. That is why copyright, for example, often provides over a century of exclusive control over original expressions of cultural works including books, music, films, video games and other kinds of software. Patents protect new, useful and unobvious inventions for up to twenty years by giving their owners a temporary monopoly in exchange for disclosing inventions instead of keeping them secret. Trademarks stop competitors from causing confusion among brands in the market, so long as the owner's words, symbols or other marks remain distinctive. Other kinds of IPRs fill in gaps by, for example, protecting the intangible assets of plant breeders, product designers or geographic regions.

According to the instrumentalist theory, countries that offer such IPR protection are believed to prosper economically as a result. These countries' businesses and citizens do better with protection than without because they are assured of returns on investments in creative expression, technological innovation and commercial goodwill. As the former director general of the influential UN agency, the World Intellectual Property Organization (WIPO), put it, IPRs are a "power tool" for economic growth (Idris 2003). Other theories suggest that IPRs are even "natural" rights, belonging innately to artists and inventors regardless of states' intervention or failure to provide formal recognition. On both justifications, the levels of protection of IPRs worldwide have been ratcheted upward for most of the twentieth century. The convergence of international trade and IPRs culminated in the mid-1990s with the TRIPS Agreement (Agreement on Trade Related Aspects of Intellectual Property Rights), which was reached when the World Trade Organization (WTO) was created.

In practice, however, the relationship between IPRs and development has long been a more complex matter than theory suggests. Historically, many countries chose not to protect IPRs, especially the rights of foreigners, opting instead to permit copying of foreign creativity and innovation (Chang 2003). The United States, for instance, did not grant copyright in foreign works until 1981. Only in the latter part of the twentieth century – after it became a net exporter of music, movies, books and other entertainment products – did the United States promote protection of its IPRs around the world (Chang 2003). The kind of free-riding on foreign creativity and innovation in which countries like the United States, Japan and Germany have historically engaged is one reason why many developing and least-developed countries are still cautious about protecting IPRs. Simply put, they need access to foreign cultural works and technological inventions and are not convinced that protecting IPRs will provide that.

Another practical reality has begun to emerge from empirical evidence, also supported by economic theory: having too much protection for IPRs is as bad as not having enough. Overprotection can create economic "gridlock" when too many IPRs are held by too many different people because transaction costs impede efficient market transactions

(Heller 2008). This is in addition to worries about potentially adverse impacts that IPRs might have on much broader issues like access to medicines, crop seeds, learning materials or clean energy technologies. Debates around these issues are essentially about distributive justice; IPRs can facilitate the concentration of wealth in the hands of large corporations (often multinationals), leaving local citizens at the mercy of the monopoly powers that IPRs provide.

Of course, opinions vary widely about the significance of these risks, the severity of their implications (if indeed even the worst fears are true) and the difficult tradeoffs that must inevitably be made in any case. That is why many developing country governments have struggled to set coherent policy frameworks for the protection of IPRs or, perhaps worse, have ignored these issues altogether. Those developing countries that have taken action have done so pursuant to diplomatic/economic pressures or technical advice from developed countries that are acting mainly in their own self-interest.

Concerns that developing and least-developed countries were being coerced into adopting inappropriately high levels of protection for IPRs coalesced into a call for changes to the way international policy is made and implemented. This led to the establishment in 2007 of a development agenda for WIPO – an effort to make the organization more responsive to the needs of developing countries, a kind of counterbalance to the TRIPS Agreement (de Beer 2009; WIPO 2007).

As if the relationship between IPRs and development were not complex enough, another variable has created new and even more difficult challenges – as well as profound opportunities – for virtually everyone in society: the widespread proliferation of radically transformative ICTs throughout the world, including within developing countries. Other chapters in this book demonstrate the myriad ways in which ICTs impact development. Looking specifically at IPR-related aspects of ICTs and development, especially pertaining to mobile telephony and to the Internet, this chapter emphasizes two disruptive developments.

First, ICTs threatened to – and, in fact, did – massively alter consumer behavior and, therefore, business practices. The rise of ICTs in the 1980s and 1990s and their use to effortlessly copy and distribute digital content challenged the predominant business models on which publishing, music, movie and other cultural industries depended. ICTs are still causing significant structural changes to occur within these industries (Castells 2009). Technological changes and corresponding economic challenges sparked a wave of "modernization," i.e., further strengthening of IPRs around the world to respond to the commercial threats posed by digital technologies (Sell 2003).

Second, ICTs have created unprecedented opportunities to re-imagine the place of individual citizens in the knowledge production process. No longer are consumers confined to the role of passive recipients of information. Anyone with access to appropriate ICTs is technically able to participate actively in the creation – and not just consumption – of cultural information and technological innovation (Lessig 2007). Benkler, in his 2006 book *The Wealth of Networks: How Social Production Transforms Markets and Freedom*, explains the possibilities of peer production as the key driver of a profound shift from a hierarchical industrial economy to a networked knowledge society.

The duality of ICTs as both a threat to established interests and an opportunity for socio economic restructuring, as well as the role of IPRs in those contexts, has made it an ideal topic around which to orient a robust program of research. Undoubtedly there were multiple ICT-related aspects of IPRs that could have been studied. The so-called smart phone patent wars that have made headlines lately could have been studied while the problem was in its infancy. The implications of trademark and branding strategies, such as registering domain names in cyberspace "landgrabs," might have been another topic of fruitful research. Instead, most IDRC ICT4D-supported research during the past 10 years has focused on copyright, rather than other IPRs. Why might that be?

In hindsight, one explanation for the focus on copyright could be the emergence of a sociolegal movement advocating for "open" licensing of IPRs, particularly the free and open source software (FOSS) and the Creative Commons movements (Wong and Sayo 2004). Although the FOSS movement first appeared in the 1960s and 1970s, the Creative Commons movement was just beginning to build a following in 2001. Both FOSS and Creative Commons shared, and still share, several common features: an underlying ethos of sharing and collaboration, a belief that ICTs will yield more social and economic benefits with IPR systems that facilitate sharing and a re-imagination of the role of licensing contracts to accomplish these aims within existing legal frameworks.

More specifically, FOSS licensing allows the free use, reuse, redistribution and remixing of source code – often free from royalty obligations – as long as there is attribution and recognition of authorship and previous contributors. What FOSS is to software, Creative Commons aspires to be for other expressive content, including literary, musical, dramatic and artistic works. Creative Commons licenses provide a flexible array of licensing options intended to loosen the "all rights reserved" model of traditional copyright, licensing greater liberties for users.

The characteristics of these open licensing models put them somewhere in the middle of divisive legal and policy debates about whether developing countries should provide more or less, or stronger or weaker protection for IPRs. They demonstrate that the issues call for much more nuanced and complex analysis than these binary positions permit. Given these characteristics, one might see how IDRC and its partners' interests in studying these topics have stemmed from more than just coincidental timing.

The practical tools of open licensing alone, however, were not enough to support an entire program of research. An overarching theoretical framework was needed. The instrumentalist and natural rights theories discussed above seemed inadequate; they were either empirically unreliable or normatively contentious. So research interests gravitated toward a then newly emerging way of framing the issues: access to knowledge or "A2K" (Kapczynski 2008). An A2K framework presumes that free and open flows of information, accelerated by an increasingly networked world, benefit societies overall. It anticipates a sea of change in the way societies are able to share information within and without and supposes that existing IPR paradigms require reform to adjust to these socioeconomic and technological transformations. This theoretical framework therefore rests on the principle of balance in IPR policy, weighing the need to protect authors and inventors on the one hand and the public interest as well as other citizens' countervailing rights on the other. This requires a focus on flexibility in IPR regimes. From a development perspective, one size of IPR system does not fit all countries or communities.

The A2K theoretical framework and the practical tools of open licensing were together viewed as having real development potential, offering a different, freer route for cultural and technological development (Lemos and Rossini 2005). The idea of a commons-based production that encompassed everything from "open source software, to initiatives for affordable, community-created educational materials, to architectural designs for reliable and cheap housing, to methods that allow artists, musicians and filmmakers from around the world to succeed even without access to commercial media distribution services," was associated with development potential (Lemos and Rossini 2005). It was viewed as a way of facilitating collaboration across borders, universal participation in the cultural and knowledge domains and sustainable products that could be adapted to suit the needs of local communities (Lemos and Rossini 2005). It was along these lines of thinking that IDRC's ICT4D program built its approach to IPRs and development.

Reviewing the Research

Exploring open source and development

IDRC's ICT4D program's main activities in the field of IPRs essentially grew out of its work on ICT tools and software capabilities. To understand the field of IP more fully, however, it was necessary to first identify the interests of developing country researchers in the field and to build networks of researchers, experts and policymakers working in the area.

The International Open Source Network (IOSN), for example, was initially funded by IDRC in partnership with the United Nations Development Programme (UNDP) to raise awareness of open source software as a tool for development. Along with a number of FOSS training guides and programs, support and advocacy, the project established a network of FOSS experts, policymakers, organizations and communities of practice through email lists, virtual spaces and other online collaborative tools. Over the time frame of the project (2003–2005), FOSS shifted from the periphery of development research to a major consideration in ICT4D discourse (IDRC 2005, 8–9).

Although the potential of FOSS and other flexible licensing systems was a focal point of much of IDRC's work on IPRs, research results led to mixed conclusions. In some circumstances where the FOSS model might have been appropriate, it was not being used to its full potential. It also became clear that FOSS licensing is not an appropriate choice in all circumstances. A 2005 study conducted by Bridges.org and funded in part by IDRC noted that neither the cost savings nor the advantages of source code availability of FOSS could, in reality, be taken advantage of in many African contexts. This study of computer labs in Namibia, South Africa and Uganda found that the widespread use of pirated proprietary software and the availability of donated proprietary software meant that FOSS generated few cost savings for computer lab operators. It also found that the local programmers could not take advantage of the availability of source code or did not have the ability to modify it. Proprietary software held several advantages over FOSS: it was generally more widespread, training courses and experience were easier to access, technical support was more widely available and support services were more competitive and less expensive. On the other hand, the study found that proprietary and mixed software could be combined in useful ways according to the priorities of given projects (Bridges.org 2005).

A focus on access

Given the expanding importance of IP issues in ICT4D's research portfolio, IDRC started to look beyond open source licensing to broader issues of access to knowledge. An IDRC-supported project, "Access to Knowledge: Copyright as a Barrier to Accessing Books, Journals and Teaching Materials" that was led by Consumers International identified copyright as a key barrier to knowledge production and dissemination. Researchers observed that, although the current global copyright regime provided certain limitations and exceptions to copyright, most countries included in this particular study had not taken advantage of the flexibilities afforded by international law. The project concluded that these policies priced access to knowledge out of reach of consumers in these countries through expensive copyrighted educational materials (Consumers International 2008). Interestingly, these research results foreshadowed similar findings from a much larger empirical analysis of media piracy in emerging economies (Karaganis 2011); the findings are discussed below.

The Consumers International project successfully promoted policy change. Researchers were able, through their work on this project, to influence the WIPO as well as various national governments. Consumers International argued that WIPO had helped to encourage inflexible IP systems in developing countries, rather than promoting the use of flexibilities in international treaties. Consequently, the *Financial Times* ran headlines such as "Bad copyright advice stunts learning" (Williams 2006a) and "UN body gives poor nations misleading copyright advice" (Williams 2006b). The study, combined with other pressures, drew a commitment by WIPO to change draft laws (Consumers International 2008).

The importance of the issue of IP flexibility is not limited to Africa, so the research by Consumers International was also useful in other developing regions of the world. For example, the alternative law forum in India used data and recommendations from this research to prepare its own submission to India's national copyright office and the intellectual property office of Mongolia sought Consumers International's assistance to comment on draft legislation in that country (IDRC 2009).

Meanwhile, in Africa, the "Commons-Sense: Copyright Alternatives, Education and Innovation in Africa" project responded (as had the A2K initiative) to debates at WIPO about appropriate IP protections in developing countries. Like many other research-related developments around the same time, this project was inspired by various academics' and NGOs' *Geneva Declaration on the Future of WIPO*, which called on WIPO to adopt a development agenda in line with its position as a United Nations agency (May 2007; de Beer 2009). Given the push toward more creative and flexible approaches to

IP issues, the project aimed to study the effects and implications of such systems on educational materials in Africa (IDRC 2004a, 4).

The scoping study on copyright-related barriers to accessing educational materials and the corresponding primer on possible alternative access mechanisms were widely discussed at events including a conference featuring renowned scholar Lawrence Lessig. In addition to the multimedia training materials developed from the underlying research (IDRC 2004b), concrete outcomes included the customized South African version of the Creative Commons license.

These were important developments. They not only opened the box on several IP issues that had until then been ignored in southern Africa, they also integrated new networks of civil society and scholarly researchers into the community of people working on these topics (IDRC 2007a). Several researchers involved in early projects like Commons-Sense eventually proposed and led the much larger-scale activities that have had sustainable impacts on practice and policy, not to mention IDRC's own research agenda. It was this growing community more than particular projects that fostered ongoing empirical research, robust policy dialogue and successful influence on development through IPR and ICT systems in national and international contexts.

In Africa, for instance, a large segment of the IDRC-supported research community came together under the umbrella of the African Copyright & Access to Knowledge (ACA2K) network. Formally established in 2007, this pan-African network built on the earlier work of the Commons-Sense and other projects and complemented concurrent research being done throughout the continent. A group of over thirty people from at least eight countries in Africa connected with experts on every other continent for this elaborate, empirical research project.

The topic of research – access to learning materials – was one with which IDRC was already somewhat familiar from Consumers International's work in Asia. The spark that lit this fire in southern Africa, however, came not from IDRC but from other organizations that included the International Centre for Trade and Sustainable Development (ICTSD), the United Nations Conference on Trade and Development (UNCTAD) and the Trade Law Centre for Southern Africa (TRALAC). These organizations supported a study by Rens et al. in 2006 on intellectual property, education and access to knowledge. This eventually became a model for the much broader internationally comparative research conducted through the IDRC-funded ACA2K project. The lesson learned here is how important connections with other organizations – international agencies, think tanks and NGOs – can become, even if the real value of such relationships is not fully apparent until sometime after a sponsoring research program has wound down.

The ACA2K project was both network building and methodologically pioneering. Researchers developed a replicable methodology to track the real world impact of African copyright laws and policies (Armstrong et al. 2010). Most research on IP and development employs either legal research methods that focus almost exclusively on desk analysis of legal documents such as treaties, statutes and case decisions or on econometric models that use statistical data and computational analysis. This project forged a new path because it took methods from other social sciences and humanities research (for example, impact assessment interviews and focus groups) and combined these with legal research on IP frameworks to gather empirical evidence of copyright's practical impacts in the selected study countries. These data were then analyzed comparatively to reveal common themes or significant distinctions in either law or practice, answering the overarching research questions around the role of copyright in access to knowledge through learning materials.

The research revealed that any problem copyright poses for access to legal materials is not primarily a legal one; it is a practical one. Copyright legislation in all of the study countries around Africa meets or exceeds international standards. That, no doubt, is a product of the technical assistance activities of foreign governments and international agencies; studies like those done by Consumers International revealed this in other regions of the world. While copyright enforcement in most African countries is weak, arguably undermining incentives for authors and publishers to invest in these markets, the real concern is the dramatic disconnect between the law "on the books" and the behavior "in the real world." Economic, social and cultural circumstances make it literally impossible for people to comply with copyright legislation based on Western legal systems and standards that are applicable in the world's high-income countries. Unrealistic laws do not only exacerbate enforcement efforts; even worse, they are perceived as foreign and unfair, thus undermining any potential that a healthy, balanced copyright system might have for all stakeholders in these countries.

Because of the ACA2K project, national governments, international organizations, grassroots activists and reputable academics better understand the nature of copyright challenges in Africa and potential solutions to them. The project produced dozens of published reports and policy briefs, as well as events in eight African countries, in Europe and in North America (IDRC 2010). Commentary on the research can, however, be summarized by reference to a review of one of the project's main outputs, a book. In 2011, May, a world-renowned leader on the political economy of IP, made these remarks in the prestigious journal *African Affairs*:

> This study is clearly intended to act as a spur to further comparative work to substantiate its conclusions for a wider set of countries. Moreover, there is nothing to stop the pluralist methodology employed across these cases being used more widely in the study of the gap between copyright law and its actual effects/outcomes. [...] [T]his is a valuable contribution to the discussion of copyright's role in education and development, which use fully (and explicitly) seeks to place laws in their social context. (May 2011, 655)

The research has had impact beyond academia with organizations including WIPO not only inviting consultation and engagement with project researchers, but even publishing the project's findings in its widely circulated magazine (Kawooya 2011). This was a welcomed *volte-face* for an organization so heavily criticized for its IP promotional activities and perspectives when IDRC began researching these issues.

In hindsight, perhaps it is not surprising that the research has been so well received and influential among stakeholders, given the careful monitoring and assessment of impact strategies throughout the lifespan of this project – a valuable tactic for future projects to focus on

Research across Access, Production and Publication

The shift in focus from flexibility and access to innovation and production was rooted in work supported in Asia and Africa. Research in both regions initially experimented with the open source paradigm as a tool for the production and adaptation of software in local languages, termed "software localization."

In Asia, localization projects had found that Chinese, Hindi and Urdu are highly complex languages with unique input symbols and so were not well served by technological frameworks originally designed in western languages (IDRC 2007b). IPRs could impede localization efforts if source code were proprietary; open source models present a possible solution here. That is one reason the UK Commission on Intellectual Property Rights in 2002 recommended that developing countries consider low-cost and open source software in their software procurement processes (Commission on Intellectual Property Rights 2002). IDRC's localization work, therefore, adopted FOSS development models.

In Africa, IDRC-supported partners also made use of open source software in projects related to ICTs in health, proving the broad sectoral relevance of the IPR/ICT issues being studied. In 2006, the "Developer Network and Open Source PDA Software for Health Data Collection" project, for example, began exploring the possibility of producing open source software applications for health data collection on handheld computers for developing countries. This was followed in 2007 with projects to integrate FOSS computerized health medical records systems in southern Africa and to develop and publish an open eHealth architecture using FOSS.

This research on open source licensing models helped to bridge the divide, not only between the policy and practice of copyright, but also between the consumption and production of copyright-protected ICTs. The potential of open access licensing, as further research revealed, is not limited to software.

Several projects focused on the potential of open access to research, i.e., unrestricted access via the Internet to peer-reviewed scholarly journal articles and other academic publications. These projects were focused not only on access to works in developing countries; indeed, they were more concerned with the production and dissemination of works coming from developing countries.

The projects "Access to Knowledge Southern Africa: Universities," "Open Approaches to Research in an Internet Age," as well as the Scholarly Communication in Africa program addressed the difficulties African countries face in participating fully in the knowledge society. Despite various factors inhibiting access to African research, these projects showed how open source technologies and platforms could be tools to encourage local scholarly publishing in African countries. Indirectly, therefore, these models could encourage indigenous approaches to research and could foster communities with less dependent and more productive relationships with foreign researchers (Creative Research & Development 2008, 6; IDRC 2007c, 4).

Another project – "Publishing and Alternative Licensing Models (PALM) in Africa" – acknowledged that, like the music industry, the publishing industry was experiencing dramatic shifts as it incorporated new ICTs. In 2007, the project established a collaboration between publishers in Uganda and South Africa to explore the use of alternative licensing models and online publishing tools. PALM Africa piloted business models ranging from free, online open access that might be sustainable with public funding to more complex models combining the commercial and free access in various ways. Some of the most innovative publishers in both countries began experimenting with these strategies to complement existing print versions of publications. Like several other IDRC-supported projects, PALM revealed a real potential for partnerships between commercial publishers and universities to extend and increase the impact of African research. Another insight gained by the PALM project was that African publishers were more interested in producing new local content than in making international content more accessible (IDRC 2011, 10). Later studies would build on this insight, focusing on domestic innovation rather than access to international materials.

Of course, the project encountered roadblocks such as a lack of capacity among participants to implement experimental business models using unfamiliar technologies. But one benefit of the PALM project was the clear identification of this kind of barrier. Five years later, in 2012, researchers involved in that project are making great progress. Members of the Ugandan research team, for example, are about to host an important regional meeting of the Creative Commons in collaboration with the "Open African Innovation Research" (Open A.I.R.) project. Once again, it is only now becoming apparent how IDRC's early investments in particular projects have helped to sustain and grow an interconnected research community working toward positive changes in business and policy environments.

Exploring Open Business Models in Latin America and the Caribbean

Meanwhile, in Latin America, places like Brazil were home to some early adopters of alternative and open IP practices. This provided fertile ground for research into how such new practices were created and adopted. Of particular interest was the idea of "open business" models. "Open business" for IDRC-supported Brazilian researchers describes a particular way of doing business related to information, knowledge and culture in which IPRs are neither primary economic incentives nor primary sources of remuneration. Open business models include, for instance, possibly giving away or making content or services available to some degree and then charging for value-added products or services around the content. Researchers in Latin America observed that such practices were common, for example, in informal cultural industries, from street vendors to online peer-to-peer networks. They appropriated technological tools to create their own networks for the production, distribution and consumption of culture.

A good illustration of an alternative business model is a music scene called *tecno brega* that, loosely translated, means "cheesy techno" in Portuguese. It emerged in the city of Belém in Brazil and has achieved significant success resulting in yearly revenues of

$20 million (Anderson 2009). *Tecno brega* records by local artists are released every year by the hundreds with both the production and distribution taking place outside of the formal music industry; 90 percent of the artists have no record contract and no label (Anderson 2009). Instead, the *tecno brega* model can be described as follows: artists freely release their music online and through local street vendors to market live events called "sound system" parties. Every weekend, these parties attract thousands of people to the outskirts of Belém, resulting in significant revenues for the artists from charging for admission, as well as for food and drinks. Other revenue streams include artists recording their live concerts and subsequently selling these recordings at the conclusion of the event.

Among the major, unresolved challenges following this research are concerns about mediating tensions between the legal and illegal – or formal and informal – aspects of open business models. Regulatory reforms may be needed to deal with these challenges. One example is the complexity of IP issues that arise within the *techno brega* business model. It is clear that producers do not rely on IP protection to earn revenue from their product outputs; they charge admission fees for live performances instead. But some, if not most, of the music performed during these performances and distributed before and afterwards is remixed from popular artists whose work is protected by copyright. If Brazilian producers are profiting financially by using copyright-protected content in their commercial business operations, how is this different – if it is different at all – from other kinds of activities decried as piracy? The complexities around the meaning of piracy and its impact in developing countries have been another major theme of IDRC-supported work during the past decade.

Understanding Media Piracy in Developing Countries

Beginning in 2007, IDRC collaborated with the US-based Social Science Research Council (SSRC) to support a research project called "Towards Détente in Media Piracy" that focused on the accessibility of foreign works. It also emphasized the productive contribution of piracy and informal markets by producing a multi-country comparative study of media piracy entitled *Media Piracy in Emerging Economies* (Karaganis 2011) funded by IDRC and the Ford Foundation. In finding that "high media prices, low local incomes, technological diffusion and fast-changing consumer and cultural practices" had combined to produce soaring piracy, the researchers concluded that expanded enforcement of intellectual property would do little to change the underlying market dynamics. These dynamics show that international media companies kept prices high to protect their price structures in their main markets while leaving space for piracy and informal economies to flourish, thereby meeting market demand for lower prices (Karaganis 2011 ii–iii). Much like the "Access to Knowledge" studies funded in the past by IDRC's ICT4Dprogram, the study concluded that consumers were being priced out of access to foreign works.

But the Media Piracy project also broke new ground in a number of ways. It provided concrete and objective quantitative data in an area that had, until the study, relied on industry-sponsored and methodologically flawed studies based on undisclosed data tied to an industry lobbying agenda (Karaganis 2011, 4–7). By moving away from examining educational materials and formal economies, this study was innovative in its consideration of informal economies and a range of entertainment products. Remaining consistent with past IDRC objectives, Media Piracy responded to contemporary policy developments; it was inspired by the emergence of the enforcement agenda – a policy agenda that attempts to encourage or coerce greater enforcement of intellectual property. Focusing on access, as well as on the failure of globalization to democratize media access (Karaganis 2011, 1), the study effectively examined the economically productive aspects of informal economies and the business models of both the informal and formal media industries. The main findings show that piracy has served a market that was otherwise underserved while contributing economically to developing countries (Karaganis 2011, 16–18). Media Piracy sought to address many of the prevailing myths around software piracy. Contrary to frequent assertions that there were strong links between organized crime and piracy, findings show no evidence of a relationship. The researchers conclude that "decades-old stories are recycled as proof of contemporary terrorist connections, anecdotes stand in as evidence of wider systemic linkages, and the threshold for what counts as organized crime is set very low" (Karaganis 2011, 39). Furthermore, there is no proof that antipiracy education programs have an impact on consumer behavior. The authors documented over three hundred antipiracy education programs but were unable to uncover benchmarks or even efforts to discover whether the programs work.

Finally, the study rejected the conventional wisdom that stricter punishments provide strong disincentives to piracy activities. It is recognized that judges are generally more concerned with violent crime such as murder and assault and tend to let cases focusing on economic damages to copyright holders take a backseat to home-grown criminal activity that poses threats to public health and safety.

Through years of rigorous study of piracy in emerging economies, this initiative has shown that piracy is not a legal problem but a result of market failure. As the popular iTunes "$1 per song" strategy shows, making creative goods more affordable could go a long way in diminishing piracy. Moreover, ineffective government enforcement strategies to curtail piracy may prove too costly and, in fact, outweigh the intended benefits to society, especially in developing and least-developed countries.

Conclusion

Over the past decade, a new framework for analyzing the relationships among ICTs, IPRs and development has emerged around the concept of access to knowledge. While leading scholars and activists from highly developed regions of the world – such as, for example, the United States, Europe and Canada – were instrumental in explaining and promoting theoretical aspects of the access to knowledge paradigm, IDRC-funded researchers in less-developed regions of the world have breathed life into this framework by empirically exploring its implications for development.

Initially, developing country researchers concentrated their attention on the applicability and appropriateness of open source software licensing. More recently, researchers in Asia and Africa have expanded their studies to examine open source software localization, copyright and access to educational materials and openly accessible scholarly publishing. In Latin America, researchers focused more specifically on open business models. Researchers from all regions joined forces to support groundbreaking research in media piracy that, along with outputs on copyright and education, has been among IDRC's most highly cited and widely praised work.

In this process, a shift in and broadening of interests occurred, moving from a focus on mechanisms that might be used or transformed to foster access to (often foreign) works to a focus on policy choices that might nurture local innovation, creativity, networking and collaboration within developing countries. The popularity of recent research is likely linked to its clear applicability to policy debates, as well as its convincing use of qualitative and quantitative evidence to inform recommendations. Continuing engagement with policymakers will help ensure that developing country researchers' work has maximum impact (Armstrong et al. 2010, 354–5).

The growing popularity in less-developed countries of open and online business models offers a variety of opportunities and risks that have not yet been fully explored or understood. While the increasing digitization of content, the virtualization of economic transactions and new, networked forms of economic organization offer opportunities for more distributed development, they also pose risks of unemployment, marginalization and exploitation. Continuing work should therefore explore how new business models and new models of IP management and policy can contribute to social and economic gains in developing countries; how the value of innovation, formerly bottled up within firms in part by IP laws and practices, can be more broadly dispersed; and how developing country entrepreneurs can use open business models to the greatest benefit. In this endeavor, a strong commitment to robust, empirical research methods is essential to ensure not only credibility but, more importantly, real world impact.

References

Anderson, C. 2009. *Free: The Future of a Radical Price*. London: Random House.

Armstrong, C. et al., eds. 2010. *Access to Knowledge in Africa: The Role of Copyright*. Cape Town: University of Cape Town Press.

Bannerman, S. 2007. *Intellectual Property Issues in ICT4D*. Ottawa: IDRC.

Benkler, Y. 2006. *The Wealth of Networks: How Social Production Transforms Markets and Freedom*. New Haven: Yale University Press.

Bridges.org. 2005. "Comparison Study of Free/Open Source and Proprietary Software in an African Context: Implementation and Policy-Making to Optimise Public Access to ICT." Online: http://idl-bnc.idrc.ca/dspace/bitstream/10625/44830/1/131304.pdf (accessed 13 July 2012).

Castells, M. 2009. *Communication Power*. New York: Oxford University Press.

Chang, H.-J. 2003. *Kicking Away the Ladder: Development Strategy in Historical Perspective*. New York and London: Anthem Press.

Commission on Intellectual Property Rights. 2002. *Integrating Intellectual Property Rights and Development Policy: Report of the Commission on Intellectual Property Rights*. London: Commission on Intellectual Property Rights.

Consumer Project on Technology. n.d. "Geneva Declaration on the Future of WIPO." Online: http://www.cptech.org/ip/wipo/genevadeclaration.html (accessed 17 July 2012).

Consumers International. 2008. "Final Narrative Report: Access to Knowledge Copyright as a Barrier to Accessing Books, Journals and Teaching Material." Unpublished and archived at IDRC.

Creative Research & Development. 2008. "Scholarly Publishing and Access to Knowledge in Africa Project: Project Planning and Scoping Proposal." Unpublished and archived at IDRC.

de Beer, J., ed. 2009. *Implementing the World Intellectual Property Organization's Development Agenda.* Ottawa: IDRC.

Heller, M. 2008. *The Gridlock Economy: How Too Much Ownership Wrecks Markets, Stops Innovation, and Costs Lives.* New York: Basic Books.

Idris, K. 2003. *Intellectual Property: A Power Tool for Economic Growth.* Geneva: World Intellectual Property Organization.

IDRC. 2004a. "Access to Knowledge Copyright as a Barrier to Assessing Books, Journals and Teaching Material: Rolling Project Completion Reports." Unpublished and archived at IDRC.

_____. 2004b. "Commons-Sense: Copyright Alternatives, Education and Innovation in Africa: Project Approval Document." Unpublished and archived at IDRC.

_____. 2005. "International Open Source Network: Rolling Project Completion Reports: Stage III Interview." Unpublished and archived at IDRC.

_____. 2007a. "Commons-Sense: Copyright Alternatives, Education and Innovation in Africa: Rolling Project Completion Reports: Stage III Interview." Unpublished and archived at IDRC.

_____. 2007b. "PAN Localization Phase 1 (February 2004 – April 2007) Final Report." Unpublished and archived at IDRC.

_____. 2007c. "Proposal by Southern African Regional Universities Association: Access to Knowledge Southern Africa: Universities, Open Research and Open Science in the Internet Age." Unpublished and archived at IDRC.

_____. 2009. "Report of Pan All 'Unconference' 2009: Innovation Processes for Identifying the State of Play and Priorities of ICT4D Research in Asia." Internal report to IDRC from Penang, Malaysia, 12–14 June.

_____. 2010. "ACA2K Project Outputs: High Quality Findings." Unpublished and archived at IDRC.

_____. 2011. "Publishing and Alternative Licensing Models Africa: Rolling Project Completion Reports: Stage III Interview." Unpublished and archived at IDRC.

Kapczynski, A. 2008. "The Access to Knowledge Mobilization and the New Politics of Intellectual Property." *Yale Law Journal* 117, no. 5: 804–85.

Karaganis, J., ed. 2011. *Media Piracy in Emerging Economies.* New York: Social Science Research Council.

Kawooya, D. 2011. "Access to Knowledge in Africa: The Role of Copyright." *WIPO Magazine*, February, 24. Online: http://www.wipo.int/wipo_magazine/en/pdf/2011/wipo_pub_121_2011_01.pdf (accessed 17 July 2012).

Lemos, R. and C. Rossini. 2005. "iCommons: Share the Past, Create the Future: Proposal to IDRC." Unpublished and archived at IDRC.

Lessig, L. 2007. *Code and Other Laws of Cyberspace. Version 2.0.* New York: Basic Books.

May, C. 2007. *The World Intellectual Property Organization: Resurgence and the Development Agenda.* New York and Abingdon: Routledge.

_____. 2011. "Access to Knowledge in Africa: The Role of Copyright." *African Affairs* 110, no. 441: 664–5.

Rens, A. 2006. *Intellectual Property, Education and Access to Knowledge in Southern Africa.* Geneva: ICTSD, UNCTAD and TRALAC.

Sell, S. 2003. *Private Power, Public Law: The Globalization of Intellectual Property Rights.* Cambridge: Cambridge University Press.

Williams, F. 2006a. "Bad Copyright Advice 'Stunts Learning.'" *Financial Times*, 20 February. Online: http://search.ft.com/search?queryText=%22bad+copyright+advice%22 (accessed 30 June 2012).

_____. 2006b. "UN Body 'Gives Poor Nations Misleading Copyright Advice.'" *Financial Times*,
    20 February. Online: http://search.ft.com/search?queryText=%22gives+poor+nations+misle
    ading%22 (accessed 30 June 2012).
Wong, K. and P. Sayo. 2004. *Free/Open Source Software: A General Introduction*. Kuala Lumpur: UNDP-
    APDIP.
WIPO (World Intellectual Property Organization), ed. 1997. *Introduction to Intellectual Property: Theory
    and Practice*. London: Kluwer Law International.
_____. 2007. *Development Agenda for WIPO*. Geneva: WIPO.

Chapter 4

ICTs AND SOCIAL INCLUSION

Chaitali Sinha and Raymond Hyma[1]

According to a growing number of reports, conferences, academic papers and popular media sources, more and more people are living in an "information society." Wikipedia, arguably an archetypal result of the information society, defines this term as "a society where the creation, distribution, diffusion, use, integration and manipulation of information is a significant economic, political and cultural activity."[2]

But what does an information society look like? Does it look, behave and respond the same way for everyone? Who is part of the information society and who is not? How does participation vary by gender, ability and literacy? How can information and communications technologies (ICTs) worsen existing inequities and further marginalize disadvantaged groups? As with any society, an information society is composed of individuals and groups occupying a shared territory – a virtual one, in this case – and is characterized by relationships, expectations, institutions and varying levels of influence and participation. This chapter examines two central questions that are closely linked: how can inequities of access to ICTs be redressed and how can access to ICTs potentially facilitate or inhibit social inclusion?

It would be foolish to assume that just using ICTs alone could redress inequities that persist within and among these groups.[3] There are myriad factors and complex dependencies underlying if, how and to what extent social exclusion is experienced. Similarly, the ways in which social inclusion can be made possible through the use of ICTs are equally complex, interdependent and non-linear in nature. Social disadvantages and vulnerability can be examined along several different axes, many of which can be experienced simultaneously. The focus of this chapter, which draws on over a decade and a half of action research supported by the International Development Research Centre (IDRC), is on asking how men and women, youth and people of different cultures and languages experience exclusion from the information society or gain opportunities for social inclusion through the use of ICTs.

Conceptual Framework

ICTs are embedded in a complex array of factors that range from physical ability, education and literacy, community and institutional structures to social resources and relationships (Warschauer 2003). Accordingly, it is not sufficient to merely determine whether different groups have the capability to access and use ICTs in different environments. There is also a significant need to examine (i) the context and trends of use (*the nature of use*), (ii) the common uses (*the purpose of use*) and (iii) whether these result in social inclusion or exclusion (*ends of use*) (Mann 2003). This chapter will review these dimensions of use in relation to gender, language and youth, which were three areas where IDRC concentrated its focus regarding social inclusion and the information society in the developing world. (See Appendix 1 for a description of this conceptual framework model.)

In the field of development, ICTs can be seen by some as paradoxical. On the one hand, they can serve as a means to amplify and aggregate the voices of those people that may be otherwise left behind or be unheard altogether (Kenny 2002). On the other hand, ICTs can be used by the powerful elite to filter information, alter perceptions or persecute those who are already largely excluded and marginalized (Deibert et al. 2012). Social inclusion and exclusion have been important in research in information and communications technologies for development (ICT4D). This is because, as ICT use and digitization continue to spread throughout the world, the need to research and understand the nature and extent of the relationship between ICTs and disadvantaged citizens assumes greater significance. Social inclusion can be defined as the extent to which "individuals, families and communities are able to fully participate in society and control their own destinies, taking into account a variety of factors related to economic resources, employment, health education, housing, recreating, culture and civic engagement" (Warschauer 2003). Looking at the flip side, social exclusion can be defined as a result of multiple deprivations, the breaking of family ties and social relationships and loss of identity and purpose (Silver 1995). The scope of these concepts does not have to be restricted to the area of financial poverty; their use in this chapter will be broader than that. Moreover, the relationship between inclusion/exclusion and different social change processes will be shown as one that is complex and often non-linear in nature.

These relationships involve issues that affect critical services and rights, including health, education, employment, security and political participation – in short, the benefits of citizenship. Moreover, the growing prevalence of ICTs in the development discourse makes it essential to conduct research on the nature and extent of change to which ICTs contribute. These changes can be negative or positive, intended or unintended. ICTs, in their own right and to varying degrees, can contribute to greater or lesser participation in the benefits of the information society. What is noteworthy here is that ICTs should not be perceived as neutral tools that are introduced into a complex situation. Rather, ICTs themselves are socially constructed and are therefore imbued with social values. The reasons for studying ICTs and how they reflect or counter the dominant value systems in which they are used are based in the demand for more informed and contextually appropriate interpretation of ICTs when influencing design, technological innovations, social structures and policy processes.

IDRC has been supportive of World Summit on the Information Society (WSIS) principles of equity and inclusion since IDRC began supporting research in developing countries in 1970. In the last fifteen to twenty years, IDRC has been actively supporting researchers to carry out rigorous and action-research studies that examined the relationships between ICTs and different aspects of society. ICT4D values were espoused at the groundbreaking WSIS in Geneva, whose first principle declared:

[...] our common desire and commitment to build a people-centered, inclusive and development-oriented Information Society, where everyone can create, access, utilize, and share information and knowledge, enabling individuals, communities and peoples to achieve their full potential in promoting their sustainable development and improving their quality of life. (World Summit on the Information Society 2003, 1)

IDRC's research portfolios in Asia, Africa, the Middle East, Latin America and the Caribbean have focused on socially disadvantaged groups. Each study involved significant local engagement, local leadership and a focus on participatory development, design and learning. This helped ensure the research processes and findings were shaped by the pressing needs of the populations involved in the study and reflected local realities. Supported projects demonstrated and documented both positive outcomes (social inclusion), as well as negative outcomes (social exclusion) through ICT4D interventions. Findings presented in this chapter span a range of changes in policy, social and technology realms and should be considered relative to the knowledge gaps and particular circumstances present when the studies were funded and when the findings were communicated.

Gender Relations, ICTs and Social Inclusion

Social analysis in general and gender analysis in particular are indispensable when addressing equity issues regarding access to resources and, subsequently, how the level of access influences social inclusion or exclusion. Researching gender issues implies examining the intersection of race, ethnicity and class as they pertain to masculine and feminine behaviors. According to Kabeer (2003), "gender" refers to the rules, norms, customs and practices by which biological differences between males and females are translated into socially constructed differences between men and women and between boys and girls. Although discrimination according to gender can be experienced by both men and women, gender discrimination globally is significantly more pronounced toward women and girls – notably in low- and middle-income countries (Mohanty 1991; Kabeer 1994). IDRC supported many of the early studies done in low- and middle-income countries that gathered sex-disaggregated household-level data on ICT usage. These findings, discussed later in this section, help provide important baseline knowledge when it comes to examining the gendered nature of ICT access and use. Findings from other studies provide insights on the second central question of how access to ICTs can potentially facilitate or inhibit social inclusion. By exploring the purpose of use and the ends achieved, these findings illustrate the range of outcomes that the use of ICTs can influence – some outcomes that arguably increase social inclusion and others that suggest reinforcing or creating new forms of power asymmetries.

Some questions come to mind when thinking about gender issues in an information society: (i) What types of gender sensitivities need to be considered when introducing a new ICT into a community? (ii) To what extent does the introduction of certain ICTs influence the underlying contributing factors for gender inequities? (iii) Do ICTs have the potential to reshape or break societal norms and cultural practices as they pertain to gender roles and equity? (iv) How are issues of mobility, geography, literacy and responsibilities differentially influencing how women and men use ICTs? These questions are among the many presented to IDRC over the years as pressing research concerns from researchers in developing countries.

Gender and ICTs: Nature of use

The ability to unpack and contextualize gendered differences and similarities requires a sound explanatory basis of sex-disaggregated data, something that is woefully lacking (Kabeer 2003; Hafkin and Huyer 2008). Although the act of disaggregation is not equivalent to conducting gender analysis, it is a necessary step to providing context and to detecting patterns and correlations that are essential for gender analysis and interpretation. Given this lack of evidence, researchers and policymakers alike are confronted with challenges when building a case for changes that support gender-sensitive policy toward redressing rampant inequities that persist. Findings emerging from IDRC-supported studies over the years show that, across the regions, technological access and usage remain uneven across women and men despite the increasing prevalence of ICTs in developing countries.

IDRC's ICT4D program provided support for the development and analysis of ICT frameworks and measurement across 192 countries. The publication *From the Digital Divide to Digital Opportunities*, which examined data in these countries for the period of 1995–2003, provided the global community with measurements and analysis never before produced (Sciadas 2005). A dedicated chapter "Women in the Information Society" was included in this publication as a response to the absence of sound sex-disaggregated data. As one might expect, relationships between ICT availability and access are not linear when it comes to examining availability and use across women and men (Sciadas 2005; Hafkin and Huyer 2008). The study found that the "relationship between the gender divide[4] and the overall digital divide is very tenuous and does not support the argument that the two move in tandem" (Huyer et al. 2005, 145). For example, data analyzed from the study indicate that, although countries such as Djibouti, Guinea, India, Nepal and Yemen have both low Internet penetration rates and low female Internet usage rates, other countries like the Philippines, Thailand and Mongolia show female Internet users exceeding male users. The non-linear nature of relationships between ICT availability and use (see Figure 4.1) conveys the information that other factors – some of which could be structural in nature – are influencing this complex dynamic.

In the case of conventional Internet use (i.e., largely text-intensive with terminals often located in workplaces or community centers), some factors besides sex that could influence usage rates include literacy, mobility, income, livelihood and cultural norms (Hafkin and Huyer 2008; Hafkin and Taggart 2001). The rising availability, affordability and use of mobile phones among women and men of different age groups, class and ethnicity have introduced different ways of socially positioning mobile phones as means of connecting, contesting and (re)creating social structures, processes and power dynamics. As mobile

Figure 4.1. Relationship between Internet penetration and proportion of female Internet users

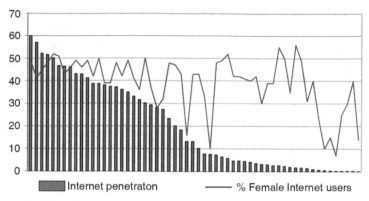

Source: Hafkin and Huyer (2008).

phones are tools that carry social values, they can lead to, for example, facilitating women to mobilize in front of Zambian courts to advocate for women's rights (Abraham 2009) or perhaps to reinforcing practices of women needing to ask for permission in Pakistan to use mobile phones (Siegmann 2010).

Figure 4.1 shows the trend line in the percentage of female Internet users is downward sloping. While this provides some support at a macro level for the conclusion that the gender digital divide moves in the same direction with the overall Internet penetration, the relationship is tenuous at best and related to other factors (Huyer and Hafkin 2007). This demonstrates the clear need for more quantitative and qualitative analysis along different social, economic and political factors. A central consideration for policymakers is that high inequality in ICT adoption can increase pre-existing socioeconomic inequalities (DiMaggio et al. 2004).

To gain a better understanding of the nature of ICT use by women and men, IDRC's ICT4D program supported several studies that examined supply-side aspects of ICT use through an examination of regulatory frameworks and policies, as well as demand-side aspects of usage patterns at the household level (Samarjiva and Zainudeen 2008; Gillwald and Stork 2008; Galperin and Mariscal 2007). In a project led by LIRNE*asia*, sex-disaggregated data proved useful in contextualizing analysis and defining gender gaps across ICT usage in order to compare and contrast across six countries (Bangladesh, India, Pakistan, the Philippines, Sri Lanka and Thailand). The study involved a random sample of 8,660 face-to-face interviews – with 50 percent keeping diaries – and six focus group discussions with 30 participants each. Findings showed that, in some South Asian countries like Pakistan, India and Sri Lanka, a significant gender divide in mobile phone usage existed; it was most pronounced in Pakistan. However, in the Philippines and Thailand, there was virtually no divide. Despite the assumption that the gender divide should close as penetration increases, this research concluded that it may not be the case – at least not in the short or medium term – for countries with significant gaps. This is possibly due to specific cultural and social contexts (Zainudeen et al. 2010). Once this evidence is available, a deeper understanding of the phenomena is necessary. This might require more in-depth frameworks and tools to understand gender dynamics. One of the questions asked in the survey was about who made the decision to get women connected using mobile phones. In South Asia, 74 percent of those decisions were made by men, whereas in Southeast Asia, the number dropped significantly to a mere 9 percent of the decisions being made by men and 91 percent made by women (Zainudeen et al. 2010).

The Research ICT Africa (RIA) project, which implemented several longitudinal household surveys in 17 African countries in East, Central, South and West Africa, sought to quantify and index ICT usage patterns. In a RIA policy paper on gendered aspects of the household data, findings indicate the need for communication regardless of income level, gender or location (Gillwald et al. 2010). Diverse strategies are used to achieve these ends, strategies ranging from using a mobile phone that belongs to a friend or neighbor to owning only a SIM card and not a handset to using public access phones to using "missed calls."[5] Continuing to examine mobile phones, it was found that, when other factors were held constant, there were no significant differences in mobile phone ownership. However, it should be noted that women generally have less access to education and employment, both of which could increase the likelihood of mobile phone ownership (Gillwald et al. 2010). Therefore, access to mobile phones is not equal between men and women based on existing inequities. The survey also found that women spent a greater proportion of their monthly income on mobile usage while men spent a greater amount in absolute terms. In more specific country-level studies (statistically significant only in South Africa and Mozambique), women were more likely than men to adopt mobile phones. The same set of results indicated that women in Senegal, Tanzania and Burkina Faso were less likely to adopt mobile telephony (Gillwald et al. 2010).

In Latin America and the Caribbean, the body of literature on how women and men use ICTs is virtually nonexistent (Navarro 2010). The "Observatory for the Information Society in Latin America and the Caribbean" (OSILAC) project was created to promote the gathering of ICT statistics in the region. Based on household survey data across six countries – Brazil, Chile, Costa Rica, Honduras, Mexico and Paraguay – the analysis revealed sex-disaggregated usage patterns. For example, in Brazil, Chile, Costa Rica and Mexico, female usage rates were found to be between 7 and 16 percent lower than male Internet use rates. This difference was relatively smaller in Paraguay and, in Honduras, female usage rates exceeded male usage rates by 5 percent (Navarro 2010). Further analysis on demographic and socioeconomic characteristics showed differences by sex; differences in Internet use varied with factors such as education, age, area of residence and labor market variables. The discrepancy favoring male over female users was more pronounced in urban areas than in rural areas. Moreover, older women, regardless of their formal education levels, had disproportionately lower usage rates. Interestingly, the divide was shown to be more prominent among the upper and middle class households. The study concluded that the gender digital divide is, to a large extent, a consequence of pre-existing gender inequalities.

These studies supported by ICT4D addressed a dire gap in available data on the supply of ICTs and the demand on ICTs as expressed at the household level. Disaggregation of the data by sex provides a foundation from which to conduct additional quantitative and qualitative analysis that could help shed light on relationships between ICT usage, sex and a range of other pertinent factors such as education, age, location and livelihood. Gender inequities in access to ICTs cannot be addressed through ICT policies alone; they require policy interventions that would help to correct existing inequities experienced by women, men, boys and girls. Such interventions would require a deeper understanding of how ICTs are used and how gender influences use or non-use. The following section moves from a focus on inequitable access to ICTs to one that examines how access to ICTs can influence degrees of social inclusion.

Gender and ICTs: Purpose of use

It is critical to gain insights into the intersection of ICT supply and demand of users, as discussed in the previous section. However, without knowledge about why there are differences in use and how use is manifested among different groups, it is difficult to generate and communicate evidence that could influence more inclusive policies and practices. This section presents findings from studies seeking to understand use patterns and behaviors as shown by women and men using ICTs. Evidence of this kind can help inform how access to ICTs can be made more equitable. Moreover, it can shed some light on how access to ICTs can either facilitate or inhibit social inclusion. Given the complexity of these questions, it is not surprising that the findings presented here do not provide a definitive answer to either of these questions; however, they manage to reveal some insight into how these questions could be responded to.

A research project in Mumbai India, home to some of the largest urban slums in the world, was designed to analyze sex-disaggregated access and usage patterns of micro-enterprises as they relate to gender relations. In-depth interviews were conducted with 329 male owners or managers of micro-enterprises and 231 female owners of micro-enterprises from April through June 2009. The study conducted a second survey of 102 men and women in September and November of the same year. According to the study, many female and male micro-enterprise owners or managers who used a mobile for business communication reported that the year-over-year income of their business had risen. When the researchers tried to compare male-owned with female-owned micro-enterprises, the findings indicated that the growth reported by female-owned businesses was modest compared with the growth of male-owned businesses (Chew et al. 2010). They also found a positive correlation between women business owners with a self-perception of positive status and power and the likelihood of incorporating ICTs within the business. These findings demonstrate some patterns that have emerged from a relatively large dataset that included questions about self-esteem, mobility, income generation and other social and economic variables. Sex-disaggregation and econometric analysis makes it is possible to gain useful preliminary insights into how sex, gender roles and livelihoods interact with one another.

Another project carried out in rural Pakistan underscored the drastic differences in levels and quality of ICT access that remain between men and women despite the exponential increase in the availability of ICTs (Siegmann 2010). The study used an extreme-case sampling methodology to select districts from Battagram (former northwest frontier province), Bolan (Balochistan), Muzzafargarh (Punjab) and Tharparkar (Sindh). Findings showed that more than 40 percent of all female respondents needed permission to use ICTs from their husbands, fathers or brothers who typically owned the ICT equipment. When exploring women's technological skills, female respondents expressed a more negative perception of their own technological abilities compared with male interviewees. The researchers claim that availability and gendered use of ICTs are two different things altogether. They state that social norms related to women and girls' access to social determinants of ICT access (e.g., education, mobility) prevent them from using ICTs (Siegmann 2010).

Another study focusing on the gendered division of labor was undertaken as part of the ICT4D-supported "Uganda Health Information Network" (UHIN) project. UHIN's work started in 2003 as a research project. In its first phases, it sought to assess changes in gender division of labor arising from the use of ICTs, changes in access to and use of technologies and shifts of power relations between men and women in households and communities involving users and adopters of the new technologies. A survey of 103 health workers (out of 600 in 174 health centers) in five Ugandan districts was carried out. Several of the women included in the study had their first contact with ICTs in the context of this project. Many of them believed the personal digital assistants (PDAs) were crucial sources of information. The respondents noted that the PDAs saved them time when they needed to refresh their medical training and when transmitting medical reports to central reporting centers (Madanda and Hafkin 2010). The attitudes of health workers also changed, giving women greater motivation to pursue future computer training and advanced ICT skills. Women more than men reported reduced work-related communication and information costs as a result of using the PDAs (shorter travel distances, increased income generation from their new skill). This study, part of a larger one focused on ICTs and health, provides a comprehensive example of how gender analysis can help reveal important social dynamics that address gender inequities even when that was not the primary intention.

A similar project in the Caribbean region looked at how the capacity of nurses and student nurses to use PDAs could be strengthened. The introduction of PDAs had a range of demonstrable impacts on nursing knowledge, nurses' self-reported feelings of empowerment and on staff retention. The initiative provided groups of nurses and nursing students in Dominica, St Kitts, St Lucia, Barbados and the Dominican Republic with wireless access – and often their first instance of computer access – to the latest nursing knowledge, diagnostic tools, treatment options and networking resources. In conjunction with the handheld units, the nurses were also able to send data back to central computers, ultimately contributing to further improvements in the region's patient care and services delivery planning. When examining usage patterns and behavior, the theory that older nurses would be resistant to participation in the program was disproved; there was no significant variance in the performance or integration of the ICTs with respect to age. In addition, it was shown that children of nurses played a significant role in coaching the nurses on how to use the device in innovative ways.

These findings clearly show that gendered use of ICTs is strongly influenced by social norms. Thus, these norms must be afforded the attention they deserve when policies are being developed or interventions designed to strengthen access and beneficial use of ICTs by women and girls.

Gender and ICTs: Ends of use

Evidence was presented in earlier sections on the nature of ICT use by women and men – specifically, sex-disaggregated demand-side statistics that were further examined along different social and economic variables. This section presents findings that further explain why usage rates vary by sex, income, education and geography, among other variables. It focuses on what can be achieved – or what transformative outcomes are contributed to – by the use of ICTs. These types of changes often take several years to surface, many times after a project is legally closed. Gender-transformative changes can be understood in comparison with gender-specific interventions, where gender-transformative changes address the underlying causes of gender inequality (Kabeer and Subrahmanian 1999).

Transformative gender outcomes, as observed through research on the information society, require deep analysis, reflective and responsive research methodologies and clear and intentional capture of changes in behavior among researchers. One such example can be found in the project "Gender Research in Africa into ICTs for Empowerment" (GRACE). Starting in 2005, the GRACE network grew to involve 18 countries in Africa and the Middle East in an effort to understand how the use of ICTs contributes to improving the lives of women, as well as understanding the barriers in this process and related outcomes. The research network adopted a qualitative approach. In looking at ICTs in different contexts, the research uncovered relationships with women's empowerment, gender discrimination, access, entrepreneurship and advocacy (Buskens and Webb 2009). Many of the noteworthy findings from the first phase of the GRACE network are published in Buskens and Webb's 2009 book *African Women & ICTs: Investigating Technology, Gender and Empowerment*.

One particularly salient finding comes from the University of Zimbabwe. The findings from this study (Mbambo-Thata et al. 2009) demonstrated that perceived environments of gender equality may not necessarily bear close scrutiny. For example, the University of Zimbabwe had a first come, first served policy for the use of library computers. What was perceived to be an equitable policy was, in fact, far from equitable because of underlying inequities between female and male users. The findings showed that males tended to crowd out or intimidate women who were earlier in the queue in a "survival of the fittest" male-dominated atmosphere (Mbambo-Thata et al. 2009, 71–2). The GRACE network's research made this situation visible by speaking to a variety of pertinent actors in leadership roles at the university. The primary focus of these interactions was the evidence-based message that the first come, first served policy – which was designed to be gender neutral – was in fact gendered in a way that disadvantaged women students. These findings, when communicated to the university leadership, led to computers being installed in the hallways of the women's residences on campus (Sey et al. 2010).

This example from Zimbabwe is one of many captured in *African Women & ICTs* that demonstrate different experiences and outcomes when looking at the mutual shaping of gender relations and ICTs. Other examples include observations about transformative outcomes for women gaining more control of their time and space to increase their earnings in Kenyan micro-enterprises (Munyua 2009); gaining a stronger understanding of the value of the cell phone for women trapped in violent marriages in Morocco in which the only lifelines were "God and the cell phone" and how mobile phones influence matters of "illiteracy, poverty, unawareness and their husband's authority over them" (Tafnout and Timjerdine 2009, 95). Buskens and Webb also explored discrimination among women in *African Women & ICTs*. In Zambia, it was found that women who had the resources to send text messages in a campaign to mobilize women at a courthouse to advocate for women's rights felt more empowered than those who did not have enough airtime to send text messages but could only receive them, causing an intragender divide (Abraham 2009). The findings coming from this work illustrate that access to ICTs have precarious and often complex effects in helping women become included in the information society – on terms they are comfortable with and have some role in negotiating.

The GRACE project demonstrates that women's use of ICTs was dependent on their particular circumstances. Often in environments where gender inequality was strong, empowerment was seen as a socially disruptive force. Women tended to weigh both the positive and the negative impacts that they foresaw if the status quo was changed. Findings proved that a larger structural change in society needs to happen to enable equal benefit for women.

Research to learn more about how gender relations influence the nature of ICT use, the purpose of use and the ends achieved has shown mixed results. Not surprisingly, the outcome really depends on the structural factors and social determinants that influence if, how and for what ends a woman, man, boy or girl accesses ICTs. Although there are no simple answers, a consistent conclusion from these findings is that failing to consider these structural and social conditions when designing ICT-based policies or programs can have grave consequences on socially inclusive outcomes.

Cultural Diversity: Using Local Language to Access ICTs

Culture and language are symbolic systems that are very closely connected. Culture can be conveyed through the use of language and language is an integral part of culture (Brown 1994; Emmitt and Pollock 1997). Variances in meaning can be found across languages and are closely related to differences in cultural norms and practice (Nida 1998). According to UNESCO, there are over 6,000 languages spoken in the world (UNESCO 2010). As communication evolved from its oral beginnings to more complex forms by means of symbols and writing, so too have the ways in which information has been recorded and shared. While some languages successfully expand into new media such as the Internet, many others are compromised or lost entirely to be replaced by a more dominant language (UNESCO 2003). This section examines IDRC's choice to focus on local language computing as means to address the growing divide between English and local languages in developing countries. It explores both how the availability of local language computing can influence accessibility of ICTs and how accessing ICTs through local language computing can potentially facilitate or inhibit social inclusion.

One can argue that, with globalization, the world is losing many local and indigenous cultures that have shaped societies. The use of ICTs to capture and convey local languages can influence the nature and extent of a language's ability to flourish within and among different groups. Intergenerational language transmission could also be constrained if languages cannot be transmitted in digital forms – for instance, through text messages or emails between family members and friends, sharing documents written in the native language and supporting discussion forums on specific topics of interest across different generations. The use of ICTs can also be used to crowd out minority languages due to content in a dominant language being more readily available and spread.

IDRC's ICT4D programming responded to such challenges. For instance, Cambodia's population (14 million) is too small a market for software companies to localize fonts, software and hardware. IDRC played an important role in pre-market investment to build capacities in Cambodia to localize the languages and to create locales to enable the software to fit with standards and local time, measurement and use norms and keyboard interfaces.

As defined by Hussain and Mohan (2008), localization is the process of developing, tailoring and/or enhancing the capability of hardware and software to process input and output information in the language, norms and metaphors used by the community. Localization can be seen as having three main components: language, technology and their sociocultural contexts (Osborn 2010). The scope of localization is not limited to text-intensive interactions. In fact, text-to-speech systems can provide access for non-literate populations; automatic speech recognition can help create local language and culturally meaningful content more quickly and optical character recognition (OCR) systems can help convert print material into electronic content that can be more easily exchanged (Hussain 2004). When important information on health or education is provided in only a few dominant languages that are inaccessible to the poor, this lack of access to information can threaten the poor's ability to stay healthy, access government services and to meet other welfare needs. The poorest of the poor, who are in most need of adapted ICTs, likely have not been reached by the information society and lack the opportunity to enhance their knowledge with the most vital information. Thus, localization cannot be separated from broader development and education efforts (Osborn 2010).

Some research questions guiding work in this area are the following: what does it mean when communications technologies are limited to a few dominant languages? What wide-ranging effects can occur when such tools prevent people from using technology and from benefitting from the knowledge society in their mother tongue? Does localization of ICTs lead to increased content generation and use? Do the creation of skills and resources and the lowering of barriers to localization lead to an increase in localization activity and the creation of a localization network that can sustain that localization activity?

Referring to the conceptual framework for this chapter, local language computing will be examined using the following questions as a guide: how can inequities of access to ICTs be redressed? How can access to ICTs potentially facilitate or inhibit social inclusion? The focus on addressing the dearth of useful and locally relevant technologies (fonts, locales, etc.) to capture and transmit local language translates into a greater emphasis on the earlier guiding question regarding inequities of access to ICTs. The first subsection – on the nature of use – will look at the landscape of localization in the countries where IDRC later supported research. Findings in the "purpose of use" subsection will highlight specific examples of how localization outcomes and outputs were used. The final section discusses innovative models such as "crowd sourcing" efforts, which are akin to outsourcing specific tasks to a larger community of interest.

Culture and ICTs: Nature of use

There is limited evidence of systematically collected and analyzed data about localization (Osborn 2010). Thousands of languages in the world cannot be used to send an email or to read a website. The consequences of this extend beyond the ability to read, write and communicate in one's own language. It influences matters of culture that are inherently political, economic and social in nature. Therefore, discussions about localization comprise many aspects that cannot be examined in isolation. For example, the generation of web content cannot be separated from the user interface (operating systems, word processors, web browsers, etc.) through which individuals access the content. Similarly, aspects of the user interface cannot be separated from the capacity of the hardware to encode and decode elements of language or from how networks can transmit and receive data between pieces of hardware. And perhaps most significantly, each of these components is inextricably linked to the community of language users who will be innovating, testing, using and producing content and advocating for necessary policy change and engagement to sustain the efforts brought about by technological innovation.

Asia is home to thirty-five hundred different languages, over half of all the languages spoken in the world.[6] And there is significant variation just in Asia. When contemplating what this means in terms of localizing language for using ICTs, let us take a few examples. For instance, Japanese, Chinese and Korean languages are ideographic/pictographic in nature, which requires complex multi-key input methods when typing characters. Lao, Thai and Khmer (spoken largely in Cambodia) are languages that do not contain spaces between words, which makes digitizing fonts complicated when it comes to line breaks, etc. Languages following the Devanagari script (e.g., Hindi and Nepali) do not use a baseline, but rather "hang" when written. Moreover, Tibetan, Dzongkha (spoken largely in Bhutan), Lao and Khmer can stack characters up to five levels over and under base characters. These are just a few examples of the complexities encountered when discussing the digitization of certain languages.

Africa has more than an estimated two thousand different languages spoken by over a billion people. There are nearly fifteen languages in Africa that each have more than ten million speakers. According to Prah (2002, 2003), between 75 and 85 percent of Africans speak 12 to 15 core languages.

Many African languages can be written with an extended Latin script, such as many languages in southern and eastern Africa (Osborn 2010), but other languages such as Arabic use non-Latin scripts. The use of Unicode[7] for these languages has opened up many new possibilities. For any language to thrive – regardless of script – complete fonts, standardized and user-friendly user interfaces, localized keyboard layouts and special software such as speech recognition software can strengthen its vitality and thus mitigate the possibility of endangerment or extinction. In cases of African languages that are experiencing decline or a certain degree of contraction, localization could be a tool for language revitalization (Osborn 2010).

To address these opportunities and challenges, IDRC developed a multi-country research network on local language computing in Asia. The process, findings and lead researcher of this project, Dr Sarmad Hussain, helped form the foundation for a seven-country research network called Pan Localization or PANL10N.[8] The initial countries in the first phase (2004–2007) were Afghanistan (Pashto), Bangladesh (Bangla), Bhutan (Dzongkha), Cambodia (Khmer), Laos (Lao), Nepal (Nepali) and Sri Lanka (Sinhala, Tamil). The second phase (2007–10) added Tibetan, Urdu, Tamil and Mongolian. These represent Asian languages with little to no computing characters for local alphabets with which to exchange digitized text. The development of the research network was not only remarkable for the localization work it undertook, but also with respect to how it conducted research. PANL10N was IDRC's first foray into creating multi-country research networks to address specific research issues. Up until then, research had been supported through competitive calls or direct grants to local institutions. PANL10N brought together institutions across Asia working on local language computing in order to address common research capacity building and technical, as well as development, goals. As a result of the success of the network, IDRC's ICT4D program adopted research networks as a principal modality to tackle ICT4D problems in most of the areas it supported. IDRC helped forge the African Network for Localization to address local language computing challenges in Africa, much the same way it had in Asia.

Africa as a continent is known for its strong oral tradition, with some exception such as the Arabic and Berber languages in North Africa and the languages in the Horn of Africa that use the script originating with Ge'ez. However, oral tradition does not imply a lack of literate tradition (Osborn 2010). These statements do not take into account the widespread use of symbols for a number of purposes (Mafundikwa 2004) and the adaptation of the Arabic script to writing many languages where Islam is important, notably in the Sahel and for Swahili (Mafundikwa 2004). In fact, "over the last century, the writing of African languages, mainly in alphabets based on the Latin script outside North Africa and the Horn, has become more common, even as oral traditions continue" (Osborn 2010).

In Africa, the idea of creating a network of people and organizations capable of the technological challenge of making computers work in more languages began with IDRC support in 2006. The ensuing outcome, the African Network for Localization (ANLoc), has since focused on the linguistic diversity of the continents to create tools and resources to make possible the adaption of computer and mobile phone interfaces and digital languages. These include tools such as locales, which are master files that define for a given language the character sets to use, the direction in which text is written, as well as ways in which symbols, measurements and names of days, weeks and months are constructed and used. Other tools include terminologies, spell checkers and translation tools. The vision of ANLoc is to empower Africans to participate in the digital age by removing "the last inch" barriers to language usage in ICT. The term "last inch" in this context can be compared with the term "last mile" that is used when discussing the reach of ICT infrastructure. The last inch refers to the ICT interface through which a user will engage with an ICT.[9] The nature of localized ICT use can be seen as a proxy, or perhaps as a precursor, for equity in accessing ICTs. Developing technology, interoperability and content using ICTs for local languages addresses critical issues because, without these in place, it would be difficult to strengthen community ties, encourage use and influence decision makers.

Culture and ICTs: Purpose of use

This section presents findings of how some outputs from the Asian localization network, PANL10N and ANLoc have been shared and used. This can include use by people in Asia and Africa, as well as others living outside the continent but actively using and/or contributing to the improvement of the digitization of specific languages. The specificity of language construction and interpretation were carefully considered in developing tools to localize language. For instance, as discussed in Hussain and Durrani (2008), in the case of the Lao language, text comparison is not done at the character level. Instead, the string is divided into syllables upon which the sorting is done. To complicate matters further, there are no explicit syllable markings; syllabification is carried out using a complex set of rules. This is just one of many examples of how meticulous the process of localization needs to be to address specificities of language construction – and thus expression of culture – and how these need to be considered for basic computation functions such as sorting, collation, grammar and spellchecking. This type of attention to cultural specificity requires strengthening local capacities for individuals and institutions that have a deep understanding of both linguistic and technological aspects of the localization process.

By 2007, the end of the first phase of PANL10N, the network had produced concrete tools to enable speakers of certain languages to begin using computers in their own tongue. In Bhutan and Nepal, localized Linux distributions in Dzongkha and Nepali respectively were launched. Optical character recognition (allowing handwritten text images to be encoded for computer use) was developed for Sinhala, Bangla and Lao. In addition, spellchecking and lexica (vocabulary, including words and expressions) were developed in Bangla, Dzonghka, Khmer, Nepali and Lao. Other innovations include text-to-speech systems in Sinhala, as well as keyboard and collation standards for several of the languages (Hussain and Mohan 2008). Figure 4.2 provides a screenshot of some Dzongkha terms that have been translated from English.

This effort was led by the Department of Information Technology in Bhutan and the Dzongkha Development Commission. Over five thousand basic computing-related words and phrases were translated from English to Dzongkha. This output is freely available on PANL10N's website.[10] Other outputs address important issues such as localization on mobile platforms, collation practices in different languages, a guide to localization for open source software, implementing international domain names (IDNs), policy papers, as well as a series of working papers.

The second phase of PANL10N extended the scope of the project more concretely in the realm of the end users who could use localized technology to produce and consume local language content. This included examining means to enhance local capacities to produce content; supporting sufficient human resource capacity in the research and development, as well as technical maintenance and support of local language computing; and contributing evidence to the policy discourse about education, ICT access and social development more broadly. Issues of gender were carefully considered in this second phase and were the impetus for PANL10N to innovate on the outcome mapping evaluation methodology to create gendered outcome mapping (OMg).[11]

Figure 4.2. Dzongkha terms

Canyon	གེན་ཡོན།	Card	སོག་བྱང་། ཌ་སེ།
Capabilities	ནུས་པ་རྣམས།	Cardbus	ཀ་ཌི་བྱུས།
Cape Verde	གེཔ་ཝར་ཌི།	Cards	ཌ་སེ།
Capitalize	ཚུགས་ཡིག་བཟོ།	Career	ལས་གཡོག
Cappella	གེ་པེ་ལ།	Carefully	དྲན་ཤེས་ཀྱི་སྒོ་ལས།
Capplet	གེཔ་ལེཊི།	Caret	ཀེ་རེཊི།
Caps Lock	ཚུགས་སྟེ།	Carpet	ས་གདན།

ANLoc had a number of sub-projects such as font development, keyboard development, locale development, development of tools for localization, terminology development, localizing software, training development and delivery, spellchecker development, language and ICT policy and network activities. The network activities as part of ANLoc successfully brought together interested people who were willing to strengthen their capacity to make the technical aspect of ICT localization a reality. For Arabic speakers, a professional certification course was developed and implemented to assist in building a group of professionals in engineering, translation and localization capable of getting ICTs further localized. In South Africa, a similar program was developed to enable localization for a country that has 11 national languages. When software is developed in a language, computers need to be able to read the language and country parameters and other standards such as date formats. To achieve this, a locale is necessary; it serves as a master file across applications to identify the language of origin and to allow functions such as searching and spellchecking in the appropriate code. ANLoc aimed to develop 100 African locales within 12 months. It achieved locales for Africa that were included in the Unicode common locale data repository. These provided the building blocks for future software that will allow more people to work on computers in their own tongue (ANLoc 2009b; Paré et al. 2010). As software is localized into more languages, a precise and consistent use of technological terminology is essential in ensuring a smooth translation process. Having recognized the importance of standardized terminology, ANLoc was able to consolidate a glossary of 2,500 terms in 10 languages spoken in Africa.[12] This work has opened the door for more languages to conform to an established standard that is working for these first languages at present. The terminology was developed in collaboration with the translation bureau of the Government of Canada for French and English.

The next section moves away from the specific outputs of these two localization efforts and examines some ends achieved through the use of innovative models to strengthen capacities, employing networks and "crowd sourcing" methodologies.

Culture and ICTs: Ends of use

Transformative change with respect to social inclusion, contributed to by localization, is a process that will likely take several more years to surface. In this section, we use some proxy indicators for this type of change. We examine outcomes of local capacity strengthening that can help ensure local engagement, mobilization and achievement of results toward advocating for greater access to information and knowledge using ICTs and thus contributing to the strengthening cultural integrity and diversity.

For example, ANLoc saw to the localization of Firefox and other OpenOffice software into Luganda and Northern Sotho. It also had teams working on Akan, Krio, Lingala, Luganda, Northern Sotho, Shona, Songhay, Swahili, Wolof and Zulu. In an open source style, innovative tools –Virtaal and Pootle – were developed to manage and track progress and enable natural language translation without programming language requirements. With these tools, the ANLoc community developed its networking web.[13] When ANLoc was looking for volunteers to develop locales – it wanted to achieve this in 100 languages – it turned to Facebook. Soon, through "crowd sourcing," several native speakers – many living and working abroad – were involved in collaborating and contributing to agreed-upon terminologies and other aspects of localized ICTs. ANLoc partnered with the Localisation Research Centre at the University of Limerick in Ireland to adapt the training program and to offer courses in Africa in Arabic, English and French. ANLoc also explored the development and deployment of language technology such as local language fonts, keyboards, local language web browsers, terminology databases and dictionaries to end users and tried to address the issues that challenge the success of the adoption of indigenous languages in the digital sphere.

Since 2003, IDRC's ICT4D program has been supporting research on local language computing to generate more knowledge about the nature of their use, the ways in which they are used and what ends are achieved vis-à-vis facilitating or inhibiting social inclusion. Localization alone cannot solve the exclusion that exists among those that feel culturally isolated by the lack of local language content and computing capacity that is currently available. However, the social and technical innovations, as well as the strengthening of technical capacity at the local level, can help more deeply embed and nurture the need for local language computing to influence the policies and practice that can enhance cultural expression and inclusion.

Youth: Responding to Demands

The United Nations World Youth Report (2011) indicates that the global youth unemployment rate stands at 12.6 percent, nearly three times the global adult unemployment rate of 4.8 percent. And female youth unemployment is more pronounced than that of male youth, specifically in certain parts of the world such as the Middle East and North Africa.[14] Developing countries are home to 87 percent of the world's youth, many of whom are underemployed, unemployed or working in the informal economy under poor conditions. As global economic insecurity increases, young people are seeking to establish their identities and carve out a living. An unsatisfied supply of youth labor is one of many factors that can exclude young people from active participation in society and from the ability to seize social, political and economic opportunities.

Young people are often found at a crossroads in development. On one hand, they can be more vulnerable, more easily exploited and marginalized in numerous contexts. On the other, they often have an advantage in that they adapt faster and can be more open to change. As youth make up a large proportion of the population in the developing world, they can benefit greatly from ICTs due to their advantage in adoption. For example, they can use ICTs to generate dialogue on pertinent issues for youth, or access more opportunities for better employment. Socially inclusive ICT solutions can bring about significant change by employing strategies that appeal to young people. These can provide tangible benefits to improve the livelihoods of youth and connect them to each other in order to come up with creative and unique ways of dealing with relevant issues. With the increasing popularity of ICTs – particularly, the Internet and mobile phones – young people have never been so connected to their peers both at home and outside of their borders. The question is: how equitable is this access and how does access influence outcomes of social inclusion or exclusion?

Examples of research questions to be examined include the following: what groups of young people are more likely to use ICTs? How are social networks and social networking practices influencing the way existing divides are exacerbated or bridged? What role do youth see for themselves in actively shaping ICTs and their use to improve their livelihoods? Are ICTs displacing traditional types of engagement among youth? If so, what are the implications of this shift? IDRC's ICT4D program has supported the work of various research partners in the developing world to answer these questions. Specific research projects have included the support for dialogue about sensitive issues such as female genital mutilation (FGM) in West Africa; HIV/AIDS among teenagers, initially in Peru and then in other countries in the LAC region; civic engagement and education in the Caribbean; and matters of youth employability. Under the "nature of use" section, findings will be highlighted that provide useful context for the types of challenges faced by youth. The different uses of ICTs by young people will be discussed under the "purpose of use" section. Finally, policy and practice changes that can lead to ongoing attention and response to the needs of young people will be highlighted in the "ends of use" section.

Youth and ICTs: Nature of use

Given the growing number of youth, notably in developing countries, it is crucial to learn more about how young people use ICTs in different situations. In LAC, ICT4D supported an existing training network, Entra21, to help create opportunities and skills for disadvantaged youth between the ages of 16 and 20 years across 18 countries in the region. Beginning in 2001, this program conducted research for 10 years to understand how ICTs could be used to support youth employment opportunities that complement existing training strategies. The findings showed that including ICT-based training does not replace traditional employment training approaches nor does it lessen the importance of the relationship between trainers and the targeted youth job seekers. At the same time, ICTs were found to motivate and enhance employability through improving computer skills that are often a requirement for entry into the modern labor force.

A project entitled "From Words to Action: ICT, Youth and Gender Equity," also in LAC, used social imagery and ICTs as a means to construct the term "youth" as both a category and a social group. The applied research study on digital literacy programs for youth in Latin America examined the dominant educational discourses and practices that encourage access to technology by the excluded or at-risk youth population. It also analyzed the ways in which those programs characterize and implement a gender equity approach. The project developed one of the first online courses for the "Regional Training Program for Specialists on Gender and Public Policies" (PRIGEPP in Spanish) for the Faculty of Social Sciences in Argentina. PRIGEPP prepares specialists in the area and is considered to be the most renowned masters-level program in gender and public policy in the region.

Youth and ICTs: Purpose of Use

Around the world, more and more work environments include computers and other ICTs. Mobile phones are becoming common tools for work in developed and developing countries alike. Opportunities abound, particularly for youth who are part of a generation more and more accustomed to working online to complete their tasks. IDRC's ICT4D program supported a number of studies to gain a more nuanced understanding of how young people are using ICTs and for what purpose.

Testing the assumption that youth could benefit most from the digital revolution, IDRC supported research in Africa that explored how male and female youth, using ICTs as a strategic community intervention tool, could work together against the practice of female genital mutilation (Mottin-Sylla and Palmieri 2010). The research in Burkina Faso, Mali and Senegal explored ICTs and female genital mutilation in a way that surpassed these issues alone. The project focused on the capacity of young people to exercise their citizenship to engage in dialogue with different groups – including among themselves. (See Figure 4.3.) The findings demonstrated that African youth, both male and female, find themselves caught between the tradition of remaining polite before their elders and the modernity of being able to speak out about issues that affect them directly – in this case, female genital mutilation. Moreover, with this issue, there is a need to have youth at the center of the debate through the use of ICTs in order to initiate and encourage dialogue (Mottin-Sylla and Palmieri 2010).

Political engagement is one area in which ICTs have often been seen as appropriate to reach out to youth and encourage more active participation. IDRC-supported research

Figure 4.3. Poster against the practice of female genital mutilation

in Asia focused on these issues across the region. In Malaysia, social media has been particularly effective in connecting people to "discover" each other through general interests enabling greater mobilization, supported by mass distribution applications that convey events and information instantly (Zhang et al. 2011). In Bangladesh, where youth are often seen as already politically active, ICTs and further access to information have produced a sense of growing transparency and potential for government to function more democratically (Zhang et al. 2010, 14).

Youth and ICTs: Ends of Use

Diverse strategies, tailored to different contexts and issues, are needed to examine ways in which ICTs could promote social inclusion among young people. Some findings from IDRC-supported projects point to longer-term change processes that have been influenced. For example, the Punto J portal on HIV/AIDS that began in Peru was taken up and adopted in other countries such as Argentina, Bolivia, Colombia, Ecuador and the Dominican Republic. The online portal created a space for people to come together and provided some degree of anonymity to individuals so that a useful dialogue and promotion of education about HIV/AIDS could take place. These issues are taboo and difficult to broach face to face. ICTs help mediate youth access to information and provide a platform for social exchange and networking in a safe environment. Punto J revealed that "youth to youth" education within a secure and confidential portal was an effective way to engage users and spark dialogue among participants around health and social issues. Youth counselors, professional health practitioners and engaged users contributed the momentum. More than five thousand users have received peer guidance and over a million have accessed the portal. It also received awards and demonstrated success in engaging young leaders within regional and international dialogue on youth and HIV/AIDS issues.

The "Partnership in Opportunities for Employment through Technologies in the Americas" (POETA) project in the Eastern Caribbean acknowledged the challenges youth face in securing employment and addressed the need to strengthen the integration of civic education and life training with ICT skills. This project provides "youth at risk" with counseling and support to promote value-based decision making and a greater respect for law through an interactive web portal set up to foster dialogue and knowledge exchange. It found that young people saw technology as an important tool to facilitate their self-development and for self-empowerment. The POETA Caribbean web portal has had over 392,000 hits worldwide since its launch in February 2009.

Conclusion

The global promise of citizenship is always undermined by inequality (Wallace 2001). Discussion of the ways in which ICT use among different disadvantaged groups can lead to varying levels of social inclusion or exclusion is both a process and a goal, which lie on a continuum. The findings in this chapter demonstrate the wide-ranging outcomes that can result. While some assert that there is a positive correlation between ICTs and reduced poverty and inequities (e.g., Duncombe 2001; Kenny 2002; Gerster and Zimmermann 2003), others warn that ICTs can actually increase existing inequalities and asymmetric power relations between the rich and the poor and urban and rural areas, as well as among generations (Nulens 2000; Bollou and Ngwenyama 2008). The purpose of this chapter is not to take a definite position in this particular debate, but rather to acknowledge the different perspectives, related evidence and the merit they carry when discussing matters of social inclusion and/or exclusion in the information society. Beyond accessing ICTs, the nature, purpose and ends achieved by using ICTs were discussed, where possible, in each of the three sections: gender, culture and youth.

The projects IDRC supported across Asia, LAC and Africa have consistently addressed important questions on how inequities around access and use of ICTs can facilitate or hinder men and women, youth and diverse languages in the information society. The researchers' aims were to better understand and reduce these barriers as a result of rigorous, grounded and useful studies. Recognizing that ICTs are tools that need to be understood in their social, political, economic and cultural contexts, IDRC-supported researchers analyzed and communicated research findings and recommendations to improve equity and promote inclusion and, indeed, a sense of citizenship in the global information society.

ICTs can provide great advantages to groups that were formerly bypassed by changes in economic circumstance. Women, linguistic minorities and youth can accelerate their social and economic possibilities if they have the opportunity to participate in the information society on appropriate terms for different groups. This beneficial outcome doesn't happen without addressing systemic issues in the social and cultural systems of the developing world. ICT4D-supported research helped to elevate these issues for improved understanding and new inclusive policy and program approaches.

Appendix 1. Conceptual Framework

This figure provides an overview of the conceptual framework used for this chapter. The two central questions for this chapter are shown on the far left, along with the overlap between them (indicated by the lighter shaded area). This is followed to the right by the three specific types of social phenomena/conditions examined in this chapter (gender, culture and youth). Findings and outcomes from IDRC-supported projects are discussed along with the nature of use, purpose of use and the ends achieved by the use.

Figure 4.4. Conceptual framework for ICTs and social inclusion

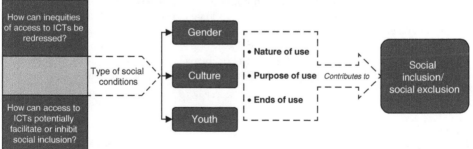

Notes

1 This chapter is inspired by the hard work of IDRC-supported researchers who conceived and implemented ICT4D research projects to better understand the complex dynamics of social inclusion and exclusion. It is dedicated to all populations and individuals around the world that struggle from being excluded in their societies with the hope that it may contribute to fostering more inclusive lives and livelihoods. We are grateful for thoughtful contributions from Kathleen Diga, Adel El Zaïm, Alicia Richero and Ramata Thioune. We also thank Katie Bryant and the book editors for their inputs and guidance during the writing process.

2 http://en.wikipedia.org/wiki/Information_society (accessed 12 April 2012).
3 The Internet and mobile phones are quickly spreading around the world. In developing countries, mobile telephony is becoming the communication of choice to connect people through voice and data applications. The developing world now has a mobile subscription rate of 73 percent compared with its 53 percent rate in 2005 (International Telecommunication Union, *The World in 2010: ICT Facts and Figures*, Geneva: ITU, http://www.itu.int/ITU-D/ict/material/FactsFigures2010.pdf [accessed 30 March 2012]).
4 The "gender digital divide" can be defined as gaps in access between men and women which can manifest themselves through various societal axes such as race, ethnicity, class and age (Hafkin and Taggart 2001; Gurumurthy 2003).
5 "Missed calls" (also known as "beeping" or "flashing") is the practice of dialing someone but hanging up before the call is connected. This type of communication does not incur a cost for either the calling or receiving party. In addition to cost savings, missed calls allow for discreet exchanges and can sometimes be used as a code language between the sender and recipient. A system can be devised to use sequential or sporadic beeping to communicate simple messages.
6 http://www.ethnologue.com/ethno_docs/distribution.asp?by=area (accessed 28 March 2012).
7 Unicode (ISO10646) is a computing industry standard for the consistent encoding, representation and handling of text expressed in most of the world's writing systems (http://en.wikipedia.org/wiki/Unicode [accessed 12 April 2012]).
8 http://www.panl10.net (accessed 12 April 2012).
9 It should be noted that the terms "first inch" and "first mile" are often used instead of "last inch" and "last mile" to reorient the matter from the demand side (the users' perspective) rather than the supply side.
10 A full list of outputs from PANL10N can be accessed at http://www.panl10.net/english/outputChart.htm (accessed 12 April 2012).
11 More information about outcome mapping and the innovations by PANL10N on OMg can be found in Chapter 10 of this book.
12 http://www.africanlocalisation.net/anloc-ict-terminology-available-download (accessed 12 April 2012).
13 Virtaal is a free software computer-assisted translation tool that was developed and is maintained by Translate.org.za (http://en.wikipedia.org/wiki/Virtaal [accessed 20 April 2012]). Pootle is a free software online translation management tool with translation interface that was originally developed and released by Translate.org.za (http://en.wikipedia.org/wiki/Pootle [accessed 20 April 2012]).
14 Total youth unemployment rate is reported as 25.5 percent in the Middle East and 23.8 percent in North Africa. Female youth unemployment rates in these regions are 39.4 percent and 34.1 percent respectively (UN 2011a).

References

Abraham, K. B. 2009. "The Names in Your Address Book: Are Mobile Phone Networks Effective in Advocating Women's Rights in Zambia?" In *African Women & ICTs: Investigating Technology, Gender and Empowerment*, edited by I. Buskens and A. Webb. Ottawa: IDRC / London and New York: Zed Books.

Agyemang, N. et al. 2007. *Opportunities and Challenges of ICTs for Youth Development in Ghana: Policy and Programme Implications for the Ghana ICT4D Process*. Kumasi: Youth Development Foundation.

ANLoc. 2009a. "Interim Technical Report." Ottawa: IDRC.

_____. 2009b. "Unicode CLDR Includes 54 new African Locales." Press release, Mountain View, 17 March. Online: http://www.africanlocalisation.net/unicode-cldr-includes-54-new-african-locales (accessed 12 March 2012).

Bollou, F. and O. Ngwenyama. 2008. "Are ICT Investments Paying Off in Africa? An Analysis of Total Factor Productivity in Six West African Countries from 1995 to 2002." *Information Technology for Development* 14, no. 4: 294–307.

Brown, H. D. 1994. *Principles of Language Learning and Teaching*, 3rd edition. Eaglewood Cliffs: Prentice Hall Regents.

Buskens, I. and A. Webb, eds. 2009. *African Women & ICTs: Investigating Technology, Gender and Empowerment*. Ottawa: IDRC / London and New York: Zed Books.

Chen, M. et al. 2005. *Progress of the World's Women 2005: Women, Work & Poverty*. New York: UNIFEM.

Chew, H. E. et al. 2010. "The Economic Impact of Information and Communication Technologies (ICTs) on Microenterprises in the Context of Development." *Electronic Journal of Information Systems for Developing Countries* 44, no. 4: 1–19.

Deibert, R. J., eds. 2012. *Access Contested: Security, Identity and Resistance in Asian Cyberspace Information Revolution and Global Politics*. Cambridge, MA: MIT Press.

DiMaggio, P. et al. 2004. "Digital Inequality: From Unequal Access to Differentiated Use." In *Social Inequality*, edited by K. M. Neckerman, 355–400. New York: Russell Sage Foundation.

Donner, J. 2008. "Research Approaches to Mobile Use in the Developing World: A Review of the Literature." *Information Society* 24, no. 3: 140–59. Online: http://www.tandfonline.com/doi/abs/10.1080/01972240802019970 (accessed 11 March 2012).

Duncombe, R. A. 2001. "Information, Technology, and Small, Medium and Micro Enterprise Development in Botswana." PhD dissertation, Gaborone, University of Botswana, Institute for Development Policy and Management.

Emmitt, M. and J. Pollock. 1997. *Language and Learning: An Introduction for Teaching*, 2nd edition. Melbourne: Oxford University Press.

Galperin, H. and J. Mariscal, eds. 2007. *Digital Poverty: Latin America and Caribbean Perspectives*. Ottawa: IDRC and Practical Action Publishing.

Gerster, R. and S. Zimmermann. 2003. "Information and Communication Technologies (ICTs) and Poverty Reduction in Sub-Saharan Africa: A Learning Study." Gerster Consulting report. Online: http://www.gersterconsulting.ch/docs/Synthesis_report.pdf (accessed 15 January 2012).

Gillwald, A. et al. 2010. "Gender Assessment of ICT Access and Usage in Africa 2010" Research ICT Africa Network, Towards Evidence-based ICT Policy and Regulation 1, paper no. 5. Online: http://www.researchictafrica.net/publications/Towards_Evidence-based_ICT_Policy_and_Regulation_-_Volume_1/RIA Policy Paper Vol 1 Paper 5 - Gender Assessment of ICT Access and Usage in Africa 2010.pdf (accessed 12 March 2012).

Gillwald, A. and C. Stork. 2008. "ICT Access and Usage in Africa 2008" Research ICT Africa Network, Towards Evidence-based ICT Policy and Regulation 1, paper no. 2. Online: http://www.researchictafrica.net/publications/Towards_Evidence-based_ICT_Policy_and_Regulation_-_Volume_1/RIA Policy Paper Vol 1 Paper 2 - ICT Access and Usage in Africa 2008.pdf (accessed 12 March 2012).

Grunfeld, H. and S. Hak. 2009. "Gender Empowerment through ICTs, iREACH, Cambodia: iREACHing the Unreached," *i4d (Information for Development)*. Online: http://i4d.eletsonline.com/gender-empowerment-through-icts-ireach-cambodia/ (accessed 13 March 2012).

Gurumurthy, A. 2003. *Bridging the Digital Divide: Issues and Insights on ICT for Women's Economic Empowerment*. New Delhi: UNIFEM.

Hafkin, N. J. and S. Huyer. 2008. "Women and Gender in ICT Statistics and Indicators for Development." *Information Technologies & International Development* 4, no. 2: 25–41. Online: http://itidjournal.org/itid/article/view/254/124 (accessed 7 January 2012).

Hafkin, N. and N. Taggart. 2001. *Gender, Information Technology, and Developing Countries: An Analytic Study*. Washington, DC: United States Agency for International Development (USAID).

Hussain, S. 2004. "Developing Local Language Computing." *i4d (Information for Development)*. Online: http://i4d.eletsonline.com/pan-localisation-regional-initiativedeveloping-local-language-computing/ (accessed 13 March 2012).

Hussain, S. and N. Durrani. 2008. *A Study on Collation of Languages from Developing Asia.* Lahore: Center for Research in Urdu Language Processing and the National University of Computer and Emerging Sciences. Online: http://idl-bnc.idrc.ca/dspace/bitstream/10625/42566/1/129903. pdf (accessed 12 January 2012).

Hussain, S. et al. 2007. "Developing Lexicographic Sorting: An Example for Urdu." *ACM Transactions on Asian Language Information Processing* (TALIP) 6, no. 3, article 10.

Hussain, S. and R. Mohan. 2008. "Localization in Asia Pacific." In *Digital Review of Asia Pacific 2007–2008,* 43–58. Montreal: Orbicom, IDRC and Sage Publications India.

Huyer, S. et al. 2005. "Women in the Information Society." In *From the Digital Divide to Digital Opportunities: Measuring Infostates for Development,* edited by G. Sciadas. Montreal: Orbicom. Online: http://www.orbicom.uqam.ca/projects/ddi2005/index_ict_opp.pdf (accessed 1 March 2012).

Huyer, S. and N. Hafkin. 2007. *Engendering the Knowledge Society: Measuring Women's Participation.* Montreal: Orbicom.

IDRC. 2009a. "Project Success Story: Teleworking and the Disabled (Latina America)." Online: http://www.idrc.ca/uploads/user-S/12561450781SS2_Tlwrk_Disabld_eng.pdf (accessed 11 February 2012).

———. 2009b. *Success Story of the Project "Punto J: Phase II– Adolescents, Young People and ICT in Response to the HIV/AIDS Epidemic in Latin America and the Caribbean."* Ottawa: IDRC.

———. 2010. *Connectivity and Equity in the Americas Program Initiative Final Report 2006– 2009.* Ottawa: IDRC.

Kabeer, N. 1994. *Reversed Realities: Gender Hierarchies in Development Thought.* London and New York: Verso.

———. 2003. *Gender Mainstreaming in Poverty Eradication and the Millennium Development Goals: A Handbook for Policy-Makers and Other Stakeholders.* Ottawa: Commonwealth Secretariat, IDRC and CIDA.

Kabeer, N. and R. Subrahmanian. 1999. *Institutions, Relations, and Outcomes: A Framework and Case Studies for Gender-Aware Planning.* New Delhi: Kali for Women.

Kenny, C. 2002. "Information and Communication Technologies for Direct Poverty Alleviation: Costs and Benefits." *Development Policy Review* 20, no. 2: 141–57.

Loh-Ludher, L. L. et al. 2006. "Homeworkers and ICTs: Malaysia, Final Report." Online: http://www.aseanfoundation.org/documents/homeworkers/Malaysia -I- Fin Report. pdf (accessed 11 January 2012).

Madanda, A. and N. Hafkin. 2010. *Assessing Women's Empowerment through the Uganda Health Information Network. Uganda Health Information Network, Phase IV, November 2007 – April 2010.* Kampala: Makerere University.

Mafundikwa, S. 2004. *Afrikan Alphabets: The Story of Writing in Africa.* New York: Mark Batty Publisher.

Mann, C. L. 2003. "Information Technologies and International Development: Conceptual Clarity in the Search for Commonality and Diversity." *Information Technologies and International Development* 1, no. 2: 67–79.

Mbambo-Thata, B. et al. 2009. "When a Gender-Blind Access Policy Results in Discrimination: Realities and Perceptions of Female Students at the University of Zimbabwe." In *African Women & ICTs: Investigating Technology, Gender and Empowerment,* edited by I. Buskens and A. Webb, 67–76. Ottawa: IDRC / London and New York: Zed Books.

Mitter, S. 2004. "Globalization, ICTs, and Economic Empowerment: A Feminist Critique." *Gender, Technology and Development* 8, no. 1: 5–29.

Mohanty, C. T. 1991. "Cartographies of Struggle: Third World Women and the Politics of Feminism." In *Third World Women and the Politics of Feminism,* edited by C. T. Mohanty et al., 1–50. Bloomington: Indiana University Press.

Mottin-Sylla, M. H. and J. Palmieri. 2010. *Excision: Les jeunes changent l'Afrique par les TIC.* Dakar: Endatiers-monde. Online: http://idl-bnc.idrc.ca/dspace/handle/10625/44631 (accessed 15 December 2011).

Munyua, A. W. 2009. "Women Entrepreneurs in Nairobi: Examining and Contextualizing Women's Choices." In *African Women & ICTs: Investigating Technology, Gender and Empowerment,* edited by I. Buskens and A. Webb, 119–32. Ottawa: IDRC / London and New York: Zed Books.

National University of Computer and Emerging Sciences, Regional Project Secretariat. 2007. "PAN Localization Phase 1 (Feb. 2004 – Apr. 2007): Final Report." Online: http://idl-bnc.idrc.ca/dspace/handle/10625/44052 (accessed 10 February 2012).

Navarro, L. 2010. "The Impact of Internet Use on Individual Earnings in Latin America." IDRC-ECLAC. Online: http://www.inesad.edu.bo/bcde2010/contributed/b21_16.pdf (30 March 2012).

Ngolobe, B. 2010. "Women in Uganda: Mobile Activism for Networking and Advocacy." *SMS Uprising: Mobile Phone Activism in Africa*, edited by S. Ekaine, 105–15. Cape Town: Pambazuka Press.

Nida, E. 1998. "Language, Culture, and Translation." *Foreign Languages Journal* 115, no. 3: 29–33.

Nulens, G. 2000. "Information Technology in Africa: The Policy of the World Bank." In *Information Technology in Context: Studies from the Perspective of Developing Countries*, edited by C. Avgerou and G. Walsham. Aldershot: Ashgate.

Osborn, D. 2010. *African Languages in a Digital Age: Challenges and Opportunities for Indigenous Language Computing*. Cape Town: HSRC Press / Ottawa: IDRC. Online: http://www.idrc.ca/en/ev-145920-201-1-DO_TOPIC.html (accessed 3 April 2012).

Paré, D. et al. 2010. *External Review of the IDRC Acacia Program*. Ottawa: IDRC.

Prah, K. K. 2002. "Language, Neo-colonialism, and the African Development Challenge." *TRIcontinental* 150.

_____. 2003. "Going Native: Language of Instruction for Education, Development and African Emancipation." In *Language of Instruction in Tanzania and South Africa (LOITASA)*, edited by B. Brock et al., 14–35. Dar-es-Salaam: E&D.

Samarajiva, R. and A. Zainudeen, eds. 2008. *ICT Infrastructure in Emerging Asia: Policy and Regulatory Roadblocks*. New Delhi and Ottawa: Sage Publications and IDRC.

Sciadas, G., ed. 2005. *From Digital Divide to Digital Opportunities: Measuring Infostates for Development*. Montreal: Orbicom, ITU and NRC Press. Online: http://www.itu.int/ITU-D/ict/publications/dd/material/index_ict_opp.pdf (accessed 10 January 2012).

Sen, A. 1999. *Development as Freedom*. New York: Anchor Books.

_____. 2005. "Human Rights and Capabilities." *Journal of Human Development* 6, no. 2: 151–66.

Sey, A. et al. 2010. "Narrative Report," Acacia Research and Learning Forum in Dakar, Senegal, 4–8 October. Online: http://idl-bnc.idrc.ca/dspace/bitstream/10625/45413/1/131877.pdf (accessed 10 May 2012).

Shams, S. and S. Hussain. 2011. "Strategies for Research Capacity Building in Local Language Computing: PAN Localization Project Case Study." Presentation at the Conference on Human Language Technology for Development in Alexandria, Egypt, 2–5 May. Online: http://www.hltd.org/pdf/HLTD201130.pdf (10 February 2012).

Siegmann, K. A. 2010. *The Gender Digital Divide in Rural Pakistan – To Measure and to Bridge It*. Final technical report. Ottawa: IDRC.

Silver, H. 1995. "Reconceptualizing Social Disadvantage: Three Paradigms of Social Exclusion." In *Social Exclusion: Rhetoric, Reality, Responses*, edited by G. Rodgers et al., 58–80. Geneva: Institute of International Labour Studies.

Tafnout, A. and A. Timjerdine. 2009. "Using ICTs to Act on Hope and Commitment: The Fight against Gender Violence in Morocco." In *African Women & ICTs: Investigating Technology, Gender and Empowerment*, edited by I. Buskens and A. Webb, 88–96. Ottawa: IDRC / London and New York: Zed Books.

Telecapacitados: Teletrabajo para la inclusión laboral de personas con discapacidad. 2009. Ottawa: IDRC. Online: http://www.telecapacitados.tic.org.ar/telecapacitados.pdf (accessed 11 February 2012).

"Telework, New Forms of Work and Employment Opportunities." 2008. Post-project summary on IDRC Development Research Information Service (IDRIS), project no. 103239. Online: http://idris.idrc.ca/app/Search?request=directAccess&projectNumber=103239&language=en (accessed 19 February 2012).

UNESCO. 2003. "Language Vitality and Endangerment." Document submitted by the Ad Hoc Expert Group on Endangered Languages to the International Expert Meeting on the UNESCO Programme Safeguarding of Endangered Languages in Paris, 10–12 March. Online: http://www.unesco.org/culture/ich/doc/src/00120-EN.pdf (7 February 2012).

———. 2010. "Atlas of the World's Languages in Danger." Online:http://www.unesco.org/culture/languages-atlas/ (accessed 18 February 2012).

United Nations. 2003. "World Youth Report 2003: The Global Situation of Young People." Online: http://www.un.org/esa/socdev/unyin/documents/worldyouthreport.pdf (accessed 12 March 2012).

———. 2011. "Factsheet – *World Youth Report 2011*." Online: http://www.un.org/esa/socdev/unyin/documents/wyr11/factsheet.pdf (accessed 15 March 2012).

United Nations Enable. 2011a. "Factsheet on Persons with Disabilities." Online: http://www.un.org/disabilities/default.asp?id=18 (accessed 4 April 2012).

———. 2011b. "Priority Themes." Online: http://www.un.org/disabilities/default.asp?id=33 (accessed 15 March 2012).

Wallace, C. 2001. "Youth, Citizenship and Empowerment." In *Youth, Citizenship and Empowerment*, edited by H. Helve and C. Wallace, 11–30. Aldershot: Ashgate.

Warschauer, M. 2003. *Technology and Social Inclusion: Rethinking the Digital Divide*. Cambridge, MA: MIT Press.

World Health Organization. 2011. *World Report on Disability*. Geneva: WHO Press. Online: http://whqlibdoc.who.int/publications/2011/9789240685215_eng.pdf (accessed 17 February 2012).

World Summit on the Information Society. 2003. "Declaration of Principles." WSIS Geneva Phase in Geneva, Switzerland, 10–12 December. Online: http://www.itu.int/wsis/docs/geneva/official/dop.html (accessed 4 March 2012).

Zainudeen, A. et al. 2010. "Who's Got the Phone? Gender and the Use of the Telephone at the Bottom of the Pyramid." *New Media & Society* 12, no. 4: 549–66.

Zhang, W. et al. 2011. "PANeGOV: Understanding Democratic eGovernance in Asia: Youth, ICTs and Political Engagements in Asia." Final technical report. Online: http://idl-bnc.idrc.ca/dspace/handle/10625/48362 (accessed 4 April 2012).

Chapter 5

ACCESS AND USAGE OF ICTs
BY THE POOR (PART I)

Kathleen Diga[1]

Poverty reduction has been a key focus of development interventions and development research. Global levels of poverty have declined in the last decade, but there still remain many who cannot afford their basic food requirements for the day. Statistics illustrate that, in 2008, developing regions were home to nearly 1.4 billion people identified as being income poor (Chen and Ravallion 2008). Finding innovative ways to reduce poverty therefore continues to be a pressing goal. It is in light of this goal that IDRC's "Information and Communications Technologies for Development" (ICT4D) program sought to support research that investigated the role of information and communications technologies (ICTs) in reducing multi-dimensional poverty or addressing its root causes. In order to do so, IDRC partners focused much of their research on understanding the circumstances and conditions under which the poor accessed and used ICTs.

While studying this issue, a second focus emerged that was related to definitions and conceptualizations of poverty. A key aspect of poverty research has been to develop a realistic measure of poverty (where, if you are below a certain poverty threshold, you are considered poor). The rationale for a poverty line or threshold is that governments would then be able to have a statistical estimate of deprivation within their country. Using this guideline, governments could make decisions about the eligibility, costs and allocation of welfare resources to the families most in need (i.e., social protection programs such as child and social grants). Questions and studies about how best to measure poverty have emerged as a key facet in this field of research because the dimensions developed to measure poverty lines are contested. For example, an institution like the World Bank uses the simple $1 or $2 a day absolute poverty line to measure poverty across countries. Some researchers criticize this official poverty measure, arguing that it is a limited way of measuring and understanding poverty.

The limitations of these measurement tools were investigated with poverty researchers suggesting that poverty needs to be measured by an individual's or family's access not only to income, but also to other needs such as human, financial, social and physical capital (Moser 1998). This new, multi-dimensional exploration of poverty has opened the door to exploring the relationship between ICTs and poverty, since ICTs are thought to potentially facilitate the acquisition of these other forms of capital. This thinking has led a small group of developing country researchers who work in the interdisciplinary research area of poverty and ICTs to start exploring other possible new dimensions of poverty, such as digital poverty (Barrantes 2007) and investigating how this concept fits into a multi-dimensional poverty index (May 2012). They are also exploring possible impacts of ICTs on poverty reduction over time (May et al. 2011). The purpose of this chapter is therefore to summarize the main findings from these studies. First, the chapter looks at research IDRC sponsored on the relationship between ICT access and various economic indicators. Following that, it delves into the findings that reveal how and why the poor access ICTs. Then, attention is drawn to more nuanced aspects of the ICT-poverty nexus and how this idea has contributed to new theoretical developments and applied research in the last decade[2] to get a better understanding of the complex relationship between ICTs and poverty.

Background on ICT and Poverty Research: Moving from the Digital Divide to Digital Poverty

> IDRC was one of the first development agencies that embraced ICTs as key for development and poverty alleviation. (Muirhead and Harpelle 2010, 206)

IDRC's ICT4D program embraced the idea that ICTs could play a role in addressing development challenges early on. Within the scope of this work, IDRC-supported researchers focused on the relationship between the digital divide and economic growth. IDRC-supported research took two interrelated approaches to explore the digital divide, a macro- and micro-level analysis. The first approach began by exploring the digital gap from a macro-level perspective and the digital gap relationship between countries. An important project emerging from this particular research focus was conducted by Sciadas (2005). Sciadas used the International Telecommunication Union's (ITU) country-level data about a country's access to ICTs to examine the direct relationship between a country's access to ICTs and its population's productive capacity (defined as labor and capital). To measure the relationship between ICTs and productive capacity, Sciadas used an innovative conceptual framework (see Figure 5.1) of the info state, which was seen as composed of info density and info use. In this framework, Sciadas tried for the first time to incorporate ICT skills into the measure of the "digital divide."

Info density involved the ITU's data on ICT infrastructure and ICT skills while info use employed the data on ICT uptake and ICT intensity of use. The information was combined to develop a score for each country: the country's info state. The results from this first-of-its-kind analytical macro-study showed that major ICT info density and info use gaps exist among countries with access to ICTs and those without. The study demonstrated that all countries experience a positive change in info state status over time but the intensity of these changes differed; countries with bottom-end info state statuses have higher rates of growth than the top-end info state status countries. The middle and upper-middle info states are improving their rankings and closing the narrow digital divide between them and the status of top info state countries. Unfortunately, even though countries in the bottom info state tier (especially countries in Africa) have higher rates of growth,

Figure 5.1. A schematic of the conceptual framework of an info state

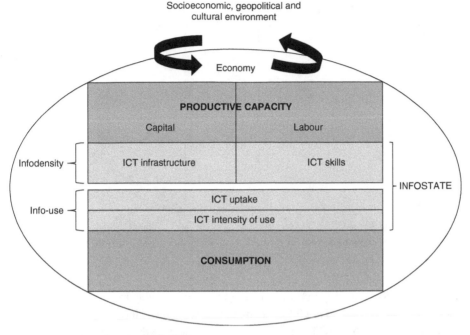

Source: Adapted from Sciadas (2005, 301).

they see much less and slower progress in catching up to the top info state countries. This is mainly because those in the bottom tier are starting at near-zero baselines of info density and info use. Sciadas' study was significant because it provided a new and realistic picture of the digital divide from an aggregate supply-side perspective. Soon after, many studies tried to adopt this analytical model. Yet, as Sciadas recommends, further work could be done from the demand side and at a micro household level to see if digital divide results are similar.

More important for our focus, the Sciadas report also took the info state concept and questioned the relationship between various levels of info state and gross domestic product (GDP) growth over time. The info density in 1995 and 2003 (see Chart 5.1) was found to be highly correlated with per capita GDP (expressed in US$ and in purchasing power parity [PPP] terms), with a correlation coefficient of 0.95 (Teltscher and Korka 2005).

This finding confirms the "strong linkage between the level of ICT advancement of a country and its level of income" (Teltscher and Korka 2005, 46). Moreover, Sciadas found that this responsiveness increases over time at higher ICT levels. Interestingly, a more nuanced analysis showed that countries benefited more from ICTs if they had a certain minimum level of info density. However, countries that started off with low levels of info density did not benefit as much in terms of economic growth when info density grew. This, according to the study, is potentially explained by the "still-low absolute levels of ICT uptake (and implicitly inadequate diffusion among economic sectors, including small businesses), and the less efficient incorporation of ICTs in their production processes" (Teltscher and Korka 2005, 55). The revelation that there is a relationship between ICT

Chart 5.1. Info density and per capita GDP

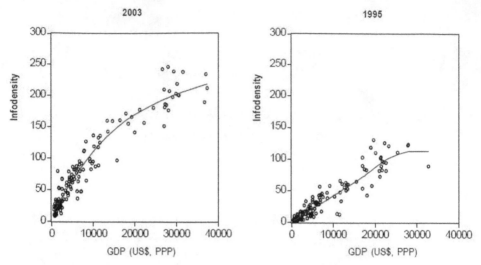

Source: Teltscher and Korka (2005, 46).

access growth (or info density) and economic growth at the macro-indicator level is important. However, it does not fully explain the more nuanced levels of causality between poverty and ICTs or how ICTs play a role in economic growth. To answer that question, researchers needed to focus on more specific user or household surveys – preferably over time – to get a better grasp of how these relationships function. As such, IDRC sought to address this research gap by devoting a significant amount of resources to this issue.

IDRC supported household surveys and analysis by LIRNE*asia* (Learning Initiatives on Reforms for Network Economies Asia), RIA (Research ICT Africa) and DIRSI (Diálogo Regional sobre Sociedad de la Información) to report on the micro-level household demand side of ICT access and use in the three regions of the world, focusing specifically on how the poor used ICTs. This descriptive reporting from the household and individual perspective was unique as it provided the ICT4D community with insights into how ICTs were being used by the poor. The work done around this approach can be broken into three separate yet interrelated issues: the poor's access to and use of ICTs, their reasons for using ICTs and the affordability of ICTs in various countries in these three regions. The following section discusses key findings of research studies on these three issues. The findings provide context for the development of conceptual frameworks and applications around the research work on the nexus between ICTs and poverty, which is the third focus of this chapter.

The poor's access to and use of ICTs

Table 5.1 summarizes the most significant IDRC supported studies on this topic. The following section describes the main findings that emerged from these studies.

The first study listed, from DIRSI, examined access and use of mobile telephony in Latin America. Researchers from the DIRSI network attempted to better understand poor

Table 5.1. Summary of IDRC projects on ICTs and the poor

Project Name	Organization	Duration	Region/ Countries	Methodology	Sample
Poverty and Mobile Telephony in Latin America and the Caribbean (LAC)	DIRSI	2006–2008	Jamaica, Brazil, Trinidad and Tobago, Peru, Mexico, Colombia, Argentina	Survey	Low-income households: ages 13–70; n=7,000
Teleuse@BOP (Asia)	LIRNE*asia*	2005–2011	Bangladesh, India, Indonesia (Java), Pakistan, Philippines, Sri Lanka, Thailand	Survey, face-to-face interviews, focus groups, mini-ethnographies	Low-income households: ages 15–60; n=29,162
Towards an African-Index: Household and Individual ICT Access and Usage*	RIA	2004–2012	Benin, Botswana, Burkina Faso, Cameroon, Côte d'Ivoire, Ethiopia, Ghana, Kenya, Mozambique, Namibia, Nigeria, Rwanda, Senegal, South Africa, Tanzania, Uganda, Zambia	Household and individual survey: focus groups	Nationally representative; n=22,446
Poverty and Information & Communication Technology Systems in Urban and Rural Eastern Africa	PICTURE-Africa	2006–2010	Kenya, Uganda, Rwanda, Tanzania	Household and individual survey, focus groups, panel data	Low-income households: poorest enumerating areas, rural and urban; n=1,600

*Research ICT Africa has finished their 2011 household survey (n=14,100), but analysis was still in progress at the time of this publication.
Source: Adapted by the author from Rashid and Elder (2009).

households' access to and use of mobiles (Galperin and Mariscal 2007). The researchers analyzed surveys of over 7,000 face-to-face interviews with individuals aged 13 to 70 residing in low-income households in the study's seven countries – Argentina, Brazil, Colombia, Jamaica, Mexico, Peru, and Trinidad and Tobago. The study demonstrated significantly high, but also very different, national percentages of ownership of mobile phones by

Chart 5.2. Mobile usage and ownership Latin America (% of total)

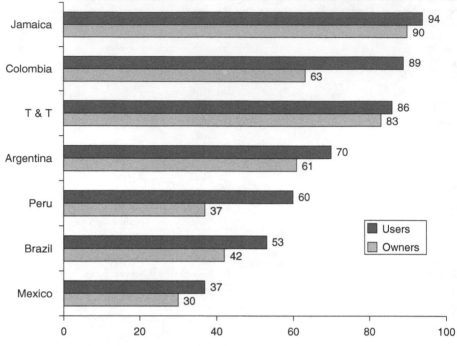

Source: Adapted from Galperin and Mariscal (2007).

Chart 5.3. Bottom-of-the-pyramid (BOP) mobile and fixed phone ownership (2006) (% of BOP teleusers)

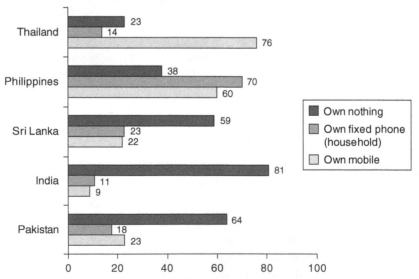

Source: Adapted from de Silva and Zainudeen (2008, 30).

low-income households. For example, Chart 5.2 indicates that all of these countries had some level of mobile ownership among the selected poor households. Yet there were very different levels of ownership when comparing countries. Some had remarkably high percentages of ownership, such as Jamaica and Colombia; both countries had approximately 90 percent ownership. Other countries, however, had much lower ownership levels; Mexico, for example, had about 30 percent (Galperin and Mariscal 2007).

In contrast, a study by LIRNE*asia* – the Teleuse@BOP program that ran from 2005 to 2011 – focused much of its attention on understanding poor (identified as the "bottom of the pyramid" or BOP population) teleusers[3] and the effects of ICTs on this segment of the population. The study found relatively lower levels of ICT ownership – specifically mobiles – in certain Asian countries in 2006.[4] (See Chart 5.3.) For example, in Pakistan, India and Sri Lanka, mobile ownership was below one-quarter of BOP teleusers; these individuals relied either on a household fixed phone (still only available to a similarly low number of BOP teleusers) or on shared phones – either through paid public access phones or shared with other people within their household or their social network (de Silva and Zainudeen 2008). Other surveys in Thailand, Sri Lanka and the Philippines found much higher levels of mobile ownership among the poor, similar to levels in many of the DIRSI Latin America studies.

The following 2008 studies by LIRNE*asia* showed significant improvements in mobile phone ownership across the four revisited Asian countries with small numbers even taking up services beyond voice, such as SMS-based information alerts, m-voting, etc. (Zainudeen and Ratnadiwakara 2011). However, awareness and use of the Internet has been very low among the BOP in all of the Asian countries studied across the time periods, suggesting that mobiles were potentially a much more appropriate technology for poorer communities.

On the African continent, Research ICT Africa (RIA) completed a demand side, nationally representative survey in 18 African countries in 2006–2007 to determine the social factors that lead to mobile phone adoption. In the population surveyed, RIA found that income and education factors increase the chances of mobile adoption while gender, age and membership in asocial network have no significant impact (Gillwald and Stork 2008). Their findings were also relatively consistent with the findings from Latin America in that there were significant national divides in mobile ownership across the continent with 62 percent of people in South Africa having access to mobile phones while only 3 percent of people in Ethiopia own phones. Research by RIA also focused on people's access to computers and the Internet and determined that the highest rate for ownership of home computers was 15 percent in South Africa with all other African countries having a much smaller computer adoption (Gillwald and Stork 2008).

Why the poor use ICTs

Understanding the extent to which the poor in developing societies have access to ICTs gives a better picture of who can potentially benefit from ICTs. However, an important factor for explaining the relationship between ICT usage and improving people's livelihoods is revealing why they use ICTs. The 2007 poverty and mobile usage study

Chart 5.4. Mobile phone ownership 2006–2008 by individuals (% of BOP teleusers)

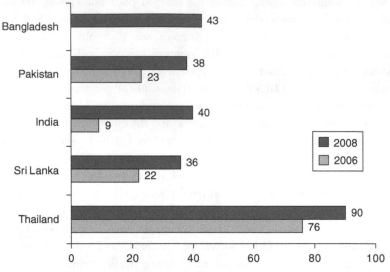

Source: Adapted from de Silva and Zainudeen (2008, 30) and Sivapragasam and Kang (2011, 38).

in Latin America, for instance, revealed that mobile telephony is highly valued by the poor as a tool to strengthen social ties and increase personal security. Mobile usage is also beginning to prove useful for enhancing business and employment opportunities (Galperin and Mariscal 2007). Overall, the results in Latin America suggest that the economic impact of mobile adoption by the poor is mediated by social capital variables such as the strengthening of trust networks and improved coordination of informal job markets. The greatest perceived benefits of the mobile phone by low-income households are contacts with family and friends, followed by the phones' usefulness during emergencies. In all regions – looking at both the poor and non-poor – the benefits of using ICTs for earning or saving money (or what some would consider "instrumental" purposes) were seen to be lower. However, in poor settings, social relationships with family and friends are intrinsically linked to economic issues; people usually get jobs or loans from family and friends. Therefore, separating the two reasons for using mobile phones – maintaining social relationships and economic purposes – may be false or might at least need to be further interrogated.

Affordability of ICTs

Research was also carried out on the amount of money the poor were spending to have access to ICTs. In Latin America, average monthly spending on mobile telephony by the poor appeared to range from US$6.10 in Colombia to US$15.70 in Mexico; costs in Caribbean nations were considerably higher. The significant level of expenditures on mobile handsets and services by these low-income populations has major implications for mobile phone use as it lowers households' frequency or penetration of use or burdens low-income households with high costs. In his 2008 research brief, Agüero took a closer look at Peru and showed that telecommunications services (mobile and fixed telephony and the Internet) were viewed as luxury goods by those surveyed. In 2007, Gamboa noted similar perceptions about mobile telephony in Colombia between 2001 and 2006. In contrast, Agüero et al. (2011) show that, by 2008 in the six Asian countries studied by LIRNE*asia*, mobile phone services had become necessities for BOP users. Barrantes and Galperin looked at the affordability of mobile phone services in 2008 and came up with three regional findings: first, most poor people pay a premium for mobile phone usage because most of the poor use higher-cost prepaid mobile airtime rather than postpaid; second, the affordability of phones can help predict whether a country has high mobile phone penetration; third, by using 5 percent of personal income as the affordability threshold and by using a low-volume mobile phone user basket (or the best approximate usage of mobiles by the poor – about 24 outgoing calls for less than two minutes and thirty text messages [SMS] per month), they discovered that Brazil, Mexico and Peru with their high basket cost have lower mobile penetration than Colombia, Argentina, Uruguay and Chile, where the basket cost is low (Barrantes and Galperin 2008). When the researchers tested different scenarios, they also noted that, if costs were set using a micro-prepayment (paying smaller amounts for airtime) as well as per second call billing, poor mobile users would lower their mobile expenditures by up to 24 percent – like they did, for example, in Colombia (Barrantes and Galperin 2008). Finally, Brazil and Peru have the highest monthly costs of the low-volume mobile basket as a percentage (30 to 45 percent) of their average income, far beyond the 5 percent affordability threshold (Barrantes and Galperin 2008). An update from Galperin (2010) produces similar findings in Latin America with some of the highest mobile telephony tariffs in the world, rates that range from US$2.20 (in Jamaica) to US$45.00 (in Brazil) with an average tariff of US$15.00 for the low-usage basket. These regional findings reveal an urgent need to rethink public policies that are premised on the mobile phone as a luxury good. Since affordability is the most significant barrier to extending the reach of mobile services, as well as the range of services offered to the poor, priority should be placed on policies aimed at reducing tariffs.

In terms of affordability, 70 percent of selected Indian and Sri Lankan respondents surveyed in 2005 thought the cost of mobile telephony service was "high," "very high" or "extremely high' as they spent at least four percent of their monthly income on such communication expenses (Moonesinghe et al. 2007). In LIRNE*asia*'s 2008 survey – sampling over 9750 representatives of the BOP in India, Pakistan, Bangladesh, Sri Lanka, the Philippines and Thailand – the poorest respondents in the survey were found to be spending over twenty-five percent of their income on mobile telephony services (Agüero et al. 2011). In contrast, the highest income groups of the BOP spend between 3 and 6 percent. In terms of income elasticity of demand, which measures the responsiveness of the demand for a good to a change in the income of the people demanding the good, LIRNE*asia* found that demand for mobile services was not very sensitive to changes in income. It appears that these respondents view mobile phones as a necessity rather than a luxury item. In the case of India, this contrasts with the earlier findings of Moonesinghe et al. (2007) (though using different methodology) that identify mobile services as luxury items at the BOP. Agüero et al. (2011) suggest that this change of status for mobile phone services in India could be due to the improvement in market conditions through increased competition.

In a specific study of migrant workers in the same six countries in 2008, mobile remittances were examined to gauge whether mobiles were gaining traction as a tool to send money back to family. The study found that usage was at near-zero levels so the poor were not benefitting from these types of mobile applications. At the time of the study, Thailand and the Philippines offered mobile remittances or mobile money and banking, but only forty to sixty percent of migrant workers in the study were aware of such services in these countries (Sivapragasam et al. 2011). Researchers found that, as income, educational level and access to financial services increased, awareness of mobile remittances improved as well (Sivapragasam et al. 2011). However, those who were aware of mobile remittance services hesitated to use them due to their satisfaction with current financial services (Sivapragasam et al. 2011). In selected African household studies, RIA found that the mobile platform has become an acceptable method for banking, especially since many of the mobile phone users surveyed were without formal bank accounts either due to bank accounts being perceived as unnecessary from lack of regular income or as being unaffordable (Comninos et al. 2008).

The RIA team also estimates the bottom seventy-five percent of mobile phone users in Africa spend approximately eleven to twenty-seven percent of their household income on mobile communications (Gillwald and Stork 2008). These figures match the levels found by Agüero et al. (2011) in Asia. Across regions, most mobile phone subscribers are using prepayment for mobile airtime (Gillwald and Stork 2008; Mariscal and Rivera 2006; Samarajiva 2007). RIA found that the lower the income of a household, the higher the proportion of income that will be spent on mobiles compared with those with higher income (Chabossou et al. 2008).

Positive and negative aspects of ICT use

Another IDRC-supported project, "Poverty and ICTs in Urban and Rural East Africa" (PICTURE-Africa), took a different look at the relationship between ICT use and poverty. In comparing 2007 with 2010, it found various positive and negative aspects of ICT household use. In Kenya, for example, during a recession, many households went from non-poor to poor status between 2007 and 2010; yet, the few that did improve from poor to non-poor status had increased their income through enhanced use of ICTs (Waema and Okinda 2011). Their findings also showed a significant increase in the respondents' sum of assets, human capital and access to services and infrastructure, but insignificant change when looking at social inclusion or participation in social networks (Waema and Okinda 2011). In Kenya, through the Research ICT Africa data, they further found that income, education level and available infrastructure were good predictors for Internet use in urban areas. As for development outcomes, mobile phones and the Internet were perceived to improve social development, especially for communication between family members and friends (Ndung'u and Waema 2011). Finally, mobile money or transfers had gained popularity in the country with over fifty percent of the respondents transferring mobile airtime. The respondents started using the mobile money service due to the low cost of transactions and for reasons of safety. However, negative outcomes have also been found in Kenya: mobile phones have been used for crime and they also are the cause of job losses for those who cannot cope with adapting to new technologies (Ndung'u and Waema 2011).

In Tanzania, PICTURE-Africa discovered that ICT use had the greatest impact on welfare through savings of time and money as ICTs replaced the need for physical travel. For example, Amina, a Tanzanian small businesswoman, saved money on the transport of goods. Before she used a mobile phone, she would have to pay for a return trip by scooter taxi to the town of Mlandizi to purchase her supplies. Today, she calls in the order to her supplier and the scooter taxi picks it up. She saved half of what she used to pay and she could spend the time on other activities instead of travelling (Mascarenhas et al. 2010, 19). Nevertheless, as was seen in a Ugandan case study (Diga 2007), the costs of mobile services and repair remain high for the poor and tend to divert money from other essential household food expenses.

The studies by these research networks provided some of the first micro-level research findings on ICTs and the digital divide on the three continents. However, the key assumption underlying this work – that the poor could be moved out of poverty simply by providing them with ICT and information access and usage – was a limited one. Just comparing the haves and have-nots was not enough to understand the broader development issues of poverty. As work in this field moved forward, the effects of ICTs on the lives of the poor were identified as key issues that were missing and that required the attention of researchers in this area. Thus, as research studies progressed and attempted to complement earlier research done in the digital divide field, researchers started to investigate the effects that ICT demand could have on poverty in developing world contexts.

In the early conceptualization of ICTs and understanding of their role in poverty reduction, IDRC teamed up with international groups such as the UN Task Force for Science, Technology and Development to draw out the most important impacts of technologies and its systems, particularly on the ICT access to the poor. This led to important poverty discussions through two Harvard forums (in 2003 and 2009) entitled "A Dialogue on ICTs, Human Development, Growth and Poverty Reduction" (Spence 2003; Spence and Smith 2009). Within these forums, researchers acknowledged how the tremendous access to mobile phones in the developing world has increased their reach to those who previously had no connection with new information technologies (Spence and Smith 2010). The widespread use of mobile phones by even the poor started to help researchers take the next step on the ICT-poverty nexus issue and begin to investigate whether ICT use was helping to lift people in the developing world out of poverty. Several case studies mentioned in Chapter 6 on local economic opportunities and livelihoods reflect on the social and economic changes in small non-farm enterprises and agricultural farming as a result of ICT use (especially mobile phones). Yet, on a larger scale, questions began to emerge about whether these case studies could be calculated through overall country-level surveys that could then aggregate these life changes of the poor at the household level to understand whether there is a trend of moving out of poverty due to ICT use.

Figure 5.2. ICT, poverty and livelihoods framework

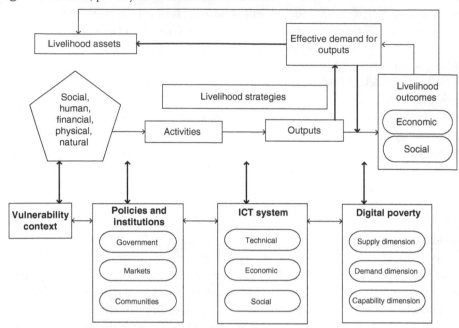

Source: Adapted from May (2010), Carney (2003) and Dorward et al. (2003).

Understanding the Relationship between Poverty and ICTs: Analytical Frameworks

Part of the difficulty of exploring the relationship between ICTs and poverty stems from the complexity involved in conceptualizing that relationship. IDRC therefore supported a body of work to try to better understand that relationship. By 2005, studies had developed that improved the conceptualization of poverty and the place of ICTs within a multi-dimensional poverty framework, as well as innovative measurements and applied analysis of poverty reduction and ICTs. In East Africa, IDRC-funded researchers have attempted to build a conceptual framework of digital poverty as a predictor in the multi-dimensional aspect of poverty measurement. This framework derives from the sustainable livelihoods framework (May 2010), which has been useful in understanding poverty and the process of livelihood change. It includes Moser's 1998 asset portfolio of social, human, financial, physical and natural capital; PICTURE-Africa later contributed the sixth capital – digital capital. The framework incorporates an enhanced ICT system (especially the technical, economic and social aspects), which can affect the livelihood strategies and outcomes result in the everyday choices of the poor. (See Figure 5.2.)

As previously mentioned, PICTURE-Africa established, through a unique analysis of household consumption and expenditure levels, that access to information and communications technologies contributed to reducing poverty in eastern Africa. This analysis is a more accurate measure of household asset wealth rather than only income and develops poverty measurement over time through a panel longitudinal study.

Just over one thousand households in the poorest areas of each country were interviewed, first in 2007–2008 and again in 2010 to form the region's (and the world's) first "ICT4D & Poverty" panel data survey.

Digital poverty

In addressing the ongoing development debate about the limits of financial poverty measurements and the inclusion of other multiple dimensions of poverty, one conceptual innovation is to incorporate the possible dimension of digital poverty. Developed with IDRC support, the Latin America team DIRSI produced a book entitled *Digital Poverty*, which enhances the ideas of information poverty by including the attributes of connectivity, communication and information. In this text, Barja and Gigler (2007) examine a concept called "information and communications poverty," revealing these enhanced factors that bring about the digital divide. They interpret Sen's 1999 work, *Development of Freedom*, by hypothesizing that "freedoms will strengthen the individuals' capability to participate in the information society and therefore the communication and information poverty is a lack of the basic capabilities needed to participate in the information society" (Barja and Gigler 2007, 15). They theorize first that there is a set physical location in a country – the information and communication poverty baseline. Barja and Gigler then try to calculate an economic cost for locations to meet that poverty baseline through a function of current local capabilities plus local, usage and technological constraints. Elements of an information and communication poverty dimension, which is conceptually location-based and uses mainly supply-side data, can be taken further to a household-level measurement as was done by Barrantes (2007). (See Figure 5.3.) The concept of digital poverty is located through "the minimum ICT use and consumption levels, as well as income levels of the population necessary to demand ICT products" (Barrantes 2007, 33). Barrantes tries to incorporate the listed attributes (age, education, available infrastructure and functionality accomplished) within the measurement of digital poverty. Barrantes developed the concept of digital poverty by breaking down the poverty level into four classifications: extremely digitally poor, digitally poor, the connected and the digitally wealthy.

The extremely digitally poor are households that are deficient in all forms of ICT connectivity and that have little capability or means to accept or deliver electronic messages or to participate actively with information. The digitally poor are passive receivers of radio or television media. The connected can engage in two-way reception and delivery of voice communication, mainly through mobiles. The digitally wealthy are full participants in electronic media, both in terms of receiving or sending information, usually through the Internet (Barrantes 2007). Using these categories, digital poverty can be explored to see whether a group of households or individuals falls within a category of digital deprivation or digital wealth. In a sample of over seventeen thousand Peruvian households with access to ICTs (from a 2003 national living standards survey), Barrantes identified 68 percent of the sample as being mainly "extremely digitally poor." The study also found that, at the time, there were many in the survey who may have access to telecenters but no telephone access (Peru had poor telephone service penetration in 2003). Through this analysis, Barrantes confirms that the lower the poverty level of the household, the higher the likelihood for the

Figure 5.3. Digital poverty framework

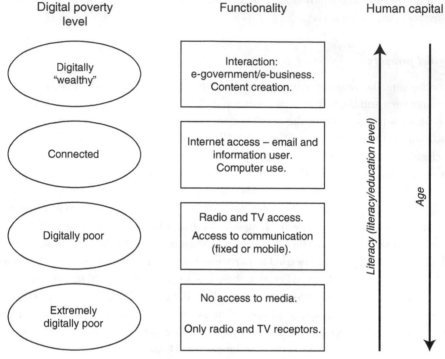

Source: Adapted from Barrantes (2007, 36).

household to be connected either via Internet access or mobile phone. With urban or male youth in the household, the probability of being connected increased.

Applying Theory – The Nexus of ICTs and Poverty

PICTURE-Africa likely went the furthest in exploring the use of a multi-dimensional poverty assessment tool to understand the ICT-poverty relationship in East Africa. The study investigated six types of capital (including the new digital capital), developed proxies and indices for the poverty line and included a discussion on vulnerability. The study shows a 2.5 percent improvement away from poverty by the poor in all countries who accessed ICTs between 2007 and 2010 (May et al. 2011). The study used an econometric model to demonstrate a causal link: access to ICTs contributes a small but positive effect toward reducing poverty. This poverty change is also in a pro-poor direction and shows that the proportional expenditure change experienced per person in a household with ICTs between 2007and 2010 was felt more strongly (or two times more) by the poorest than the non-poor who were surveyed (May et al. 2011). The findings by May et al. (2011) suggest the poorest benefit the most from ICTs. Finally, mobile phones were seen to be a key tool in ensuring people's more sustainable resilience to socioeconomic vulnerabilities.

Discussion

IDRC's partners have focused on two particular area of research with respect to ICTs and poverty: (i) enhancing the concept of the "digital divide" and its relationship to economic growth and measurements of the access and use of ICTs and the poor; and (ii) developing the theoretical underpinnings and applied research on the nexus between ICTs and poverty. Given that IDRC partners have demonstrated a positive impact of ICTs on the reduction of poverty in East Africa and have shown that the poor pay proportionally more than the non-poor for ICT services, one would advocate for social equity for ICTs, especially mobile phones. However, further research is recommended to complement the current research on ICTs and poverty. In Asia as well, we see the significant change from ICTs being a luxury item to being a necessity – a change that may be important to follow, especially in the other regions of the world. Using this evidence, one can advocate for lower-cost ICTs for the poor and seek lower tariffs or find mechanisms to ensure the poor can access ICTs as well. Failure to do these things could exacerbate problems of growing socioeconomic inequality, particularly in countries where economic growth has recently been significant, such as Brazil and India.

To complement ICT access, social protection mechanisms will continue to provide poor households with consistent and necessary resources to help them out of poverty. For example, most developing countries have poverty reduction plans but, given the expansion of ICT use, policymakers may need to consider how ICTs can play a role in poverty eradication if they see such relevance (Diga et al. 2013). Social policy research has shown that government policies in developing country contexts can play a significant role in changing levels of poverty. This has been demonstrated in social protection programs that are having a positive effect on reducing poverty through social grants, such as those in Brazil through the "Bolsa Família" programs (Soares et al. 2010; as cited in Machado et al. 2011). In this instance, the direct cash transfers reach the poorest households, along with various support programs for health, childcare, children's education and work and have contributed toward the dramatic reduction of poverty. ICTs could play a complementary role in lowering the costs for poor families to receive such grants or services. Nevertheless, an environment that can help promote decent employment and improved incomes will also help those who can transition out of social protection services to the workplace.

Much of the research mentioned in this chapter was carried out by researchers within developing countries and IDRC continues to support the capability enhancement and strengthening of research methods and approaches coming from the global south. While such local ICT and poverty studies have made significant contributions to the field, further work can also examine the use of the PICTURE-Africa conceptual framework as well as more participatory methods of poverty and ICT measures to complement aggregate macro-level research. In other words, how could the poor assess their own well-being changes in light of ICT access or usage? In pushing for up-to-date poverty reduction strategies, initiatives can be developed to help balance the information deficit in poor areas and help to find ways for the poor and their families to become better able to use the available tools to meet their livelihood needs.

Finally, there was little demand for the Internet among the poor households and there was slow progress toward improving its affordability and access. Current studies question the relationship between poverty and the Internet – notably broadband access – in the developing world (Kenny 2011). However, the reality is that Internet access has only recently started to reach poorer communities, mainly through mobile Internet access and with broadband connectivity in locations of enhanced reach and lower Internet costs. Hence, very few rigorous studies have been conducted in the developing world. But current research does tend to suggest that increasing mobile affordability and access may be a better policy choice than increasing broadband Internet penetration in poor communities, at least in the short term. Further research is needed though to confirm this policy stance.

Conclusion

From the research, it can be suggested that ICTs are a resource when addressing problems of systemic poverty. Today, the key device accessed and used by the rural poor has been the mobile phone – despite the higher costs, in many cases in the global south, that are being paid by resource-constrained households. This seems, however, to be a rational choice since new evidence reveals that access to ICTs can have significant effects on alleviating poverty, especially for the very poor. Finally, in expanding the debate about the multi-dimensions of poverty, developing country researchers helped to contribute another innovative concept of digital deprivation in today's knowledge society.

To date, statistical agencies across the developing world are now incorporating certain ICT access and usage indicators into their national household surveys. Much of this trend was spurred on by the research networks supported by IDRC. The next steps are to continue training developing country researchers to (i) complete further analysis and see whether ICT access and use have any effect on poverty reduction and (ii) further the conceptual thinking and frameworks around digital poverty and its incorporation within the current multi-dimensions of poverty. This way forward would make substantial contributions to a field dedicated to tackling the war against poverty.

It comes as little surprise that access to and use of ICTs affects poverty outcomes. These technologies have become indispensable elements of livelihoods in the more developed regions of the world. However, this process rolls out differently at the "base of the pyramid." First, a "threshold of use" has to be achieved in the society before income effects from ICT use can be seen. Once achieved, low-income earners at the base of the pyramid are willing to expend much higher proportions of their much lower incomes to retain access to ICT services, especially mobile telephony. They clearly understand that these tools are indispensable in their social and economic lives, which is among the reasons that ICT4D had such an active program of applied research in this area at IDRC.

Notes

1 I would like to thank Katie Bryant and Laurent Elder for their contributions to shaping this chapter. My thanks also go to Raymond Hyma, Alicia Richero, Geneviève Lefebvre, Shalini Kala, Delphine Larrousse and Edith Adera for their initial contributions and to Rohan Samarajiva, Ranjula Perera and Ayesha Zainudeen (the LIRNE*asia* team), Christoph Stork and Roxana Barrantes for their editorial reviews. This chapter contributes substantial insight into the author's current PhD thesis.
2 See Muirhead and Harpelle (2010) for a more in-depth historic narrative of IDRC's work on ICTs and poverty alleviation.

3 Teleusers are those who have made or received a call from any phone in the three months preceding the survey.

4 The 2005 study was non-representative; therefore, national BOP numbers cannot be drawn from the data. From 2006 onwards, the data are nationally representative of the BOP in each respective country.

References

Agüero, A. 2008. "Telecommunications Expenditure in Peruvian Households." DIRSI research brief.

Agüero, A. et al. 2011. "Bottom of the Pyramid Expenditure Patterns on Mobile Phone Services in Selected Emerging Asian Countries." *Information Technologies & International Development* 7, no. 3: 19–32.

Barja, G. and B. S. Gigler. 2007. "The Concept of Information Poverty and How to Measure It in the Latin American Context." In *Digital Poverty: Latin American and Caribbean Perspectives*, edited by H. Galperin and J. Mariscal, 11–28. Ottawa: IDRC.

Barrantes, R. 2007. "Analysis of ICT Demand: What is Digital Poverty and How to Measure It?" In *Digital Poverty: Latin American and Caribbean Perspectives*, edited by H. Galperin and J. Mariscal, 29–53. Ottawa: IDRC.

Barrantes, R. and H. Galperin. 2008. "Can the Poor Afford Mobile Telephony? Evidence from Latin America." *Telecommunications Policy* 32, no. 8: 521–30.

Carney, D. 2003. *Sustainable Livelihoods Approaches: Progress and Possibilities for Change*. Toronto: Department for International Development (UK).

Chabossou, A. et al. 2008. "Mobile Telephony Access and Usage in Africa." *Southern African Journal of Information and Communication* 9: 17–49.

Chen, S. and M. Ravallion. 2008. "The Developing World Is Poorer than We Thought, But No Less Successful in the Fight Against Poverty." Policy research working paper WPS4703. Washington, DC: World Bank.

Comninos, A. et al. 2008. "M-Banking the Unbanked." Research ICT Africa Network, Towards Evidence-based ICT Policy and Regulation 1, paper no. 4. Online: http://www.researchictafrica. net/publications/Towards_Evidence-based_ICT_Policy_and_Regulation_-_Volume_1/RIA Policy Paper Vol 1 Paper 4 - M-banking the Unbanked.pdf (accessed 12 January 2012).

de Silva, H. and A. Zainudeen. 2008. "Teleuse at the Bottom of the Pyramid: Beyond Universal Access." *Telektronikk* 2: 25–38. Online: http://www.telektronikk.com/volumes/pdf/2.2008/ Tel_2-08_Page_025-038.pdf (accessed 17 December 2011).

Diga, K. 2007. "Mobile Cell Phones and Poverty Reduction: Technology Spending Patterns and Poverty Level Change among Households in Uganda." Paper prepared for master's in development studies. Durban: University of KwaZulu-Natal.

Diga, K. et al. 2013. "ICT Policy and Poverty Reduction in Africa." *info* 15, no. 5: 114–27.

Dorward, A. 2003. "Markets, Institutions and Technology: Missing Links in Livelihoods Analysis." *Development Policy Review* 21, no. 3: 319–32.

Fosu, A. K. 2011. "Growth, Inequality, and Poverty Reduction in Developing Countries: Recent Global Evidence." WIDER working paper no. 2011/01, United Nations University, World Institute for Development Economics Research. Online: http://www.wider.unu.edu/ publications/working-papers/2011/en_GB/wp2011-001/. (accessed 14 December 2011).

Galperin, H. 2010. *Tariffs and the Affordability Gap in Mobile Telephone Services in Latin America and the Caribbean*. Lima: DIRSI and IDRC.

Galperin, H. and J. Mariscal. 2007. *Mobile Opportunities: Poverty and Mobile Telephony in Latin America and the Caribbean*. Lima: DIRSI and IDRC.

Gamboa, L. F. 2007. *Patterns of Access and Analysis of Spending on Cellular Mobile Telephone Service in Colombia, 2001–2006*. Lima: DIRSI and IDRC.

Gillwald, A. and C. Stork. 2008. "ICT Access and Usage in Africa." Research ICT Africa Network, Towards Evidence-based ICT Policy and Regulation 1, paper no. 2. Online: http://www.researchictafrica.net/publications.php (accessed 12 January 2012).

Kenny, C. 2011. "No Need for Speed." *Foreign Policy*, May. Online: http://www.foreignpolicy.com/articles/2011/05/16/no_need_for_speed?page=0,0 (accessed 29 November 2011).

Machado, A. F. et al. 2011. "Assessment of the Implications of the Bolsa Família Programme for the Decent Work Agenda." Working paper no. 85, UNDP International Policy Centre for Inclusive Growth (IPC-IG) in Brazil.

Mariscal, J. and E. Rivera. 2006. "Mobile Communications in Mexico in the Latin American Context." *Information Technologies & International Development* 3, no. 2: 41–55.

Mascarenhas, O. et al. 2010. *Tanzania Country Report: 2010 Poverty & Information and Communications Technology in Urban and Rural Eastern Africa (PICTURE-AFRICA)*. Ottawa: IDRC.

May, J. D. 2010. "Digital and Other Poverties: Exploring the Connection in Four East African Countries." School of Development Studies Seminar Series, School of Development Studies, University of KwaZulu-Natal in Durban, South Africa.

———. 2012. "Digital and Other Poverties: Exploring the Connection in Four East African Countries." *Information Technologies & International Development* 8, no. 2: 33–50.

May, J. D. et al. 2011. "Information and Communication Technologies as an Escape from Poverty Traps: Evidence from East Africa." Online: http://ces.univ-paris1.fr/Traps/papers/julian may.PDF (accessed 25 January 2012).

Moonesinghe, A. et al. 2007. "Telecom Use on a Shoestring: Expenditure and Perceptions of Affordability amongst the Financially Constrained." In *Diversifying Participation in Network Development: Case Studies and Research from WDR Research Cycle 3*, edited by A. Mahan and W. H. Melody. Montevideo: LIRNE.net.

Moser, C. O. N. 1998. "The Asset Vulnerability Framework: Reassessing Urban Poverty Reduction Strategies." *World Development* 26, no. 1: 1–19.

Muirhead, B. and R. Harpelle. 2010. *IDRC: 40 Years of Ideas, Innovation, and Impact*. Waterloo: Wilfrid Laurier University Press.

Ndung'u, M. N. and T. Waema. 2011. "Development Outcomes of Internet and Mobile Phones Use in Kenya: The Households' Perspective." *info* 13, no. 3: 110–24.

Rashid, A. and L. Elder. 2009. "Mobile Phones and Development: An Analysis of IDRC-Supported Projects." *Electronic Journal of Information Systems in Developing Countries* 36, no. 2: 1–16.

Samarajiva, R. 2007. "Preconditions for Effective Deployment of Wireless Technologies for Development in the Asia-Pacific." *Information Technologies & International Development* 3, no. 2: 57–71.

Sciadas, G. 2005. "Infostates Across Countries and Over Time: Conceptualization, Modeling, and Measurements of the Digital Divide." *Information Technology for Development* 11, no. 3: 299–304.

Sen, A. 1999. *Development as Freedom*. Oxford: Oxford University Press.

Sivapragasam, N. 2011. "The Potential of Mobile Remittances for the Bottom of the Pyramid: Findings from Emerging Asia." *info* 13, no. 3: 91–109.

Sivapragasam, N. and J. Kang. 2011. "The Future of the Public Payphone: Findings from a Study on Telecom Use at the Bottom of the Pyramid in South and Southeast Asia." *International Technologies & International Development* 7, no. 3: 33–44.

Soares, S. et al. 2010. "Os impactos do beneficio do Programa Bolsa Família sobre a desigualdade e a pobreza." In *Bolsa Família 2003–2010: Avanços e desafios* 2. Brasilia: IPEA.

Spence, R. 2003. "Information and Communications Technologies (ICTs) for Poverty Reduction: When, Where and How?" IDRC background paper for discussion, research, collaboration. Ottawa: IDRC.

Spence, R. and M. Smith. 2009. "Harvard Forum II: Information and Communication Technologies, Human Development, Growth and Poverty Reduction: A Background Paper." Ottawa: IDRC.

———. 2010. "ICT, Development, and Poverty Reduction: Five Emerging Stories." *Information Technologies & International Development* 61: 11–17.

Teltscher, S. and D. Korka. 2005. "Macroeconomic Impacts." In *From the Digital Divide to Digital Opportunities: Measuring Infostates for Development*, edited by G. Sciadas, 45–55. Montreal: Orbicom.

Waema, T. and O. Okinda. 2011. "Policy Implications of the Relationship between ICT Access and Usage and Well-Being: A Case Study of Kenya: Research Paper." *African Journal of Science, Technology, Innovation and Development* 3, no. 3: 30–56.

Zainudeen, A. and D. Ratnadiwakara. 2011. "Are the Poor Stuck in Voice? Conditions for Adoption of More-Than-Voice Mobile Services." *International Technologies & International Development* 7, no. 3: 45–59.

Zainudeen, A. et al. 2006. "Telecom Use on a Shoestring: Strategic Use of Telecom Services by the Financially Constrained in South Asia." WDR Dialogue Theme 3rd Cycle discussion paper, WDR0604, version 2.0. Online: http://ssrn.com/abstract=1554747 (accessed 3 November 2011).

Chapter 6

LOCAL ECONOMIC OPPORTUNITIES AND ICTs: HOW ICTs AFFECT LIVELIHOODS (PART II)

Kathleen Diga[1]

With the growing reach of mobile telephony, an inquiry into how information and communications technologies (ICTs) affect the livelihoods of the poor may seem unnecessary in the second decade of the twenty-first century. People all over the world, and especially in the developing world, are now "voting with their wallets" and paying to adopt mobile telecommunications technology in their business, personal and educational lives. When the "Information and Communications Technologies for Development" (ICT4D) program at the International Development Research Centre (IDRC) was first introduced in 2000, mobile phones were far from being the "everywhere" technology they have since become. Like the Internet, mobile phones in the developing world were – and, in some cases, still are – prestige technologies available only at a premium price. What role could they possibly have in helping peasant farmers and micro-entrepreneurs make more money and develop more productive enterprises? This chapter continues the discussion in the earlier chapter on ICTs and poverty, but focuses more squarely on the role of ICTs as tools of productivity for farmers and small entrepreneurs.

Applied research within the ICT4D program at IDRC understood that social policy programs were a necessary, but not necessarily sufficient tool for lowering levels of poverty in a country over the long term. Other complementary approaches, such as building economic opportunities for the poor in targeted and focused ways, were equally important, especially in a developing country's poverty reduction strategies. Whether it is stimulating local institutions to create new jobs or building an enabling market environment for budding micro-entrepreneurs, the fostering of economic opportunities provides many options to help citizens participate in productive income-generating or cost-saving activities.

With the rates of employment growth slowing throughout the world (ILO 2012), these kinds of focused employment strategies are even more important today. In keeping with this particular issue, this chapter focuses on the economic participation of citizens. It examines how governments and institutions have used ICT4D initiatives to enhance the livelihoods of two specific groups of economic actors – farmers and micro-entrepreneurs – and their link to income-generation activities. The research also examines the link of

ICTs to income generation within these groups and whether access to information has led to either enhanced productivity or more effective enterprises, especially for underserved communities.

This chapter looks at numerous case studies of small-scale farmers in agriculture or fishing and of entrepreneurs who are developing their own micro-businesses. Research in this field has shown that, by expanding such local opportunities, there has been an increase in household income in various developing country contexts. This financial increase has helped families pay for their needs – for example, improving their children's education and getting satisfactory healthcare services – and has overall improved their livelihoods.

The chapter is structured as follows: first is a profile of the farmer and micro-entrepreneur, typically from within the informal economy, to give a picture of the type of individual this research attempts to support; second, it reviews what we know about how ICTs have helped enhance relevant and timely knowledge for farmers and micro-entrepreneurs. We examine the contexts in which ICTs have helped to improve the information reaching farming communities and small businesses. Lastly, we discuss IDRC-supported studies showing that, when information access improves for local citizens such as farmers and small business owners, they can make better informed decisions that can result in tangible economic benefits. The research illustrates that the broader use of ICT tools can have real possibilities in improving livelihoods through lowering a business's operating costs or expanding current operations. Researchers, working with community-based organizations or industry and government partners, have seen how rural agriculture and non-farm practices and processes have, in many instances, adapted positively to today's increased use of ICTs.

Informal Employment Profiles: Farmers and Micro-entrepreneurs

Before discussing the research findings and outcomes that have emerged from IDRC's work in this field over the past fifteen years, it is important to profile the small-scale farmers and non-farm micro-entrepreneurs. We provide insight into various characteristics of the informal employment segment of the population that is highlighted in much of IDRC's research support in these sectors. These beneficiaries depend on opportunities in what is usually classified as informal employment.

While there is great debate around the concept and measurement of informal employment, the International Labour Office (ILO) defines it as a "job-based concept and encompasses those jobs that generally lack basic social or legal protections or employment benefits and maybe found in the formal sector, informal sector or households" (ILO 2011, 2). ILO states that, in some developing countries, between 35 to 90 percent of total employment is based in the informal economy (ILO 2011). Many in informal employment receive low pay and are highly vulnerable in work situations. In a 2009 OECD report, Jütting and de Laiglesia debate whether such informality means low levels of productivity or, on the upside, flexibility for innovative growth. Nevertheless, in environments where formal jobs are limited, informal employment provides some income upon which households depend. This is especially true for women and youth who work in the informal economy to avoid falling into extreme poverty (Jütting and de Laiglesia 2009).

Farmers

Rural agriculture, deeply rooted in informal employment, has undergone a wave of innovation and reform and it is important to determine if the use of information technologies plays an economic role. The last decade has seen a Green Revolution that has tried to revive existing practices of agricultural services to improve productivity, but it has seen mixed results. More recently, the global food price crisis of 2008 – which reappeared in 2012 – caused instability in food prices and trade throughout the world. Within this context, the agricultural value chain in rural areas affects in many different ways the variety of stakeholders who contribute to seasonal harvests. While we acknowledge that an urban agricultural trend exists – particularly in trying to address food insecurity within the growing sprawl of larger cities – the rural population continues to be most involved in subsistence production, putting them at high risk for poverty.

We turn our attention to the start of the value chain: small-scale farmers or those who care for small agricultural plots that are usually household-based or for communal production. Here, a few crops are grown – mainly for subsistence, but sometimes a good harvest can allow farmers to bring their surplus to market and generate additional income. Munyua, in her 2007 study *ICTs and Small-Scale Agriculture in Africa*, defines small-scale farmers in Africa as deriving "their livelihood from holdings of less than 2–5 hectares (usually less than 2 hectares); and around 10 to 20 head of livestock (although often they have less than 2 or none at all)" (Munyua 2007, 9). The category of farmer can also include the day laborers (generally family members) who help to harvest every season and may not necessarily be paid for their work or receive any other benefits. Together, they will grow familiar crops, using familiar techniques and inputs, and then sell their output at the market or to people with whom they have previously interacted. There are multi-faceted factors that curtail success for farmers with small-scale farms.

In Africa, Munyua (2007) cites factors such as poor access to agricultural inputs, the use of traditional tools and poor market experience as characteristics of subsistence farmers. With limited training available to poor or rural people, their businesses are run with only the information available at hand, information that usually comes from their personal social circles. Within these groups, ICT access and usage among farmers is on the rise; for example, nearly one hundred percent of farmers in a 2008 Kenyan study had seen or heard of mobile phones and 84 percent had used a mobile phone. In the same sample, 36 percent owned mobile phones, with the phones purchased mainly by the farmer (Okello et al. 2009) and used for social purposes. Of the people who identified themselves as phone users, 35 percent used their phone to obtain information on agriculture, but had to depend on phones owned by other people (Okello et al. 2009). Most of the usage was with voice systems for communication; very few used SMS (short message service). The high cost of airtime prevented many from using mobile phones; the difficulty of charging the phone battery was the second biggest obstacle (Okello et al. 2009).

Table 6.1. Characteristics of small and medium enterprises

Informal operator/ survivalist	• No employees • Does not distinguish between business and personal finances • Does not keep records • Does not pay taxes • Is not registered with any authority • Engages in business activities to pay for daily and weekly activities
Informal micro- or small business	• Less than 10 employees • May not distinguish between business and personal finances • May not keep records • May not pay taxes • May not be registered with any authority • Has physical address and contact details
Formal micro- or small business	• Between 10 and 49 employees • Keeps records • Has separate bank account • Pays taxes • Is registered with all required authorities • Has physical address and contact details

Source: Esselaar et al. (2007, 89).

Small-scale farmers are attempting to enter a digitally connected society. However, the barriers of their own farming experience, market choices and the cost clearly can hinder full participation and usage of ICTs for agricultural purposes.

Micro-entrepreneurs

Besides farming, other income-generating non-farm activities include running micro- or small and medium enterprises (MSMEs or SMEs) in both urban and rural areas. Characteristics of these businesses vary within and between countries. While farming has contributed greatly to growth in developing countries, the practices of local micro- or small businesses have become entrenched as a way to earn complementary non-farm income. Non-farm activities help to diversify activities in the non-farming season or when there is a run of poor crops. As well, non-farm activities can be a good area in which to invest profits from agricultural production. This extra income-generating activity can help lower the risk of shocks and thus the vulnerability of households. Accordingly, informal micro-enterprises in developing countries have gained much attention as an approach to dealing with local economic growth as the number of formal jobs has declined, especially following the recent economic downturn (ILO 2012).

In one African survey, 47 percent of informal business owners started a business because they had not found work (Esselaar et al. 2007). When salaried jobs are scarce and difficult to obtain, local innovation is brought to the fore to develop products and services that not only meet the needs of communities, but also help small businesses thrive. International organizations have their own definitions for SMEs. In Africa's case, one

Table 6.2. Suggested categorization of informal ICT sector activities

Sector	Telecommunications	Computers/Internet	Digital audiovisual
Primary	N/A	N/A	N/A
Secondary	Production of goods and equipment	Antenna manufacture	Assembly of computers and peripheral devices
Tertiary			
Commerce	Sale of computer accessories	Sale of accessories	Sale of accessories
	Sale of recharge cards	Sale of computer hardware	Sale of audiovisual equipment
	Sale of telephones and accessories	Sale of software and firmware	TV program distributors
Services	Sale of telephones	Advisory services	Sale of CDs, VCDs, DVDs
	Access (call centers, cybercenters, call boxes)	Office electronics (photocopies, data input, scanners, downloads, burning CDs, etc.)	
	Hardware repairs	Hardware repairs	Hardware repair
	Antenna installation		
	Mobile phone decoding	Networking and wiring	
	Maintenance and servicing	Maintenance and servicing	Maintenance and servicing
	GMS telephone chargers	Application developers and website designers	
	Fleet collectors-payers	Webmaster	
	Training courses	Training courses	Training courses
	Advisory services	Advisory services	Advisory services
			Audiovisual productions
			Video libraries

Source: Ouédraogo (2009); also found in Konté and Ndong (2012).

research network used similar characteristics as the ILO in classifying small businesses as informal, semi-formal or formal. (See Table 6.1.)

As is the case for micro-businesses, business owners may choose a few products and services to sell, imitate other local sellers' products and marketing techniques or identify the easiest and least-risky way to make an income. In both the agricultural and micro-business cases, poorly informed capital investments or low marketable skills can keep any profit gain marginal and may perpetuate a condition of persistent poverty (Barrett 2008; Barrett and Swallow 2006).

As with agriculture, an understanding of the connection between ICTs and improved business practices of small (generally informal) businesses has been limited to date. With the little evidence available, we are aware that micro-enterprises in the informal sector are increasingly using ICTs. IDRC-supported research has explored whether ICT use has helped to build some economic growth within these businesses and communities. In Senegal and Burkina Faso, mobile phone activities dominate the informal sector for employment (Bayala et al. 2010; Ndiaye et al. 2010). The Yam Pukri team in West Africa categorized this growth within the informal sector of ICT activities (Ouédraogo 2009). (See Table 6.2.)

In Senegal, the majority of the surveyed group who worked in the informal ICT sector received their remuneration at irregular periods and had to use their own resources to finance their ICT business activities (Konté and Ndong 2012). Those surveyed list four types of obstacles in the informal ICT sector: technical, financial, human and institutional. Examples of ICT issues resolved by the micro-entrepreneurs range from repairing faulty ICT merchandise to sourcing costly imported parts to shortages of technical staff (Konté and Ndong 2012).

In summary, informal employment such as farming and other micro-level non-farm activities constitute small enterprises that are a substantial part of many developing countries' economies and that contribute considerably to the maintenance of household livelihoods. Nevertheless, one must note the lack of social protection in such small-scale unregulated work, which can leave poor workers in a vulnerable state without knowing their worker rights or ways to improve their way of life. How then have ICTs helped to complement or even enhance the current agricultural and non-farm work of local community members?

Information Level Changes with Use of ICTs

Today, the availability of information and network relationships can help these farmers or micro-entrepreneurs go beyond their previous circles of knowledge, which may have been small and limited. Before access to ICTs, citizens were left with few ways to obtain information such as where to find the best markets to sell their products, which traders demand their goods and the latest updates on the ever-changing market price – a deficiency of information that some researchers term "asymmetric information."

Asymmetric information is a one-sided information flow in a transactional exchange and, in many cases, the farmer or small business owner lacks suitable information for the trade. Not knowing crucial information for their business, small informal enterprises such as farmers and micro-business owners are left making intellectual guesses about the best price on the market exchange floor. Individuals with reliable information on price and product demand, such as the market's "first handlers" of the farmer's produce, have been known to take advantage of the farmer by using the information to keep the greater profits or benefits for themselves. Researchers explore whether providing information access to the wider public through ICTs could reduce this information asymmetry, thereby leading to improved economic opportunities.

IDRC sponsored several ICT4Dprojects on building capacity of micro-businesses by testing ways to improve information reach in Africa, Latin America and Asia. IDRC research projects have helped to demonstrate how ICT use can be integrated to gain quality and timely content for agricultural prices, marketing, productivity and knowledge-sharing practices.

As mentioned earlier, farmers can have limited local information about market prices or the prices of their goods bought at the local market. Farmers can therefore unknowingly sell to traders or intermediaries for their stated price offer without knowing the real market price. These traders would buy produce from the farmers in various remote villages, then transport and sell the farmers' products at more central distribution centers at substantially marked-up prices. Realizing this inequitable division of profits, one of the first ICT4D agricultural projects was to test whether better market information for fishermen could provide them with better selling prices. In a preliminary case study, the researchers explored whether better real time weather reports and market prices through technology use (using SMS and WAP technology) could improve information reach to a Senegalese fishing community.

This early, turn of the century pilot project by the Senegalese organization Manobi focused on data collectors updating market prices and then enabling fishermen, using mobile phones, to access the accurate price on local markets in a timely manner. The project then expanded the project to a similar program for agricultural produce in the capital city of Dakar. "Know your market" (or *xam marsé* in Wolof) became the management information system that allowed farmers to access market price information instantly via SMS (Annerose and Sène 2005). A review (Annerose 2005, 107) of the project concluded that the selected Senegalese farmers who were studied increased their incomes by a significant fifteen percent on average. Manobi believes that farmers made better production and bargaining choices within this specific experience.

This first pilot project in West Africa spurred further research on improving state and private sector delivery of market extension and market information services in other IDRC projects. The lesson from this first study was that some of the most important information communicated through ICT devices was identified by the agricultural communities themselves and used in a context suitable to their needs. With the growing trend to decentralized extension systems, IDRC also explored the possibility of providing information through several participatory action research projects. More specifically, the question arose of whether local farmers could produce their own agricultural content and use ICTs for dissemination strategies that would lead to better farming practices. Local research was conducted to better understand the intricacies of this information value chain and to understand whether ICTs could be incorporated into improving community ownership of agricultural systems and in meeting the evolving information needs of farmers.

In a small coastal town eighty kilometers from Lima, Peru, a small farmers' organization helped to create 11 agrarian information system telecenters in the Huaral Valley areas. This helped to provide local information on water management and cultivation monitoring. Local acquisition and adoption of the system provided the basis of sustainability for such systems as the local farmers' organizations are flexible enough to shape the project within a locally changing environment and to speak directly to policymakers for support and guidance (Bossio and Sotomayor 2008).

The African Highlands Initiative, Acacia, (Masuki et al. 2011) is another example of providing additional information resources and centers to local farmers through an information delivery system in Kabale District, Uganda. The project rearranged the way information was communicated through the decentralized institutional system. The assessment drew together the most important needs of the targeted farming communities; these were mostly related to agricultural information, various produce production, soil erosion and soil water conservation (Masuki et al. 2011). The information centers hosted the locally produced content that was developed from the assessment. However, those who generally used the information were the demonstration farmers who had already bought into the new information system. Clearly, the new systems and information had to find ways to integrate into the community. Lessons from agricultural information systems show that tailor-made community content, adaptable technologies and active local participation were the most important factors – always, of course, within the limited resources and an affordable and maintainable infrastructure.

The Knowledge Access for Rural Interconnected People Network (KariaNet) in North Africa and the Middle East region was another example of testing local network building for enhanced information to farmers. KariaNet's pilot focus of five countries was to empower poor farmers through learning and experience exchange using innovative tools and practices. In improving the electronic knowledge management tools and use within each country's project, KariaNet found that the most important aspects of knowledge stock were participatory approaches to rural finance, technology transfer and rural enterprise development (Breard 2006). Today, KariaNet continues with phase two: aiming to better understand the socioeconomic effects of improved knowledge-sharing techniques among its rural farmers and its networked organizations.

In another case study of information reach, the "Informatics for Rural Empowerment and Community Health" (iREACH) project in Cambodia developed a rural network of 20 community-owned ICT and Internet hubs. The hubs provided ICT services between 2006 and 2010 in two pilot areas, the coastal village of Kep and the border town of Kamchai Mear (Grunfeld et al. 2010). The project incorporated a community-driven operation using locally elected management committees and learning programs that were based on locally requested and culturally appropriate video and audio materials. The information resources included information on issues like agriculture – for example, the use of the right fertilizer for rice production, how to plant gourds and ways of animal husbandry (Grunfeld et al. 2010).

Assessing the impact of the iREACH initiative, the selected group of respondents emphasized the most significant change or positive improvement in knowledge was the chance to learn new farming methods, especially about new crops, organic farming and pest and disease control (Grunfeld 2011). Some respondents went on to say that the information obtained through iREACH had helped to improve agricultural yields and the choice of new crops and also lower costs of farm inputs (Grunfeld 2011). Furthermore, respondents stated that the iREACH program also provided complementary on-demand services after they had finished farming training with other organizations.

For example, one young group from Kep had trained with one NGO on how to use alternative methods to harmful pesticides and several went to iREACH to seek further information on this subject area (Grunfeld 2011). As mentioned by Rashid and Elder (2009), farmers may also use mobile phones to complement face-to-face meetings or opportunities. The participants saw improved ways of farming and better production yields from this newly acquired information. For example, one farming group found information on the web about mushroom growing and was able to start an experimental plot. The information level change also spilled over from learning more about agricultural prices through to family-level topics.

In Bangladesh, a small study on 100 farmers was conducted where a free SMS agricultural price service gave the selected individuals the market and wholesale price of various products in a timely manner (Islam and Grönlund 2010). In the first test of this service, it was noted that 80 percent of its users had a difficult time using Roman script on the basic mobile phone. The team then refined the product by using a live phone operator to provide the prices; this was fully acceptable to the farmers (Islam and Grönlund 2010). Improving access to information to the previously unconnected, whether they are living in rural areas or are socioeconomically disadvantaged, works better when projects are flexible, incorporate locally driven content and community participation and react positively to the needs of their targeted beneficiaries.

Livelihood Outcomes with Use of ICTs

In addition to better information reach, using ICTs within the informal employment sector can have potentially great economic benefits for the lives of the poor. Even in the early days, IDRC-supported research investigating whether small-scale producers could get better and more timely information on local agricultural or fish prices by mobile phone. It was assumed that this information could then help farmers get better prices and could lower costs. In making information available to farmers promptly, much of the research concluded that certain implementations or interventions of ICTs have helped farmers to receive modestly better incomes and livelihoods.

The next section will reveal these cost-saving measures resulting from better information access, whether through lowering travel costs or by saving time in searching. Some projects also demonstrate increased productivity such as less wastage of produce. Researchers investigated further whether there are livelihood changes resulting from better information for farmers and micro-entrepreneurs, such as overall improvements in household income.

Information costs

Information was clearly now reaching farmers and micro-entrepreneurs through the use of ICTs, but to what extent could we measure the changes in costs or savings? In investigating the importance of agricultural prices and where the costs and prices change

Figure 6.1. Components of the agricultural value chain

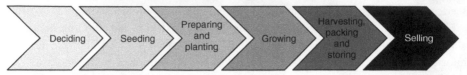

1. **Deciding:** At this stage, farmers decide what crop to grow, how much land to allocate for each crop, and also arrange for financing.
2. **Seeding:** During this stage, farmers either purchase seeds or prepare their own seeds and possibly prepare a seed bed.
3. **Preparing and planting:** During this stage, there is land preparation using labour or machines and actual planting happens.
4. **Growing:** At this stage, applying fertilizer, pesticides and water takes place.
5. **Harvesting, packing and storing:** During this stage, finding labour for harvesting, finding storage and packing are the main activities.
6. **Selling:** In the final stage, (some) farmers check prices at the market, find a transportation method, and transport the packed produce to the market and sell it.

Source: Adapted from Ratnadiwakara et al. (2008).

in the production line, this inquiry led to studies to better understand this value chain. As IDRC-supported researchers had been some of the first to help guide our thinking around value chains (Kaplinsky and Morris, 2001), it was natural to see Ratnadiwakara et al. (2008) conduct a pioneering study on the agricultural value chain as it applies to transaction costs for farmers. Figure 6.1 is the conceptualization of this agricultural value chain and applies the concept to a research project on small-scale farmers in Sri Lanka and the quantification of the "cost of information" for these farmers. As seen in Figure 6.1, Ratnadiwakara et al. (2008) broke the agricultural value chain into six stages from decision making or planning all the way to the product being sold to the market.

After laying the foundation of the stages of the agricultural value chain, the LIRNE*asia* researchers examined 314 small-scale farmers through these various stages plus their information costs in each stage. The research reveals some of the information asymmetries in the agriculture market cycle that have led to information search costs (the main component of transaction costs for the farmer) of nearly eleven percent of farmers' total costs from the time of deciding what to grow to the time of selling. In other words, information search costs were incurred as a result of poor information availability along the agricultural value chain.

While complexity can be embedded in many of these communities, the above study still underscored how ICT tools could help farmers make more informed decisions with fewer transactional costs (Ratnadiwakara et al. 2008). In a different Bangladesh study that tested both a "pull" (where farmers would initiate the request for information and be refunded at the end of the month) and "push" (where farmers are regularly sent the information for free), the following complexity was observed: the "pull" service drew very few participants because it would mean paying for usage but not being able to wait until the end of month to be reimbursed (Islam and Grönlund 2010). It can therefore be argued that even simple contextual observations about mobile phones and payment for services can change how farmers incur costs to obtain information. This complicates the idea of market efficiency

Figure 6.2. The effect of transaction cost on market participation

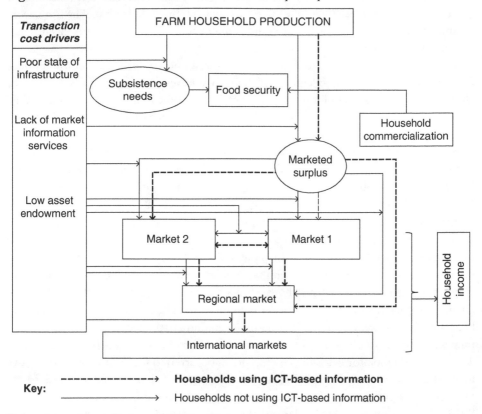

Source: Adapted from Okello et al. (2010a, 44).

in a value chain. With this awareness of some of the cost and contextual implications in a value chain, the case studies on small enterprises (farm and non-farm) and ICTs' effect on livelihoods were continued in longitudinal studies to further explore the ICT system's role in farmer's productivity and in small business sectors' market efficiency and income.

Income and profitability

Okello et al. (2010a) built a framework that explains how improved income is derived within complex market information services that uses ICT intervention (Figure 6.2). The framework assumes that transaction costs of production and marketing are reduced and that an improved income can help farmers move to more formal commercial farming. Households with surplus production can then use market information services to get the best price for selling produce in the markets. However, some households will have no access to information from a market information system and little surplus from their production (low assets). Or, they may live in a place with poor infrastructure, thereby keeping them from participating in the advancing information market. All the while, other farmers with access to ICT-based market information services can market their goods better and increase their new sales, leading to commercialization. The framework assumes that, at the end, there is an improvement of food security status given better income and production.

In all its learning about information asymmetries and complex market frameworks, LIRNE*asia* also tested a mobile platform called TradeNet that provided free basic price alert services through SMS for up to five vegetables in three markets as well as an online "trading post" for produce. Research on the TradeNet service showed that providing real time information on fruit and vegetable pricing through mobile phones has empowered farmers in the study. Farmers perceived themselves as better aware of price trends – being as knowledgeable as traders dealing in their specific produce – and had better interactions with their networks (including farmer groups, relatives and neighbors). They also obtained higher profits (average daily price increases of 23.4 percent or an increase of US$0.045 to $0.09 per kilogram of produce above the average price for the day) for the products of the 55 farmers who were studied when they were using the price information to decide when to sell (Lokanathan et al. 2011). The group of farmers that did not have the TradeNet intervention saw a much lower average increase per kilogram of produce. Other projects have shown similar profit. For example, in Bangladesh, the farmers believed the free SMS/voice agricultural price information increased their profit between ten and twenty percent (Islam and Grönlund 2010). Farmers also believed that they made better decisions about timing their trips to market to get the best market price. They started to monitor when higher crop prices occurred to see whether it was lucrative to increase their crop selection. Research also discovered that middlemen traders can find these new mechanisms disruptive to their market power at first (Islam and Grönlund 2010). Farmers realized that traders would be less inclined to offer farmers the lowest prices once the farmers had improved information access; slightly better prices were therefore ensured. However, traders did continue to have an important relationship with farmers regardless of the better information; for example, traders provided farmers with non-interest emergency loans.

In Asia, IDRC teamed up with the International Fund for Agricultural Development to support ENRAP (Knowledge Networking for Rural Development in Asia Pacific), which provided evidence of how ICT usage and rural knowledge exchange can help to support poverty reduction. If rural communities were not effectively engaged in rural knowledge systems, there were fewer positive changes through livelihood activities. ENRAP supported seven research studies using the sustainable livelihoods framework and was able to demonstrate a measurable impact on income and savings through the use of ICTs (Grimshaw and Kala 2011). However, the studies reveal that farmers' use of ICTs was successful only when the devices or applications were most appropriate to the needs of their pricing strategies and fell within their specific agricultural context.

One example of an ENRAP project was a system of advisory services in India delivered by mobile phones whereby farmers were able to access information related to crop and nutrient practices to improve their yields. This information, tailored to the needs of 450 farmers in the villages of Sirkali Taluk, Nagapattinam District, India, helped them increase their income by 15 percent (Raj et al. 2011). This research confirmed that mobile phones were effective tools in reaching rural people and those in exceptionally isolated areas.

Similarly, Lifelines, a telephone-based advisory service for Indian farmers, showed that its selected Lifelines users had an average increase of 37 percent in their income compared with non-users (Rizvi 2011). The services' acceptance by users was also encouraged by signs of positive impact on health through improvement in nutrition. Farming families depend primarily on the income generated from their agricultural sales for their livelihoods. However, research in the Philippines demonstrated that ICTs contribute even more to the livelihoods of farmers if ICTs are used for expanding employment opportunities, thus complementing their agricultural interventions in terms of income generation. By enabling farming households to diversify the resources that sustain the household, they become less vulnerable (Barrios et al. 2011).

Following the ENRAP, LIRNE*asia* and Manobi project on ICTs and agricultural prices, a further surge of interest by researchers drew in work on how ICT use affected the marketing of farmers' produce. An action research project in Kenya attempted to determine whether improved farming methods, better access to international markets and electronic-based information systems led to empowered farmers. This project was dubbed DrumNet, where the mobile phone represented the traditional drum that once communicated events throughout villages in Africa.

The DrumNet project provided around two thousand resource-poor farmers in Kenya with marketing, finance and information advice through low-cost technologies consisting of an Internet connection, a whiteboard and a mobile phone application platform. The DrumNet research revealed that farmers who were the first to adopt ICTs improved their incomes by 32 percent because of increased adoption and marketing of export crops (Ashraf et al. 2009). The farmers found they could lower their transaction costs, search and screening costs, negotiation costs and the costs of monitoring and enforcing terms of agreement; this improved their income (Ashraf et al. 2009). Farmers were also seen to share more food with neighbors which was a sign of food surplus and thus an improvement of livelihood. Through DrumNet, farmers were able to access credit for seed and fertilizer inputs and have better links to buyers who could advise on markets and technical aspects (Okello et al. 2010b).

On the downside, researchers in various projects also discovered that major socioeconomic, market, physical, legal and environmental factors had dampening effects on the success of the livelihood changes of improved income and savings. For example, the farmers' low incomes led them to employ several different strategies to purposefully default on their loans, with no intentions of repaying the borrowed money (Okello 2010). While farmers may benefit in the short term from borrowed money, the micro-finance system thus becomes unsustainable in coping with lack of repayment. Additionally, farmers were also found to react poorly when reorganizing to meet the ever-changing and costly European health and safety traceability regulations on fresh produce. The farmers also responded weakly when dealing with crop pests and there was a poor legal framework to enforce cooperative group agreements taken by the DrumNet groups. These failings all acted as barriers to the sustainable performance of ICTs in management information system projects (Ashraf et al. 2009; Okello 2010).

These externalities proved to be major limitations to a sustainable market information system. In Cambodia, the use of ICTs for demand information of market prices saw a few farmers stating that they tried negotiating for a better price for their goods (Grunfeld 2011). In one example, the farmer learned about the true market price of rice and, despite knowing the new price, had to wait a few days before finally convincing the trader to move the price from 900 riels/kg to 1020 riels/kg, thus gaining about US$30 for one ton of rice (Grunfeld 2011). Clearly there is a disruptive adjustment between stakeholders before behavioral change takes place. Cambodian farmer respondents also were not forthcoming in stating that the information about new crops or fertilizer inputs had led them to then experiment or try out these new techniques (Grunfeld 2011). The reluctance could be the short-term result of the project or that the farmers' ability to develop bargaining skills or to use information for the benefit of their livelihoods may not come right away for all farmers. Therefore, information may need to be complemented with other programs or the evaluation extended over a longer term to eventually uncover the change in income or savings.

From these results, we must take into account the many factors that could make an ICT intervention result in unexpected outcomes that deviate from the original aim of income generation or cost savings. Nevertheless, the research supported through the ICT4D program at IDRC has helped to expand some of the thinking around such outcomes and to provide scenarios of how to improve the multiple accesses to knowledge for farmers and all stakeholders who benefited from improved technological skills and, in some modest cases, increased incomes.

Productivity

At the market end of the agricultural value chain, the final end product can result in either sales or wastage. When poor sales continued, farmers received little feedback as to why this was happening. A project in Asia used a "last mile traceability system," providing farmers in the northwestern province of Sri Lanka with local data on gherkins, as well as information on buyers' acceptance or rejection of the gherkins. With this information, the farmers could react immediately and lower the rejection rate (Soysa 2008). The farmer could increase the use of water and pesticides right away, thus lessening the possibility of deformed fruits and produce infected with melon fly (two major reasons for rejecting product) and improving the quality of the gherkins sent to market. However, it should be noted that quality improvements in the case of gherkins can be made fairly quickly by adjusting inputs (Soysa 2008). ICT use helped improve the farming choices of small-scale farmers through their better understanding of the demands at the end of the agricultural value chain (Soysa 2008). In the Senegalese Manobi project, the researchers also found up to thirty percent waste reduction (Batchelor et al. 2003).

As shown by these IDRC research projects, such crucial agricultural information can not only help farmers decide where and at what price to sell their produce, but can also help reduce the high search costs associated with locating available suppliers, traders and buyers. Overall, it is shown that farmers' benefits in income and production can increase significantly if they can use a stable phone-based ICT platform to link their selling decisions with the decision to grow a particular product. Successfully localizing information to incorporate the community farmer's information needs throughout the various stages of the value chain has big advantages for a well-designed and sought-after platform. Finally, while intermediaries or middlemen have not disappeared as a result of the platforms, research has revealed they continue to hold crucial roles in the system. Research has also shown that middlemen have adjusted their profit-seeking behavior because they know their farmer clients have now improved their information access.

Local micro-entrepreneurs

Improvement in the lives of micro-entrepreneurs when they are able to successfully make use of information or ICTs for their business practices is also noted. In Latin America, local researchers recognized the lack of research on ICTs and MSMEs in the region (Botelho and Alves 2007). Monge-González and his team (2005) sought to understand the effects of ICTs on competitiveness in Costa Rica, El Salvador, Guatemala, Honduras and Nicaragua. Some findings showed that low e-readiness in the country was also reflected in low competitiveness (Monge-González et al. 2005).

As for access to ICTs, the five countries, unlike other regions, all reflected high levels of fixed phoneline access (71 to 95 percent) followed by access to mobile telephony. However, as in other regions, SMEs viewed access to computers and the Internet as a low priority. For example, Honduras had 75 percent of its SMEs not adopting ICTs. Yet the SMEs surveyed in the five countries mostly believed that ICT adoption would affect their labor productivity and then their sales and profitability. In the African studies, the reasons *not* to have ICTs in the business were the high costs, the lack of knowledge about how to use ICTs and the perception that these tools were unnecessary for productivity. In Africa, Research ICT Africa (RIA) used a survey of small and medium enterprises (SMEs) in 14 countries to get a general sense of the impact of ICTs on private sector development and the contributions that ICTs could have in developing country economies (Esselaar et al. 2007). RIA investigated the possibility of building ICT-SME indices around the possession, usage and usage intensity of ICTs. (See Table 6.3.)

From the average of various types of businesses, it was found that the more formal the SME, the greater the possession and usage of ICTs. However, the usage intensity was greater the more informal the SME. Furthermore, with regard to profits and labor productivity, the research found that informal SMEs have a much greater profitability (after-tax profit divided by total fixed assets) than many of the semi-formal or formal businesses surveyed. The survey found that ICT use contributes toward increased labor productivity (Esselaar et al. 2007). Most of the selected African SMEs limited to the use of mobile phones for their businesses because fixed lines were considered expensive; this was also the perception about computer and Internet costs. There seem to be a number of SMEs that choose to run their businesses without ICTs. Yet, those who do

Table 6.3. Mean rank comparison for ICT usage, ICT possession and ICT usage intensity

	Formality	N	Mean rank	Chi-square	df	Asymp. sig.
ICT possession index:	Informal	1,504	1,195	1,214.8	2	0.000
	Semi-formal	1,139	1,968			
	Formal	1,048	2,648			
	Total	3,691				
ICT usage index:	Informal	1,504	1,275	947.1	2	0.000
	Semi-formal	1,139	1,924			
	Formal	1,048	2,580			
	Total	3,691				
ICT usage intensity index:	Informal	1,358	1,844	19.5	2	0.000
	Semi-formal	1,104	1,690			
	Formal	1,037	1,691			
	Total	3,499				

Source: Esselaar et al. (2007, 93).

use ICTs – particularly those operating in the informal sector – seem to find substantial benefits in profit and labor productivity.

In a more in-depth case study of Ghana (Frempong 2009), 600 SMEs were examined on their perception of mobile phone usage. The majority, 84 percent, owned mobile phones with an average of US$10 to US$20 spent on business calls per month. The top four uses of the business-related calls were to (i) check on orders, (ii) check on prices in the market, (iii) order raw materials and (iv) check on those who owed them money. The cost effectiveness of the phone over travel was highlighted among the Ghanaian SMEs. The study found SMEs perceived profits to be "good" with use of the mobile phones. The major recommendation of the study was to explore further the possibility of developing mobile business applications that focus on meeting the needs of the SMEs – for example, inventory tracking or cash flow analysis. At the more regulatory side, recommendations for lower ICT costs as well as improved accessibility will help to propel the link between ICT usage and micro-business profits.

Business growth

Since this study, Chew et al. (2011) have developed frameworks (Figure 6.3) on micro-entrepreneurship, ICTs and business growth. To examine business growth, the researchers also developed a revised theoretical model to look at the independent variables of formality, total ICT access and business use of mobile phones. The team tried to test whether business use of mobile phones was correlated to business growth.

Figure 6.3. Model for micro-enterprise growth

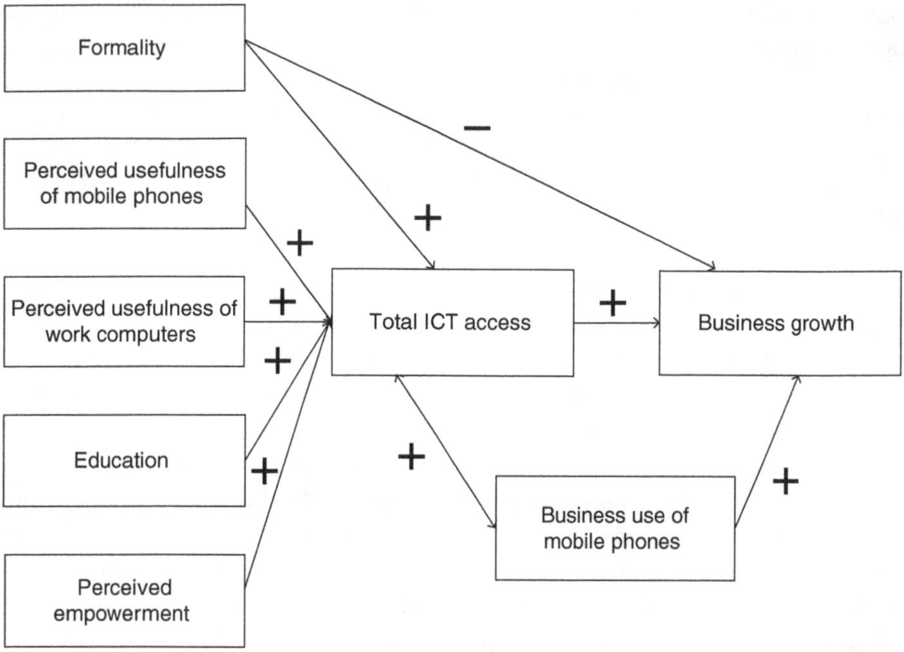

Source: Adapted from Chew et al. (2011, 8).

Chew et al.'s (2011) work with female micro-entrepreneurs in urban India complements RIA's findings in that entrepreneurs within the informal sector have a higher rate of micro-enterprise growth, and those using mobile phones for business purposes had an association with business growth (Chew et al. 2011, 8). In the case of Asia, Africa and Latin America, all case studies on micro-enterprises have noted that electronic or mobile banking is of interest to most SMEs in the future.

Poverty Reduction through Informal Employment

It is important to investigate the ways in which ICTs are helping small enterprises become more efficient businesses and grow accordingly (Mascarenhas et al. 2010). In an East African case study from 2007–10, the researchers asked the following question: "How has the increased use of ICTs contributed to the growth and reduction of poverty among the MSEs in Tanzania?" The study looked at micro- and small entrepreneurs based in two small towns in Tanzania. One town's micro-businesses received a mobile with airtime and email access for five months; the other town's did not receive the same benefits. The researchers looked at the multi-dimensions of poverty and were able to see that, in 2008, both groups had been identified as poor and both had approximately the same poverty level – around fifty-five percent. In 2010, the town with the micro-entrepreneurs that had received the mobile and Internet access reported a drop of poverty to 16 percent; the town without the benefits also saw its poverty level drop, but only to 38 percent (Mascarenhas et al. 2010).

Out of seven dimensions of poverty, the group that was given email and phone resources had improvements in five dimensions while the group without the benefits saw improvement in only two. The study concluded that the changes in poverty as a result of ICTs usage were effected very easily and quickly in the short term. However, it also stated that education and the increase in savings would need growth to maintain the reduction of poverty through ICTs (Mascarenhas et al. 2010).

The iREACH project in Cambodia had also examined whether users of the telecenters had attempted to use the facilities to develop new enterprises; many who replied had not. While this study did not concentrate specifically on micro-entrepreneurs, it asked whether there was the chance to use the telecenters to spark a new wave of business people. One example was given of a male respondent who started typing letters and invitation cards as a business after computer training from iREACH (Grunfeld 2011). Respondents also stated that they would encourage their children or students to use the computers to improve their economic opportunities and their chances of joining the formal economy (Grunfeld 2011). The researcher also pointed out a possible limitation: if local Cambodians in the town were to find cheaper local produce in border towns in Vietnam through improved information and find it viable to get a better price even with transport costs, then what would be the implications for local production (Grunfeld 2011)? Again, the expansion beyond local markets can provide possible opportunities and drawbacks for the lives of the most poor.

The chapter examines developmental levels of change when looking at farmers' and micro-entrepreneurs' information access to asymmetrical information; studies show changes of market prices, product marketing and coordination of business activities. It also looks at livelihood outcomes translating into improved income and productivity. In summary, ICTs have certainly played a role in the informal employment activities of local farmers and business people, especially in these specific cases affecting profitability, productivity, growth and poverty. The research has certainly challenged future researchers and policymakers to think further about information costs and what farmers and micro-businesses would need to complement their ICT use to ensure improved economic opportunities. In the case of both the farmer and micro-business owner, mobiles were highlighted. However, recommendations dealt with the need to customize well-designed local applications and content to meet their agricultural or enterprise needs, including financial mobile services.

Government Policy

ICTs alone cannot have a lasting impact on the livelihoods of farmers and micro-entrepreneurs. Aspiring farmers or young entrepreneurs should not only be left with a few ICT resources. They should be supported by local economic development initiatives ranging from legal frameworks, business regulations, access to financing, building space and amenities to stimulate innovative enterprise. Specialized local training in technical skills could help to fill jobs or create new employment, meet the ICT needs of communities and improve operation of farms or small businesses (Jütting and de Laiglesia 2009). Can ICT usage help create better jobs and decent work, especially given the current growth of informal employment?

In addition to determining ways in which information asymmetry could be addressed in small businesses through ICT access, IDRC-supported research projects hoped to provide evidence to influence policies as well as local economic development strategies. With respect to these issues, research has demonstrated that governments need to consider small-scale farming regulations and non-farm diversification activities to meet the needs of the world's most vulnerable communities.

As was found in cases such as DrumNet, while the use of technology for improved marketing information worked well, there were greater infrastructural and regulatory issues that needed to be addressed, especially when expanding production into exports. Great dedication is required by various stakeholders to collaborate and negotiate for trade regulations beyond the ICT system to build a more conducive and enabling environment. The local market could be supported by the government helping to match local sellers with local or foreign buyers of produce or goods. In line with foreign markets, governments could help to support local businesses meet the various overseas regulations such as produce quality control and improve trade relations for a smooth transition to the international marketplace. Such institutional mechanisms and policies on trade promotion can help boost confidence in local products for export. Farmers also need protection from risks taken in crop production, whether it is trying out new products or adapting to the changes in the environment. Governments and institutions can complement the role of ICTs and protect businesses and local farmers from unpredictable changes in the market by working to develop regulations about financial mobile intermediation and mechanisms to improve weather predictability and by providing local incentives for consumers to grow and buy locally.

Globally, preparation for future volatility in global food prices and changes in climate is necessary and ICT4D research continues to be needed in the area of ever-adapting agricultural value chains and micro-enterprises. Finding ways, such as the use of ICTs, to expand the work of farmers and non-farm business activities can be a complementary method to reduce poverty. However, a broader goal of formalizing informal work so that workers are socially protected is also important so that the most vulnerable are sheltered with human rights and decent work.

These challenges include the need to acknowledge issues of inclusion and marginalization that exist at the local level; the depth of coordination and communication among communities, institutions and authorities at all levels; the persistence of barriers to access; and the amount of capacity necessary to undertake action in the future. So, even if technically sound projects are identified for the rural context, this does not mean that the priorities of vulnerable communities are being met. Research needs to go beyond the technical promise of tools and instead relate the projects closely to broader development challenges in the global south, including local livelihoods, capabilities and governance. Further research is required to better understand their challenges, techniques and knowledge on adaptation at the local level in the various scenarios of strong or weak government regulation and enforcement, as well as low or high capacity level. With better research on these topics, we hope that one can minimize the negative effect of external events on poorer communities and allow them to continue or even improve their day-to-day routines.

Conclusion

IDRC's ICT4D-supported research asked specifically how communication technologies and processes are reaching farmers and small businesses and what development outcomes result from their use. ICTs can be used as potentially life-changing tools that could assist farmers in gaining new knowledge to improve their practices and further employment. Some research results from the projects showed that ICTs facilitate and indeed accelerate the acquisition and application of appropriate knowledge leading to increased agricultural productivity and household income and assets. Nevertheless, the research findings on the profit and productivity changes through use of ICTs over time have been modest. Provision of price information using ICTs was found to increase efficiency or performance of agricultural markets. Nevertheless, several lessons have been learned from these projects, including the need for long-term commitments and holistic development analysis of projects as opposed to simple technological implementation. Despite the great enthusiasm for technology, agricultural information projects are hands-on initiatives that need constant monitoring, contextual adaptation and design adjustment according to the changing external environment. Moreover, frequent staff turnover and difficult access to communication infrastructure are difficult challenges to overcome, especially in resource-poor settings.

As noted earlier, IDRC research in this area was guided by the assumption that farmers' and micro-entrepreneurs' use of ICTs to get timely information could lead to actions that would help them improve their income or their livelihood. ICTs and improved access to information are clearly contributing to a shift in some activities of farmers, intermediaries, buyers and sellers in the agricultural value chain and of some micro-entrepreneurs.

We are seeing examples of activities that improve the efficiency and transparency of economic interactions, leading to lower transaction costs and stimulating innovative methods of market expansion. IDRC's ICT4D program has supported many agricultural mobile phone and market interventions. In the future, one would like to see that contextual and locally driven mechanisms are in place to ensure that the information most needed by farmers and small businesses is available to help them make better decisions. Further research questions include whether the usual consumers of information (farmers, micro-entrepreneurs, etc.) will use their newly developed ICT savvy to also become the producers of information – either to contribute to the aggregate information flow or to improve their opportunities for economic prosperity. And, given the high number of unemployed and underemployed individuals in developing countries, how are we monitoring the changes in meaningful employment as a result of our digital society? Much hinges on understanding these expanding changes, especially in light of the recent food price crisis and high demand for certain key agricultural commodities. Given this prospect, how will ICTs play a role in the future in the local food systems within developing countries?

Research showed that intermediaries do not in fact disappear when an ICT system is in place to improve information within communities. Their roles change and, although hardly formalized, this may offer other benefits to farmers, such as small no-interest loans or the purchase of produce at closer to market prices. As the intermediary–farmer relationship is often hidden, intermediaries are sometimes not considered as important for large-scale country- or regional-level programming. Reconsideration of this integral factor in the agricultural value chain should be noted for future research in this field.

Further research work is imperative in local economic development and ICT adoption to gain an understanding of the changing face of agricultural extension services. For example, will the electronic interface become transformative in meeting greater distributive justice within an agricultural value chain? Research is also required on the externalities or on the unintended outcomes that occur with ICT usage in a community. For example, once the usefulness of ICTs is established in farming communities, one research project recommended that integrated loan support to small-scale farmers for production and farm infrastructure include finances to purchase cell phones (Okello et al. 2010b). While some ongoing research topics can follow the adoption of ICT usage by farmers and extension services, the transition to adoption still requires close monitoring and integration of face-to-face interaction with the technology for sustainable practice.

Research is still useful in understanding how to improve the ability of farmers to utilize all the information that they gather locally to improve their decisions in the future. Further investigation is needed to find a way to ensure there is a systematic and easy method of disseminating information using ICTs on agriculture, animal husbandry, fisheries, forestry and food. Such information needs to be readily accessible, low cost, comprehensive, up-to-date and localized with good reach, particularly in rural areas. More specifically, a research question for the future includes determining which process is best for farmers to adjust their input purchases or planting techniques given better analysis of previous agricultural data. Ongoing projects such as participatory geographic information systems (PGIS) for land reform and natural resource management in West Africa is one example of local players taking historical data to redress land claim issues of the most poor. The major factor being examined is whether the information is successful in working in favor of the poor if the access to such information is free, open and available to the most disadvantaged.

With respect to new research exploring the concepts of openness and ICTs, particularly regarding rural development, some researchers include the rural context within an expanded national innovation system. "In the rural and remote regions of developing countries, it is not so much the collaboration between firms, customers and suppliers that is critical for learning, but collaboration between agencies, institutional structures and community networks" (Turpin and Ghimire 2010, 15). What should those public–private networked partnerships look like in order to maximize the use of ICTs as instruments to improve production (quantity and quality)? And when such a relationship is in place, what is necessary for a just society under conditions of open data to rural government services? As more rural citizens gain access to ICTs, a possible research question could be how informal indigenous data from various new and existing sources (crowd sourcing) can be transformed or filtered in a way to be useful to decision makers and policymakers at both the local and international level? What are the options in the future of open data and content that include all possible data sources and do not repress data availability or local contributions that may arrive from marginalized groups?

In a globalized environment with surmounting pressures of weather unpredictability, economic crisis and the promise of erratic changes to the livelihoods of the poor, we envision the transformational power of ICT usage through the improvement of work, and one day, helping informal employment transition towards more formal means of social protection.

It is commonly understood that ICTs enhance productivity and, thereby, increase incomes within large and medium enterprises. This understanding was less known for micro-entrepreneurs and small enterprises in the developing world. Beyond agriculture and fisheries, ICTs were also quickly adopted by non-farm actors across the informal economy. The findings showed quick ICT implementation which led to opportunities towards further productivity and income generation.

Research supported within IDRC's ICT4D program helped to demonstrate this, as well as what types of interventions had the greatest likelihood of success. Informed, pro-poor ICT public policy and an increasingly competitive and diverse telecoms market supports lower ICT costs to small business. In turn, entrepreneurs can expand their range of services that can be of benefit to improved micro-enterprise and livelihood opportunities.

Note

1 I would like to thank Katie Bryant and Laurent Elder for molding this chapter; Raymond Hyma, Alicia Richero, Geneviève Lefebvre, Shalini Kala, Delphine Larrousse, Priyanka Mohan and Edith Adera for their initial contributions; and Rich Fuchs, Rohan Samarajiva, Ranjula Perera and Ayesha Zainudeen (the LIRNE*asia* team) for their editorial review.

References

Annerose, D. 2005. "MANOBI: Increasing the Incomes and Life Quality of Farmers in Senegal through a Multimedia Mobile Phone MIS." Paper presented at the "Expert Consultation on Market Information Systems and Agricultural Commodities Exchanges: Strengthening Market Signals and Institutions" in Amsterdam, 28–30 November. Online: http://ciat-library.ciat.cgiar. org:8080/jspui/bitstream/123456789/5308/1/expert_consultation_market_information. pdf (accessed 11 February 2012).

Annerose, D. and E. Sène. 2005. "Receiving Market Prices by SMS." *ICT Update* 9 (November). Online: http://ictupdate.cta.int/en/Feature-Articles/Receiving-market-prices-by-SMS (accessed 25 February 2012).

Ashraf, N. et al. 2009. "Finding Missing Markets (and a Disturbing Epilogue): Evidence from an Export Crop Adoption and Marketing Intervention in Kenya." *American Journal of Agricultural Economics* 91, no. 4: 973–90.

Barrett, C. 2008. "Small Holder Market Participation: Concepts and Evidence from Eastern and Southern Africa." *Food Policy* 33, no. 4: 299–317.

Barrett, C. and B. Swallow. 2006. "Fractal Poverty Traps." *World Development* 34, no. 1: 1–15.

Barrios, E. B. et al. 2011. "Impact Assessment of the E-AGRIKultura Project: Philippines." In *Strengthening Rural Livelihoods: The Impact of Information and Communication Technologies in Asia*, edited by D. J. Grimshaw and S. Kala, 89–108. Ottawa: IDRC.

Batchelor, S. et al. 2003. *ICT for Development: Contributing to the Millennium Development Goals: Lessons Learned from Seventeen infoDev Projects*. Washington, DC: World Bank.

Bayala, S. et al. 2010. "Dynamiques et rôle économique et social du secteur informel des TIC en Afrique de l'Ouest et du Centre: Cas du Burkin a Faso, du Cameroun et du Sénégal."

Yam Pukri / IDRC working document for DT-TIC-INFOR 2.3 SN, Ouagadougou, Burkina Faso. Online: http://tic-infor.burkina-ntic.net/wp-content/uploads/2008/06/Version-finale-TICINFOR_format-livre-bv.pdf (accessed 20 February 2012).

Bossio, J. F. and K. Sotomayor. 2008. "Public Access to Information & ICTs: Peru." Public access landscape study final report, presented by Alfa-Redi to the University of Washington Center for Information & Society (CIS) in Seattle.

Botelho, A. J. and A. D. S. Alves. 2007. "Mobile Use/Adoption by Micro, Small and Medium Enterprises in Latin America and the Caribbean." Background paper for "Mobile Opportunities: Poverty and Telephony Access in Latin America and the Caribbean" project. Lima: DIRSI and IDRC.

Breard, P. 2006. *Knowledge and Information Assessment Report: Karia Net.* Final version, February. Ottawa: IFAD/IDRC. Online: http://idl-bnc.idrc.ca/dspace/bitstream/10625/47683/1/IDL-47683.pdf (accessed 6 February 2012).

Chew, H. E. et al. 2011. "The Limited Impact of ICTs on Microenterprise Growth: A Study of Businesses Owned by Women in Urban India." *Information Technologies & International Development* 7, no. 4: 1–16.

Esselaar, S. et al. 2007. "ICT Usage and Its Impact on Profitability of SMEs in 13 African Countries." *Information Technologies & International Development* 4, no. 1: 87–100.

Frempong, G. 2009. "Mobile Telephone Opportunities: The Case of Micro- and Small Enterprises in Ghana." *info* 11, no. 2: 79–94.

Grimshaw, D. J. and S. Kala. 2011. *Strengthening Rural Livelihoods: The Impact of Information and Communication Technologies in Asia.* Ottawa: IDRC.

Grunfeld, H. 2011. "The Contribution of Information and Communication Technologies for Development (ICT4D) Projects to Capabilities, Empowerment and Sustainability: A Case Study of iREACH in Cambodia." PhD dissertation. Melbourne: Victoria University. Online: http://vuir.vu.edu.au/19359/1/Helena_Grunfeld.pdf (accessed 6 February 2012).

Grunfeld, H. et al. 2010. "Lessons from a Community Owned ICT network in Cambodia." In *ICTs for Global Development and Sustainability: Practice and Applications*, edited by J. Steyn et al., 302–28. Hershey: Information Science Reference.

ILO (International Labour Organization). 2011. *Statistical Update on Employment in the Informal Economy.* Geneva: ILO. Online: http://www.ilo.org/wcmsp5/groups/public/---dgreports/---stat/documents/presentation/wcms_157467.pdf (accessed 15 March 2012).

_____. 2012. *Global Employment Trends 2012.* Geneva: ILO. Online: http://www.ilo.org/global/research/global-reports/global-employment- trends/WCMS_171571/lang--en/index.htm (accessed 15 March 2012).

Islam, M. S. and A. Grönlund. 2010. "An Agricultural Market Information Service (AMIS) in Bangladesh: Evaluating a Mobile Phone Based E-Service in a Rural Context." *Information Development* 26, no. 4: 289–302.

Jütting, J. P. and J. R. de Laiglesia, eds. 2009. *Is Informal Normal? Towards More and Better Jobs in Developing Countries.* Paris: OECD.

Kaplinsky, R. and M. Morris. 2001. *Handbook on Value Chain Research.* Ottawa: IDRC. Online: http://sds.ukzn.ac.za/files/handbook_valuechainresearch.pdf (accessed 11 February 2012).

Konté, A. and M. Ndong. 2012. "The Informal ICT Sector and Innovation Processes in Senegal." UNU-MERIT working paper no. 2012-009, Maastricht, the Netherlands.

Lokanathan, S. et al. 2011. "Price Transparency in Agricultural Produce Markets: Sri Lanka." In *Strengthening Rural Livelihoods: The Impact of Information and Communication Technologies in Asia*, edited by D. J. Grimshaw and S. Kala, 15–32. Ottawa: IDRC.

Mascarenhas, O. et al. 2010. *Tanzania Country Report: 2010 Poverty and Information and Communications Technology in Urban and Rural Eastern Africa (PICTURE-Africa).* Ottawa: IDRC.

Masuki, K. F. G. et al. 2011. "Improving Small Holder Farmers' Access to Information for Enhanced Decision Making in Natural Resource Management: Experiences from Southwestern Uganda." In *Innovations as Key to the Green Revolution in Africa*, edited by A. Bationo et al., 1145–59. Dordrecht and New York Springer.

Monge-González, R. et al. 2005. *TICs en las PYMES de Centroamérica: Impacto de la adopción de las tecnologías de la información y la comunicación en el desempeño de las empresas.* Ottawa: IDRC.

Munyua, H. 2007. *ICTs and Small-Scale Agriculture in Africa: A Scoping Study.* Ottawa: IDRC.

Ndiaye, S. 2010. "État des lieux du secteur informel des TIC au Sénégal. Recherches sur les dynamiques et rôles économiques et sociales du secteur informel des TIC, TICINFOR AFRIQ." March. Yam Pukri, Ouagadougou, Burkina Faso. Online: http://tic-infor.burkina-ntic.net/wpcontent/uploads/2010/12/RAP-R.TIC-INFOR-1.3-SN_dec10.pdf (accessed 6 February 2012).

Okello, J. J. 2010. "Does Use of ICT-Based Market Information Services (MIS) Improve the Well Being of Developing-Country Small Holder Farmers? Evidence from Kenya." Paper presented at the 4th ACORN-REDECOM Conference in Brasilia, 14–15 May.

Okello, J. J. et al. 2009. "Awareness and the Use of Mobile Phones for Market Linkage by Small Holder Farmers in Kenya." In *E-Agriculture and E-Government for Global Policy Development: Implications and Future Directions*, edited by B. M. Maumbe, 1–18. Hershey: IGI Global.

———. 2010a. "A Framework for Analyzing the Role of ICT on Agricultural Commercialization and Household Food Security." *International Journal of ICT Research and Development in Africa* 1, no. 1: 38–50.

———. 2010b. "Using ICT to Integrate Small Holder Farmers into Agricultural Value Chain: The Case of DrumNet Project in Kenya." *International Journal of ICT Research and Development in Africa* 1, no. 1: 23–37.

Ouédraogo, S. 2009. "Dynamiques et rôle économique et social du secteur informel des TIC au Burkina Faso, au Cameroun et au Sénégal. Le sous-secteur informel des TIC: éléments méthodologiques pour une recherche sur la question." Yam Pukri, Burkina Faso. Online: http://tic-infor.burkina-ntic.net/wp-content/uploads/2010/12/DT-TICINFOR-METHOD_dec10.pdf (accessed 6 February 2012).

Raj, D. A. et al. 2011. "A Crop Nutrient Management Decision Support System: India." In *Strengthening Rural Livelihoods: The Impact of Information and Communication Technologies in Asia*, edited by D. M. Grimshaw and S. Kala, 33–52. Ottawa: IDRC.

Rashid, A. and L. Elder. 2009. "Mobile Phones and Development: An Analysis of IDRC-Supported Projects." *Electronic Journal of Information Systems in Developing Countries* 36, no. 2: 1–16.

Ratnadiwakara, D. 2008. "Transaction Costs in Agriculture: From the Planting Decision to Selling at the Wholesale Market: A Case-Study on the Feeder Area of the Dambulla Dedicated Economic Centre in Sri Lanka." Paper presented at the 3rd Communication Policy Research South Conference in Beijing, December.

Rizvi, S. M. H. 2011. "Lifelines: Livelihood Solutions through Mobile Technology in India." In *Strengthening Rural Livelihoods: The Impact of Information and Communication Technologies in Asia*, edited by D. J. Grimshaw and S. Kala, 53–70. Ottawa: IDRC.

Soysa, S. 2008. "Traceability in Agricultural Markets: Using ICTs to Improve Traceability of Gherkins: Presentation of Initial Learnings." Paper presented at the "Workshop on Transaction Costs and Traceability: Potential for ICTs in the Agricultural Value Chain" in Kandalama, Sri Lanka, 21–23 February.

Turpin, T. and A. Ghimire. 2010. "The Internet and Social Capital: Experiences of Openness in Remote and Rural Areas in Least Developed Economies." Paper presented at the Open Development Workshop 2010, sponsored by IDRC, March.

Chapter 7

RESEARCH ON eHEALTH ACROSS HEALTH SYSTEMS: CONTRIBUTIONS TO STRENGTHEN A FIELD

Chaitali Sinha and Dominique Garro-Strauss[1]

The International Development Research Centre's (IDRC's) "Information and Communications Technologies for Development" (ICT4D) program supports research on the use of information and communications technologies (ICTs) in health systems – often referred to as electronic health or eHealth. Since the late 1990s, IDRC's eHealth research portfolio has been driven by priorities stated by researchers and practitioners from low- and middle-income countries (LMICs). Specifically, these studies respond to a clear and steady demand for applied research on how the use of ICTs could influence changes in behavior, service delivery, planning and policies at different points and at different levels of a health system. The scope of the studies extended beyond the financial bottom line to include ones that examine varied experiences of integrating eHealth in different health systems contexts. This chapter presents lessons and outcomes from IDRC-supported eHealth projects that helped strengthen the capacities of researchers and research networks, influence policies and practices and shape the body of literature on eHealth from a LMIC perspective.

The World Health Organization (WHO) defines eHealth as the use of ICTs for health in order to accomplish a wide variety of tasks, such as treating patients, pursuing research, educating students, tracking diseases and monitoring public health.[2] Although the term "eHealth" is increasingly recognized by many working in the field of health, this was not the case when IDRC's ICT4D program first started supporting projects in the early 1990s. These research projects – based in communities across Africa, Asia, and Latin America and the Caribbean (LAC) – examined a broad range of research questions about the expected and unexpected influences that ICTs have had on health services and health outcomes. The projects ranged from exploratory proof-of-concept studies, efforts to strengthen communities in LMICs to collaborate in the development and implementation of software, to systematic reviews and multi-country studies carried out by research networks. Early project titles included "Development of an ICT-Based Telemedicine System for Primary Community Healthcare in Indonesia," "Information and Communication Technology for Monitoring and Treating Diabetes in Senegal" and "Pilot Project Using ICTs to Monitor Chagas Disease in Argentina and Bolivia." Although not all of the projects explicitly used the term "eHealth," each project examined the relationships between eHealth and health outcomes, which entail changes in health processes, health behaviors and/or changes in the state of health and well-being.

This chapter presents evidence, outcomes and some initial impact resulting from IDRC-supported research and researchers working on eHealth in LMICs. The first section provides key definitions and the conceptual framework for the chapter. The second section briefly describes IDRC's approach to supporting eHealth research. The third section looks at relevant literature and specific research outcomes from IDRC-supported projects. The portion on health outcomes is divided into three categories: evidence contributing to potential outcomes, process outcomes and health status outcomes. The research for development outcomes look at the areas of capacity development, fostering networks and networking and influencing policy. The fourth section concentrates on the contributions of these outcomes toward strengthening the field of eHealth. A final section describes IDRC's vision for future eHealth research support. It is followed by a short conclusion, which emphasizes a health systems research approach with particular attention on issues of governance, equity and systems integration.

Definitions and Conceptual Framework

Strengthening health systems involves considering and examining the nature and extent of how different parts of the system interact with and depend on each other. These include, but are not limited to, the six building blocks of a health system as outlined by WHO: health information systems; health workforce; leadership and governance; service delivery; medical products, vaccines and technologies; and health systems financing. Beyond these, there are social determinants of health, which are defined by WHO as the conditions in which people are born, grow, live, work and age, including the health system. The relationships and interactions among these different components have to be examined since evidence shows that strengthening one or more components within a health system does not necessarily strengthen the system as a whole (Swanson et al. 2010). Researching the effects of integrating eHealth into a health system can take place in multiple ways and at many levels. Two such examples are: examining the effects of introducing an eHealth tool within an existing system to study how workloads are affected in the short-term, medium-term and longer-term time frames and investigating how ICT-enabled feedback loops within a health system can promote or impede data validation and influence accountability and governance for different actors at multiple levels in the system.

eHealth and mHealth

The 58th World Health Assembly in May 2005 adopted Resolution WHA58.28, urging member states to develop eHealth strategies and to plan for appropriate eHealth services. Within the resolutions were specific recommendations, which included developing a strategic plan for eHealth; reaching communities, including vulnerable groups; and evaluating and sharing knowledge about eHealth activities to promote equity, equality, as well as to protect privacy and confidentiality of information. The resolution is indicative not only of the rapid spread of ICTs; it also shows the pressing need to develop and implement appropriate eHealth strategies and plans to help ensure the growing number of eHealth applications and services are relevant, informed and equitable in how they meet the health needs of different populations.

As is usually the case with new terms, "eHealth" conjures up different images for different people. Oh et al.'s 2005 paper, "What Is eHealth: A Systematic Review of Published Definitions," was dedicated entirely to the term "eHealth" and how it was defined and treated in different publications. The review revealed 51 unique definitions for the term but the definition by Eysenbach (2001)[3] was the one most commonly cited. However, in this chapter, we will be using the WHO definition that was mentioned earlier. Therefore, the use of the term "eHealth" goes well beyond issues of automation, digitization and securing stable power supplies. It involves context-specific, politically aware and socially sensitive examinations of how different ICTs are being appropriated and who is being included and/or excluded in the process. Above all, the understanding of eHealth encompasses how different processes and outcomes influence how health systems are designed and planned and how they function. Moreover, eHealth should not be seen as synonymous with electronic medical records (EMRs). Although EMRs represent one particular example of eHealth, overlooking other forms of eHealth can lead to an overly narrow sense of eHealth as primarily serving individual clinical health purposes. There are many important applications of eHealth to the field of public health. Examples of different ways in which eHealth can be involved in a health system include the following:

- Collecting, storing, transmitting and using data within health information systems (Braa et al. 2007; Fairall et al. 2008)
- Continuing medical education offered to the health workforce (Hoppenbrouwer and Kanyengo 2007; Geissbuhler et al. 2007)
- Extending access to health services by providing care from a distance (Wootton et al. 2009; Durrani and Khoja 2009)
- Providing interactive means to engage with citizens at all levels in order to strengthen governance (Freifeld et al. 2010; Chetley et al. 2006)
- Tracking the distribution of medical products and vaccines through responsive supply chain management systems (Berger et al. 2007; Fraser et al. 2006)
- Providing alternate means for health financing (Nishtar et al. 2011; Mechael et al. 2010)

The demand for, and development and spread of, eHealth solutions has been heavily influenced by substantial increases in mobile phone availability and affordability. There is growing attention on and resource allocation to the use of mobile technologies in health systems. According to the International Telecommunication Union's (ITU) World Telecommunication/ICT Indicators database, global penetration of mobile phones in 2011 reached an estimated eighty-seven percent and seventy-nine percent in the developing world.[4] Furthermore, it is expected that, by 2012, half of all individuals living in the world's most remote areas will have mobile phones (Vital Wave Consulting 2009). Mobile health (mHealth) – defined as the use of mobile telecommunications and multimedia technologies within increasingly wireless healthcare delivery systems (Istepanian and Lacal 2003) – can provide new ways of communicating and can complement existing communication channels. In developing country contexts specifically, it can foster direct voice and data communication where wired infrastructure is limited or nonexistent. And mHealth can extend the reach of health services at the point of care by leveraging the growing wireless infrastructure (Mechael et al. 2010).

Although there is no universal way of conceptualizing eHealth, Figure 7.1 depicts the way in which eHealth is thought of for the purposes of this chapter. This representation is not meant to be absolute. Scholars, practitioners and policymakers may conceive of the field differently based on their particular disciplinary, sectoral and/or personal backgrounds. Figure 7.1 proposes mHealth as a subset of eHealth. Mobile devices (wireless devices) are considered a type of interface or mode of access. Although to date mHealth has been dominated by mobile phones, there are other mobile devices (such as mobile ultrasound machines) that can also be included as a mobile device. This categorization allows for continued use of the conceptual framework as technologies and interfaces evolve and respond according to different environmental, political, social, economic and legal factors. For instance, an increasing amount of research is being conducted on embedded medical technologies such as "smart pills" and subcutaneous chips.[5] Therefore, although there are changing interfaces and modes of access, the overarching use of ICTs remains unchanged. This is why eHealth is shown conceptually to include mHealth.

Depending on the interface and mode of access, there are different types of functions that can be performed to improve individual and public health outcomes. Some examples are provided under the broad categories of telehealth and health informatics, but these represent a handful of potential examples that could have been presented. Dotted bidirectional arrows represent connections, overlaps and interdependencies. For instance, conducting household surveys using mobile devices can serve as an example of decision support that would require the use of common and open data standards when reporting the data to the district level. At the district level, when these data are compared with other data such as water quality and drug supply, it would require wider coherence that would be supported by enterprise architecture across different data sources in the system. The resulting analysis at district, provincial and/or national levels can inform how health workers are trained using distance learning applications (mobile phone-based interfaces included) to meet the health needs that were captured in the household survey.

Health outcomes

Outcomes are defined as the intended or unintended changes in the behavior, relationships, activities or actions of the people, groups and organizations that a research study influenced.[6] These changes should be reasonably linked to the research strategies and activities, albeit not necessarily directly caused by them. The need to determine and document health outcomes is obvious; however, the ability to measure them systematically

Figure 7.1. Conceptual diagram of eHealth

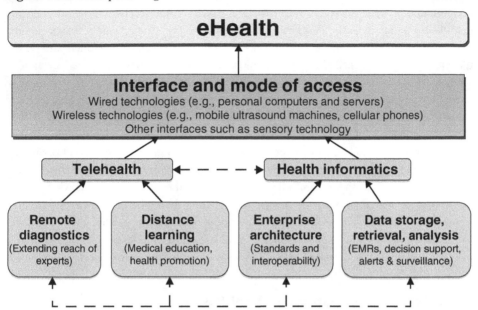

and meaningfully and make a reasonable link to the research activity being undertaken can be less than straightforward.

Health outcomes can be defined as "a change in the health status of an individual, group or population which is attributable to a planned intervention or series of interventions, regardless of whether such an intervention was intended to change health status" (WHO 1998).[7] These outcomes include changes in the health status, as well as relevant health process outcomes, which can be defined as changes in processes that can lead to improved health outcomes. Despite the increased adoption of eHealth, strong evidence linking eHealth solutions to health outcomes is limited (Scott and Saeed 2007; Mechael et al. 2010). Sinha and Clarke (2010) allude to sound, context-specific evidence about eHealth related to health outcomes as the "holy grail" of eHealth research. Findings from rigorous research studies show correlations or unearth critical patterns and behaviors but have not yet led to measurable outcomes (process or health status) that are significant. These will be discussed in this chapter. Since the value of findings or outcomes depends largely on their orientation and use (CIHI 2008), health findings and health outcomes discussed below are subsequently linked to research for development outcomes – specifically, capacity strengthening, networks and networking and policy influence. When examined collectively, these outcomes are shown to contribute to strengthening the field of eHealth research in low-and middle-income countries.

Field building

The concepts of "field" and "field building" are recognized as being complex, abstract and without precise definitions (Bernholz et al. 2009). A field can be framed as a discipline in academia, a field for philanthropic efforts, a space for semi-structured debate or some combination of these and other framings. The Robert Wood Johnson Foundation defines field building as building "leadership and capacity by strengthening infrastructures, supporting research and encouraging linkages among researchers, practitioners and policy-makers" (Ottoson et al. 2009, S38). Melinda Fine (2001) defines a field as "an area of specialized practice encompassing specific activities carried out by trained practitioners in particular settings." Fields of study generally have several subdisciplines or branches and the distinguishing lines demarcating these are often both arbitrary and ambiguous (Abbott 2001). The field of eHealth is found at the intersection of several other fields – health sciences, medicine, information systems, public health, computer science and operations research, among others. Discussing eHealth as a field recognizes the different theories and frameworks that are drawn from other fields, while at the same time acknowledging the emergence of shared language, professional education, theory-based knowledge base and standards of practice (Fine 2001). Discussions about field building in this chapter will focus on the area of eHealth (as shown in Figure 7.1) with special emphasis on the state of the field in LMICs as this was the focus of IDRC's mandate to support research for development.

IDRC Approach to Supporting eHealth Research

Discussions about eHealth research projects at IDRC begin with the health challenges being addressed in a given project. Such challenges can take a variety of forms, which can include limited awareness and promotion of positive health behaviors, insufficient access to health services for those in need or poor coordination of processes in one or more parts of a health system. The projects were designed to examine eHealth within and across different national and sub-national contexts in ways that acknowledge and respond to differences in how health systems are organized, how clinical and public health workflows are carried out and how different parts of the system interact with one another (Bates and Wright 2009; de Savigny and Adam 2009).

The potential for the use of eHealth to contribute to influence or change – which can lead to transformational change in some cases – needs to be researched in a way that reveals both positive and negative effects of ICT use. Carrying out research on eHealth can include, but is not limited to, the following:

- Researching how the technologies are socially constructed, perceived and used by different user groups (focus on behavioral change)
- Examining eHealth with respect to specific processes within health service delivery and how these can influence health outcomes (focus on implementation research or implementation science)
- Looking across different processes and structures within a health system to understand how the system works and the different interrelationships it embodies (focus on process modeling, functional and systems analysis)

As IDRC funds research for development, IDRC-supported researchers drew from existing literature and past experiences to design their specific studies. In addition to the

Figure 7.2. mHealth initiatives in Uganda

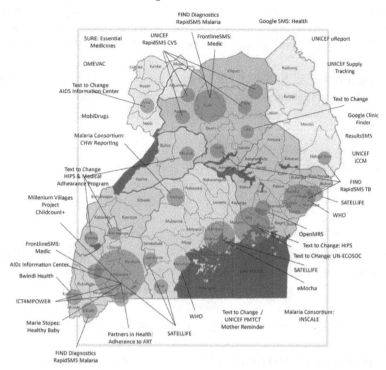

Source: Sean Blaschke (UNICEF Uganda, http://www.flickr.com/photos/texttochange/5178727492/ [accessed 9 June 2012]).

standard activities of conducting literature reviews, testing and retesting instruments and acquiring necessary approvals and engagement from different stakeholders, the informed project development process also involves due diligence through learning about and connecting with relevant organizations and initiatives working on similar issues. This can help avoid what Bates and Wright (2009, 1) refer to as the norm: "Every group moving ahead in this [eHealth] area has to reinvent the wheel, creating an enormous amount of rework. Furthermore, even when an organization finds a solution, different organizations are not communicating their success stories with each other." The "Strengthening Community Health in Uganda" (STRETCH-Uganda) project is an example where this was considered and actively addressed in the project's design and implementation.

This project arose from two different project ideas that were shared with IDRC related to the use of mobile phones and how village health teams (also called community health workers in other parts of the world) acquire training and provide health services. Each involved the improvement of maternal and newborn health through the use of mobile phones by village health teams (VHTs). Recognizing the multitude of other mHealth projects in Uganda (as shown in Figure 7.2), IDRC began discussions with the proposing institutions to explore how some research could be done to help mitigate a harmful dependence on isolated and siloed pilot studies. The project pursued research questions that could provide evidence for greater alignment with national health priorities, workload and incentive structures of VHTs, the availability of ICTs, as well as the different mobile phone-based solutions currently in use. There is a lack of standardization in eHealth within countries, which is further exacerbated by the isolation of systems and scant sharing of experiences (Bates and Wright 2009; Moodley et al. 2012).

The research design for STRETCH-Uganda was developed by different organizations in Uganda representing different sectors; non-governmental organizations or NGOs, for example, (Uganda Chartered Health Net, Uganda National Association of Community and Occupational Health and FHI-SATELLIFE), academe (Makerere University) and government (Ministry of Health). The project was designed to conduct a systematic review and field surveys and to convene different VHT projects (funded by different donors) across Uganda to discuss the policies, practices, incentives and innovations as they relate to VHTs using mobile devices to provide health services to their respective communities.

A survey of 221 members of village health teams (VHTs) plus 86 key informants and 8 focus group discussions of men and women was carried out in 2011 in 10 districts.[8] The findings, complemented by a policy and stakeholder analysis and face-to-face workshops, provide more clarity on what types of projects are underway, how they align with national health priorities and whether data across the different sites can be shared and analyzed based on standardized requirements and interoperability[9] across systems. (See Box 7.1.)

The approach taken by STRETCH-Uganda resonated with a memorandum issued on 17 January 2012 by the director-general of health services from the Ugandan Ministry of Health. This document communicates the need for greater harmonization and coordination of all eHealth projects in the country. So, all eHealth initiatives have to acquire the necessary approvals and comply with national standards on interoperability, ownership and guidelines on sustainability.

STRETCH-Uganda illustrates a number of strategies used by IDRC, such as the following:

- Encouraging an evidence-based and use-oriented approach to action research
- Strengthening research capabilities at individual and organizational levels
- Nurturing research networks and networking activities that can foster dialogue, cultivate synergistic efforts and stimulate debate
- Supporting knowledge translation to influence policy and practice

These outcome areas are discussed below in the third section along with examples drawn from other IDRC-supported projects. The ways in which these outcomes contribute to building the field of eHealth in LMICs are discussed in the fourth section.

Different eHealth study designs

Despite the growing body of eHealth research, there are gaps between the predicted and the observed benefits of eHealth technologies (Black et al. 2011). Moreover, there is

---

Box 7.1. Interoperability

The increasingly interconnected world we live in necessitates working with others. This collaboration requires sufficient common ground to reliably exchange messages in a way that minimizes errors and misunderstandings. In the world of eHealth, this is referred to as interoperability. If one were to relate this concept to spoken language, it would include discussions about dictionaries, punctuation, structured grammar and the ways in which language is spoken and understood among different individuals and across different groups. Interoperable health systems are the foundations behind collaborating to strengthen health systems in a way that minimizes fragmentation, error and misunderstandings. This often involves establishing common ground when it comes to structuring data and selecting standards to exchange them.

---

limited use of the existing evidence base (Clamp and Keen 2007). When the millennium development goals (MDGs) were first developed in 2000, eHealth research studies were predominantly pilot projects and proof-of-concept efforts. Given that the field of eHealth was just emerging at this time and that the use of ICTs in health, especially in LMICs, was not a prevalent topic, many of these early projects were ambitious and often lacked sufficient longer-term planning relating to the integration with existing systems and finding appropriate ways to achieve scale. Some were driven more by the determination of selected donors and technologies than by what would work best on the ground and align best with local and national priorities.

There is still value in supporting pilot eHealth research studies on particular aspects of a health intervention, policy or process. However, with more than a decade of experience with these types of initiatives, there is a growing recognition that the influence of ICTs in health should take a more nuanced and grounded perspective on how various dependencies within a system respond and react when ICTs are introduced (Black et al. 2011; Chong 2011). There will always be an important role for pilot studies in the field of eHealth (and ICT4D in general) – notably for exploratory research to establish foundations for other types of studies. Pilots can be a necessary step to systematically capture lessons in order to inform larger-scale efforts. As such, pilots themselves are not the problem; the problems stem from pilots that are conceived and implemented without adequate attention paid to local context, community engagement and voice, alignment with pressing health priorities, and models to enable longer-term sustainability and potential to scale.

In the context of rigorous and sound eHealth research, researchers should situate the study and its design so findings build on past evidence and avoid the needless repetition of pilot studies – or other types of studies, for that matter – that do not contribute new findings and knowledge to the body of evidence. The topics, study designs and funding mechanisms used by IDRC's ICT4D program to support eHealth research in LMICs shifted from the early pilot studies – many of which aimed to prove the feasibility of using ICTs in low-resource health settings – to research projects that were more focused on addressing health challenges in an integrated way. This shift and growth in IDRC funding over the years should be seen as a gradual progression due to the time and effort needed to strengthen individual and organizational research capacities, the emergent nature of development research and the fast-changing landscape of ICT innovations (most notably the sharp increase in the diffusion of mobile telephony).

Outcomes Contributing to Strengthened eHealth Research

As a funder of development research, IDRC places a strong emphasis on measuring outcomes in the research projects that it supports. Outcomes can carry positive and negative values vis-à-vis the desired development change, as well as values that are unintended in the project's design and implementation. In the case of eHealth, the use of ICTs within health systems could lead to positive outcomes such as improving adherence to drug regimens or enhancing budgeting practices due to timely and validated data harvesting and analysis. The use of eHealth could also lead to negative outcomes such as contributing to delays in service delivery due to bottlenecks in training or the frustration of health workers who are already stretched to perform their duties. Several experiences have shown that implementation of poorly designed eHealth systems cannot only fail to meet the anticipated objectives, but can also waste scarce resources and perhaps compromise the quality of health service provision (Ammenworth and Shaw 2005; Catwell and Sheikh 2009). As a research funder, IDRC is equally interested in supporting researchers examining positive and negative outcomes of the different uses of eHealth.

Considering the importance of the design, deployment and use of technology to eHealth outcomes, projects funded by IDRC look first to relevant existing technical infrastructure, hardware, software and processes that can be made accessible to the stakeholders involved. The appropriateness of ICTs for any eHealth intervention is crucial for the project's acceptance by various stakeholders and for its efficacy, utility and viability. For example, the stability of power supplies and costs associated with alternative sources of energy are fundamental considerations when selecting ICTs that can be widely adopted as part of an eHealth project. Similarly, adapting data entry methods to local needs may entail forgoing mobile devices with the standard numeric keypad in favor of alternatives such as touch-screen interfaces, optical character recognition or quick response codes (Waidyanatha 2010). Beyond technical and economic appropriateness, important political and cultural considerations of using eHealth must be studied. These considerations are often the ones that can seal the fate of a project.

This section follows the conceptual model shown below in Figure 7.3. Each subsection will define the outcome being examined, discuss relevant literature and unveil some pertinent outcomes from IDRC-supported research. In the following section, these findings will be discussed collectively as they pertain to field building.

Health outcomes

Changes and improvements in information availability, processes and behaviors can contribute to improved health outcomes and quality of life indicators. At present, the majority of IDRC's work on eHealth research has produced an ample body of evidence on outcomes related to data, process and practice. A formative evaluation study on IDRC's eHealth research portfolio from 2005 to 2010 states that "the majority of the program implementation and intervention evaluation focused on process improvement and its potential impact on health outcomes and overall quality of care" (Mechael 2011). Measuring changes in health status outcomes as influenced by eHealth interventions is not straightforward, as relationships and correlations tend to be complex and non-linear in nature.

In Asia, the search for a better understanding of how eHealth influences health outcomes was at the heart of the IDRC-funded "Pan Asian Collaboration for Evidence-based eHealth Adoption and Application" (PANACeA), a multi-country research network that worked on eight projects in twelve countries. The objectives and design of PANACeA were informed by a study done of previous IDRC eHealth research grants, including grants provided through the competitive Pan Asia Networking (PAN) research and development grants program. This study (Scott and Saeed 2007) examined projects supported in India, Indonesia, Mongolia, Nepal, Pakistan and the Philippines and analyzed them with respect to five categories: knowledge production, research targeting, adoption or integration, informing policy, and broader benefit and health benefits. The resulting scores were consistently high when measuring "knowledge production" and "informing policy," but lower for "health benefits" and "adoption or integration" (Scott and Saeed 2007). Recognizing that this was likely due in part to the early stage of using ICTs for health in many of the organizations leading the projects, the message came through loud and clear that there is a lack of evidence – notably from researchers in Asian LMICs – that provides correlative findings relating eHealth to health outcomes and integration into health systems. The purpose of the PANACeA network was to help fill this gap.

Despite the challenges in measuring health outcomes, eHealth projects supported within IDRC have shown a number of significant outcomes leading to sustained process improvements, enhanced decision support through triangulation and feedback loops, as well as evidence of how the use of eHealth can influence diagnoses and compliance to care. Examples of health outcomes are presented below in three categories:

- Evidence contributing to potential outcomes
- Process outcomes
- Health status outcomes

This section will conclude with how these health and process outcomes are linked to research for development outcomes. Figure 7.3 presents the framework for how different outcomes discussed in this section relate to one another, as well as how they relate to the broader discussion about field building. The figure clarifies the lack of a hierarchy

Figure 7.3. Outcomes contributing to the field of eHealth research in LMICs

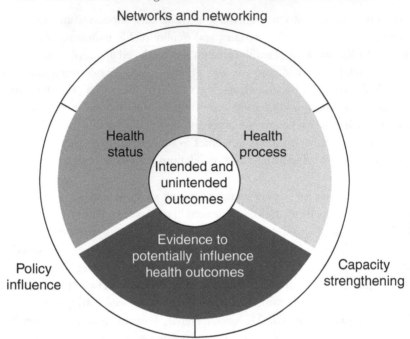

of health outcomes or of research for development outcomes. Each among them fulfills different and important functions in contributing toward the field of eHealth in LMICs. The circle in the middle of Figure 7.3 indicates that the diagram is centered around outcomes, both intended and unintended. This circle is then surrounded both by health outcomes (health status, health process, and evidence to potentially influence health outcomes) and by research for development outcomes (networks and networking, capacity strengthening and policy influence). Overlaps and complementarity exist among the different outcomes.

Evidence contributing to potential outcomes

The process of influencing outcomes can be unpredictable. It can be shaped by various forces – at times occurring simultaneously, at other times influencing action to go in different directions. These forces can range from general ones, such as an enabling environment, to more specific ones, such as networks and networking to support advocacy efforts. In an evidence-based decision making framework, research findings have great significance in informing the change process. Examples of this type of evidence include findings about bottlenecks in the system, findings that identify recurring behavioral or technical patterns and those that provide insights into the costing of different events or interactions in a health system.

The PANACeA network in South Asia and Southeast Asia consists of research projects that operate in at least two different countries. The projects address specific health challenges and examine outcomes that may be facilitated or inhibited through the use of eHealth. One such project, "Economic Evaluation Framework of Computerization in Hospitals," examined the cost implications of computerizing hospitals in Afghanistan, India, Pakistan and the Philippines. As with all PANACeA projects, this study employed a quasi-experimental research design with a control group and high levels of engagement with the participating communities. Seven hospitals were selected, including public and private sector hospitals, as well as hospitals from large urban centers and rural areas. This diversity helped make the cost–benefit analysis tool (CBAT), developed by the researchers, both robust and broadly applicable. Preliminary findings from two of the hospitals in Pakistan show the cost for a glucose test is 14 cents in the computerized hospital compared with 26 cents at the non-computerized hospital – nearly double the cost. However it was found that computerization leads to cost savings and efficiency gains only in relatively large hospitals (Jan et al. 2011). These results, which include the methodology and the CBAT tool, can serve as a foundation to generate additional methodological innovations and evidence. The findings can also incorporate additional relevant social, political and economic factors that, when analyzed using locally appropriate methods, can further shed light on matters of costing in a broader systems-oriented perspective. Thus, this evidence can be used in the future to influence changes in processes and to potentially improve health status through the provision of more affordable and timely laboratory testing, and potentially other types of testing, within hospital settings.

A particular aspect of a research project supported in South Africa's Free State from 2004 to 2008 is another example. In addition to the health process and health status outcomes (discussed in subsequent passages in this chapter), the project generated evidence that could inform several other such outcomes in the future. The researchers supported the development and analysis of a comprehensive information system to support the administration of free anti-retroviral treatment (ART) in the Free State. With this development, they aimed at improving and optimizing data captured on structured medical records that were used for routine care and clinical information systems at multiple primary care clinics. They also implemented and eventually transferred to the Free State Department of Health a clinical data warehouse[10] that, as of 2009, housed information for at least 77,000 infected children and adults. Data from the warehouse were used for monitoring and evaluating patients and conducting research (Fairall et al. 2008). Generating this sound base of evidence led to ongoing research, which can often have considerable influence down the line on health process and health status outcomes.

Process outcomes

The term "process outcome" as used here refers to cases where sound evidence is used to change processes in the health system. This type of outcome can go by many names, such as "implementation research outcomes" and "operational research outcomes." Given the different inflows, outflows and processes involved in a functioning health system, the value of process outcomes is clear. A concrete example of a process outcome includes

Box 7.2. FOSS (free and open source software)

Did you know that free and open source software (FOSS) is all around us? FOSS drives many prominent websites, large web browsers (such as Firefox) and web servers (such as Apache). So, what is FOSS and what isn't FOSS? According to the Free Software Foundation, when thinking of FOSS, one should "think of free as in free speech, not as in free beer." This means the term FOSS refers to the freedom to download, copy, modify, reuse and contribute software back to the community, rather than the price of the software. Resources, both human and financial, are often required to customize, deploy and maintain a FOSS system. These tasks are increasingly being carried out by a locally trained and highly skilled workforce in LMIC countries.

a reduction in wait times when seeking care. A large proportion of IDRC's eHealth research projects yielded process outcomes (Mechael 2011). The specific examples highlighted here relate to diagnosis, treatment and reporting functions within a health system.

Within the PANACeA network, a study was carried out in Pakistan and the Philippines to examine the diagnosis of tuberculosis (TB) through the use of diagnostic committees. Specifically, the project sought to provide evidence on the effectiveness of online TB diagnostic committees (TBDCs) when compared with face-to-face TBDC decisions. The results demonstrated that electronic decisions showed greater accuracy (sensitivity of 32.4 percent) compared with face-to-face accuracy (27.6 percent). Using a two-month clinical follow-up as the gold standard, face-to-face decisions correlated more closely with improvement in patient symptoms and weight when compared with ICT-based decisions. This demonstrates the potential of integrating eHealth into a system that retains other non-eHealth-enabled processes. Therefore, the integration of eHealth need not displace other non-eHealth parts of a process. Since the goal is to improve health processes and health outcomes, integrating eHealth should be carried out in a manner that facilitates achieving this goal. The free and open source software (FOSS) (see Box 7.2) "iPath," which was used in the Philippines for the electronic TBDCs, was shown to have a cost- and time-saving potential. Using iPath, TBDCs could review cases, diagnose and confer remotely, thus potentially reducing the diagnosis and treatment delay when compared with conventional care (Marcelo et al. 2011).

As part of the Free State project mentioned earlier, a clinical data warehouse was established. In the context of this project, the data warehouse was able to link data from the South African Death Register,[11] Electronic Tuberculosis Register[12] and National Health Laboratory Service (NHLS).[13] Due in large part to the integrated system, quarterly reports were produced that accounted for the progress of the ART rollout and provided a realistic estimate of the number of patients receiving treatment in Free State, South Africa. The project was one of the first demonstrations of the use of data integration from routine health information systems (RHIS) for public health policymaking, of the use of mobile devices for data collection and of a clinical data warehouse for data integration and reporting. According to a formative evaluation conducted of IDRC's eHealth projects, this example points to IDRC's role in helping to improve data triangulation and decision support by funding research on the development of a comprehensive patient management system for HIV/AIDS (Mechael 2011).

Another example can be found in a research network funded by IDRC in Sub-Saharan Africa. The "Open Architectures Standards and Information Systems" (OASIS) project began in three countries (Mozambique, South Africa and Zimbabwe), expanding in its second phase to Rwanda and a number of other countries in Sub-Saharan Africa. OASIS focuses on strengthening local capacities to design, develop, analyze and improve eHealth systems, specifically through the use of FOSS. This includes work on mobile phone interfaces and usage, training programs, electronic medical records, enterprise architecture and policy analysis among other things related to strengthening health systems through appropriate use of eHealth.

The OASIS project node in Mozambique, a predominantly Portuguese-speaking country, has leveraged local capacities in computer science and health informatics to build robust, locally relevant eHealth software while simultaneously providing a point of convergence and trust for different eHealth project funders, developers and key stakeholders, including the Ministry of Health. A flagship project for the Mozambican OASIS node (M-OASIS) was a registration system for hospital deaths (SIS-ROH). Originally designed and deployed for the central hospital in Maputo, the registration system has been approved for deployment in 14 other hospitals.[14] The system produced the first systematic data collected routinely in hospitals and allows deaths to be coded using the international ICD-10 standard. Data collected in SIS-ROH are being used to improve the monitoring of morbidity, mortality and prevalence of disease. The process improvements in monitoring and registration have led to more effective planning and resource allocation at district and subdistrict levels. The M-OASIS team is also discussing mortality measurement with the National Department of Statistics in Mozambique that is ultimately responsible for mortality data.

At first glance, the significance of adopting ICD-10, an international mortality coding standard adapted for a LMIC context, may not be apparent. With the woeful lack of data on vital statistics (e.g., births and deaths) in LMICs, having the ability to code and thus analyze mortality can influence many different types of changes. For example, resource allocation can be informed by the burden of mortality in different locations. Seasonal and other patterns of disease can be researched based on mortality data. There are also a number of administrative matters related to mortality coding that can affect the families of the deceased. The issue of poor data on vital statistics and civil registration was one that was prioritized as part of the Commission on Information and Accountability for Women's and Children's Health, which is part of the "Every Woman Every Child" (EWEC) global initiative.[15]

Measuring process outcomes is of tremendous importance when trying to understand and improve health systems. The different examples illustrate how evidence can shed light on certain aspects of complex systems and hopefully catalyze additional research to gain a more complete and nuanced understanding of different processes, dynamics and tensions within a given health system.

Health status outcomes

Generating findings and improving processes in a health system can influence outcomes in the health status of both individuals and larger populations. These types of outcomes – the focus of this section – point to a measurable change in behavior and/or action that is linked to health status. Two such examples will be examined here, one focusing on behavioral change communications at the individual level and the second on treatment practice for individual and public health.

The PANACeA network supported a project in Indonesia, Pakistan and the Philippines on the use of eHealth to improve safe motherhood promotion. The project, "Community-based eHealth Promotion for Safe Motherhood: Linking Community Maternal Health Needs with Health Services System," examined the effectiveness of using SMS (short message service) messages for behavioral change communication for safe motherhood promotion (SMP). Using a case-control study design, the study examined the changes in behavior when comparing a group that received SMP text messages on their mobile phones with others that did not. The study arm in Pakistan was carried out in the Mardan district in the province of Khyber Pakhtonkhwa – an area of 1.9 million where 44.4 percent of births are attended by a trained health worker (PAIMAN 2009). Lady health workers (LHWs) were trained to use Java-enabled mobile phones to send messages to the 433 women in the intervention group (375 women were in the control group). Analyzing the data collected over 18 months revealed an increase in deliveries at health facilities from 35 percent to 55 percent among the intervention group and a significantly smaller increase in facility-based deliveries for those in the control group (from 38 percent to 40 percent). Data collected for antenatal care (ANC) visits demonstrated similar patterns. Among the intervention cases, there was an increase from 65 percent to 73 percent of women attending at least one ANC visit (a decrease from 68 percent to 63 percent was found among the control group) (Khoja et al. 2012). Quantitative and qualitative analysis showed an increase in contact with health providers, increases in ANC visits and a greater number of deliveries at health facilities for those in the intervention group relative to the control group.

Building on the evidence and process outcomes generated in the Free State ART project in South Africa, the results also influenced health status outcomes. Specifically, by bringing to light the high mortality rate among people awaiting treatment, the project contributed to the decision at the provincial level to explore alternative ART delivery strategies.

The impact of this decision was felt at the level of individuals, families and communities. The use of nurse-initiated ART in the STRETCH (Streamlining Tasks and Roles to Expand Treatment and Care for HIV) system of training and support[16] is an example of an alternative delivery strategy. This project was among the first that was able to demonstrate that adherence of HIV-positive individuals to ART in LMICs could lead to controlling the HIV virus, essentially reorienting the disease from an acute illness to a chronic one. The use of ICT innovations in the project – notably mobile handheld devices – served as the rationale for starting a consortium for mobile-based applications for healthcare. This experience sowed the seed for the OpenRosa consortium of mHealth software that forms the JavaRosa code base. JavaRosa, a product of the OpenRosa consortium, is a FOSS platform for mobile device-based data collection and exchange. Several leading mobile phone-based eHealth applications draw from the code base and also contribute back to it. This unintended outcome of the research project in the Free State province of South Africa contributed to a strong development outcome related to strengthening networks, collaboration and ownership of mobile device-based software that is used to collect and share health data in LMICs.

The findings and health outcomes described in this section are closely linked to research for development outcomes. In addition to networks and networking practices to convene and mobilize efforts – illustrated through the OpenRosa example – other research for development outcomes include strengthening a wide range of individual and organizational capacities to design, implement and communicate research, as well as influencing practices and policies.

Research for development outcomes

The focus of IDRC work is on research *for* development, as opposed to research *on* development. The distinction is a subtle one, but one that is important to make. The term "research on development" can be construed as somewhat extractive, with limited involvement and even less ownership of the communities meant to be the beneficiaries. In contrast, the term "research for development" is focused more on working alongside researchers living in the beneficiary countries and communities. These researchers drive the process and benefit from demand-driven support to facilitate the strengthening of their capacities, the influence of their networks and the intended contributions to policy and practice. In this section, three areas – networks and networking, capacity development and influencing policy – will be discussed vis-à-vis the outcomes achieved.

Networks and networking

IDRC's eHealth programming has often approached its support of research projects in a networked modality. IDRC's "Corporate Strategy and Program Framework 2005–2010" suggests that the network modality, "when properly executed, is an efficient way to transmit knowledge across a wide range of groups or regions."[17] IDRC's network approach to programming does not generally involve creating new organizations. It aims to work with existing organizations and to strengthen weak institutions (Earl 2004). However, in certain cases, IDRC responds to the need to support the creation of organizations that fill a clear niche and have a sound business model. For example, in the first phase of OASIS, the scope of the project outgrew the organization hosting it. As a result, an NGO (Jembi Health Systems) was formed from OASIS with non-monetary support from IDRC. The first phase of OASIS was managed by the Medical Research Council in South Africa, which continues to work closely with Jembi. Today, Jembi is a thriving South African NGO that seeks to improve global health through advances in health information systems.[18]

A strong contribution from IDRC to eHealth research comes from its support for networks and community building (Mechael 2011). This includes supporting communities of practice such as the OpenMRS Implementers Network and the OpenRosa Developers Network. According to Bates and Wright in their 2009 article "Evaluating eHealth", when a critical mass of participants in a community works collectively on a solution, there is a higher likelihood that a successful and relevant solution will emerge, especially in an open source environment. They go on to note that a global interchange can lead to significant economies of scale, as the cost of adapting and customizing software is far lower than developing it from scratch. The OpenMRS community is a strong example of this.

IDRC has provided support for LMIC-based participants to attend OpenMRS meetings as a forum for capacity development, knowledge sharing and networking among developers, implementers and users of OpenMRS and other FOSS-based electronic medical records (EMRs).[19] OpenMRS comprises a core web application that allows for the management of basic patient and clinical encounters, to which additional functionality can be added by installing optional modules. Implementers[20] configure and implement the system while developers[21] in different countries can customize the EMR by independently adding their own functionality without having to make changes to the main application; they can also share and collaborate on such modules (Seymour et al. 2010). The main aspect of OpenMRS supported by IDRC was the community development aspect that has been instrumental in making OpenMRS almost certainly the largest community developed and maintained open source health application in the world (Seebregts et al. 2009, 2010). As of 2010, OpenMRS had been implemented in at least twenty countries and was supporting the care of more than one million patients, more than a hundred thousand of whom were HIV/AIDS patients receiving anti-retroviral treatment (Seymour et al. 2010). Thus, OpenMRS is an example of a project that has not only developed functionally appropriate ICTs for the context in which it is being implemented, but has also helped build the competencies required for local staff to maximize the system's functionality. In 2011–12, OpenMRS Ltd was registered as an NGO. It has grown into a large grassroots open source community with over four hundred contributing participants and implementations hosted in over forty-two countries around the world.

IDRC has also supported eHealth research networks such as PANACeA, OASIS and eSAC (Public eHealth Innovation and Equity in Latin America and the Caribbean), to name a few. In her 2011 report, *Evaluation of IDRC-Supported eHealth Projects*, Mechael asserts that "IDRC's support for the PANACeA research network has led to the development of an emerging community of supportive and motivated eHealth researchers. [...] There [is] a strong feeling that the community part of the PANACeA network would lead the dialogue on eHealth policy in the region." In the case of OASIS, IDRC is supporting research across existing projects and contributing to generalizable enterprise architecture (EA) frameworks, capacity development practices and policy influence. In the area of enterprise architecture, IDRC's support is "leading the dialogue for designing an open enterprise architecture framework for eHealth in developing countries through projects such as the Open Architecture and Standards Information System (OASIS)" (Mechael 2011). The eSAC research network[22] in the LAC region is supporting a fertile environment for innovation through the use of an integrated approach. This includes examining incentives, facilitating networking among practitioners and policymakers and developing a cadre of young professionals in the region to act as knowledgeable and networked ambassadors for issues at the confluence of public health, health equity, social determinants of health and innovation.[23]

Contributions by IDRC-supported research studies to networks and networking in the field of eHealth include seeding innovative network approaches that were based on previous evidence. The OpenRosa network emerged from findings in the Free State ART project. Specifically, there was obvious need for exchange and coherence among mobile devices used in health. The foresight of such a network is evident as it continues to be the largest and most widely respected mobile health repository of code and forum of exchange. Networks such as OpenMRS exemplify the central importance of developing a community from which to build, implement and use software that is grounded, relevant, effective and affordable. There have been different releases of the OpenMRS software over the years. What has remained unchanged during this process is a deep commitment to local ownership, capacity development and dialogue and debate about health data and how it is used to improve health processes and status outcomes. The different types of research networks supported by IDRC, which have responded to felt needs, demonstrate how working with peers toward goals can help contribute to greater clarity, leverage innovative modes of working, stimulate much-needed debate and strengthen individual and collective capacities.

Capacity development

A central objective of IDRC is "to assist the developing regions to build up the research capabilities, the innovative skills and the institutions required to solve their problems" (IDRC Act 1970). Capacity development can be defined as the process by which individuals, groups, organizations, institutions and societies increase their ability to identify and analyze development challenges and to conceive, conduct, manage and communicate research that addresses these challenges over time and in a sustainable manner (Taylor and Ortiz 2008). IDRC support of eHealth research projects includes strengthening organizational capacity, human resources capacity and researcher and stakeholder capacity to use eHealth and to carry out rigorous and useful eHealth research studies (Mechael 2011). The formative evaluation study highlights three main types of capacity development activities supported by IDRC: developing the capacity of in-country specialists to conduct quality eHealth, health information system (HIS) and mobile technology research; developing the capacity of in-country specialists to design, develop, program and maintain eHealth (including mobile-based) devices and software; and using eHealth technology to improve the knowledge and skills of front-line health providers and educators.

In keeping with IDRC's strong emphasis on research capacity development, every eHealth study supported by IDRC addressed this form of capacity development outcome. The 12-country PANACeA research network in Asia, described earlier in this chapter, is a powerful embodiment of this outcome. Results from a utilization-focused evaluation of PANACeA indicate that the different network members achieved the following (Sajwani et al. 2011):

- Developed their capacity in designing research studies
- Improved their readiness for conducting independent eHealth projects through mentorship activities, courses, workshops and training sessions
- Benefitted from opportunities for collective learning and sharing
- Acquired new skills to develop communication plans, as well as monitor and evaluate indicators
- Strengthened their ability to formalize, reflect and disseminate research results and lessons learnt

Members of the PANACeA network have already produced peer-reviewed publications and conference papers, with more expected in the near future (http://panacea-lr.eu/en/project/publications/ [accessed 15 March 2012]).

The OASIS network and the Health Enterprise Architecture Lab (HEAL), both focused on Sub-Saharan Africa, are examples of in-country specialists designing, developing, programming and maintaining eHealth devices and software. The first phase of the OASIS network (2007–2009) was designed to develop capacities through open approaches to improving access to eHealth in Mozambique, Zimbabwe and South Africa.[24] Specifically, this involved establishing OASIS nodes at national universities in each of the three countries and providing theoretical and hands-on, in-country capacity development and training to the OASIS node members. The result of this model allowed members to respond to local eHealth design and implementation needs, including, but not limited to, those of the Ministry of Health.

The second phase of OASIS (2009–12) continues to be based on open principles, data standards and interoperability (see Box 7.1). The project's aim is to gather evidence on how to move away from information silos organized vertically by disease and toward an interoperable system in which data are made securely available to individuals and organizations within the health system (including care providers and public health officials) through common enterprise architecture.[25] (See Box 7.3.) In addition to the OASIS nodes, which continue to deepen the local capacities to design, implement and provide training on eHealth solutions, OASIS Phase II also includes a dedicated project to strengthen health informatics capacity in Rwanda, "eHealth: Software Development and Implementation (EHSDI)." Moreover, OASIS II included capacity building components that strengthened a network of eHealth specialists working with the Millennium Villages Project across different countries in Sub-Saharan Africa. It also nurtured a network of community health workers in Tanzania working with mHealth tools to improve health processes and outcomes related to maternal and newborn health (MNCH).

The EHSDI training program has provided support to two cohorts of students to complete a nine-month program.[26] Ten Rwandan students completed the first training program and, after their graduation in October 2009, were matched with jobs in

---

Box 7.3. Enterprise architecture

How does one plan a health system? What are the different components and how do they interact with one another? Similar to how a building would need a "blueprint" to allow the architects, plumbers, electricians and contractors to understand how it is built and functions, the role of enterprise architecture (EA) is to illustrate a health system by showing the component subsystems as well as the relationships among them. Understanding these relationships and how they contribute to broader goals of improving health is central to strengthening health systems. This allows information systems to be less fragmented and work more effectively in a well-designed and harmonized environment.

---

the Rwandan Ministry of Health (MoH), the Clinton Foundation and the Rwanda Development Board – Information Technology. Most of the students are now working for the MoH and are currently developing modules for OpenMRS and supporting preparations for a national rollout (Fraser and Seymour 2010). As initially intended, the second course has drawn from Rwandan expertise to build a team of mentors for the new cohort of students. While these students were being trained, other IDRC-supported eHealth projects in Rwanda were examining the use of ICTs for continuing medical education for nurses, as well as exploring a national health enterprise architecture framework (HEAF). Focusing on building capacities in parallel with applied research in Rwanda represents awareness of and attention placed on different parts of the system, which is required for sustained, locally-driven and appropriate eHealth systems in the country.

HEAL[27] places capacity development at the core of its mandate. HEAL was established at the School of Computer Science at University of KwaZulu-Natal in South Africa to support researchers working on health enterprise architectures (see Box 7.3) for developing African countries. This project helps to fill a gap in the current implementation landscape by creating a relatively neutral space in Africa to continuously reflect on and innovate architectures and technologies for African HIS (Moodley et al. 2012). It aims to develop and curate a repository of expertise, knowledge and human capabilities that contribute to the EA-related challenges and opportunities in low-resource contexts. HEAL presented the first round of awards to graduate students in computer science with a specialization in health informatics. Graduate students working at HEAL focus their projects on relevant eHealth work underway in the region. For example, the national-level enterprise architecture project in Rwanda (as part of OASIS II) is serving as a real life example for the HEAL students. Initial results include the analysis and design of an Open Health Information Mediator (OpenHIM) for the Rwandan Health Information Exchange (HIE) by a HEAL student (Crichton et al. 2012). The HIE has initially been applied to improve interoperability among systems for maternal and child health in the Rwamagana district of Rwanda. However, the OpenHIM not only enables interoperability among existing health information systems in Rwanda but can be gradually expanded to incorporate new systems as the Rwandan eHealth rollout progresses. A fundamental feature of OpenHIM is its generic design and next steps include exploring its potential for deployment in other domains of healthcare in Rwanda and other African countries.

A number of different projects supported by IDRC over the years have focused on improving the knowledge and skills of front-line health workers with the use of ICTs (including mobile devices). The two-way electronic communication system known as the Uganda Health Information Network (UHIN) is an example of an IDRC-supported project. It began as a pilot in the early 2000s and was implemented in multiple districts. The project demonstrated significant improvements in how information was used by the rural health districts to deliver healthcare services more efficiently to the community members (AED-Satellife 2008, 5–6). The UHIN project was conceived in response to a dearth of current health and medical information among public healthcare providers, especially in rural districts, as well as a lack of timely communication of information necessary to plan for the healthcare needs of rural residents. From 2003 to 2010, IDRC supported the project through funding and other capacity building initiatives, including training in evaluation. In 2010, IDRC facilitated the transfer of UHIN to the Ugandan Ministry of Health.

Like many other countries, Uganda in the 1990s had envisaged health reforms that would shift the focus of care toward primary healthcare, with the main responsibility for health service delivery falling to districts and subdistricts. In the following decade, the Ugandan government stated its desire to integrate ICTs in healthcare delivery. In Uganda's second national health policy, one of the strategies for strengthening the organization and management of national health systems is to plan, design and install ICT infrastructure and software for the management and delivery of care (Ministry of Health 2010, 15).

In light of this decentralized healthcare structure and the circumstances highlighted above, the impetus for the UHIN project came from reported inadequacies of the paper-based reporting system used by the Ministry of Health, especially data loss, variable data quality due to transcription errors and slow transmission of clinical information to those who required it for planning purposes. With respect to the continuing education of healthcare providers, it was reported that there was limited access to relevant and timely health information, particularly in rural areas, due to a lack of libraries and limited or no access to telephones, fax machines and the Internet. All of these challenges presented an opportunity for UHIN to make relevant and up-to-date health and medical information available electronically to health practitioners in rural Uganda and to facilitate communication between rural health centers and the Ministry of Health for the purpose of reporting more quickly on various facets of healthcare delivery.

Strengthening capacities is a fundamental component of research for development. Responding to capacity needs – be they at the level of research design and implementation or at the level of organizational practices, facilitating brokering of relationships with key stakeholders or through the provision of technical assistance within a project – supports a process of change that is essential to address the complex nature of researching eHealth within health systems. Developing local capacities through providing continuing medical education, formal training of graduate students or by collective learning and publication of findings can serve as an effective means to buttress continuous local learning, reflection and improvement.

Influencing policy

Influencing change in policy is a non-linear process that can be shaped by a range of factors. A lack of an enabling policy environment for eHealth policy change was brought up repeatedly in the lessons-learned workshops carried out as part of the formative eHealth evaluation study that was completed in 2011. Specifically, several respondents noted the challenge of securing government participation and commitment for continued presence and appropriation (Mechael 2011). In this section, policy influence will be discussed at the different levels of influence – local, national, regional and international.

Local level: Health planning and service delivery in the Philippines is decentralized to the level of municipalities, meaning that decisions to invest in health systems are influenced at the local level. The growing use of the Community Health Information Tracking System (CHITS) in different cities and provinces of the Philippines is an excellent example of local policy influence that has received international recognition and acclaim. CHITS is an open source electronic medical records (EMR) system that was initially supported by IDRC as part of the Pan R&D grants program. It works at the primary healthcare level to integrate the tracking of national disease-specific health programs at the community level (Tolentino et al. 2005). CHITS was designed in collaboration with the staff at the Lagrosa Health Center, Pasay City, where it was first deployed in 2004 and is still used today. Two years after its initial deployment, CHITS was chosen as one of the leading projects by the Asia Pacific Economic Digital Opportunity Center in Taiwan and was also a finalist in the Stockholm Challenge, a competition of ICT applications for people and society. Capacity building of government health staff is central objective of CHITS (Fernandez-Marcelo et al. n.d.). Specifically, CHITS introduces and strengthens ICT skills for health and deepens the appreciation for better quality data to serve the public, notably the poor. As of June 2011, CHITS has been deployed in 50 rural health units in the Philippines.

The successful implementation of an epidemiological monitoring and surveillance system for the Chagas disease in selected municipalities in Argentina and Bolivia was directly linked with support the project received from the local Ministries of Health and Science and Technology (Cravero et al. 2011). The tracking system was incorporated into the HIS of ministries of health from the participating municipalities. As well, the Health Ministry of Cordoba and the Hospital de la Rioja (Argentina) have expressed interest in adapting the ICT applications developed for this project (both mobile and web software for data collection) to respond to the Dengue epidemic affecting the region. This interest in the adaptation and use of the Chagas surveillance model to respond to other diseases demonstrates the positive influence that the project is generating at both the local and national levels (Cravero et al. 2011).

National level: At the national level, IDRC-supported research has been influential in a number of countries, such as Mozambique, Peru and Uganda. In some cases, successful results during project implementation can lead to endorsement and even direct support from ministries of health at the national level. Ministerial support through formal agreements, as in the case of Peru and Mozambique, can strengthen project outreach and impact. The M-OASIS project has an agreement with the Ministry of Health (MoH) in Mozambique in which M-OASIS develops software and systems on behalf of the MoH. This agreement was reached as a result of successful implementation of the SIS-ROH mortality registration application; it also formed the basis for subsequent grants from bilateral donors and WHO.

In Peru, a framework agreement between the MoH and the Institute of Education and Health (IES) (an IDRC grantee for the Punto J project) was agreed upon and has been submitted to the General Directorate of People's Health within the MoH for final approval. Punto J is a project that developed a youth-to-youth participatory approach to produce and disseminate online information and social media to tackle HIV/AIDS prevention and to raise awareness of sexual and reproductive rights among young people in Latin America and the Caribbean. The aim of the agreement between MoH Peru and IES is to set the general conditions for mutual cooperation and exchange between the MoH and the IES to promote the overall health of adolescents and young people, contributing to improving their quality of life and promoting their full development. This agreement is the result of a close collaboration between the MoH and the IES throughout the implementation of the Punto J project. The MoH participated as sponsors in all project-related events and is promoting the Punto J web portal within the ministry itself and even internationally (Hidalgo et al. 2010).

In Uganda, the UHIN implementing partners worked in consultation with the Ministry of Health to convert patient registers[28] to electronic forms that could be transmitted more expeditiously to higher levels of administration for processing. They also surveyed healthcare providers in the participating districts about the health topics most relevant to their patients' needs and compiled and distributed material pertinent to them on a regular basis. Policy influence is a process that requires sustained engagement with the different stakeholders. According to Mechael (2011), the UHIN project is an example of gradually changing policy. As a result, UHIN "has become a part of the country's National Health Information System Strengthening Team to inform policy on eHealth." It also "influenced the MoH to hire staff focused on developing eLearning materials" (Mechael 2011).

Regional level: The Punto J project was also able to achieve policy influence at the regional level. Originally established as a pilot project in Peru beginning in 2005, five countries in the region (Argentina, Bolivia, Ecuador, Mexico and the Dominican Republic) by 2010 had adopted the strategy that included the creation of a regional network and web portal featuring the communication products of all the countries[29] (Hidalgo et al. 2010). Government officials in Argentina, Mexico, Bolivia and Peru supported the project implementation, recognizing the importance of the participation of young people and the social use of ICTs in promoting healthy sexualities and HIV/AIDS prevention.

International level: At the international level, IDRC-supported researchers and research organizations are central to discussions and implementations on EA and data standards.

Specifically, IDRC's early investment in OASIS (beginning in 2007), the formation of Jembi and the reference implementation of EA in Rwanda as part of OASIS II have contributed considerably to the body of experts from LMICs on matters of EA. Beyond helping to strengthen the body of respected researchers and research findings, early results from these projects have helped mobilize funding from many funders. For example, the success of the Free State ART project in resistance genotyping[30] led to a grant from the European Union that will help the research partners implement a WHO-recommended drug resistance surveillance program. Other examples include attracting myriad different funders in Mozambique to fund M-OASIS work due to the success demonstrated with projects like SIS-ROH, among others.

IDRC has also sponsored research on data privacy and security in eHealth, research that can have implications on an international level. A recent IDRC-supported study examining this issue in developing countries brought to light several areas of research that should be considered in future eHealth projects. The final report indicated that "any 'solutions' to medical privacy or health information security in these contexts will need to incorporate both technological means such as directed identifiers, access controls and encryption, as well as appropriate organizational, legal and policy responses" (Hosein and Martin 2010). This IDRC-supported study was extensively cited in a 2012 WHO report, "Legal Frameworks for eHealth."[31] For instance, key findings from this report were cited in the WHO report, including the fact that many LMICs are unequipped to address basic needs for patient privacy and this is in contexts where it is most needed. The WHO report uses evidence from the study to highlight appropriate legislation and privacy systems as core pillars of good eHealth practices.

The different examples of influencing policy process and outcomes at local, national, regional and international levels point to the longevity of IDRC's support in the field of eHealth research in LMICs, as well as the non-linear path and unpredictable amount of time this type of influence can take. Recognizing that policy change is complex, dynamic and, at times, erratic, sound research for development outcomes highlights the hard work done by researchers to broaden policy horizons, expand policy capacities and affect policy regimes in their respective contexts (Carden 2010).

Contributions to Strengthening the Field of eHealth Research

The collection of health outcomes and research for development outcomes discussed in previous sections can be seen as contributing to strengthening the field of eHealth research in LMICs (as shown in Figure 7.3). The emphasis on a LMIC perspective is an important distinction as there as a relatively large body of literature on eHealth in well-resourced contexts, mostly in Europe and North America. Although some of these findings can be relevant for resource-constrained LMICs, they cannot replace the value of much-needed research from a LMIC perspective. Research conducted by LMIC-based researchers and research organizations has arguably much stronger value given the complexities of health systems, policies in health, ICT and other relevant domains and the careful process of change that needs to be managed and fit the purpose.

Discussing a field in this context should not be perceived as a rigid classification. Fields and field building are complex concepts and, not surprisingly, not accompanied by precise definitions (Fine 2001; Bernholzetal 2009; Hay 2010). The approach in this section focuses on some key attributes or characteristics of fields and field building – specifically, with a focus on the field as defined and strengthened in a LMIC context. The attributes to be examined include research and knowledge contributions, leaders and mentors, strengthening individuals and organizations, supporting spaces and forums and mobilization of resources.

Research and knowledge

Contributions toward bolstering the body of evidence and knowledge in eHealth research in LMICs are arguably among the strongest made by IDRC toward strengthening this field. Of the respondents to the IDRC eHealth evaluation study (Mechael 2011), 44 percent of grantees published one to two manuscripts in open access (OA) peer-reviewed academic journals; 44 percent published one to four manuscripts in non-OA, peer-reviewed journals; and 11 percent published one manuscript in non-OA, non-peer-reviewed journals. Ninety-nine percent of respondents indicated that they had presented at least once at a regional conference. Beyond the contributions, the availability of the resources through open access journals is a noteworthy attribute of a growing number of publications supported by IDRC. IDRC is a strong proponent of OA publishing and encourages researchers to publish in high-impact OA journals as much as possible.

Leaders and mentors

Over the years, IDRC has had the distinct opportunity to support researchers from their first foray into the world of eHealth research and to witness their growth into national and international leaders in the field. One such example is Dr Alvin Marcelo from the Philippines, who has been an IDRC research partner since 2004. Beginning with a small grant for the CHITS project, Dr Marcelo continued his research activities with IDRC through the international open source network (IOSN) and the PANACeA eHealth research network. He has produced an impressive number of publications in peer-reviewed journals, conferences, blogs and newspaper articles over the years. As of late 2011, he assumed the position of chief information officer of PhilHealth, the national health insurance organization of the Philippines. It is expected that Dr Marcelo's deep knowledge of the health system in the Philippines, field experience across the country and across the region, sound understanding of interoperability and enterprise architecture, and strong capacities in understanding the social, economic and political aspects of eHealth will serve him well in his new position.

Another strong example of leadership is shown by Dr Chris Seebregts. As early as 2004, Dr Seebregts was carrying out IDRC-supported research studies. Since his work on the ART project in the Free State, he has served as project leader in OASIS Phase I, Open Source Digital Assistant Software for Health Data Collection (the precursor to OpenRosa), OASIS II and then as co-principal investigator for HEAL, which began in 2011.

Throughout the years of leading research projects supported by IDRC, Dr. Seebregts has delivered increasing numbers of presentations, authored many publications (several of which are peer-reviewed) and nurtured future leaders in the field of eHealth. The role of mentorship is critical to foster future leaders. As a network, OASIS II has maintained an implicit focus on mentorship.

The PANACeA project included a dedicated mentorship component in the network structure, an advisory and mentoring/monitoring team (AMT). Each AMT member was assigned one to two projects to provide regular mentoring and facilitation and to provide demand-driven technical assistance to carry out the eHealth research projects. This also involved field visits and working with the researchers during face-to-face workshops. According to an evaluation study done of the network, the network membership indicated that the mentorship model was a strong component in how it was designed and implemented (Sajwani et al. 2011).

A new generation of leaders in the field are being groomed within the eSAC project. Five researchers and practitioners – referred to as young professionals (YPs) in the project – are being trained on issues that fall at the intersection of public health, health equity and eHealth. These YPs, based in the region and each corresponding to one of five subregions, build on their existing experience and expertise through targeted and interactive training sessions. These individuals are to act as ambassadors in the region and are mandated to initiate and nurture discussions through social media and through face-to-face interactions.[32]

Strengthening individuals and organizations

It is difficult for a field to flourish without informed, passionate and skilled individuals and organizations. As part of IDRC's capacity-strengthening mandate, a number of specific examples can be shared as they pertain to strengthening individuals and organizations in the field of eHealth in LMICs. For example, the UHIN project in Uganda trained over seven hundred health workers in five districts on use of ICTs. In Rwanda, the EHSDI project trained several Rwandans in computer science and health informatics so they could form a strong foundation of skilled local resources to address the eHealth demands in the country. The HEAL project is positioned to train graduate-level students (masters and doctoral level) in computer science with a focus on enterprise architecture. Based at an African higher education institution, this skill set is of paramount importance in addressing the need for local institutions to build strong local capacities that can strengthen health systems. At the organizational level, the South African NGO Jembi Health Systems provides an excellent example of how solid in-country organizational capacity can help coordinate different efforts to deliver similar services in a way that provides continuity and opportunities for ongoing growth for the staff. Jembi focuses on eHealth interventions with systems-level impact and has successfully leveraged grants totaling several million dollars to date. The OASIS node in Mozambique is an entirely Mozambican institution and is a strong example of eHealth capacity building in low-resource settings. The M-OASIS example demonstrates how an innovative business model and a strong focus on delivering results can allow the institution to work closely with different stakeholders such as the Ministry of

Health and other government departments, the Universidad Eduardo Mondlane, different donors and several implementing partners. In response to the significant work being done by Jembi and local staff in Rwanda, a Jembi office in Kigali, Rwanda was officially opened March 2012.

Supporting spaces and forums

The presence of forums and spaces to discuss and debate an emerging discipline is a central component of a strong field of study. This is an area that has matured significantly from the time when IDRC began its eHealth investments. There are now a number of new organizations, alliances, networks and conferences in the field of eHealth, even in the field of eHealth in LMICs. It would be foolish to suggest a simple count metric indicates high-quality discussions or fruitful collaborations and action. However, it does show a growing awareness of the role that eHealth plays in health systems. With continued focus on strengthening the field of LMIC eHealth researchers and research evidence, one can expect steady movement toward more informed debates, grounded analysis and aligned efforts with local and national health priorities.

Funding provided to support LMIC community participation at the OpenMRS implementers meetings enabled African (in large part) and other LMIC representatives to attend meetings and to forge face-to-face relationships that have since strengthened over the active OpenMRS listserv and other online spaces for exchange and growth. According to Mechael (2011), the OpenMRS community of practice is an example of a model that has advanced the development and adoption of a FOSS application relevant to low-resource contexts. Networks such as OpenMRS for EMRs and OpenRosa for mobile device software development continue to thrive and have become sustainable due to the intellectual input and unrelenting enthusiasm of the membership. Other donors continue to fund them alongside IDRC.

Mobilization of resources

With IDRC as an early investor in eHealth research in LMICs, several IDRC-supported researchers have been able to demonstrate early results and have thus garnered trust and respect from other donors wishing to support eHealth projects in Asia, Africa and the LAC regions. The formative evaluation study by Mechael (2011) indicates that IDRC projects have mobilized over CDN $7.3 million in funding from other donors, including the PEPFAR, CDC, the European Union and the Rockefeller Foundation. Beyond the dollar figures, IDRC acts as a broker of knowledge and relationships. This role has facilitated conversations between researchers and prospective donors at opportune moments.

Contributions made by IDRC-supported projects to the field of eHealth in LMICs should not be seen as the end goal. There remains a great deal to be researched in the field of eHealth. However, given the maturity of the field and its growing recognition among policymakers, public health professionals, economists, software and hardware industry bodies, sociologists and global health researchers alike, there is an opportunity to forge ahead in strengthening eHealth research as a critical component of health systems research. The use of appropriate frameworks, methodologies and paradigms from a range of different disciplines working on eHealth can serve only to strengthen and enrich the endeavor.

Future of eHealth Research Support at IDRC

Research and researchers supported by IDRC "have been instrumental in catalyzing critical pathways within eHealth" (Mechael 2011, 9). As IDRC continues funding research on eHealth as part of its "Governance for Equity in Health Systems" (GEHS) program, it plans to support contributions that strengthen the field of eHealth research and to make the implicit links to central considerations such as health equity, health governance and health systems strengthening more systematic and explicit. This type of analysis will help break down perceived and/or actual silos that exist between the world of eHealth research and that of health policy and systems strengthening research.

As ICTs become increasingly embedded in health systems, it becomes exceedingly important to explore and understand how eHealth is shaping the health system and the values and norms it embodies. However, data by themselves will not transform outcomes; neither will information or analysis. Instead, a combined and context-specific examination of power relations, capabilities, governance structures, social mobilization and collaboration will shed light on the linkages between eHealth policy and practice and changes in health outcomes, services and systems. Health systems have context-specific norms and social values embedded in them, which can sometimes sustain suboptimal practices that contribute to health inequities (Gilson et al. 2007); such is also the case for the use of eHealth within health systems. Continuing to support eHealth initiatives without considering health equity, governance processes and systems integration can contribute to worsening inequities, asymmetrical power dynamics and suboptimal health system outcomes.

Supporting research on how ICTs are used by different actors within health systems is of critical importance because it allows exploration into how existing and emerging social and structural determinants of health can influence eHealth implementations and resultant health outcomes. Researching the role of eHealth with respect to timely, accurate and reliable analysis across different districts, health functions and public service sectors is proving extremely relevant given the growing recognition of the interdependencies among different systems and sectors (de Savigny and Adam 2009). If these systems are not appropriately designed and validated, they could lead to fragmentation, multiple data sources and parallel systems not adhering to common standards and practices (Braa et al. 2007). Recognizing the realities of resource scarcity and complex interdependencies within and among health systems, examination of eHealth efforts requires political, social and economic analyses just as much as technically oriented ones.

IDRC's continued support of research on eHealth includes a project entitled "Strengthening Equity through Applied Research Capacity Building in eHealth (SEARCH)." This five-year project involves consultative processes with researchers living and working in LMICs to inform the trajectory of the research agenda, as well as the activities it can support to deepen the evidence base for eHealth and health systems research. The geographic scope for SEARCH stretches across the three regions where IDRC's eHealth research had been supported to date. The premise of SEARCH is based on the realization that the use of eHealth should not be seen as an end in and of itself. Research on eHealth should focus on understanding how to enhance its application to reduce inequities and help avert situations in which the use of eHealth can exacerbate inequities. The SEARCH vision, which was collectively crafted as part of a consultative process, is "to maximize and accelerate the transformational potential of eHealth to promote and strengthen equity in health systems that are more dynamic, participatory and responsive in addressing equitable power distribution, decision making, allocation and use of health information and resources." All research activities supported by SEARCH will focus on health inequities and embrace a health systems perspective.

Conclusion

The trajectory of IDRC's research support for eHealth in LMICs has evolved over the years in response to pressing health priorities, shifting policy contexts and changes in technological and social innovations. Along the way, this support has enabled researchers to generate and share knowledge about eHealth from a LMIC perspective, nurture networks of vibrant and insightful exchanges, cultivate leaders in the field and mobilize interest and resources to carry forward their research agenda toward improved health outcomes and strengthened health systems. This overview of some of these experiences, lessons and outcomes to date from IDRC-supported projects is intended to provide a snapshot of a handful of experiences in the field of eHealth in LMICs. This snapshot is meant to simultaneously depict the complexities of researching the use of eHealth in health systems, as well as highlight some significant accomplishments over many years that could contribute to the work of others in the growing field of eHealth in LMICs.

As eHealth research continues to be supported, there is much to be gained from methodological innovations that adopt a health systems approach. Today, the use of eHealth in health systems demonstrates the multiplier effect through, among other examples, the rapid increases in mobile phones and thriving communities of innovative health and ICT practitioners. The spread of these phenomena necessitates a strong focus on research that explores the different system-wide implications of eHealth. At IDRC, the trajectory of eHealth research support in the future will build on the strong past achievements and will continue supporting efforts that examine matters of health equity, governance processes and systems integration.

IDRC's "research for development" approach in the health sector supported the start-up of important individual ICT innovations in the healthcare systems of a wide range of countries. Over time and with patient, committed and networked support, it helped contribute substantially to field building in this demanding and fast changing domain of inquiry.

Notes

1 We are deeply indebted to the IDRC-supported researchers who have designed and carried out studies that have strengthened the field of eHealth research in low- and middle-income countries. These findings form the foundation of this chapter. We would like to acknowledge Patty Mecheal and her team for their work on a formative eHealth evaluation study for IDRC, Katie Bryant for her guidance during the writing process and Jennifer Vincent for her initial contributions to the chapter. We are grateful to Antoine Geissebuhler, Shariq Khoja, Alex Jadad, Alvin Marcelo, Portia Fernandez-Marcelo, Deshen Moodley and Christopher Seebregts for their thoughtful comments on the chapter.

2 http://www.who.int/topics/eHealth/en/ (accessed 1 March 2012).

3 According to Eysenback (2001, e20), eHealth is "an emerging field in the intersection of medical informatics, public health and business, referring to health services and information delivered or enhanced through the Internet and related technologies. In a broader sense, the term characterizes not only a technical development, but also a state-of-mind, a way of thinking, an attitude, and a commitment for networked, global thinking, to improve health care locally, regionally, and worldwide by using information and communication technology."

4 http://www.itu.int/ITU-D/ict/facts/2011/material/ICTFactsFigures2011.pdf (accessed 1 March 2012).

5 Smart pills can be defined in a number of ways. The sense of the term in this context is a pill that, once swallowed, can transmit data to the patient or care provider. More information about smart pills can be found at http://www.economist.com/node/15276730 (accessed 15 March 2012). A subcutaneous chip is a chip embedded beneath the skin.

6 Adapted from IDRC's outcome mapping definition. See http://www.idrc.ca/en/ev-26586-201-1-DO_TOPIC.html (accessed 4 April 2012).

7 Emphasis in the original.

8 Arua, Oyam, Nakasongola, Hoima, Kyengegwa, Mpigi, Ntungamo, Manafwa, Tororo and Masindi.

9 Interoperability, defined in Box 7.1, is discussed later in the chapter.

10 A data warehouse is a database used to store structured data that can be analyzed and used for reporting purposes.

11 This was the first time a national death register was used to evaluate survival in a Sub-Saharan African cohort. This linkage proved important because as many as eighty percent of deaths were determined through linkage alone. Free State has signed an agreement with the Department of Home Affairs to obtain this information on an ongoing basis, paving the way for other provinces and researchers in South Africa.

12 Tuberculosis is an opportunistic infection. As such, for patients with active tuberculosis or other serious opportunistic infections, HAART (highly active anti-retroviral therapy) was deferred until they were clinically stable or until the intensive phase of tuberculosis treatment was completed (Fairall et al. 2008).

13 An agreement is being finalized between the province of Free State and the NHLS to obtain laboratory data – critical in formation feedback for clinicians – with a view to this serving as a template for other provinces.

14 Three central hospitals (Maputo, Beira and Nampula), seven provincial hospitals (Lichinga, Pemba, Quelimane, Tete, Chimoio, Inhambane and Xai-Xai) and four rural hospitals (José Macamo, Mavalane, Chamanculoh and Machava).

15 More information about the commission and the EWEC Global Strategy can be found at http://www.everywomaneverychild.org/resources/accountability-commission (accessed 15 July 2013).

16 For more information on this initiative, see http://www.doh.gov.za/docs/hiv/stretch/pdf (accessed 13 March 2012).

17 IDRC, "Corporate Strategy and Program Framework 2005–2010" (2004), section 5-4, paragraph 13 (http://idl-bnc.idrc.ca/dspace/bitstream/10625/26335/1/121985e.pdf [accessed 4 April 2012]).

18 Jembi Health Systems, www.jembi.org.

19 IDRC does not favor one EMR over another. The appropriateness of the EMR is what should drive any decision to adopt and adapt it to a particular community. For instance, IDRC has supported work related to OpenMRS, Community Health Information Tracking System (CHITS), TeleHealth and Health Informaics for Rural and Remote Areas (THIRRA), among others.

20 OpenMRS implementers are technical non-programmers who do not necessarily contribute to the development (Seebregts et al. 2010).

21 Developers contribute code to OpenMRS, either in the core application or modules (Seebregts et al. 2010).

22 http://new.paho.org/ict4health/index.php?option=com_content&view=category&layout=blog&id=21&Itemid=23&lang=en (accessed 15 July 2012).

23 There are five young professionals working with the eSAC project, corresponding to the five subregions – notably, Central America, the Caribbean, the Andrean region, Southern Cone and Brazil.

24 Open technologies are liberally licensed innovations that grant the right to users to use, study, change and improve the design of said technology through the availability and transparency of its source code, process, etc.

25 The ways in which health systems are currently fragmented and unable to interface and share data among the different composite information systems can be mitigated by an EA development approach (Stansfield et al. 2008). The role of such an EA in the domain of health systems is indispensable, as it acts as the conceptual scaffolding that holds together various data flows and interfaces among different elements of a national health system.

26 The first cohort of students finished an 11-month course in October 2009. The second iteration of the training has been reduced to 9 months.

27 This project is co-funded with the Rockefeller Foundation.

28 Examples include registers pertaining to child health, HIV counseling and testing, anti-retroviral therapy and antenatal care and prevention of mother-to-child transmission of HIV.

29 See web portal at www.jovenlac.com.

30 The research partners note that drug resistance is an important indicator of treatment failure and can be effectively monitored using cost-effective assays and routine blood samples.

31 http://whqlibdoc.who.int/publications/2012/9789241503134_eng.pdf (accessed 4 April 2012).

32 More information about the project can be found at http://esacproject.net/.

References

AED-SATELLIFE and Uganda Chartered Health Net. 2008. "Uganda Health Information Network (UHIN), Phase-IV: User Needs Survey."

Abbott, A. 2001. *Chaos of Disciplines*. Chicago: University of Chicago Press.

Ammenwerth, E. and N. T. Shaw. 2005. "Bad Health Informatics Can Kill – Is Evaluation the Answer?" *Methods of Information in Medicine* 44: 1–3. Online: http://iig.umit.at/dokumente/z29.pdf (accessed 24 September 2011).

Bates, D. W. and A. Wright. 2009. "Evaluating eHealth: Undertaking Robust International Cross-Cultural eHealth Research." *PLoS Medicine* 6, no. 9.

Berger, E. et al. 2007. "Implementation and Evaluation of a Web Based System for Pharmacy Stock Management in Rural Haiti." In *Proceedings of the AMIA Annual Symposium*. Bethesda: AMIA. Online: http://proceedings.amia.org/1amo9q/1amo9q/1 (accessed 13 March 2012).

Bernholz, L. et al. 2009. "Building to Last: Field Building as Philanthropic Strategy." The MacArthur Foundation Series on Field Building. Online: http://www.scribd.com/doc/26742690/Building-to-Last (accessed 25 June 2011).

Black, A. D. et al. 2011. "The Impact of eHealth on the Quality and Safety of Health Care: A Systematic Overview." *PLoS Medicine* 8, no. 1. Online: http://www.plosmedicine.org/article/info%3Adoi%2F10.1371%2Fjournal.pmed.1000387 (accessed 27 February 2012).

Braa, J. et al. 2007. "Developing Health Information Systems in Developing Countries: The Flexible Standards Strategy." *MIS Quarterly* 31, no. 2: 381–402.

Canada Health Infoway. 2011. "About *Infoway*." Online: https://www.infoway-inforoute.ca/lang-en/about-infoway (accessed 27 June 2011).

Carden, F. 2010. *Knowledge to Policy: Making the Most of Development Research*. New York: Sage Publications.

Catwell, L. and A. Sheikh. 2009. "Evaluating eHealth Interventions: The Need for Continuous Systemic Evaluation." *PLoS Medicine* 6, no. 3.

Chetley, A. et al. 2006. "Improving Health, Connecting People: The Role of ICTs in the Health Sector of Developing Countries." *info*Dev framework paper, grant no. 1254, 31 May, 1–65.

Chong, A., ed. 2011. *Development Connections: Unveiling the Impact of New Information Technologies*. New York: Palgrave Macmillan.

CIHI (Canadian Institute for Health Institute). 2008. *A Framework for Health Outcomes Analysis: Diabetes and Depression Case Studies*. Ottawa: CIHI.

Clamp, S. and J. Keen. 2007. "Electronic Health Records: Is the Evidence Base any Use?" *Medical Informatics and the Internet in Medicine* 32, no. 1: 5–10.

Cravero, C. et al. 2011. "Sistema de Vigilancia en Chagas facilitado por tecnologías de información y comunicación." *Revista de Salud Pública* 15, no. 2: 56–69. Online: http://www.saludpublica.fcm.unc.edu.ar/sites/default/files/art6_0.pdf (accessed 4 April 2012).

Crichton, R. et al. 2012. "An Interoperability Architecture for the Health Information Exchange in Rwanda." In *Proceedings of the International Symposium on Foundations of Health Information Engineering and Systems* (FHIES), August 27–8.

de Savigny, D. and T. Adam, eds. 2009. *Systems Thinking for Health Systems Strengthening*. Geneva: WHO.

Durrani, H. and S. Khoja. 2009. "A Systematic Review of the Use of Telehealth in Asian Countries." *Journal of Telemedicine and Telecare* 15, no. 4: 175–81.

Earl, S. 2004. *A Strategic Evaluation of IDRC-Support to Networks*. Ottawa: IDRC. Online: http://idl-bnc.idrc.ca/dspace/bitstream/10625/47641/1/IDL-47641.pdf (accessed 12 September 2011).

Eysenbach, G. 2001. "What Is E-Health?" *Journal of Medical Internet Research* 3, no. 2: e20.

Fairall, L. R. et al. 2008. "Effectiveness of Antiretroviral Treatment in a South African Program: A Cohort Study." *Archives of Internal Medicine* 168, no. 1: 86–93.

Fernandez-Marcelo, P. et al. n.d. "Community Health Information Tracking System (CHITS)." Center for Health Market Innovations. Online: http://healthmarketinnovations.org/sites/healthmarketinnovations.org/files/PIDS_case_study_CHITS.pdf (accessed 27 June 2011).

Fine, M. 2001. *What Does Field Building Mean for Service-Learning Advocates?* New York: Academy for Educational Development.

Fraser, H. and R. Seymour. 2010. *Capacity Building in Open Medical Record System – Rwanda*. Fourth interim report. Ottawa: IDRC.

Fraser, H. et al. 2006. "Forecasting Three Years Drug Supply for a Large MDR-TB Treatment Program in Peru." *International Journal of Tuberculosis and Lung Disease* 10, suppl. 1: S245.

Freifeld, C. C. et al. 2010. "Participatory Epidemiology: Use of Mobile Phones for Community-Based Health Reporting." *PLoS Medicine* 7, no. 12.

Geissbuhler, A. et al. 2007. "The RAFT Network: 5 Years of Distance Continuing Medical Education and Tele-consultations over the Internet in French-Speaking Africa." *International Journal of Medical Informatics* 76, nos 5–6: 351–6.

Gilson, L. 2007. *Challenging Inequity through Health Systems*. Final report, Knowledge Network on Health Systems 2007. Geneva: WHO Commission on the Social Determinants of Health.

Hay, K. 2010. "Evaluation Field Building in South Asia: Reflections, Anecdotes, and Qu
American Journal of Evaluation 31, no. 2: 222–31.

Hidalgo, C. et al. 2010. *Informe Técnico Final del Proyecto Punto JII Fase: Adolescentes, Jóvenes*
Respuesta a la Epidemia del VIH-SIDA en Latinoamérica y el Caribe (LAC). Ottawa: IDRC.

Hoppenbrouwer, J. and C. Kanyengo. 2007. "Current Access to Health Inform
Zambia: A Survey of Selected Health Institutions." *Health Information and Libraries* Jo
no. 4: 246–56.

Hosein, G. and A. Martin. 2010. "Research Note on Privacy and Security of Medical
in Developing Countries and Emergency Situations." Policy Engagement Network
Department of Management, London School of Economics. Online: http://www.l
management/documents/Medical-Privacy.pdf (accessed 2 March 2012).

International Development Research Centre Act. 1970. Online: http://www.idrc
AboutUs/WhoWeAre/Pages/IDRCAct.aspx (accessed 15 March 2012).

Istepanian, R. S. H. and J. C. Lacal. 2003. "Emerging Mobile Communication Techno
Health: Some Imperative Notes on M-Health." Presentation at the 25th Annual Inte
Conference of the IEEE, Engineering in Medicine and Biology Society in Cancun,
17–21 September.

Jan, A. et al. 2011. *Cost Benefit Analysis of Computerization in Hospitals: A Marginal Cost.* Fin
PANACeA. Ottawa: IDRC.

Khoja, S. et al. 2012. "Achieving Behaviour Change among Pregnant Mothers Usin
Phones." Presentation at Med-e-Tel Forum in Luxembourg, 18–20 April.

Marcelo, A. et al. 2009. "Online TB Diagnosis (SS-ve) to Improve Case Detection in the
Program." In *Global Telemedicine and eHealth updates: Knowledge Resources* 2, edited by M. J
and F. Lievens, 508–10. Grimbergen: International Society for Telemedicine & eHealth
_____. 2011. "An Online Method for Diagnosis of Difficult TB Cases for Developing C
Studies in Health Technology and Informatics 164: 168–73. Online: http://www.ncbi.nlm
pubmed?term=firaza%20%5bau%5d%20AND%20marcelo%20%5bau%5d (acc
March 2012).

Mechael, P. 2011. *Evaluation of IDRC-Supported eHealth Projects.* Final technical report. Ottaw

Mechael, P. et al. 2010. *Barriers and Gaps Affecting mHealth in Low and Middle Income Count*
White Paper. Center for Global Health and Economic Development. New York: T
Institute at Columbia University.

Ministry of Health, Republic of Uganda. 2010. "The Second National Health Policy: P
People's Health to Enhance Socioeconomic Development." July. Online: http://ww
org/uganda/The_Second_National_Health_Policy.pdf (accessed 27 February 2012)

Moodley, D. et al. 2012. "Position Paper: Researching and Developing Open Architec
National Health Information Systems in Developing African Countries." In *Foun*
Health Information Engineering and Systems, Lecture Notes in Computer Science 7151, edited
and A. Wassyng, 129–39. Berlin: Springer-Verlag.

National Epidemiology Center, Department of Health, Philippines. 2010. "FHSIS Annu
2010." Online: http://www.doh.gov.ph/sites/default/files/fhsis2010.pdf (accessed 27 Ju

Nishtar, S. et al. 2011. "Protecting the Poor against Health Impoverishment in Pakist
of Concept of the Potential within Innovative Web and Mobile Phone Technologie
World Health Report background paper 55. Geneva: WHO.

Oh, H. et al. 2005. "What Is eHealth? A Systematic Review of Published Definitio
Hospitals and Health Services 41, no. 1: 32–40.

Ottoson, J. M. et al. 2009. "Policy-Contribution Assessment and Field-Building Analy
Robert Wood Johnson Foundation's Active Living Research Program." *American*
Preventative Medicine 36, suppl. 2: S34–S43.

PAIMAN (Pakistan Initiative for Mothers and Newborns). 2009. *District Health Report: Distri*
2009. Lahore: PAIMAN. Online: http://paiman.jsi.com/Resources/Docs/distri
profile-mardan.pdf (accessed 15 April 2012).

Policy Engagement Network (PEN). 2010. *Electronic Health Privacy and Security in Developing Countries and Humanitarian Operations*. London: London School of Economics and Political Science. Online: http://www2.lse.ac.uk/management/documents/Electronic-Health-Privacy.pdf (accessed 1 October 2011).

Sajwani, A. et al. 2011. "PANACeA Formative Network Evaluation Report." Ottawa: IDRC. Online: http://idl-bnc.idrc.ca/dspace/handle/10625/48142 (accessed 3 March 2012).

Scott, R. and A. Saeed. 2007. *Project Planning for Regional Health and ICT Research Network PAN-Asia*. Ottawa: IDRC.

Seebregts, C. J. et al. 2009. "The Open MRS Implementers Network." *International Journal of Medical Informatics* 78, no. 11: 711–20.

_____. 2010. "Human Factors for Capacity Building: Lessons Learned from the Open MRS Implementers Network." *Yearbook of Medical Informatics* 13: 20.

Seymour, R. P. et al. 2010. "Training Software Developers for Electronic Medical Records in Rwanda." *Studies in Health Technology and Informatics* 160, pt 1: 585–9.

Sinha, C. and M. Clarke. 2010. "Lessons from Rwanda: A Systems Approach to eHealth Research in Developing Countries." *Healthcare Information Management & Communications* 24, no. 3: 76–8.

Stansfield, S. et al. 2008. "The Case for a National Health Information System Architecture: A Missing Link to Guiding National Development and Implementation." Presentation at the "Making the eHealth Connection" conference sponsored by the Rockefeller Foundation in Bellagio, Italy, 13 July–8 August. Online: http://www.ehealth-connection.org/files/confmaterials/The Case for a National Health Info System_0.pdf (accessed 17 June 2011).

Swanson, R. C. et al. 2010. "Toward a Consensus on Guiding Principles for Health Systems Strengthening. *PLoS Medicine* 7, no. 12. Online: http://www.plosmedicine.org/article/info%3Adoi%2F10.1371%2Fjournal.pmed.1000385 (accessed 27 June 2011).

Taylor, P. and A. Ortiz. 2008. *IDRC Strategic Evaluation of Capacity Development: "Doing Things Better? How Capacity Development Results Help Bring about Change"*. Ottawa: IDRC. Online: http://idl-bnc.idrc.ca/dspace/bitstream/10625/47606/1/IDL-47606.pdf (accessed 6 July 2011).

Tolentino, H. et al. 2005. "Linking Primary Care Information Systems and Public Health Information Networks: Lessons from the Philippines." *Studies in Health Technology and Informatics* 116: 995.

Vital Wave Consulting. 2009. *mHealth for Development: The Opportunity of Mobile Technology for Healthcare in the Developing World*. Washington, DC and Berkshire: UN Foundation–Vodafone Foundation Partnership.

Waidyanatha, N. 2010. *Evaluation of an Information Communication Technology Pilot in Support of Public Health in South Asia: Real-time Biosurveillance Program*. Final technical report. Ottawa: IDRC.

Wootton, R. et al. 2009. "Introduction." In *Telehealth in the Developing World*, edited by R. Wootton et al. London: Royal Society of Medicine Press and IDRC.

World Health Organization. 1998. *The WHO Health Promotion Glossary*. Geneva: WHO.

Chapter 8

MAKING THE GRADE: THE ROLE OF ICTs IN PROVIDING ACCESS TO KNOWLEDGE

Ahmed T. Rashid, Alioune Camara, Maria Ng and Alicia Richero

Education plays an important role in development. Basic education is at the core of national strategies aimed at enhancing human development, social and political empowerment and economic progress. The recognition of the value of education is clearly reflected in the second goal of the UN Millennium Development Goals, which aims to achieve universal primary education for children everywhere, boys and girls alike, by 2015. Achieving these goals is particularly important in this age of the global knowledge economy, where many socioeconomic groups in developing countries risk exclusion from the economic and social benefits that this new knowledge economy can potentially provide (Castells 1996).

A long-standing relationship exists between education and technology; some would suggest it began with the invention of the printing press. As new technologies emerged, educational providers have tried to integrate them into the learning process. The emergence of newer information and communications technologies (ICTs), like computers and mobile phones, has significantly widened the scope of how technologies can facilitate educational processes and there is a growing interest in using ICTs in developing countries' educational settings. Many believe that introducing ICTs into these contexts will have great impact given the systematic problems of access to quality education in the developing world. Yet evidence is lacking with regard to the actual impact of ICTs on the educational sector. Trucano, in a 2005 World Bank/*info*Dev study, found that the impact of ICT use on learning outcomes is unclear and open to much debate as reportedly very little useful data exist on several dimensions of ICT interventions in education. This chapter tries to fill some of these gaps by discussing International Research Development Centre (IDRC) supported projects across different sectors (formal and non-formal as well as primary, secondary and tertiary education settings) in Africa, Asia and Latin America. An analysis of all the projects funded by IDRC in ICTs and education is beyond the scope of this chapter.[1] Instead, this chapter aims to explore the key strategies and programmatic initiatives in the area of ICTs and education and discuss the main research findings and outcomes emerging from these initiatives.

An analysis of the projects shows that, while early projects placed a significant focus on providing schools with access to computers, it was realized that access alone was not enough to achieve important educational outcomes. Greater emphasis needed to be placed on how ICTs can contribute to pedagogical changes. This necessitated taking a more holistic look at the education sector, including the roles played by teachers and policymakers, as well as broader issues such as infrastructure, costs, regulations, institutional design and so on. The chapter is organized following these sequential learnings achieved by IDRC in its work on ICTs in education. The first section discusses some of IDRC's early projects that focused on access. The second section examines how a concern for pedagogy became central in the more recent interventions. The final section explores some emerging experiences in which social inclusion (i.e., neither access nor pedagogy) is the driver. The chapter concludes by summarizing the projects and reiterating key points emerging from the discussion.

The Challenges of Improving Access

A major obstacle for education in developing countries is equitable access to education. For example, in Asia alone, there are 560 million adults who are illiterate, accounting for more than seventy percent of the world's illiterate citizens. Of that number, nearly sixty-six percent are reported to be girls and women (Malik 2009). Similarly, in Africa, although there has been significant improvement in primary school enrollment, a large sector of African youth are excluded from education and the dropout rate of children from primary to secondary school remains a problem (Isaacs et al. 2004). During the initial phase of using ICTs in education, IDRC's entry point was the improvement of access to both education through ICTs and to ICT equipment. Therefore, access had several dimensions, including access to a computer in educational institutions, to the Internet, to digital education materials and to remote instruction.

One of the earliest IDRC interventions supported the SchoolNet Africa initiative in the 1990s (James 2004). SchoolNets were essentially national organizations that promoted learning and teaching through the use of ICTs (Isaacs 2004). Following the development and implementation of SchoolNet initiatives in Canada and Europe in the 1980s and early 1990s, the SchoolNet program took root in Africa and mushroomed across the continent. The typical national SchoolNet in Africa was a small-scale, donor-supported pilot initiative that was grassroots-based and led by local champions. IDRC-funded SchoolNet projects with varying sizes, scope and activities in several countries (Isaacs et al. 2004, 39–40). For example, in Mozambique, IDRC supported the establishment of "Internet for Schools" projects, targeting 10 schools; they received 11 computers with email and Internet connectivity, content and courseware development. In Senegal, 12 cyber youth clubs were established in schools. In South Africa, IDRC helped to establish the organization SchoolNet South Africa as an NGO.

In all these contexts, the use of schools as an access point to ICTs was considered successful, as learners, educators, administrators and members of the community were able to use computers to at least stand at the doorstep of the then-emerging information society (James 2004, xxv). In contrast, the issue of content posed a much bigger challenge, as the development of educational content online or through the use of ICTs was extremely limited despite this being part of the projects' designs. The SchoolNet project showed that the overwhelming challenge faced by most African schools was the high cost of connectivity; providing ICT access in underserved areas would be a major political, economic and logistical endeavor (James 2004). Yet the overarching story of SchoolNet is that it was a pioneering and successful attempt to apply new ICTs in resource-poor environments as a way of reducing the digital divide and enhancing education. The evolution and eventual formal establishment of SchoolNet Africa[2] is a testimony to the growth of an Africanized SchoolNet movement – a process envisioned, promoted and supported in its early days by IDRC (Isaacs 2004).

In Latin America, the approach to providing access to ICTs was different. Although the rate of ICT penetration in schools was higher in Latin America than in Africa, the scarcity of relevant content in the local language was a major barrier to the use of ICTs in education. Therefore, IDRC chose to support a regional network of national educational portals known as RELPE (Latin America Network of Education Portals) for storage and circulation of educational content among member countries. This applied to all content produced by the countries or available to them with no restrictions on intellectual property. The spirit of the initiative was to create a pool of educational content in Spanish that could be treated as a regional public good. The content, which is constantly being expanded and upgraded, is available online and accessible to all students connected to the Internet. Although this initiative provided access to content, gaining access to this content in the early days was limited because few computers were available in educational institutions of the region. Yet, as educational centers acquired ICT equipment and governments launched programs to provide computers (mainly laptops) to students, thousands of children in primary and high schools, including those in families with very limited incomes, today have access to valuable educational resources available in their national portals and other portals of the region (members of RELPE). The project has also developed a special offline portal so those schools that lack connectivity can still have access to the same resources found in these online portals. An important outcome of the project at the regional level was that the Economic Commission for Latin America and the Caribbean (ECLAC) considered RELPE as a significant model for localized multimedia content for the learning process (ECLAC 2010). This acknowledgment has led to the inclusion of RELPE as a reference in the eLAC program.[3]

The challenge of content was also a major issue for African countries; in some of these countries, IDRC supported efforts to address the issue. For example, in Uganda, the difficulties posed by the lack of appropriate content was a central concern and led to the development of a project called "CurriculumNet." The National Curriculum Development Centre developed, tested and implemented a mechanism for curriculum integration and delivery in two selected subjects for primary and secondary schools via communication networks using computer-related tools (Shore 2004). The project provided information and experiences to policymakers in the country's Ministry of

Education and clearly demonstrated how an ICT-based curriculum is not only possible, but also adds value to teaching and learning processes (Babikwa and Ssentongo 2002). In 2004, the project received formal government approval for its ICT-based curriculum materials in mathematics and geography for primary schools and mathematics and science for secondary schools (Obot et al. 2005). Government approval was significant as it meant the developed curriculum could be used by all schools in Uganda immediately, provided they had IT access and could go through the formal examination process of the Uganda National Examination Board (UNEB).

Unlike in Africa and Latin America, where the focus was on access to ICTs in the classroom, the main focus in Asia was on distance education (DE) in both formal and non-formal settings. In Asia – with its large rural and urban population with limited access to face-to-face higher education, vast geographical areas and long distances from teaching institutions – distance education has a relatively long history and spread in the region. Ten of the thirteen single-mode DE open universities in the world are in Asia, including in China, Indonesia, India, Malaysia and Thailand (Baggaley et al. 2009, 52). Based upon these factors, it became critical to investigate the extent to which technology-based distance education could be as effective as – and less expensive than – the declining post-secondary sector, particularly because of states' withdrawals of funding for public post-secondary education.

Between 1998 and 2003, IDRC supported seven DE learning technology projects in several Asian countries (Baggaley 2004). One of these projects explored the use of ICTs in student learning satisfaction and course completion at Universitas Terbuka in Indonesia. The project involved systematic research and study of the educational effectiveness of the ICT-based instruction compared with the print medium, first piloting the course conversion and offering the pilot courses to 177 districts. The project found that students' participation in online courses and tutorials increased their course completion rates significantly. Students expressed their appreciation of and satisfaction with the online services, which were considered innovative, appropriate and useful for working students. On the other hand, students complained about technical problems that frequently occurred when accessing the online services, notably low speed. Furthermore, students suggested that online services needed to be improved, especially with regard to the tutors' responsiveness. A general conclusion of the research was that large-scale, web-based course delivery is slow and problematic and it was suggested the online methods be restricted to tutorial and learning support.

From 2005 to 2008, IDRC supported a unique collaborative research network called PANdora (Pan Asian Network for Distance and Open Resource Access), which included 9 sub-projects in 13 countries. The research encompassed a wide range of issues related to policy, pedagogy and technology, including the impact of ICT-based distance higher education. It mapped the acceptability and accessibility of provisions as well as the development and testing of software and content in critical need areas – localized technology-based learning management systems (LMS), short message system (SMS) technologies, e-assessment and repositories of learning objects. PANdora's findings concluded that DE methods, standard in other parts of the world, do not work as efficiently in Asia where the necessary infrastructure, accessibility and training are lacking. In particular, the low-bandwidth Internet available to students constrains the wider use of rich media in such DE programs.

In quantifying web accessibility (measuring the time taken to access web pages), a PANdora study found that browser loading times in many locations were four times slower than what would be commonly prescribed as acceptable (Baggaley and Batchuluun 2007). So there was a dire need to upgrade the infrastructure for Internet-based education to enable educational institutions to take full advantage of it. Another sub-project evaluated a range of open-source software packages with potential value for online LMS – tools to enhance delivery and sharing of educational materials – in Asian educational institutions (Batchuluun et al. 2009). While the project researchers identified the Moodle LMS as particularly suitable for Asian needs, they recommended using offline versions of Moodle produced on CDs and for other portable media (e.g., cell phone "texting" techniques), owing to the lack of high bandwidth connections.

In Africa's tertiary sector, IDRC's focus was on access to the Internet, a pressing problem in many universities. For example, West Africa's higher educational institutions, surveyed in 2008, used 74 mbps average of total inbound bandwidth – slightly more than a Canadian household – which is far from the ideal requirements of 1156 mbps (or 15 times the existing provision) for an entire campus (Hamilton et al. 2008). With nearly 2.2 million staff and students in this region, the average bandwidth would be 0.37 kbps per head, mainly via satellite connection. At the average current price of US$2,330 per mbps per month, prices need to fall to US $120 to meet their requirement in 2013 within the given West African universities' budgets (Hamilton et al. 2008). Such substantial pricing differences encouraged the National Research and Education Networks (NRENs) to collectively influence policy in favor of negotiated bandwidth costs with service providers or to develop innovative business models to intervene in the bandwidth supply chain. IDRC's support was critical in the attempts to ensure that Africa matched their peers in other continents, as demand for academic information, increased bandwidth and lower connectivity costs are imperative for the continent's universities. (See Box 8.1 for a full description of this initiative.)

In sum, these projects, while aiming to support access, clearly illustrate that there are several other key issues requiring attention. First, many of these projects highlighted the fact that ICT-supported education cannot be used effectively unless there is sound infrastructure in place that provides reliable and relatively low-cost access to the necessary hardware, software and networks. Second, as ICTs became integrated into the teaching and learning processes across educational systems, the need for digital learning materials and content relevant to local curricula became even more critical. It became clear that the premise, "deploy first, worry about content later," needed to be rethought. Finally, the experience of the early days showed that integrating ICTs into the classroom required new ways of teaching and learning in which teachers and students needed to reformulate their roles and responsibilities in the process. This is the focus of the next round of IDRC programming.

Box 8.1. Ubuntu Net Alliance – Removing access barriers for African researchers

The state of Internet connectivity in tertiary institutions in Africa can be summarized by three characteristics – too little, too expensive and poorly managed. The average African university has bandwidth capacity equivalent to a broadband residential connection available in Europe, pays 50 times more for their bandwidth than their educational counterparts in the rest of the world and fails to monitor, let alone manage, the existing bandwidth. (Gakio 2006)

While many African countries are aiming to improve access to higher education through blended teaching that involves distance learning modules and/or remote lecturing using ICTs, it will be difficult to show results from these efforts if sufficient bandwidth is not available to universities at affordable prices. Africa had no such high-performance network to facilitate cutting-edge research and learning. This has resulted in the marginalization of higher educational institutes because of insufficient access to the necessary infrastructure.

Against this backdrop, IDRC supported the project "Promoting Research and Education Networking in Africa" (PAREN), which worked in partnership with universities and other donor stakeholders to build a mechanism to reduce the cost and improve the quality of bandwidth at universities in the Sub-Saharan African region. IDRC experimented with the idea of a dynamic regional network that could work together to enhance regional connectivity through collective bargaining with their fiber optic service providers. For example, Makerere University in Uganda was paying, at the time, $2,000 a month for 2MB of bandwidth, whereas the average university in the United States was paying $200 for 200MB. The idea that a university in the US pays a fraction of what a university in Africa does was unfair.

By May 2005, the Ubuntu Net Alliance (UA) was created – a group of national research and education networks (NRENs) established by representatives from Kenya, Malawi, Mozambique, Rwanda and South Africa – to explore regional academic networking strategies. Rather than connect to the Internet via expensive satellite access, the UA sought alternative networks to connect universities to, for example, the fiber optic networks that were deployed but not fully used by energy and rail utilities in countries. However, these network infrastructures, because of telecommunications licensing, could not be used by the public. This search for fiber, which started as a research project, resulted in many of the countries' researchers involved in the process – most of them heads of IT departments in their respective universities – as well as researchers in the Research ICT Africa network (RIA; see Chapter 2) forging an alliance with engineers seeking a solution. Thanks to the Ubuntu Net Alliance, many of these countries now benefit from dramatically reduced costs and increased access to fiber and other networks for universities. Lowering Internet costs for the universities required the involvement of many different stakeholders, such as university vice chancellors, governments and IT support services. These players needed to make important policy decisions that focused on ensuring universities' capacity to prepare for higher speeds of Internet and to find the means to ensure quality service.

Today, a critical mass of universities have succeeded in receiving subsidized rates for bandwidth, have created their own ISP and have coordinated a sustainable team of African researchers across the region to ensure that broadband opportunities come to fruition. Since the mid-2000s, IDRC supported the emergence of the Ubuntu Net Alliance as well as a staff person at the Association of African Universities. Both the alliance and the staff person work on promoting NRENs – especially in West Africa where their emergence was slower than in eastern and southern Africa. UA has had great success with the European Commission, Internet2, the ITU and other philanthropic foundations. UA is a success story of initial support for research to find local solutions leading to organizations being formed in response to countries' and regions' needs. Existing NRENS, such as Tenet in South Africa and Kenet in Kenya, were able to provide a great deal of insight for the network they helped develop. The developmental impact is that universities now have improved broadband Internet connectivity for universities in Sub-Saharan Africa.

A Shift in Focus: From Access to Pedagogy

The shift in IDRC's research programming focus from access to pedagogy was partly attributable to the experience gained from earlier interventions and partly due to the natural evolution of the introduction of ICT in schools. The potential for ICTs as a tool to bring changes in the way education is delivered was apparent in a study on the operation of six well-functioning SchoolNets in Latin America (Argentina, Brazil, Colombia, Costa Rica, Chile and Mexico). The project, REDAL (Redes Escolares de América Latina), examined the management, audience, mission, financing, infrastructure, pedagogy and regulatory context of the six countries and found that all of them considered ICTs as tools for change and as a means to achieve educational aims more effectively.

In 2007, IDRC supported a network on the Pan African research agenda on the pedagogical integration of ICTs (PanAf). This project's overarching objective was to better understand how, for whom and under what circumstances the pedagogical integration of ICTs can substantially improve the quality of teaching and learning at all levels of African educational systems. In the first phase, the PanAf network collected an unprecedented depth and quality of data with the institutions that participated in the research representing nearly 245,000 learners, along with 9,000 educators and other stakeholders. The study found that the majority of uses of ICTs fall into the category of "the subject of learning" while very few fall into the category of "ICTs to teach subjects other than computing itself" (Karsenti et al. 2011). In other words, ICTs are not used as a "way" to learn; they are "what" is taught. While the teaching of computers maybe justifiable in many remote regions of Africa where schools are the only arena for accessing and learning ICTs, paradoxically, this phenomenon was also present in cities where 75 percent of learners report frequent uses of cyber cafés and are comfortable with at least the basic functions of computers. In conclusion, the PanAf study showed that, despite the potential impact of using ICTs as a means to improve the quality of education, such pedagogical integration is rarely observed in Africa. The learners are called upon to appropriate ICTs and the data show that they are relatively successful in doing so, though practical sessions are brief and resources limited.

Research also highlighted the important role of teachers in the process. For instance, researchers underscored the need for a change in mindset to use ICTs reflectively and strategically and to leave behind the paradigms of the teacher as master (Toure 2008). Furthermore, some educators have indicated they would prefer not to facilitate this type of learning situation, as they have the impression that they would "lose control" of their classrooms. This concern reveals an attitude that ICTs present a menace to the role of the teacher. Yet, some learners are actively involved in gaining competency with ICTs rather than passively absorbing the subject matter as presented by educators. Therefore, the pedagogical effectiveness of ICTs depends more on the capacity of teachers to integrate and operate new technologies in a relevant pedagogical context than on the available information technology infrastructure.

Concerns about the role of ICTs in pedagogy recently became central in Asia as well. PANdora surveys on attitudes to DE accessibility and acceptability have shown a preference by students throughout the region for a more interactive style of education than they typically receive (Baggaley and Belawati 2007). Furthermore, these studies demonstrated that some learners preferred to complement distance education with face-to-face instruction. As such, blended learning – face-to-face instruction combined with computer-mediated instruction – could offer a more effective learning experience (Baggaley and Belawati 2007). The benefits of blended learning have been confirmed in other research. For example, a study by the Department of Education in the United States found that instruction that combined online and face-to-face elements had a greater advantage over purely face-to-face instruction or purely online instruction (Means et al. 2010).

It is increasingly recognized that the educational needs of young people are varied and that learning takes place not only in schools and colleges, but throughout an individual's lifespan in many different locations and times, something known as lifelong learning (Dighe et al. 2010). This is particularly relevant in the case of non-formal education where learning is more needs-based and flexible than formal education. Initiatives aimed at integrating ICTs into the process can help meet the various needs of individuals, minority groups, etc. For example, ICTs can be used to develop livelihood skills, link literacy to economic activities, build capacity for teachers and students and share information in the community. Therefore, it is critical to go beyond the traditional idea of content as merely textbooks to think of content with regard to second-language instruction or public health education, which are equally pressing needs for many people across different socioeconomic contexts.

Another major learning that emerged from the research in Asia is that mobile phones can play a significant role in distance learning – not just in view of the rapid growth of mobile telephony, but also because of the pedagogical processes that mobiles facilitate. Proponents of m-learning (mobile learning), who often are the mobile operators, assert that the increasing ubiquity of mobile phone penetration has the potential to reach more students than ever before (Dawes 2010). Several PANdora sub-projects experimented with mobile phones, including SMS, as a means of interactive learning; texting to inform students of schedule changes, deadlines, examination regulations, grades and to publicize social activities and job fairs; and university administration using cell phones to coordinate the admission process and disseminate emergency information, among other things (Librero et al. 2007). The field of m-learning, or learning facilitated by mobile devices, has been generating growing interest in recent times. There are enough indications, including those from IDRC-funded studies, that warrant a degree of cautious optimism regarding mobile learning as a valuable tool for supporting distant education (Valk et al. 2010).

Exploring the links between pedagogy and student performance

Integrating ICTs in a way that changes pedagogical practices is not only desirable from the perspective of a better learning experience; it can also potentially contribute to better student performance, as demonstrated in some IDRC-funded projects. For example, a pilot project initiated by the Senegal Ministry of Education in 2003 installed ICT equipment in classrooms, including access to the Internet. But, more importantly, it used ICTs as a tool for learning French and mathematics rather than a technology to learn in addition to existing courses (Sène and Sy 2009). The project promoted a more learner-centered approach based on active learning, with the emphasis on building knowledge and student creativity. The experiment helped to improve the success rate of students taking the national exam at the end of the primary cycle: the success rate before the project was 22 percent; in subsequent years, the success rate improved gradually (27 percent in year one; 33 percent in year two; 64 percent in year three; 83 percent in year four) (Sène and Sy 2009; Rioux, 2009). This competency-based approach has been a key part of the curriculum reforms in Senegal and the Ministry of Education has committed to scaling up the project in other primary schools (Sène and Sy 2009).

A project in the Philippines sought to explore the viability of SMS technologies for non-formal distance education on SMS-based modules in English and math. In the experiment, it was revealed that the mean percent correct score of passers in the SMS group was marginally higher than those in the non-SMS group. Another non-formal DE project in Mongolia had modules for health and service (bank and restaurant) workers which required SMS for completion. The pre- and post-test results revealed that, on average, both groups of learners were able to improve their scores, which the project's researchers attribute to the increased knowledge gained through the SMS-based curriculum (Ramos 2008, 28).

More recently, a pilot study in Mongolia has shown conclusively that ICTs can improve student performances. The study found that students who used different technologies (television, the Internet and mobile phones) in the learning process performed significantly better in exams than those who did not (Natsagdorj et al. 2010). For example, in the English language exam written after the completion of the pilot project, 26 percent of students who used the technologies received an A grade; 47 percent got a grade of either C or D; and 26.5 percent got an F. By contrast, only 1.8 percent of the control group students received an A, 14.3 percent got a C or D and 83.9 percent got an F.

Examining the probable factors behind how ICTs can improve student performances, it is useful to look beyond IDRC projects to the broader literature on ICTs and pedagogy (Kozma 2005; Webb and Cox 2004). One of the main processes is the increased collaborative and interactive learning experiences and instructional methods that are more learner-centered (UNESCO 2003). ICTs facilitate more classroom interaction between students and their peers and between students and their teachers (Webb and Cox 2004). Instead of mere instruction, learning becomes a process of construction as learners can engage in conversation to resolve differences, understand the experiences of others and create common interpretations and a shared understanding of the world (Sharples et al. 2007, 225–6). As mentioned earlier in the chapter, part of interactive learning requires a change in the roles of teachers, such as setting joint tasks, rotating roles, promoting student self-management and so on. ICTs facilitate designs for personalized learning in that they are responsive to difference and diversity so that learning occurs regardless of the setting. Therefore, they can be used in the field for a botany student, in the classroom for a teacher trainee or in the workshop for an engineer (Kukulska-Hulme and Traxler 2007, 184–6; Traxler 2007, 7). While some of the IDRC projects provide evidence that these processes are taking place, further research is needed to explore whether these new pedagogical mechanisms can transform teaching and learning across the globe.

From Pedagogy to Social Inclusion

Finally, to close the cycle of transformations that the arrival of ICTs in education has had around the world, it is worth highlighting that, in some more recent cases, the introduction of computers and ICTs in schools has been aimed at acting as a tool for social inclusion, rather than improving learning and better performance. These programs have been driven by political factors focused on reducing inequity for individuals and groups who have fewer resources and on creating venues for their integration into the information society. This goal is best reflected in some of the initiatives being launched in the Latin American and Caribbean region where some governments are implementing programs along the lines of Negroponte's "One Laptop per Child" (OLPC) initiative. Although not all countries have adopted the XO computer produced by the OLPC program, they have largely followed the logic and rationale that a child with a laptop has a far better chance of overcoming poverty than one without access to ICTs.

IDRC was involved in the early stages of the 1X1 programs by creating a regional working group from the six countries (Argentina, Brazil, Chile, Colombia, Costa Rica and Uruguay) that assessed the feasibility of adopting OLPC for the national educational sector. IDRC support allowed the creation of a non-partisan space where countries could express their concerns and exchange knowledge and experiences gained in the assessments they were conducting. IDRC also supported the initiative with studies that provided evidence, information and data that allowed countries to make informed decisions in this regard. Of the countries of the LAC region, the most relevant case is Uruguay, which was the first to implement the program. It has been implemented in all primary schools in the country, starting with the most remote and poorest areas and progressing to deployment to cities and better resourced areas.[4]

Until recently, research has been inconclusive with regard to the economic, social and educational impacts of these programs (Severin and Capota 2011). To fill this gap, an IDRC-funded study explored the social impact of 1X1 models in Argentina, Costa Rica, Uruguay and Colombia (Zucker and Light 2009). This study found that the greatest impact of 1X1 programs has been at the level of inclusion, particularly through mobility, i.e., the possibility of having the laptops (*Ceibalitas*) connected by WiFi. In and of itself, the opportunity to bring the technology to any scenario where the children interact creates a powerful sense of inclusion, enabling the transfer of learning and skills generation with natural and spontaneous conversations arising regardless of location (home, street, school or playground). The 1X1 projects also modify the child's relationship with the family in that the child becomes a benchmark in terms of digital skills transfer at the household level.

Conclusion

This chapter has illustrated how research supported by IDRC in the domain of education and ICTs moved from a focus on access in its early days to a greater concern for how ICTs could facilitate better pedagogical practices in the classroom.[5] For example, in the early 1990s, IDRC supported some of the earliest initiatives that focused on putting computers and the Internet into schools in Africa through the SchoolNet project. In Latin America, the focus was on access to content, the main concern of the project. In Asia, IDRC-funded research explored the effectiveness of distance education at the tertiary level. All of these projects provided important insights into the ways in which ICTs can improve educational outcomes. In some of the interventions, it was clear that a disconnect existed between the rationales most often presented to advance the use of ICTs in education (introduction of new teaching and learning practices) and their actual implementation (predominantly for use in computer literacy and dissemination of learning materials). This is to be expected given that, as a recent PanAf research study shows, the integration of technologies in a way that allows them to become effective is harder to achieve as it depends on a variety of factors. These changes require a change in teachers' mindsets, as well as a variety of other transformations throughout the educational system, such as sustained investment in infrastructure, capacity building of human resources, transformation of curricular frameworks and a permanent assessment and adjustments of progress (Light 2009). Furthermore, a multitude of actors with various and often conflicting interests are involved in the transformation and need to be integrated in a constructive way into the process. In sum, IDRC projects have shown that the introduction of ICTs in education is a holistic, complex and long-term process requiring a broad vision and a long-term commitment from those involved in this profound institutional, political and cultural shift that is transforming an area that is at the basis of human progress and development.

Appendix 8.1. Basic information of selected IDRC-funded projects on ICTs and education

Project name (IDRC project number)	Amount (CAD)	Project duration	Region/country	Lead research agency
Social Impacts Research on 1X1 Models in Latin America (104122 &106202)	200,000	2008–2011	Argentina, Costa Rica, Colombia, Uruguay	DESEM del, Uruguay
Consolidating and Integrating the Education Portals Network and Latin America SchoolNets (103811)	856,900	2006–2011	Chile, Argentina, LAC	Corporación de Investigaciones para el Desarrollo (Chile) & Fundación Evolución (Argentina)
SchoolNets Latin America (REDAL) (102073)	177,200	2003–2006	LAC	Fundación Evolución (Argentina)
Building Regional Educational Content Online (Latin America) (RELPE) (102126)	425,180	2003–2006	LAC	Fundación Chile
ICT-Supported Distance Education in Indonesia: An Effort to Enhanced Student Learning Satisfaction and Course Completion Rates (100570)	258,000	2001–2004	Indonesia	Universitas Terbuka, Indonesia
ICT-Supported Distance Education in Water, Hygiene, and Sanitation	257,180	2003–2006	Philippines	Molave Development Foundation, Inc.
PAN Distance Learning Technology (102791)	1,684,400	2004–2011	Asia	Virtual University of Pakistan
Openness and Quality in Asian Distance Education Technology (104917)	1,200,000	2009–2013	Asia	Virtual University of Pakistan
SchoolNet South Africa– Institution Building (101026)	650,000	2001–2003	Sub-Saharan Africa	SchoolNet South Africa

(Continued)

Appendix 8.1. Continued

Project name (IDRC project number)	Amount (CAD)	Project duration	Region/country	Lead research agency
Using ICTs in Primary and Secondary Curriculum Delivery (Uganda) (100739)	446,800	2000–2005	Uganda	National Curriculum Development Centre (Uganda)
Integration of ICTs into the Basic Curriculum in Primary Schools in Senegal (101581 & 103108)	952,355	2002–2010	Senegal	Senegal, Ministèrede l'éducation nationale, and Université du Québec à Montréal
Integrating ICTs in Education in West and Central Africa: Training Teachers and Innovative Education Practices (101978 &103109)	1,007,666	2003–2009	Sub-Saharan Africa	Université de Montréal, and Educational Research Network for West and Central Africa (ROCARE), Mali
Pan African Research Agenda on the Integration of ICTs in Education (103741 & 105715)	3,248,870	2007–2011	Africa	Université de Montréal, and Educational Research Network for West and Central Africa, Mali
Ubuntu Net Alliance: Consolidating Research and Education Networking (104584 & 105717)	857,930	2008–2011	Africa	University of Malawi

While the "Information and Communications Technologies for Development" (ICT4D) program at IDRC had central themes, it was squarely rooted in the regional realities where it supported research for development. In Africa, where Internet access was just developing in the major urban areas, IDRC supported some of the first SchoolNets. This accelerated educational adoption rates and concentrated the educational benefits where they might have the greatest infrastructure and technical support.

Latin America was different. It had very high rates of urbanization and Internet access was reasonably well developed. Curriculum in the local languages (Spanish and Portuguese) was in very short supply. Accordingly, primary IDRC intervention was to assist a consortium of education ministries to build an online portal for curriculum. This helped to develop educational materials across the continent – materials which the

Appendix 8.2. Conceptual map

Figure 8.1. A conceptual map of how ICTs shape educational outcomes

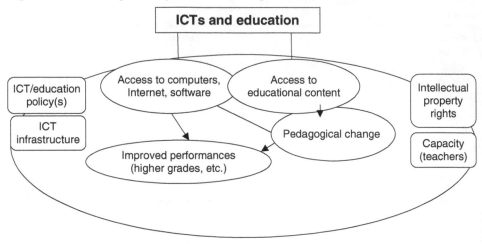

ministries themselves came to own. It also spurred online integration with existing in-situ curricula.

Asia was different again. Because of the Asian economic crisis at the turn of the century, national subsidies to public university were being withdrawn, taking post-secondary education out of reach for increasing numbers of students. Throughout the region, open universities were increasingly being seen as an alternative to their more costly "bricks and mortar" cousins.

IDRC's support helped universities across the region learn from the evidence-based experiences generated by their research. Irrespective of these regional differences, however, it became clear that the online or networked intervention was only one piece of the puzzle to sustainable adoption and change. Informed management, reliable infrastructure and reformed pedagogy were also necessary for these new approaches to have sustainable success.

Notes

1 Basic information of selected IDRC-funded ICT4E projects is given in Appendix 1.
2 See SchoolNet Africa at http://www.schoolnet-africa.org/english/index.htm (accessed 11 January 2012).
3 eLAC is an intergovernmental strategy that conceives of ICTs as instruments for economic development and social inclusion in Latin America and the Caribbean. It is based on a public–private sector partnership (Hilbert et al. 2009) and is part of a long-term vision (until 2015) in line with the Millennium Development Goals (MDGs) (http://en.wikipedia.org/wiki/Millennium_Development_Goals [accessed 2 November 2011]) and those of the World Summit on the Information Society.
4 Uruguay became the first country in the world to give laptops to all elementary school children in public schools (*Economist* 2009).
5 See Appendix 2 for conceptual mapping of how ICTs can facilitate education.

References

Babikwa, D. et al. 2008. *Computers for Schools Kenya: Evaluation Report.* Ottawa: IDRC.

Babikwa, D. and J. Ssentongo. 2002. *The Final Evaluation of the CurriculumNet Project of the National Curriculum Development Centre – Uganda.* Final report. Ottawa: IDRC.

Baggaley, J. 2004. *Distance Learning Technologies: Deploying Canadian and Southern Technology Engines to Build an Asian Research Network.* Consultant report submitted to IDRC. Edmonton: Athabaska University.

Baggaley, J. and B. Batchuluun. 2007. "The World-Wide Inaccessible Web, Part 1: Browsing." *International Review of Research in Open and Distance Learning* 8, no. 2. Online: http://www.irrodl.org/index.php/irrodl/article/view/438 (accessed 11 December 2011).

Baggaley, J. and T. Belawati, eds. 2007. *Distance Education Technology in Asia. Part 1: Past and Present.* Lahore: Virtual University of Pakistan.

Baggaley, J. et al. 2009. "Distance Education in Asia Pacific." In *Digital Review of Asia Pacific 2009–2010*, edited by R. Akhtar and P. Arinto, 51–8. Ottawa: IDRC, Sage and Orbicom.

Batchuluun, B. et al. 2009. "Open-Source Software for Learning Management." In *Distance Education Technology in Asia*, edited by J. Baggaley and T. Belawati, 195–209. PANdora: Distance and Open Resource Access project, Virtual University of Pakistan Online: http://www.pandora-asia.org/downloads/Book-2/PANdora-book2_v6-Chap8.pdf (accessed 12 November 2013).

Castells, M. 1996. *The Rise of the Network Society.* Malden: Blackwell.

Dawes, L. 2010. *mLearning: A Platform for Educational Opportunities at the Base of the Pyramid.* London: GSMA Development Fund. Online: http://www.gsma.com/mobilefordevelopment/wp-content/uploads/2012/04/mlearningaplatformforeducationalopportunitiesatthebaseofthepyramid.pdf (accessed 12 January 2012).

Dighe, A. et al. 2010. "ICTs in Non-formal Education in Asia Pacific." In *Digital Review of Asia Pacific 2009–2010*, edited by S. Akhtar and P. Arinto, 59–66. Ottawa: IDRC, Sage and Orbicom.

ECLAC. 2010. *Monitoring of the Plan of Action eLAC 2010: Advances and Challenges of the Information Society in Latin America and the Caribbean.* New York: ECLAC. Online: http://www.eclac.org/ddpe/publicaciones/xml/2/41802/LCR2165.pdf (accessed 2 November 2011).

Economist. 2009. "Education in Uruguay: Laptops for All – A Pioneering Project's Chequered Start." 1 October. Online: http://www.economist.com/node/14558609 (accessed 12 January 2012).

Farrell, G. and S. Isaacs. 2007. *Survey of ICT and Education in Africa: A Summary Report, Based on 53 country Surveys.* Washington, DC: *info*Dev/World Bank. Online: http://www.infodev.org/en/Publication.353.html (accessed 15 December 2011).

Gakio, K. 2006. *African Tertiary Institutions Connectivity Survey (ATICS).* Ottawa: IDRC. Online: http://ahero.uwc.ac.za/index.php?module=cshe&action=viewtitle&id=cshe_172 (accessed 11 February 2012).

Geddes, S. J. 2004. "Mobile Learning in the 21st Century: Benefit for Learners." *Knowledge Tree.*

Grompone, J. et al. 2009. *Impacto social de los proyectos 1 a 1 e identificación de implementación de TICs innovadoras en América Latina y el Caribe-Proyecto ILATIS–Informe final.* Final technical report submitted to IDRC. Ottawa: IDRC.

Hamilton, P. et al. 2008. *AAU Connectivity Study: Addressing the Demand for Connectivity of Higher Education Institutions (HEIs) in the West and Central Africa Region.* Accra: Association of African Universities.

Hilbert, M. et al. 2009. "Foresight Tools for Participative Policy-Making in Inter-governmental Processes in Developing Countries: Lessons Learned from the eLAC Policy Priorities." *Technological Forecasting and Social Change* 76, no. 7: 880–96.

Hosman, L. 2010. "Policies, Partnerships, and Pragmatism: Lessons from an ICT-in-Education Project in Rural Uganda." *Information Technologies and International Development* 6, no. 1 48–64. Online: http://itidjournal.org/itid/article/view/488/213 (accessed 1 February 2012).

Isaacs, S. 2004. "Foreword." In *Information and Communication Technologies for Development in Africa, Volume 3: Networking Institutions of Learning – SchoolNet*, edited by T. James, xi–xiii. Ottawa: IDRC and the Council for the Development of Social Science Research in Africa.

Isaacs, S. et al. 2004. "Contextualising Education in Africa: The Role of ICTs." In *Information and Communication Technologies for Development in Africa, Volume 3: Networking Institutions of Learning – SchoolNet*, edited by T. James, 1–23. Ottawa: IDRC and the Council for the Development of Social Science Research in Africa. Online: http://www.idrc.ca/EN/Resources/Publications/Pages/IDRCBookDetails.aspx?PublicationID=214 (accessed 15 December 2011).

James, T., ed. 2004. *Information and Communication Technologies for Development in Africa, Volume 3: Networking Institutions of Learning – SchoolNet*. Ottawa: IDRC and the Council for the Development of Social Science Research in Africa.

Karsenti, T. et al. 2011. *Pedagogical Integration of ICT: Successes and Challenges from 87 African Schools / Intégration pédagogique des TIC: Succès et défis de 87 écoles africaines*. Ottawa: IDRC. Online: http://www.ernwaca.org/panaf/IMG/pdf/PanAf-Success-and-challenges-african-schools.pdf (accessed 29 February 2012).

Karsenti, T. et al. 2009. *The Pan African Research Agenda on the Pedagogical Integration of Information and Communication Technologies, Phase 1 National Reports*. University of Montreal. Online: https://depot.erudit.org/bitstream/003305dd/1/RAP-karsenti-40-2009.pdf (accessed 2 November 2011).

Kozma, R. 2005. "National Policies that Connect ICT-Based Education Reform to Economic and Social Development." *Human Technology* 1, no. 2 117–56.

Kukulska-Hulme, A. and J. Traxler. 2007. "Designing for Mobile and Wireless Learning." In *Rethinking Pedagogy for a Digital Age: Designing and Delivering E-Learning*, edited by H. Beetham and R. Sharpe, 180–92. London: Routledge.

LeBaron, J. and E. McDonough. 2009. *Research Report for GeSCI Meta-review of ICT in Education: Phase One*. Nairobi: Global e-Schools and Communities Initiative (GeSCI).

Librero, F. et al. 2007. "Use of the Cell Phone for Education in the Philippines and Mongolia." *Distance Education* 28, no. 2: 231–44

Light, D. 2009. "The Role of ICT in Enhancing Education in Developing Countries: Findings from an Evaluation of The Intel® Teach Essentials Course in India, Turkey, and Chile." *Journal of Education for International Development* 4, no. 2: 52–66.

Malik, N. 2009. "Openness and Quality in Asian Distance Education." Proposal submitted to IDRC. Ottawa: IDRC.

Means, B. et al. 2010. *Evaluation of Evidence-Based Practices in Online Learning: A Meta-analysis and Review of Online Learning Studies*. Washington, DC: US Department of Education, Office of Planning, Evaluation, and Policy Development, Policy and Program Studies Service. Online: http://techchange.org/2010/12/06/is-e-learning-inferior-to-face-to-face-instruction/ (accessed 17 November 2011).

Motlik, S. 2008. "Mobile Learning in Developing Nations." *International Review of Research in Open and Distance Learning* 9, no. 2. Online: http://www.irrodl.org/index.php/irrodl/article/view/564/1071 (accessed 25 February 2012).

Natsagdorj, S. et al. 2010. *Blended Technology Education Program: Using Technology to Level Education Playing Field in Mongolia*. Final technical report. Ulaanbaatar: Education Channel Television of Mongolia.

Obot, D. et al. 2005. "The Uganda Knowledge and Information Society: Early Lessons from ICT Projects." In *At the Crossroads: ICT Policymaking in East Africa*. Ottawa: East African Educational Publishers and IDRC. Online: http://www.idrc.ca/EN/Resources/Publications/Pages/IDRCBookDetails.aspx?PublicationID=330 (accessed 15 December 2011).

Ramos, A. J. 2008. *Project MIND: The Viability of Mobile SMS Technologies for Non-formal Distance Learning in Asia*. Final report for sub-project no. 2. Philippines: Molave Development Foundation.

Rioux, M. 2009. "Les TIC en éducation au Sénégal." *Infobourg*, 6 February.

Sène, P. A. and A. G. Sy. 2009. *Projet d'école TICE. Synthèse de recherche*. Ottawa: IDRC. Online: http://idl-bnc.idrc.ca/dspace/handle/10625/42592 (accessed 12 January 2012).

Severin, E. and C. Capota. 2011. "One-to-One Laptop Programs in Latin America and the Caribbean: Panorama and Perspectives." Washington, DC: Inter-American Development Bank.

Online: http://idbdocs.iadb.org/wsdocs/getdocument.aspx?docnum=35989594 (accessed 29 February 2012).

Sharples, M. et al. 2007. "A Theory of Learning for the Mobile Age." In *The Sage Handbook of E-Learning Research*, edited by R. Andrews and C. Haythornthwaite, 221–47. London: Sage Publications.

Shore, K. J. 2004. *Casting CurriculumNet Wider*. Ottawa: IDRC. Online: http://www.idrc.ca/en/ev-64993-201-1-DO_TOPIC.html (accessed 15 January 2012).

Toure, K. 2008. "Introduction: ICT and Changing Mindsets in Education." In *ICT and Changing Mindsets in Education / Repenser l'éducation à l'aide des TIC*, edited by K. Toure et al. Bamenda: Langaa Research and Publishing Common Initiative Group / Bamako: ERNWACA.

Toure, K. et al., eds. 2008. *ICT and Changing Mindsets in Education / Repenser l'éducation à l'aide des TIC*. Bamenda: Langaa Research and Publishing Common Initiative Group / Bamako: ERNWACA.

Toyoma, K. 2011. "There Are No Technology Shortcuts to Good Education." Educational technology debate, January. Online: http://edutechdebate.org/ict-in-schools/there-are-no-technology-shortcuts-to-good-education/ (accessed 2 February 2012).

Traxler, J. 2007. "Defining, Discussing and Evaluating Mobile Learning: The Moving Finger Writes and Having Writ…" *International Review of Research in Open and Distance Learning* 8, no. 2.

Trucano, M. 2005. *Knowledge Maps: ICTs in Education*. Washington, DC: *info*Dev/World Bank. Online: http://www.infodev.org/en/Publication.8.html (accessed 3 February 2012).

UNESCO. 2003. "Theories Supporting the New View of the Learning Process." Online: http://portal.unesco.org/education/en/ev.php-URL_ID=26924&URL_DO=DO_TOPIC&URL_SECTION=201.html (accessed 29 February 2012).

Valk, J. et al. 2010. "Using Mobile Phones to Improve Educational Outcomes: An Analysis of Evidence from Asia." *International Review of Research in Open and Distance Learning* 11, no. 1. Online: http://www.irrodl.org/index.php/irrodl/article/view/794/1487 (accessed 15 December 2011).

Vital Wave Consulting. 2008. "Affordable Computing for Schools in Developing Countries: A Total Cost of Ownership (TCO) Model for Education Officials." Online: http://www.vitalwaveconsulting.com/pdf/2011/Affordable_Computing_June08.pdf (accessed 15 January 2012).

Vuth, D. et al. 2007. "Distance Education Policy and Public Awareness in Cambodia, Laos, and Viet Nam." *Distance Education* 28, no. 2: 163–77.

Webb, M. and M. Cox. 2004. "A Review of Pedagogy Related to Information and Communications Technology." *Technology, Pedagogy and Education* 13, no. 3: 235–86.

Weingarten, M. 2011. "Has the mLearning Moment Arrived?" MobileActive.org. Online: http://www.mobileactive.org/has-mlearning-moment-arrived (accessed 2 February 2012).

Zucker, A. A. and D. Light. 2009. "Laptop Programs for Students." *Science* 323, no. 5910: 82–5.

Chapter 9

E-GOVERNMENT FOR DEVELOPMENT: ICTs IN THE PUBLIC SECTOR AND THE EVOLVING CITIZEN–GOVERNMENT RELATIONSHIP

Tara Fischer, Matthew L. Smith and John-Harmen Valk

Since the 1990s, much attention and many resources have been spent on the application of information and communications technologies (ICTs) in the public sector – traditionally known as e-government – to improve the administration and services of government (Fountain 2001; Bhatnagar 2004). ICTs were seen as having the potential to achieve two benefits: the bureaucratic outcome of increased efficiency through digitizing administration processes and services; and the political outcomes of reduced corruption, enhanced transparency and greater civic engagement (Madon 2009). Furthermore, these benefits were regarded as key ingredients in helping to renew the public's waning trust in governments around the world (Bellamy and Taylor 1998, 63).

Canada's International Development Research Centre's (IDRC's) "Information and Communications Technologies for Development" (ICT4D) program began supporting research on e-government in the early 2000s within a global context of Western countries consolidating e-government applications – with particular progress made in digitizing government administration and the electronic provision of services. The international community was greatly interested in bringing the benefits of e-government to developing countries. This transfer of technology was a means to promote "good governance" (Ciborra and Navarra 2005; Misuraca 2007; Madon 2009), which was seen as a key ingredient in socioeconomic development (United Nations Development Programme 2002). Early optimism, however, gave way to the emerging reality that only a small portion of e-government implementations could be deemed a success (Heeks 2003). Research and capacity building activities were viewed as critical inputs to help enable e-government implementations in developing countries that would both be successful and ensure the benefits flowed to marginalized populations.

IDRC's ICT4D program investments in e-government in developing countries have, roughly speaking, followed the general trajectory of the stages of evolution of e-government, starting from a government-centric approach and eventually shifting to a broader citizen- and society-centric vision (Fountain 2001; Moon 2002; Nye Jr 2002; Kakabadse et al. 2003; Weare 2002; West 2005; Brewer et al. 2006). Each successive stage presupposes an increasingly sophisticated level of ICT integration within the government and the society at large, as well as associated reforms to public sector organizational structures and processes. The first group of projects supported by IDRC took a relatively inward-facing perspective; they were concerned with strengthening the capacity of governments through digitizing administrative processes and services. These projects aimed to improve the efficiency and effectiveness of government and to benefit and empower marginalized citizens and communities by making government services more accessible. Local levels of governments were the main focus, the rationale being that local governments are best positioned to address the interests and needs of marginalized communities.

The second group of projects focused on understanding how ICTs can be used to facilitate political participation and to strengthen democratic processes (e-participation or e-democracy). While a move toward e-democracy promises, in theory, to change the relationship between governments and citizens – even transforming the nature of democratic governance – in reality, the general experience globally has been slow and difficult (Ronaghan 2002; Andersen 2004; West 2005; Torres et al. 2006; Misuraca 2007). The desire to create new modes of civic engagement with government butts heads with long-established ways of working in public sector institutions (Chadwick 2008). Projects highlighted in this chapter show that, while e-government programs can increase participation, there are many such challenges in doing so.

The final set of projects was the broadest in scope. These explored the tensions that have emerged as a result of increased digitization and interconnections between the public sector and society, driven largely by e-government investments. These tensions underscore the Janus face of technology: ICTs can strengthen social processes that both strengthen and undermine effective democratic governance. For example, there is a tension between, on one hand, the democracy-enhancing effects of e-government through expanded civic engagement or the contribution to political mobilization against authoritarian regimes and, on the other, the chilling effects on civic participation that comes with increased and unaccountable state securitization, surveillance and censorship. These tensions threaten to curtail, and even reverse, the transformative potential of e-government to deepen and consolidate democracies around the world.

This chapter presents a selection of IDRC's investments in e-government research. It describes some of the research findings and the outcomes that highlight both the opportunities and challenges encountered by governments in developing countries as they attempt to harness ICTs as a way of improving governance processes. The chapter is divided into three sections. The first covers projects examining the use of ICTs to strengthen government administration and services. The second highlights research projects on e-government implementations to expand citizen engagement in governance. The final section presents research on some tensions between realizing the benefits from e-government and the threats to democratic rights and freedoms that emerge as ICTs become more prevalent throughout government and society.

Chart 9.1. The composite 2003 e-government readiness index

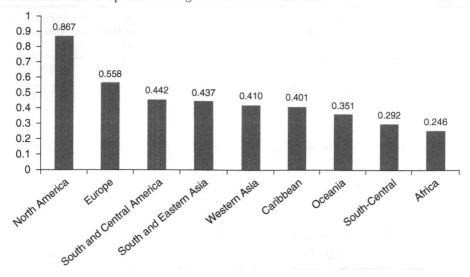

Source: Adapted from United Nations (2003, 21).

Strengthening Government Administration and Services

The first group of IDRC investments covered in this chapter was focused on improving the efficiency and effectiveness of government administrations and strengthening their capacity to deliver services to citizens. The differences between regions – in particular, regarding their readiness to implement e-government (see Chart 9.1 and Table 9.1 below) – meant that different approaches were supported in Africa, Latin America and the Caribbean (LAC) and Asia. The composite index shown in the chart below includes telecommunications infrastructure, measurement of human capital and the government's degree and sophistication of their web presence; the higher the number, the greater the readiness. The projects discussed below demonstrate the potential, as well as the challenges, of digitizing government administrations and services.

Note in Table 9.1 that Africa and South-Central Asia in 2003 had considerably lower levels of infrastructure and human capital than the other regions. In contrast, South and Central America and the Caribbean had quite high levels of human capital.

Digitizing administrative processes

eFez, Morocco

A notable success of electronic service implementation in Africa is the project "eFez" in the city of Fez, Morocco. Initiated in 2004 by Al Akhawayn University in Ifrane, the project helped the city effectively automate the internal administration, as well as the interface with citizens, of 12 bureaux d'état civil (BECs), which dispense birth certificates (Kettani et al. 2008). Research indicates that this project contributed to an increase in efficiency of the Fez local government. For instance, prior to the intervention, requests

Table 9.1. Breakdown of the three indices making up the e-government readiness index

	Web measure	Telecommunications index	Human capital index	E-government readiness index
North America	0.882	0.738	0.980	0.867
Europe	0.418	0.422	0.783	0.558
South and Central America	0.379	0.123	0.823	0.442
South and Eastern Asia	0.355	0.197	0.750	0.437
Western Asia	0.241	0.204	0.748	0.410
Caribbean	0.192	0.168	0.845	0.401
Oceania	0.217	0.138	0.697	0.351
South-Central Asia	0.195	0.035	0.268	0.292
Africa	0.137	0.036	0.521	0.246

Source: United Nations (2003, 22).

for birth certificates were processed manually and could not be delivered immediately. The digitization resulted in a drop in wait times from an average of 48 hours to only 6. Furthermore, civil servants in the BEC offices that participated in a survey two years after the rollout of the project said there were other improvements. For example, before the system was implemented, 58 percent reported that there were "a lot of errors." After the two years, no one reported "a lot of errors" and 83 percent reported that there are only "very few" errors. In addition, they had increased their certificate-processing capabilities by an average of 139 certificates per day, an increase of 20 percent from the previous daily average. This efficiency came with a decrease in the average number of employees needed from approximately ten to two and an improvement in relations with citizens, dropping the rate of tension from 58.3 percent to just 8 percent (Kettani and El Mahidi 2009).

In addition, digitizing many of the BECs' processes contributed to enhanced transparency and accountability by improving the visibility of workflows. Specifically, by automating service delivery, the process of requesting a birth certificate, processing that request and printing the birth certificate has been merged into one activity. All these steps had previously been carried out as separate activities, sometimes by different employees. As a result, if delays occurred, the reasons were not often visible to citizens. This made it difficult to initiate interventions and find resolutions.

The lack of transparency regarding the process also gave BEC employees the power to process specific requests whenever it was "convenient" for them to do so. Consequently, often small "acceleration" bribes were offered to employees to speed up processing. With the new automated service, requests are processed in real time, making it possible for citizens to monitor the progress of their requested service. This has ensured that citizens are able to access the service on a first come, first served basis and the conditions conducive to bribery have been eliminated. As a result, citizens' access to the BECs' services has become more equitable and consistent (Kettani and El Mahidi 2009). This has also helped to create a standard by which employees' performances can be judged. Employees can now be held accountable for their performance difficulties, whereas with the previous manual delivery, service performance standards were not known publicly.

One major reason for the success of the eFez project was that, over the course of its implementation, the active participation of the three local levels of government (district, city and state/province or *wilaya*) was encouraged. The organizational change needed to incorporate a new information system that digitizes records required a significant reshuffling of individuals' tasks and roles as well as on-the-job learning. The high level of local government involvement and participation was necessary to facilitate this process of change. It allowed for the diverse set of inputs required to ensure that the deployed system would meet the locally perceived needs, as well as adjusting to the local political, organizational and social context.

For example, the resulting system is multilingual and has an adaptive interface. By incorporating these elements, the e-service implementation avoided reproducing and automating previous service delivery faults and inefficiencies, resulting in high levels of acceptability, appropriation and adoption at the different levels of local government. The eFez example demonstrates that, when implemented well, electronic government services can dramatically improve the efficiency of government administration and service delivery and enhance the transparency of workflows and service delivery.

LOG-IN Africa

Unlike the relatively positive experience of eFez, the findings from research undertaken by the "Local Governance and ICT Research Network for Africa" (LOG-IN Africa) reveal the many challenges that local governments in Africa must overcome before they are able to fully reap the benefits of e-government. LOG-IN Africa was a research project that sought to investigate how ICTs could be used to (i) improve internal organization processes of local governments, (ii) provide information and deliver services, (iii) promote the principles of good governance and (iv) promote public participation and consultation.

The project assembled a network of researchers spanning nine countries that included Egypt, Ethiopia, Kenya, Mauritius, Morocco, Mozambique, Senegal, South Africa and Uganda. For example, in Mozambique, researchers studied the implementation of a land management information system (LMIS) that sought to integrate a variety of functionalities into one system. By the time the project was over, they found that the new system had had little to no net effect on the efficiency or effectiveness of their land management processes. This was due in part to the continued use of pre-existing systems, including some paper-based, that resulted in a duplication of work (Waema 2008).

Overall, the findings of the research teams demonstrated very clearly that inadequate ICT infrastructure, poor ICT knowledge and skills, limited public access to ICTs, as well as a lack of political will are, unsurprisingly, significant barriers to the successful implementation of more ambitious ICT initiatives aimed at affecting governance. Consequently, the majority of e-government implementations across the African countries

Table 9.2. Necessary conditions and obstacles for e-local governance roadmap.

Necessary conditions at the national level	Obstacles at the national level
• Existence of a governance policy • Recognition that ICTs are strategic resources in national socioeconomic development • E-local governance linked to and implemented as part of wider public service or local government reforms • Alignment of e-government strategy to the national ICT policy • Appropriate government agency or unit in charge of ICT • Successful pilot implementations of e-government projects	• Limited penetration and poor quality of the national government ICT infrastructure • E-government strategy not addressing local governments • Not promoting and publicizing e-government strategy and projects at all levels of government • Inadequate basic ICT skills at all levels of government • Inadequate financial resource allocation to local governments and to ICT • Incomplete decentralization of government • Inadequate implementation of universal access to ICT • Poor coordination of e-government implementation • Lack of political will

Source: Waema (2008).

studied by LOG-IN Africa focused on developing capacity for e-administration. A large component of this involved establishing the necessary ICT backbone infrastructure to create government intranets. However, at the time the study was completed, none of the countries studied by the network had rolled out this infrastructure to all of their ministries or at all levels of local government (Waema 2008).

The findings from LOG-IN Africa illustrate some of the difficulties in using ICTs to initiate a change process or "leapfrogging" stages of development. Generally, a considerable amount of backend work is needed to prepare governments before they can begin to digitally interact with citizens, regardless of the technological interface. To help governments avoid some of the pitfalls that often arise when implementing e-government initiatives, the LOG-IN Africa researchers created an e-local governance roadmap. The roadmap can be used to help inform national governments, multilateral agencies, local authorities and civil society about broad guidelines for investing in and developing e-government applications (see Table 9.2) (Waema 2008, 2011).

Sierra Leone project

In Sierra Leone, another project explored how ICTs can be used to improve records management and reduce corruption. This project, run by the International Records Management Trust (IMRT), began with the recognition that weak records systems open the door to fraud, corruption in procurement, misuse of resources and services and money laundering. Citizens are negatively affected by these activities as service delivery can be compromised, freedom of information can be stifled and civil society cannot hold governments to account (IRMT 2008b).

One key task of the project was to identify the issues that governments must address to introduce strong electronic records management systems (IRMT 2008a). The project involved a case study of a payroll verification exercise initiated by the government of Sierra Leone. The goals of exercise were to reduce payroll fraud, strengthen establishment controls and provide an evidence base of accurate and reliable personnel records for human resource management. The verification exercise carefully matched payroll information and employment records with information gathered through face-to-face interviews, physical head counts and payroll reconciliation (IRMT 2008a). This verification exercise revealed several anomalies within the records management system. For instance, they found a lack of education information for about three-quarters of public servants, as well as inaccurate information about their pay grades. As a result of the exercise, approximately sixteen percent of the 2,000 employees under investigation in the study were suspended from the payroll (IRMT 2008b).[1]

Common service centers

Success of electronic government services requires more than digitizing administrative processes; citizens must be able to access those services. One method for reaching out to citizens was through common service centers (CSCs), a model used in India. CSCs are public access points to ICTs that are used for delivering government e-services to citizens. In India, CSCs have been incorporated into the country's e-government strategy as a way of improving rural communities' access to government services. In 2006, the Indian national e-government strategy resulted in plans to establish one CSC for every six villages across the country.

The non-governmental organization IT for Change,[2] as part of its research on citizenship in the "Information Society for the South," explored the efficacy of this particular model.[3] Specifically, it took an in-depth look at one particular CSC, named e-gram. The objective of e-gram was to develop the *gram panchayat* (village administrative unit) within the Indian state of Gujarat to be the delivery point for a variety of e-services. These services include administering family, birth, death, caste, income and tax collection certificates. E-gram uses an offline software application with a digitized databank of family information that can be used to issue the various certificates at the *panchayat* level.

Internet connectivity – through an integrated backbone ICT infrastructure – was also being introduced as a way for villages to link with the Gujarat statewide area network and to improve two-way information flows between the various levels of government administration. This has provided a way to access, for example, Records of Rights (RoR) certificates that are needed for any transaction related to agricultural land through synchronization with the state data center (Nuggehali n.d.). The project simultaneously sought to improve rural villages' access to communication and commercial services that are dependent on computer connectivity.

The research found that e-gram helped redefine the roles of local administrative civil servants. For example, all requests for certificates are recorded in a digitized system and can be printed on demand. Therefore, civil servants cannot delay the process.

Furthermore, citizens can lodge complaints in the system. Given this new process, e-gram has also provided employees with the opportunity to focus their time and energy on other areas in their diverse work with increased efficiency (Nuggehali n.d.).

Ultimately, the efforts of the e-gram centers and *gram mitras* (community extension workers) centered on developing a strong focus on serving families that live below the poverty line. Census data on such families have been digitized at each center and the data used subsequently by the *gram mitras* to target development initiatives. Research shows e-gram to be a comprehensive and effective service delivery model, but IT for Change notes that many other CSCs in India are led predominately by the private sector. IT for Change argues that e-gram and its success serve as an example of the importance of keeping ownership within the larger local government administrative system, not with computer operators and private companies. In doing so, innovations and strategies originating from the CSCs can be driven by local government priorities, particularly addressing poverty and other issues not likely to be taken up by the profit motives of private companies (Nuggehali n.d.).

Regional e-government initiatives

In the LAC region, IDRC's approach to supporting the improvement of administration and delivery of government services through ICTs was significantly different than in Africa or Asia for several reasons. First, many countries in LAC – Brazil and Chile, to name two – had advanced considerably in their e-government infrastructure and implementations by the early 2000s. This meant there was an opportunity for "South–South" exchanges among countries in the region, rather than the countries following the lead of Western states. Second, the IDRC, through the Institute for Connectivity in the Americas (ICA), had excellent political connections and the mandate to promote ICTs throughout the region.[4] It was in this context that IDRC began funding regional e-government initiatives that sought to enhance civil servants' capacity to use e-government,[5] promote South–South knowledge exchange and ensure the issue of e-government was on the agenda of governments across the region.

RED GEALC

Perhaps the central LAC initiative was the creation of the Network of E-Government Leaders in Latin America and the Caribbean (RED GEALC),[6] developed in collaboration with the Inter-American Development Bank and the Organization of American States (OAS). RED GEALC was created in 2003 to promote horizontal cooperation in the area of e-government. The network tackled a wide range of issues that were identified as critical for the advancement of e-government by the members of the network. These issues included the facilitation of knowledge sharing of good practices, incentivizing high-quality e-government implementations, capacity building among civil servants and establishing interoperability standards.[7] One central activity that illustrates South–South sharing was the development of "eGobex,"[8] an online platform for sharing and transferring applications of e-government in which national, provincial and local governments can find solutions and share their own applications.[9]

The project leaders, understanding the critical importance of political will, sought above all to maintain e-government on the political agenda. This support was clearly achieved at several large regional forums. For instance, the declaration of Santo Domingo – "Good Governance and Development in the Knowledge-Based Society" – was adopted 6 June 2006 at the OAS's fourth plenary session. The declaration established regional commitments to promote e-government strategies, including training programs for public officials, the provision of e-services and increased levels of transparency and accountability through the use of new ICT tools. Similarly, a few years later, during the annual meeting of RED GEALC in 2009 in Uruguay, ministers, senior officials in charge of e-government policies and international experts all shared their experiences and coordinated actions to support e-government strategies in the region.

Overall, the results of the network's activities were greater than the sum of its parts. The experience of Colombia is the prime example. Colombia has been one of the most active countries since the initiation of the network (e.g., 44 percent of the online training offered through the network was taken by Colombian civil servants). The Colombian government also established an agreement with the academic team to adapt the courses to their needs. During this time, Colombia has continuously and systematically improved in the country rankings on e-government and has now become the top-ranked country in the region. The director of e-government in Colombia indicated that the key to success for the implementation was a cultural change – a change in the mentality of the civil servants that resulted from a series of activities (in particular, training and evidence of success). This illustrates how the human side of e-government implementation complements the technical issues; a bureaucratic culture conducive to ICTs and sufficient civil servant capacity are critical for the implementation and sustainability of e-government initiatives.

The network methodology used in RED GEALC also illustrates the power of collaboration and sharing between countries. Despite the differences among countries – be they financial, cultural, geographic, etc. – it proved possible to document and learn from other countries' experiences. Indeed, the financial investments made by governments to participate in the network were paid back significantly through this transfer of knowledge and solutions.

Lessons learned

As with RED GEALC, eFez demonstrated the importance of engaging decision makers at all stages of an e-government implementation. In the beginning phases of the project, researchers observed that decision makers were largely unaware of the transformative potential of ICTs. Not surprisingly, this low level of awareness translated into a lack of interest in ICTs. Consequently, ICT-related projects – including e-government – were not included in their political agendas, which meant that no funds were allocated in their budgets for such projects. However, on seeing the success of the eFez project, the municipality was compelled to improve its IT department.

The discussion above also illustrates another point: e-government implementations are deeply embedded in a context that extends well beyond the technology and even the public sector organizations themselves. There is certainly a technical infrastructure dimension, as the experience with LOG-IN Africa illustrated. eFez and RED GEALC show that there are organizational and political factors critical to shaping the ongoing process of e-government implementation. However, the development impact of implementing e-government extends even further. What research by IT for Change illustrated is that implementation cannot be removed from the broader socioeconomic development context. Context is very influential in determining the citizen's uptake and usage of the services and, ultimately, the developmental success of these projects.

In particular, the design of e-government services must take into account the day-to-day reality of marginalized populations who traditionally have had difficulties accessing government services. This is particularly true in cases like land records, where the system itself is the arbiter of the allocation of scarce resources. In one case, in Bangalore, a new land-records system created "efficiencies" through digitization; however, these efficiencies unintentionally empowered the already well-to-do to take advantage of errors in the process to remove marginalized people from their land (Benjamin et al. 2007). Thus, when it comes to assessing the success of a new e-government service, it is critical to look beyond techno-managerial assessments – such as increased efficiency – and incorporate broader social indicators that measure the impact on citizens' lives (Madon 2009).

Of course, e-government is not limited to improving administrative procedures and service delivery – or, in other words, doing what government does, but more efficiently. It is also a potential means to begin rethinking the way that government does what it does and the nature of its relationship with citizens. The following section shows how IDRC-supported research projects promoted political participation and democratic empowerment.

Facilitating Political Participation and Democratic Empowerment

An effective democracy provides space for citizens to freely express their preferences to government and to participate in decisions that affect their lives. This requires channels of communication that allow citizens both to acquire information from government and to act on that information by providing feedback to political leaders (Gasu and Akakpo 2011). ICTs have a central role to play in this process. They can facilitate the provision of relevant information in an understandable format. In addition, ICTs provide potentially new communication channels to enhance citizen participation in policymaking and decision making processes (Weare 2002; Holzer et al. 2004; Brewer et al. 2006).

Recognizing this potential, IDRC's ICT4D program funded a number of action research projects aimed at facilitating political participation through the use of ICTs. The following projects illustrate the various opportunities provided for ICTs to enable different forms of political engagement. Also discussed are the challenges ICTs face in this regard.

CITRED in Northern Ghana

One of the first projects IDRC sponsored in this area began in 2005 in northern Ghana. The project explored the role of ICTs in enhancing political inclusion and participation of marginalized groups in two local government districts, Tamale Metropolis and Tolon-Kumbungu. At the start of the project, a baseline study was conducted by the Centre for Information Technologies and Research Development (CITRED) to assess the extent of existing ICT usage, the capacity of users and the purposes for which ICTs were being used for local-level governance processes. The results of this baseline study showed that no mechanisms existed for citizens to engage with political leaders through ICTs, save for the occasional use of local FM radio stations for government announcements. They also found that computer use and literacy of the general population was quite low. In contrast, however, they did find that access to radio technology and mobile telephony was relatively pervasive, suggesting that these technologies offered the readiest means for people to acquire news and information.

In March 2006, CITRED began sponsoring interactive "breakfast shows" on Radio Savannah and Justice Radio; these shows ran until September of that year. To make the programs interactive, citizens were encouraged to call in to the radio stations with their feedback, made easier by mobile phones. The project also sponsored the creation of bureaus in the local government offices in the two districts to collect the feedback from the radio stations. This provided a quick way of compiling feedback and helping officials determine what input was most urgent and feasible to address. Ultimately, this interactive radio initiative provided new avenues for civil society to communicate with government officials and helped the officials to better appreciate their constituents' problems, as well as determine ways of addressing these problems (Gasu and Akakpo 2011).

However, not all was rosy. The project began to lose the support of political leaders and other government officials once it became apparent that the project was beginning to engender change. By establishing new technological methods for government–citizen communication and by presenting opportunities for participation in governance, the project departed quite drastically from local administrative norms where information flows were face-to-face, rather than digital and transparent. Key players suddenly became evasive and failed to honor scheduled meetings. According to the research team, the leaders' reactions reflected their fear of being overwhelmed by demands from citizens. In addition, through discussion with civil servants, it was revealed that they preferred personal contact with citizens rather than technology-mediated contact. Personal contact created a prime opportunity for government officials to supplement their income through bribes and the "out of station" allowances they were paid for leaving the office to interact with citizens. Since civil servants were one of the main implementers of the project interventions, resistance from their end held up the process significantly (Gasu and Akakpo 2011).

This project illustrates how ICT tools can be used to create new channels of communication between citizens and government; it also highlights the challenges of doing so. The experience reinforces the well-known lesson about the importance of establishing political buy-in and, in particular, the importance of this buy-in when the project begins to threaten the status quo. The research team focused predominately on aligning technologies to establish new lines of communication. However, they did not adequately address the issue that an intervention aiming to increase political participation would fundamentally alter decision making processes and civil servants' roles. This implies a shift in power, which generally provokes resistance.

Peñalolén, Chile

In the Latin America and Caribbean region, IDRC supported a similar project in the Chilean municipality of Peñalolén. The project's goal was to identify, design and analyze ICT strategies for strengthening transparency and citizen participation. Peñalolén was a particularly interesting case to test the potential for e-government in the region as it was atypical of municipal governments across Chile. Unlike most major *communas* in Chile, it has a very heterogeneous population of squatter, working-class and higher-income residents.

The political legacy of the Allende coup is also ever-present in this *communa*. One of the "torture parks" used to imprison and interrogate citizens during the coup is operated as an exhibit center and is managed by one of the former detainees. As well, the mayor of Peñalolén had been the former minister responsible for state modernization in the national government. Accordingly, "buy-in" from the top was not a problem. Indeed, the mayor, Claudio Orrego, drove the project to a great degree and wanted to use ICTs as one way to overcome the separate solitudes that characterized this heterogeneous *communa*.

One initiative was the creation of an online system to take citizens' complaints and suggestions. This system resulted in a four-fold increase in citizens' comments over the previous complaint process. However, as in Ghana, the increased number of requests generated challenges for public servants to process and respond to the requests. The research indicated the importance of developing the required capacities and internal operations to handle the new channels and amount of information flow.

Another initiative included the broadcasting and archiving of council meetings. The online council meetings resulted in a fairly dramatic increase in information requests and substantially improved the government's response rate. Furthermore, 44 percent of the citizens surveyed wanted greater diffusion of information and 33 percent indicated that they would be interested in the possibility of online citizen interaction during the council meetings.

The project also experimented with a participatory budgeting system. The system promoted the participation of some citizens in the decision making process, involving 15 percent of citizens in the city. However, there was limited participation by those people with medium to high vulnerabilities.

Asia

In Asia, IDRC supported research focusing on the relationship between ICTs and democratic participation. One such project began in 2009 by exploring the role of ICTs in facilitating political engagement among youth. This project spanned six countries – Singapore, Malaysia, India, Bangladesh, Sri Lanka and the Philippines – and aimed to understand the types of ICTs youth use to engage in political processes and how these tools are transforming the nature of their engagement. Although the study's findings differ from country to country, the results show that, generally, the majority of youth use ICTs for entertainment and personal communication. However, some youth in the region do use ICTs to engage in activism and political processes.

For example, the Malaysian research team identified and interviewed a number of youth activists, NGO members and online opinion leaders. Their research describes how youth effectively use the Internet – including blogs, social networking sites and online forums – for many political activities. These include launching major campaigns to support or counter political leaders and legislation and reporting on events that are not covered by the established media, such as the prosecution of Malaysia's deputy prime minister Anwar Ibrahim (Zhang et al. 2010).

Lessons learned

As shown by these attempts to facilitate greater democratic participation, government engagement with citizens is a tricky matter, with significant implications for public sector organizations. These implications require sustained political commitment and leadership to shepherd the required internal changes to roles and processes – in particular, the changes that open up calcified, inefficient processes to external scrutiny or input. The differences in the outcomes in northern Ghana and Peñalolén are evidence of this dynamic. In Peñalolén, this commitment helped establish a smooth working implementation process that allowed for adaptation to the emerging needs and changing conditions in the municipality. In northern Ghana, the project was not able to generate sufficient political will to sustain the continued use of the intervention; thus, not surprisingly, it had less successful outcomes.

Taking a broader perspective, implications for the public sector also arise from the slow but certain rearrangement of the citizen–government relationship that results from any e-government implementation. As we have seen, new e-government systems can bring about increased participation and inclusion as well as resistance by some and exclusion of others. As ICTs begin to shift accountability arrangements and flows of information, one can imagine that less well-intentioned people, both within and outside government, will try to use these technologies to reinforce or expand their current positions of relative advantage.

The combination of the increased prevalence and deepening of e-government implementations and the spread of ICTs throughout society suggests that the nature of the citizen–government relationship will continue to evolve and perhaps increase in complexity. The following section explores some of the inherent development tensions that emerge from this evolution.

Exploring Emerging Tensions

A variety of important issues that affect citizens' lives arises from the increased spread of ICTs, both inside and outside government. With the increased ease and capacity to gather, store, process and communicate information, there are questions as to how those data, often personal, are to be handled, whether by the state or private entities. Similarly, the technical capacity of many states to censor access to "undesirable" information raises questions about how this might limit citizens' freedom of expression or right to information. How do states' current policies on the Internet, privacy and telecommunications affect these rights? In what ways do technological choices facilitate surveillance that might be open to abuse, either by political or private actors? How can a state enact policy measures to protect the privacy and security of citizens while balancing citizens' freedom of expression, particularly when such policy measures might require regulation of the private sector? Research on these issues is needed to understand them sufficiently to inform policy and make good practice recommendations on how to reduce undesirable trends and reinforce valued ones. IDRC-funded research pursued these questions. The research has led to some important findings and outcomes and points to areas that require further research.

ONI-Asia on censorship and surveillance practices in Asia

One IDRC-funded research initiative, the OpenNet Initiative Asia (ONI-Asia), has built an important body of information regarding censorship and surveillance practices in Asia. For example, ONI-Asia uncovered extensive surveillance and censorship activities occurring through TOM-Skype, a joint venture of Skype and TOM-Online, a leading wireless provider in China. TOM-Skype was monitoring users' conversations without the users' knowledge. It was also routinely collecting and logging records that included personal information such as IP addresses, usernames and landline telephone numbers used to place or receive Skype calls. Furthermore, it collected full-text chat messages, including time and date, sent or received by TOM-Skype users. "Sensitive" words such as "Falun Gong" or "Dalai Lama" would be automatically filtered. Researchers found that the TOM-Skype software contained an encrypted file with a list of banned keywords. So, when a user sent or received a chat message with one of those keywords, the message would not be displayed. In addition, it appeared that the content of the message was uploaded to a TOM-Skype server. Translation of over 96,000 messages stored in these logfiles revealed some of the more commonly filtered keywords. (See Figure 9.1.) However, some surveillance did not seem to be driven only by keywords because many of the recorded messages contained words that were too common to log extensively. Thus, ONI-Asia believes that there must have been other triggers for filtering, such as usernames (Villeneuve 2008, 5).

These findings raise major concerns regarding the privacy and human rights of those individuals using TOM-Skype. It is unclear from the investigation the extent to which TOM-Skype was cooperating with the Chinese government to monitor the communication of political dissidents or even of ordinary citizens. Also unclear is the legal basis on which TOM-Skype was monitoring and logging communication.

The TOM-Skype findings raise issues of great relevance within the context of the emerging information society. In particular, they show the importance of the need for effective legal and policy frameworks to protect citizens' private information, including frameworks that govern interactions between the state and the private sector as pertaining

Figure 9.1. Filtered messages by keyword

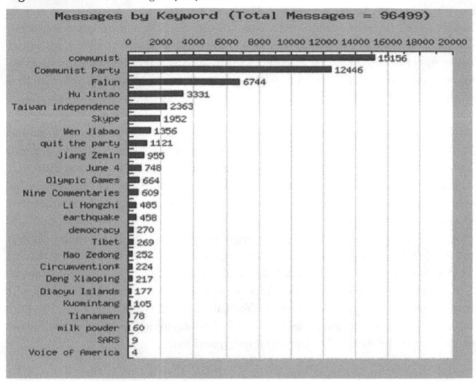

Source: Villeneuve (2008, 9).

to ICTs. The TOM-Skype discovery reveals some contours of the evolving nature of the battle over information that is taking place between governments and political dissidents through the use of new ICTs and the place of information services providers in that mix. ICTs provide a powerful platform for dissidents to spread information, but they may also provide governments with the tools to monitor and curb the influence of dissidents (Villeneuve 2008, 5, 12).

Another of ONI-Asia's significant findings resulted from an investigation of cyber espionage against Tibetan institutions. This investigation led ONI-Asia to uncover a network of 1295 computers in 103 countries that were infected with cyberspying software. Infected computers included computers at high-profile targets, such as ministries of foreign affairs, embassies, international organizations, news media and NGOs. The software enabled the attackers to send instructions to and receive data from infected computers. It was not clear who the precise attackers were, if the attackers knew the extent to which they had penetrated infected institutions or if information was ever compromised (IWM 2009, 5–6). These findings give an idea of the extent to which cyber espionage and warfare has developed. What does seem clear is that information security and privacy issues require greater attention in the information society (IWM 2009, 11, 49).

ONI-Asia research also highlighted three approaches to censorship in Asia, represented by Singapore, China and Thailand. Singapore has implemented a "light touch" model whereby state-owned media are subject to significant censorship while private media outlets are free to operate so long as they hold a license. Some critics, however, argue that the license system has led to an effective culture of self-censorship. China has implemented a system of public–private filtering partnerships, whereby local providers must filter according to state demands to maintain regulatory compliance (OpenNet Initiative 2009, 9–10). China's model is often referred to as "first generation" control. First generation controls "focus on denying access to specific Internet Resources by directly blocking access to servers, domains, keywords, and IP addresses" by targeting information flows at "key Internet choke points" (Diebert and Rohozinski 2010, 22). Thailand's model requires court approval to block a website, but the government has secured the cooperation of transnational gatekeepers such as YouTube to implement geolocational filtering – a mechanism by which Internet content is restricted in specific geographic regions – on its behalf. Accordingly, critics argue, the Thai government does not need to resort to formal or transparent legal processes. ONI-Asia suggests that the Thai model could become the norm for many other countries in Asia. For example, a Vietnamese official has expressed interest in such public–private partnerships with transnational gatekeepers like Google or YouTube (OpenNet Initiative 2009, 11). Each of these models of censorship raises questions of transparency and accountability, both on the part of the state and of Internet service providers.

Transparency versus privacy

Judicial information in Latin America and the Caribbean

A project in Latin America and the Caribbean (LAC) points to a different sort of challenge regarding the tension between transparency and privacy that takes new forms with the increasing digitization of the public sector. In this case, the project addressed a situation within the judiciary that required navigating a balance between transparency and privacy. On the one hand, ICTs facilitate the dissemination of judicial information, meeting the need for transparency, equality before the law and public scrutiny. On the other hand, there are risks to privacy that could lead to discrimination against vulnerable groups who are being processed by the justice system. For example, the bulk publishing on the Internet of judgments that are accessible via search engines potentially places witnesses' and victims' privacy at risk unless such publication is accompanied by changes in other practices, such as taking privacy considerations into account when writing the judgments.

While many LAC countries have enacted laws to protect privacy and personal data, research revealed that these laws are not effective. Only by applying child and family protection laws have the names of some individuals been removed from Internet-disseminated judgments. By replacing names with initials in sensitive cases, some private companies that disseminate judicial decisions have begun to self-regulate the spread of information (Careaga 2004, 2).

As a result of the project, several LAC judicial branches, civil society groups and academics approved the "Heredia Rules," a set of rules that establishes the minimum standards for publishing judicial information on the Internet. The rules represent the first organized attempt to strike a balance between transparency and privacy. Furthermore, the Heredia Rules are an effort to adapt both the European model (which prioritizes individual privacy, partly in response to some states' use of public records for racial and ethnic discrimination) and the American model (which prioritizes the wide and unrestricted availability of judicial information) to the situation in the LAC region (Careaga 2004, 10). The courts of justice in Costa Rica, Venezuela, Paraguay, in the Rio Grande do Sol state in Brazil and in the Rio Negro and Chubut provinces in Argentina have discussed and adapted the rules according to their own judicial traditions and contexts. Another result of the project was the development of judicial software that, while maintaining names in the sentencing texts, does not allow search engines to locate them, thus protecting the privacy of persons involved in judicial proceedings.

This project illustrates some of the challenges in the judicial sector that emerge when moving public sector activities online. In this particular case, new frameworks are needed to govern the dissemination of judicial information and the protection of individual privacy given the fact that ICTs enable dissemination of information much more widely and make it much more accessible. The judicial sector case also is evidence of a larger dynamic – namely, that the incorporation of ICTs in the public sector to bring about greater transparency often requires a renegotiation of accountability arrangements to govern the new ICT-enabled processes (Smith et al. 2010).

Citizen awareness and policy measures regarding data protection and privacy in Latin America and the Caribbean

Another project led to important findings and outcomes about the role the state could play in (i) educating citizens on the dangers of the information society and (ii) enacting policy measures to protect the privacy and security of citizens. The project also looked at the role of the state regarding the private sector and the measures it should take to act in a transparent and accountable manner. This LAC project built a body of knowledge both to facilitate informed debate on the risks generated by ICTs for vulnerable groups and to influence public policy to mitigate these risks. Research found that many social networking sites are operating with troubling practices with regard to data protection and privacy. In Brazil, for example, this lack of protection has spurred the government to confront Google about the flow of child pornography over its Orkut social network. Citizens in the country have also enacted legal action against Google, including approximately 1,300 lawsuits concerning invasion of privacy and defamation. The legal action against Google has led judges to define rights in social networks, an important step toward the creation of an overall Internet privacy regulation framework.

The "Memorandum of Montevideo"[10] is the most significant outcome of this project. It was created on 28 July 2009 by experts from a variety of LAC countries who were attending the seminar on "Rights, Adolescents and Internet Social Networks." The memorandum comprises a list of recommendations for governments on how to structure privacy-related legal frameworks, enforce legislation, implement public policies geared toward awareness-raising and further research and create mechanisms to assist victims. The memorandum also contains suggestions for educational institutions on how to educate youth about the threats posed by the social web movement. Additionally, it provides recommendations for businesses on how to protect personal data and privacy and to comply with national judicial frameworks.

The memorandum represents a significant advance toward a regulatory framework on Internet privacy issues. It contributed to the Instituto Federal de Acceso a la Información y Protección de Datos (IFAI) in Mexico and the Agencia de Gobierno Electrónico y Sociedad de la Información (AGESIC) in Uruguay, initiating processes to address some of the issues raised. For example, following discussions with researchers from the ICT4D-funded project, the Mexican Ministry of Public Education created a national website called "Clic Seguro"[11] to offer guidance and practical advice for citizens so they can use technology in safe and conscientious ways. This website incorporated recommendations from the memorandum.

Privacy issues in Asia

Another research project developed a network of researchers that examined privacy-related issues in Asia, including public understanding and perceptions of privacy; the interaction of privacy and new technologies; and the role of legal instruments, including international agreements, constitutions and national laws. It explored how Asian societies negotiate their way through their legal systems, globalization pressures, increased concerns about international crime and terrorism, greater adoption of Internet services and the spread of surveillance technologies and their adoption into national infrastructures. The project also explored what opportunities there are to introduce safeguards against abuse.

Findings thus far point to an increasing awareness about privacy-related issues among key policy constituencies in Asia. However, the research also indicates that Asians have little voice in international forums regarding the shape of privacy controls, both regionally and internationally, for two reasons. First, Asian governments have largely focused on privacy issues to enhance international trade by enabling data to flow from Europe's strongly regulated privacy environment. Second, American industry bodies often speak for Asian people at these international forums, suggesting that there is no culture of privacy in Asia in order to reduce regulatory burdens on global business (Privacy International 2009, 39).

The project outlined the juridical and regulatory frameworks pertaining to data privacy in the countries studied – Bangladesh, India, Indonesia, Malaysia, Pakistan, the Philippines, Thailand, Hong Kong and Nepal. It also proposed a comprehensive framework by which to assess privacy issues as they arise. The framework suggests exploring whether constitutional protections for privacy exist, the character of existing data protection laws and whether communications surveillance powers are authorized and overseen by an independent body to prevent abuse. It also encourages an investigation of the political risks, technological challenges, feasibility issues, costs and implications for civil liberties of identity policies. Furthermore, the framework promotes attention to the understanding of privacy in particular cultural contexts as well as the capacity of civil society to educate itself regarding privacy issues (Privacy International 2009, 46–50).

Findings of ICT4D-funded research on emerging tensions

Research funded by ICT4D, spurred on by the need to mitigate the potential negative effects of the information society, has sought to understand the changing relationship among citizens, society and the state amidst the emerging information society with the hopes of informing policymaking processes. In that regard, the research has produced some important findings about state and private sector involvements that threaten citizens' security, privacy and freedom of expression. It brought to light specific instances of the state and private sector using ICTs for surveillance and censorship. These discoveries reveal how states can and do exploit the benefits of ICTs to consolidate positions of power, just as corporations act when pursuing economic interests. Such censorship and surveillance is widespread and can have damaging effects on citizens' participation in the public sphere.

The research also resulted in significant policy-oriented outcomes that indicate how both the state and the private sector might act in more transparent and accountable ways. Specific examples include the Heredia Rules, the Memorandum of Montevideo and guidelines for the collection and storage of personal information in Asia. Each of these outcomes emphasizes the importance of personal data protection policy and regulatory frameworks and the need to include privacy considerations at the design stage of ICT systems.

It is clear that the increasing prevalence of ICTs and technological know-how, both within and outside governments, is bringing new sets of development issues to the fore. While the research presented in this section is only preliminary in nature, it does illustrate how privacy, censorship and surveillance should be seen as central development concerns in the emerging information society. More research is needed to understand these dynamics and help both developed and developing countries strike a balance between the many governance benefits and challenges that more ubiquitous ICTs raise.

Conclusion

The term e-government will soon be redundant; governments are information processing organizations (Dunleavy et al. 2006) and will use ICTs to do so. The increasing incorporation of ICTs into the public sector raises an array of governance-related issues. While the increasing pervasiveness of ICTs may strengthen the democratic nature of the citizen–government relationship – for example, by facilitating greater transparency or enabling public participation – it is also possible that ICTs facilitate anti-democratic tendencies, such as enhanced surveillance and censorship practices with chilling effects on citizens' democratic rights. The development outcomes of e-government are not preordained; they will be determined through an ongoing complex process of social negotiation and e-government-in-use rather than a linear consequence of any single implementation. What is certain, however, is that the relationship among citizens, society and the state is inexorably changing and policy and technical choices made now will shape the future space of development opportunities.

The events of the 2011 Arab Spring show how ICTs can play a role in bringing about transformative political and social change. Change was driven by actors external to government, rather than through internal reform processes. Evidence suggests that the penetration of social media technologies contributed to the uprisings through altering the media ecosystem and allowing for new flows of communication (Zuckerman 2011; Howard et al. 2011). Despite attempts to censor and intercept information and even shut down the Internet for a few days in Egypt and Tunisia, the governments failed to stop the protests and eventually fell. Indeed, early research suggests that shutting down the networks can potentially exacerbate the revolutionary movement the government wishes to quell (Hassanpour 2011). What remains to be seen – and what is a critical question going forward – is how these technologies can and will be employed in the transition process of the Arab states post-revolution.

The story of the Arab Spring, the projects in this chapter and other e-government literature make it clear that the outcomes are ultimately shaped by the context. Success or failure is strongly a "people" issue (United Nations 2008) alongside the technical challenges. In the cases of eFez and the Chilean municipality of Peñalolén, a high degree of political buy-in was key to their success. Indeed, in the case of eFez, political will helped to successfully shepherd the project through potential internal resistance despite the initial low level of ICT-related awareness within both the bureaucracy and decision makers (Kettani 2006). However, the attempt to facilitate citizens' interactions with government in Ghana resulted in a high level of resistance from the civil servants as they realized the system was threatening their particular positions of power. Such an outcome is not altogether surprising, as public sector organizational decision making always takes place within the political reality of structurally entrenched roles and power. This context will shape the nature and use of any e-government applications and associated reforms introduced (Fountain 2002). Consequently, when implementation threatens positions of power or changes the ways of working, it butts up against incompatible and entrenched public service cultures. Therefore, one would anticipate that change and acceptance of the new technologies would be at best slow, at worst met with resistance, or ultimately neutered in that the resulting outcomes perpetuate the status quo (West 2005).

The findings reviewed in this chapter also raise the importance of conceptualizing e-government as part of a larger government–society relationship rather than a means to simply improve the operations of government organizations. Democratic institutions uphold and balance a variety of sometimes conflicting values that extend well beyond improving efficiency and effectiveness (Bonina and Cordella 2010; Smith 2011). Exacerbating existing inequalities more efficiently is not an improvement. Understanding how these implementations interact with the broader socioeconomic positions of people is critical to that equation. For example, in Peñalolén, the project ran into difficulties engaging vulnerable peoples; therefore, despite increased citizen engagement at the municipal level, the voices of the vulnerable were not heard. It is critical for governments to consider issues such as inclusion from the beginning of new implementations ("inclusion by design"). This was true in the start of e-government and will continue to be true with the transition to "Government 2.0," "open government" or other future developments. If not, there is no reason to doubt that, as in the past, these new engagements will tend to favor those who already are well positioned over those who are not.

Thinking more broadly also means understanding the importance of an appropriate and enforceable legal and regulatory framework that can deal with the tensions that emerge. These tensions will undoubtedly remain – and even increase in importance – as ICTs penetrate more deeply into the daily operations of both governments and society at large. As governments realize the power of these technologies for social control, there is good reason to believe that there will continue to be those who will push for increased surveillance, censorship and securitization of the Internet. If maintaining hard-won democratic rights is desired, then governments need to protect the right to privacy and freedom of expression in the digital world to help protect citizens from emerging risks.

As the events associated with the recent "Arab Spring" demonstrate, ICTs have become a powerful tool for the promotion of transparency and participation by citizens with their governments. The numerous examples cited from Asia, Africa and the Americas all attest to this. This occurred through numerous approaches and modalities. They include focused government "e-service" centers, networks of public administrators sharing experiences across national borders, as well as through municipalities with visionary leaders who integrate ICTs into community life in exceptional ways. Long-term collaboration with local partners who drove these initiatives was a central feature of the successful projects.

But we also know that ICTs and their use by governments can have a dark side. As governments have come to adopt ICTs, they can also misuse them to stifle opposition and engender regressive surveillance. The IDRC-supported research on surveillance and privacy are examples of the need for flexible and forward-looking programming, particularly in the rapidly evolving ICT4D space. Such an approach anticipates emerging issues to be able to provide relevant evidence to inform discourse and policy decisions when the issues make it into the realm of policy discussions.

Notes

1 The project, in cooperation with the government, created a documentary video entitled *Ghost Busting: Building Payroll Integrity in Sierra Leone*, http://www.youtube.com/watch?v=LjlQetAdeAw (accessed 3 June 2012).
2 http://www.itforchange.net/.
3 IDRC ICT4D funds did not support the implementation of e-gram. Rather, support was given for a research paper produced by IT for Change as part of their work on citizenship in project 103941, "Information Society for the South."
4 ICA was established by the 2001 Summit of the Americas. See http://www.idrc.ca/EN/Programs/Science_and_Innovation/Information_and_Networks/Pages/Institute-for-Connectivity-in-the-Americas.aspx (accessed 16 July 2012).
5 One of the first projects to tackle the issue of capacity of public sector civil servants was @Campus Mexico in 2003. @Campus Mexico was designed to create a training and evaluation

framework for the government as it moved to implement the new law stipulating that promotion and hiring of public servants needed to be based on merit rather than on political influence of connection. The project also provided civil servants with an Internet-based education portal offering courses and information on certification. President Vicente Fox officially launched the project on 20 October 2004 in Mexico City.

6 http://www.redgealc.net/.

7 RED GEALC engaged in many activities that included establishing a comprehensive repository of information and documents on e-government in LAC (www.redgealc.net). Its activities include training for e-government researchers, management of an excellent e-government award (excel GOB) and management of the E-Gov monitor. In total, more than four thousand public servants were trained through online courses. The project also contributed to the *White Book of E-Government Interoperability for Latin American and the Caribbean* (www.eclac.org/ddpe/publicaciones/xml/7/37347/WhiteBook.pdf [accessed 16 July 2012]), developed in 2007 by the United Nations Economic Commission for Latin America and the Caribbean (ECLAC) and the European Union.

8 See www.egobex.net.

9 Another example of a successful transfer of an e-government solution was the "E-Government Caribbean Pilot Project." This pilot project's main objective was to transfer and adapt the Jamaica Customs Management solution (CASE) to the eastern Caribbean state of Antigua and Barbuda.

10 www.iijusticia.org/Memo.htm (accessed 13 May 2012).

11 www.clicseguro.sep.gob.mx.

References

Andersen, K. V. 2004. *E-Government and Public Sector Process Rebuilding (PPR): Dilettantes, Wheelbarrows, and Diamonds*. Boston: Kluwer Academic Publishers.

Bellamy, C. and J. A. Taylor. 1998. *Governing in the Information Age*. Buckingham: Open University Press.

Benjamin, S. et al. 2007. "Bhoomi: 'E-Governance' or an Anti-politics Machine Necessary to Globalize Bangalore?" CASUM-m working paper. Online: http://casumm.files.wordpress.com/2008/09/bhoomi-e-governance.pdf (accessed 3 June 2012).

Bhatnagar, S. 2004. *E-Government: From Vision to Implementation*. Thousand Oaks: Sage Publications.

Bonina, C. and A. Cordella. 2010. "The Internet and Public Bureaucracies: Towards Balancing Competing Values." Presentation at "Internet, Politics, Policy 2010: An Impact Assessment," Oxford Internet Institute, University of Oxford, 16–17 September. Online: http://microsites.oii.ox.ac.uk/ipp2010/system/files/IPP2010_Bonina_Cordella_Paper.pdf (accessed 6 July 2012).

Brewer, G. A. et al. 2006. "Designing and Implementing E-Government Systems: Critical Implications for Public Administration and Democracy." *Administration & Society* 38, no. 4: 471–99.

Careaga, F. L. 2004. "Research Influence on Public Policy: Case Study of the Instituto de Investigación para la Justicia." Report prepared for the Evaluation Unit and Pan America's Programme Initiative of the International Development Research Centre.

Chadwick, A. 2008. "Web 2.0: New Challenges for the Study of E-Democracy in an Era of Informational Exuberance." *I/S: A Journal of Law and Policy for the Information Society* 5, no. 1: 9–41.

Ciborra, C. and D. Navarra. 2005. "Good Governance, Development Theory, and Aid Policy: Risks and Challenges of E-Government in Jordan." *Information Technology for Development* 11, no. 2: 141–59.

Diebert, R. and R. Rohozinski. 2010. "Control and Subversion in Russian Cyberspace." In *Access Controlled: The Shaping of Power, Rights, and Rule in Cyberspace*, edited by R. Diebert et al. Cambridge, MA: MIT Press.

Dunleavy, P. et al. 2006. *Digital Era Governance: IT Corporations, the State, and E-Government*. Oxford: Oxford University Press.

Fountain, J. E. 2001. *Building the Virtual State: Information Technology and Institutional Change*. Washington, DC: Brookings Institution Press.

———. 2002. "Toward a Theory of Federal Bureaucracy for the Twenty-First Century." In *Governance.com: Democracy in the Information Age*, edited by E. C. Kamarck and J. S. Nye Jr. Washington, DC: Brookings Institution Press.

Gasu, J. and J. Akakpo. 2011. "ICTs for Political Inclusion and Good Governance in Northern Ghana." In *Local Governance and ICTs in Africa: Case Studies and Guidelines for Implementation and Evaluation*, edited by T. Waema and E. Adera. Cape Town: Pambazuka Press.

Hassanpour, N. 2011. "Media Disruption Exacerbates Revolutionary Unrest: Evidence from Mubarak's Natural Experiment." Paper presented at the American Political Science Association's Annual Meeting in Seattle, 1–4 September. Online: http://ssrn.com/abstract=1903351 (accessed 5 June 2012).

Heeks, R. 2003. "Most E-Government-for-Development Projects Fail: How can Risks Be Reduced?" iGovernment working paper series, paper no. 14, Institute for Development and Policy Management. Manchester: University of Manchester. Online: http://unpan1.un.org/intradoc/groups/public/documents/NISPAcee/UNPAN015488.pdf (accessed 27 July 2012).

———. 2004. "E-Government for Development: Basic Definitions Page." Institute for Development Policy and Management. Manchester: University of Manchester.

Holzer, M. et al. 2004. "Restoring Trust in Government: The Potential of Digital Citizen Participation." IBM Center for the Business of Government, E-Government Series. Washington, DC: IBM Center for the Business of Government.

Howard, P. N. et al. 2011. "Opening Closed Regimes: What Was the Role of Social Media during the Arab Spring?" Project on Information Technology and Political Islam Research, memo 2011.1. Seattle: University of Washington.

IRMT (International Records Management Trust). 2008a. *E-Government in Sierra Leone: Enabling Democracy and Good Governance: Electronic Government, Corruption and Records Management*. Final report prepared for IDRC. London: IRMT. Online: http://idl-bnc.idrc.ca/dspace/bitstream/10625/46371/1/132864.pdf (accessed 17 June 2012).

———. 2008b. "Sierra Leone Case Study: Evidence-Based Employment and Payroll Controls." In *E-Government in Sierra Leone: Enabling Democracy and Good Governance: Electronic Government, Corruption and Records Management*. Final report prepared for IDRC, attachment 1. London: IRMT. Online: http://idl-bnc.idrc.ca/dspace/bitstream/10625/46371/1/132864.pdf (accessed 17 June 2012).

IWM (Information Warfare Monitor). 2009. "Tracking Ghost Net: Investigating a Cyber Espionage Network." Toronto: The Munk Centre for International Studies / Ottawa: The SecDev Group. Online: http://www.nartv.org/mirror/ghostnet.pdf (accessed 13 May 2012).

Kakabadse, A. et al. 2003. "Reinventing the Democratic Governance Project through Information Technology? A Growing Agenda for Debate." *Public Administration Review* 63, no. 1: 44–60.

Kettani, D. 2006. *A Sustainable eGovernment Pilot Project for the City of Fez in Morocco*. eFez final report prepared for IDRC. Ottawa: IDRC. Online: http://unpan1.un.org/intradoc/groups/public/documents/unpan/unpan030931.pdf (accessed 4 June 2012).

Kettani, D. and A. El Mahidi. 2009. "Fez E-Government Project: An Initiative Transforming Scientific Research to Value in Morocco." *Electronic Journal of E-Government* 7, no. 4: 371–80. Online: www.ejeg.com/issue/download.html?idArticle=154 (accessed 7 June 2012).

Kettani, D. et al. 2008. "E-Government and Local Good Governance: A Pilot Project in Fez, Morocco." *Electronic Journal of Information Systems in Developing Countries* 35, no. 1: 1–18. Online: http://www.ejisdc.org/ojs2/index.php/ejisdc/article/viewFile/431/251 (accessed 4 June 2012).

Macintosh, A. 2004. "Characterizing E-Participation in Policy-Making." In *Proceedings of the Thirty Seventh Annual Hawaii International Conference on System Sciences (HICSS 37)*, held at Big Island, Hawaii, 5–8 January.

Madon, S. 2009. *E-Governance for Development: A Focus on Rural India*. New York: Palgrave Macmillan.

Misuraca, G. C. 2007. *E-Governance in Africa, from Theory to Action: A Handbook on ICTs for Local Governance*. Ottawa: IDRC.

Moon, M. J. 2002. "The Evolution of E-Government among Municipalities: Rhetoric or Reality?" *Public Administration Review* 62, no. 4: 424–33.

Ndou, V. 2004. "E-Government for Developing Countries: Opportunities and Challenges." *Electronic Journal of Information Systems in Developing Countries* 18, no. 1: 1–24.

Nuggehalli, R. K. n.d. "Building an Alternative E-Governance Model: Lessons for E-Gram in Gujarat." Bangalore: IT for Change. Online: http://www.itforchange.net/sites/default/files/ITfC/Alternative%20_E-Governance_Model-Lessons_from_e-Gram_in_Gujarat.pdf (accessed 19 June 2012).

Nye, J. S., Jr. 2002. "Information Technology and Democratic Governance." In *Governance.com: Democracy in the Information Age*, edited by E. C. Kamarck and J. S. Nye Jr. Washington, DC: Brookings Institution Press.

OECD. 2001. *Citizens as Partners: Information, Consultation and Public Participation in Policy-Making*. Paris: OECD.

Open Net Initiative. 2009. "Internet Filtering." Regional Profile: Asia. Online: http://opennet.net/research/regions/asia (accessed 7 June 2012).

Privacy International. 2009. *Final Report for "Privacy in Asia" Scoping Project*. Prepared for IDRC. Ottawa: IDRC. Online: http://idl-bnc.idrc.ca/dspace/handle/10625/40000 (accessed 31 October 2013).

Ronaghan, S. A. 2002. *Benchmarking E-Government: A Global Perspective, Assessing the Progress of the UN Member States*. New York: United Nations Division for Public Economics and Public Administration / American Society for Public Administration.

Smith, M. L. 2011. "Limitations to Building Institutional Trustworthiness through E-Government: A Comparative Case Study of Two E-Services in Chile." *Journal of Information Technology* 26, no. 1: 78–93.

Smith, M. L. et al. 2010. "Automating the Public Sector and Organizing Accountabilities." *Communications of the Association for Information Systems* 26: 1–16.

Torres, L. et al. 2006. "E-Governance Developments in European Union Cities: Reshaping Government's Relationship with Citizens." *Governance: An International Journal of Policy, Administration, and Institutions* 19, no. 2: 277–302.

United Nations. 2003. *UN Global E-Government Survey 2003*. New York: United Nations. Online: http://unpan1.un.org/intradoc/groups/public/documents/un/unpan016066.pdf (accessed 4 April 2012).

_____. 2008. *United Nations E-Government Survey 2008: From E-Government to Connected Governance*. New York: United Nations.

United Nations Development Programme. 2002. *Human Development Report 2002: Deepening Democracy in a Fragmented World*. New York: Oxford University Press, for the UNDP.

Villeneuve, N. 2008. "Breaching Trust: An Analysis of Surveillance and Security Practices on China's TOM-Skype Platform." Joint report. Toronto: Information Warfare Monitor and ONI-Asia / Ottawa: The Munk Centre for International Studies and The SecDev Group. Online: http://www.nartv.org/mirror/breachingtrust.pdf (accessed 23 July 2012).

Waema, T. M. 2008. "Local Governance and ICTs Research Network for Africa (LOG-IN Africa)." Final technical report. Online: http://hdl.handle.net/10625/42141 (accessed 4 June 2012).

_____. 2011. "Summary of Findings and E-Local Governance Roadmap." In *Local Governance and ICTs in Africa: Case Studies and Guidelines for Implementation and Evaluation*, edited by E. O. Adera and T. M. Waema. Cape Town: Pambazuka Press.

Waema, T. M. et al. 2009. "Research in African E-Local Governance: Outcome Assessment Research Framework." *African Journal of Science, Technology, Innovation and Development* 1, no. 1: 220–48. Online: http://www.ajstid.com/contents1.pdf (website discontinued).

Weare, C. 2002. "The Internet and Democracy: The Causal Links between Technology and Politics." *International Journal of Public Administration* 25, no. 5: 659–91.

West, D. M. 2004. "E-Government and the Transformation of Service Delivery and Citizen Attitudes." *Public Administration Review* 64, no. 1: 15–27.

———. 2005. *Digital Government: Technology and Public Sector Performance.* Princeton: Princeton University Press.

Zhang, W. et al. 2010. "Youth, ICTs and Political Engagement in Asia: A Six-Country Comparative Study." Workshop on "Potential for Mobile 2.0 in Emerging Asia" at the National University of Singapore, Singapore, 22 June.

Zuckerman, E. 2011. "Cute Cats and the Arab Spring: When Social Media Meet Social Change." The 2011 Vancouver Human Rights Lecture. Online: http://www.cbc.ca/ideas/episodes/2011/12/09/cute-cats-and-the-arab-spring/ (accessed 29 June 2012).

Chapter 10

INNOVATIONS IN EVALUATING ICT4D RESEARCH

Sarah Earl, Chaitali Sinha and Matthew L. Smith[1]

Approaches to evaluation can be conceptualized in several ways. Alkin and Christie (2004) categorize evaluation theory into three branches of an "evaluation tree": approaches that prioritize use, methods or valuing. Those who position themselves on the *use* branch orient evaluation toward decision making and practice change. Approaches on the *methods* branch tend to be most concerned with particular research methods guiding the evaluation. The *valuing* branch emphasizes who gets to judge the value and worth of the project, program or policy under review.

While all three approaches have value and are not mutually exclusive, the International Development Research Centre (IDRC) orients itself toward the "use" branch. All IDRC's evaluation systems and processes are designed and implemented in ways to ensure evaluation studies have a clear use and respond to the needs of a particular user whether the user is management, program staff or a group of recipients forming a research network. With *use* as its anchor, IDRC then balances the other requirements of high-quality evaluation: feasibility, ethics and rigorous methods. As a result, IDRC does not advocate any particular evaluation content, model, method, approach, theory, design or even use. Rather, it advocates employing the methodologies most appropriate to achieving the desired use. In this way, IDRC's approach to evaluation mirrors its approach to research for development; research must be *for* development and not just *about* development (IDRC 2010).

Throughout the duration of its "Information and Communications Technologies for Development" (ICT4D) program, IDRC experimented with different approaches for evaluating ICT4D research initiatives and for building evaluation capacity within the ICT4D sector. These innovations responded to different needs, contexts and opportunities. Chief among these were a community of researchers and practitioners hungry to learn about this burgeoning field and its effectiveness, a lack of identifiable ICT4D evaluation leaders and a dearth of evaluation approaches proven to be appropriate and relevant in the ICT4D sector.

This chapter will explore the main reflections and lessons that emerged from the three main areas of evaluation innovation experience within the ICT4D sector: (i) outcome mapping (OM) and the gender evaluation methodology (GEM), (ii) impact evaluations and (iii) utilization-focused evaluation (UFE). Each of these three experiences represents an attempt to develop, refine and assess the appropriateness of the evaluation approaches in ICT4D research initiatives and to build lasting evaluation capacity within the ICT4D sector.

The organization of this chapter follows these three evaluation innovation experiences, starting with OM/GEM, moving to impact evaluation and finishing with UFE. While we present these uses in a particular order, there is no implied chronology or hierarchy. These innovations were often implemented concurrently and there is no attempt to present one approach as better, of higher quality or as more useful than another. All are legitimate and each is appropriate in particular contexts. Indeed, our understanding of the need for different approaches for different purposes has only increased because of the variety of our experiences. Each approach was influenced by the swath of evaluation experiments being supported in ICT4D within IDRC and by relevant research for development experiences within IDRC and beyond. The chapter concludes with four lessons – drawn from IDRC's deep experience – that should be considered by commissioners of ICT4D evaluations, evaluators of ICT4D projects and those designing and implementing ICT4D initiatives.

Outcome Mapping and Gender Evaluation Methodology

It is often said that evaluation is used to either "prove" or "improve." Although these distinctions are not mutually exclusive, prioritizing one over the other can influence the approach, design, analysis and use(s) of the particular study. In the case of IDRC's ICT4D program, both evaluation processes and findings contributed to learning about what was effective and how to improve practices. Given IDRC's commitment to encouraging recipients to use evaluation for their own purposes and not only to comply with funders' demands, the ICT4D initiatives required evaluation approaches that were appropriate for the type of programming and contexts in which they were engaged. Where appropriate evaluation methods did not already exist, researchers engaged with evaluation thinkers and practitioners to develop them. At the time when IDRC and the Association of Progressive Communications (APC) were each developing an evaluation approach to serve particular purposes, members from the ICT4D community got involved in these experiments – specifically, OM and GEM. Several ICT4D researchers turned out to be ideal partners in this learning-oriented action research because they were willing to experiment, feed knowledge back about what worked and did not work with the methodologies and develop elements that were needed to make the approaches more useful.

Outcome mapping (OM)

In the mid- to late 1990s, IDRC was being asked to demonstrate the impact of the development research it supported. Doing so usefully and meaningfully was challenging for a number of reasons, as we will see later in the chapter. First, linear "cause and effect" approaches do not map well to development research because it is a

Figure 10.1. The 12 steps of outcome mapping

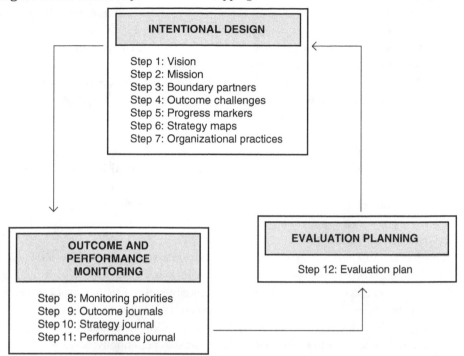

Source: Reprinted with permission from http://web.idrc.ca/openebooks/959-3/ (accessed 4 April 2012).

complex process occurring in open and dynamic systems. A cause and effect approach disregards the reality of how research processes and results improve peoples' lives via long, busy and discontinuous pathways. Second, timing is problematic. If you attempt to measure too early, the results have not yet had time to be achieved. However, if you wait too long, the research outcomes meld with a myriad of other influencing factors and can no longer be reliably untangled. Finally, IDRC understood that evaluation is not value neutral and wanted an approach that would make values explicit (Earl et al. 2001). To respond to these challenges and ensure evaluation supported iterative learning by development researchers, IDRC worked with partners in Asia, Africa and Latin America and the Caribbean (LAC) to develop an approach called "outcome mapping."

OM is an approach for planning, monitoring and evaluating social change initiatives. At a practical level, OM is a set of tools and guidelines that steer project or program teams through an iterative process to identify their desired change and to work collaboratively to bring it about. Results are measured by the changes in behavior, actions and relationships of those individuals, groups or organizations with whom the initiative is working directly and seeking to influence. Figure 10.1 illustrates the 12 steps of outcome mapping, but effective use of OM does not require all 12 steps. The way in which the steps should be used should respond to the particular planning, monitoring and/or evaluation needs being addressed.

OM has four central principles that resonated with ICT4D practitioners and made it appropriate for planning and evaluating the outcomes of ICT4D initiatives. First, OM is based on actor-centered development and behavior change. It recognizes that people and organizations drive change processes and that influencing change requires engaging with these actors, their roles, their relationships, their mindsets and motivations. By using OM, ICT4D initiatives were able to articulate and assess the social dimensions of technology, something that is particularly critical in combating the sometimes overly technology-centric approaches of ICT4D implementations.

Second, OM supports continuous learning and flexibility. The most effective planning, monitoring and evaluation activities are cyclical, iterative and reflexive. They aim to foster learning about the actors, contexts and challenges involved in influencing social change. Innovations in ICT4D initiatives were supported by the systematic incorporation of evaluative thinking from the outset. We define evaluative thinking as being results oriented, reflective and questioning; being able to articulate values; and using evidence to test assumptions (IDRC 2010).

Third, OM promotes participatory approaches and managing multiple accountabilities. By involving stakeholders in the planning, monitoring and evaluation process and by emphasizing reflection on relationships and responsibilities, participation incorporates valuable perspectives and fosters a two-way accountability that is often missing in frameworks oriented toward upward accountability. OM emphasizes building and deepening partnerships with health, education, business, community development, etc. actors so as to push for the greatest contributions possible of ICTs to social transformation.

Fourth, OM recognizes non-linearity and contribution – not attribution – and control in development. With OM, processes of transformation and change are owned collectively. They are not the result of a causal chain beginning with "inputs" and controlled by donors, but of a complex web of interactions among different actors, forces and trends. Indeed, OM positions human, social and organizational change from development interventions within a context of what has been referred to as "sequential causation" (Thompson 1993). The development intervention is one among very many internal and external realities that affect outcomes. To produce sustainable changes, projects should contribute to and influence these processes of social change, rather than focusing on controlling specific outcomes and claiming attribution (Ramírez 2007). This approach allowed ICT4D initiatives to generate a more meaningful picture of their actual contribution and role in achieving results (Jones and Hearn 2009).

A significant number of ICT4D researchers working with IDRC in Africa, Asia and LAC were engaged in developing and using outcome mapping. They were usually introduced to OM through a manual and other written resources, workshops and/or the virtual learning community.[2] OM was found to work best in this group when tackling complex problems that required understanding social factors; that benefitted from embedded reflection and dialogue to work in partnership; and that required opportunities to build capacity, generate new knowledge or influence policy.

One example of an ICT4D initiative that used OM for learning and improvement was the Uganda Health Information Network (UHIN). It introduced the use of handheld computers, or personal digital assistants (PDAs), and wireless information communications systems to send and receive regular transmissions of information critical to community health. Outcome mapping was used to track the uptake and effective use of these new communication technologies by health workers. By tracking the use of the PDAs, as well as the actual health data collected, the project was able to provide evidence of the following:

- Improved data reporting in terms of timeliness and accuracy
- Health workers' comfort with using PDAs as a result of their demand for additional content and services
- Decrease in cost of surveys and time to do data collection and analysis over paper systems
- Improved clinical care for patients with malaria, diarrhea and pneumonia as a result of receiving health information broadcast through the network and the ability of doctors to keep track of patients and treatments
- Health workers referring to literature available in their handhelds – including national treatment guidelines – to inform their practice
- Increased health worker and client satisfaction with services provided at rural health facilities (Ambrose et al. 2010).

The PDAs also helped support project monitoring. Just as they were crucial for the collection and sending of health-related data, they were also used to experiment with and improve monitoring activities. By uploading outcome mapping monitoring journals and related questionnaires on their PDAs, health workers were able to track their own and other partners' changes in behavior regarding these new communications technologies.

However, the innovation of using PDAs for monitoring and evaluation (M&E) was not without challenges. Outcome mapping was new to the participants and was filled with new terminology. It was challenging for those partners who had little previous exposure to any M&E at all. This required concurrent learning, innovating and improving on multiple planes. Adapting the terminology and helping develop their understanding of and capacities in M&E became a part of the project. The participation of partners from the planning stage helped greatly in creating a culture of evaluative thinking and practice.

There were several factors that motivated the participants to use outcome mapping. These included the development of a shared vision that in itself was sufficiently motivating, but also coincided with day-to-day activities. Other factors involved boundary partners;[3] the development of outcome challenges[4] and progress markers[5] by the boundary partners themselves; the different categories of progress markers (expect to see, like to see, love to see) to motivate boundary partners to aim for more challenging changes in their own behavior; and the fact that boundary partners were now managing their own monitoring systems instead of being "supervised" by headquarters.[6]

Gender evaluation methodology (GEM)

The effect of technology is never gender neutral as it is embedded in existing social systems with their mores. Technology very easily empowers some groups and diminishes the capacities of others. In the case of ICTs, research on how their introduction and use can reinforce or challenge dominant gender relations can be found in the example of the QWERTY keyboard and more recent examples of mobile phone use.

Most typists at the time were female stenographers who were generally perceived as "unskilled laborers." By introducing a new technology, employers effectively de-skilled the male Linotype workers and provided more opportunities for female typists to enter the printing industry. The QWERTY keyboard represents a technology that disrupted the existing male-dominated division of labor. However, as changes in technology enabled more women to enter the industry – shifting it from a male-dominated to female-dominated one – previously high wages began to fall, signaling the industry's gradual feminization (Cockburn 1985; Wajcman 1991, 37).

In the late 1990s, with ICT use increasing in all development sectors, the Association for Progressive Communications' Women's Networking Support Programme (APC WNSP) initiated what seemed to be a straightforward "lessons learned" exercise. This process quickly morphed into an action-research project on how ICT4D projects affect women's lives and their position in the community. They found that ICTs can be used in ways that support gender equality or that perpetuate gender stereotypes and biases. This led APC WNSP to explore a use-oriented way of evaluating how gender roles and practices can be systematically captured through an evaluation study of ICT4D initiatives.

GEM evolved from this work was a means of evaluating the positive and negative impacts of ICTs. Since it was first developed, the GEM tool has been tested in over fifty different contexts; translated into five languages; and adapted for specific ICT thematics such as telecenters, rural ICT initiatives and localization projects. The significance in these numbers lies in the iterative and learning-oriented nature of GEM – and of OM, for that matter.

GEM now refers both to a planning and evaluation tool, as well as a community of practitioners.[7] The GEM tool is a guide to integrating gender analysis into evaluations of ICT initiatives and to promoting gender accountability in global, regional, national and local ICT policies and initiatives. GEM provides a means of determining whether ICTs are really improving women's lives and gender relations, as well as promoting positive change at the individual, institutional, community and broader social levels.[8]

Like outcome mapping, GEM can be used from the outset of an ICT initiative to plan as well as to evaluate it later. The GEM process is divided into three phases with seven steps. The first phase focuses on integrating gender analysis by defining the intended user(s) and use(s) of the evaluation, identifying gender and ICT issues, finalizing the evaluation questions and setting gender and ICT indicators. The second phase offers options for gathering information using gender and ICT indicators by advising on data-gathering methods and tools and analyzing data from a gender perspective. The third phase suggests ways of putting evaluation results to work. (See Figure 10.2.)

GEM has proven useful to ICT4D initiatives for a variety of reasons, but the principle advantages noted from across the test cases are the following: first, GEM provides a systematic and practical way to incorporate gender analysis into ICT4D initiatives.

Figure 10.2. The seven steps of GEM illustrating how to integrate gender analysis into an evaluation of the Internet and ICTs

USING THE **GEM** TOOL

GEM is made up of seven Steps grouped into three Phases. Each Step suggests reading materials and gives examples, activities, and worksheets that lead to the expected outputs. Each expected output in turn introduces the next Step.

Phase 1   Integrating Gender Analysis   GEM

Step 1   Defining Intended Use and Intended Users

Activity 1.1 Identifying Evaluation's Intended Users
Activity 1.2 Defining Evaluation's Intended Use
Worksheet 1 Synthesising Intended Users and Intended Use

Step 2   Identifying Gender and ICT Issues

Activity 2.1 Understanding Gender Analysis and
            Concepts of ICT, Social Change and Development
Activity 2.2 Reviewing Gender Issues in an ICT Project's Life Cycle
Worksheet 2 Project Profile

Step 3   Finalising Evaluation Questions

Activity 3 Getting Familiar with Evaluation Questions
Worksheet 3 Generating Questions

Step 4   Setting Gender and ICT Indicators

Activity 4 Asking Questions
Worksheet 4 Creating Gender Indicators

**Phase 2   Gathering Information
            Using Gender and ICT Indicators**

Step 5   Selecting Data Gathering Methods/Tools

Activity 5 Exploring Examples of Practitioners' Methodologies
Worksheet 5 Developing Your Data Gathering Strategy

Step 6   Analysing Data from a Gender Perspective

Phase 3   Putting Evaluation Results to Work

Step 7   Incorporating Learning into the Work

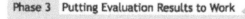

Source: Reprinted with permission from APC (2005).

Whether at the outset or the end of an initiative, GEM uses dialogic questioning and evidence to ensure that ICT4D initiatives are not treated as gender neutral. While GEM has a strong theoretical basis, it is presented in a very approachable manner so that it can complement any evaluation design, approach or purpose by helping bring focus to the gender impacts of ICT4D initiatives. Second, GEM helps uncover hidden structural barriers to women's use of ICTs that often exist below the radar of project organizers. Early on, GEM studies found that some telecenters were located where it was not safe for women or where women would not necessarily be welcome. Using GEM, they had probed why women did not use the telecenters rather than assuming it was due to a lack of interest in technology. Finally, GEM does not prescribe content and permits the development of outcomes and indicators that are specific to the context.

Among the different users of GEM is D.Net (Development Research Network), a not-for-profit research and advocacy organization that works on mainstreaming ICTs for poverty alleviation and economic development in Bangladesh. As part of the "Gender Evaluation Methodology II: Building Gender and Evaluation Practice within the ICT for Development Community" project, D.Net used GEM to document the gender issues in the implementation of the Pallitathya.

Helpline project (see Raihan et al. 2005). D.Net first conceptualized Pallitathya in 2001 as an action-research project. The central idea was to find out if access to information and knowledge – together with complementary support and use of ICTs – had any role in addressing poverty. It was also important for the project to understand gender dynamics between and among the users, the service providers and other stakeholders.

Table 10.1 shows a selection of the evaluation questions D.Net had developed using GEM and the corresponding indicators. The process of using GEM – which includes engaging with the materials and also participating in online and face-to-face dialogues – contributed to the development of questions and indicators that were better aligned with understanding gender and ICT dynamics related to the project. As a result, the questions and indicators are much more focused on unearthing and addressing gender and ICT issues compared with the broader objectives and questions of the Pallitathya action-research.

D.Net also discovered that rural male users felt uncomfortable discussing their private problems (often reproductive and sexual healthcare issues) with "mobile ladies" or sharing them with female help desk researchers. Hence, there was a need to hire men as help desk and mobile operators. The evaluation conducted using GEM showed that, even though mobile operators were only women, men in general had used the helpline services more often than the women. So, a mobile operator being female did not prevent men from using the helpline services, though it may have restricted the kinds of questions asked (Kuga 2011).

Evaluation processes that support learning by ICT4D implementers are often more challenging to implement because they require significant amounts of people's time, the most precious of all resources. Not all the testers who initiated evaluation processes completed them to a degree that was useful. But, for those who did, our experience demonstrates that both OM and GEM provide a means for ICT4D initiatives to be

Table 10.1. Examples of GEM evaluation questions and indicators developed by D.Net (the examples given here are indicators that emerged as a result of using GEM)

Evaluation questions	Corresponding indicators
Has the helpline generated employment and increased income for women in the community?	• Level of increase in income of women employees of the project • Level of satisfaction regarding increase in income • Level of mobile lady's authority over decisions regarding spending of the increased income
Has the helpline been able to empower women through access to information?	• Methods available to access information before helpline and the level of gender bias of those methods • Level of access to information by male vs. female before helpline • Distribution of topics to which women need access • Information sources of information on various topics available to women before helpline • Level of access to information by women through helpline distribution of topics on which they require information from helpline • Nature of use of information gathered from helpline for empowerment • Kinds of information queries that have not been addressed well
Has the helpline made any impact on the perception of women's role in society?	• Nature of perception about women's role in society before helpline • Nature of perception about mobile operator's role in society after helpline

Source: (Raihan and Hasan 2007).

more precise about intended and emergent outcomes, to build capacities and engage in evaluative thinking throughout implementation and to use evaluation findings to support improvement.

Some partners even used their ICT skills to introduce innovations into the methodologies. In an "open source" approach, ICT4D colleagues in the Pan Localization network – including Sana Shams in Pakistan – developed a hybrid of GEM and OM called gendered outcome mapping (OMg). OMg is an online tool that infuses gender analysis into outcome mapping through online project development, reporting and remote monitoring.[9] Dr Christoph Stork, working with Research ICT Africa in South Africa, designed a database for the collection, storage and analysis of outcome mapping data. These examples uncover different layers of use and reuse that were explored and innovated on by IDRC research partners as a result of their experiences with OM and GEM. Moreover, the way in which the research partners assumed leadership and ownership of new innovations is something noteworthy, as the process and outputs from these innovations have been discussed and shared back with the ICT4D community and development evaluation community.

Evaluating impact

The focus of IDRC's ICT4D program, broadly speaking, followed a trajectory that began with a focus primarily on foundational issues of user access and readiness, and then transitioning over time to take a greater focus on uptake and impact. The concern about impact emerged as there was an increasing realization that ICT4D projects were not as successful as originally touted and as funders became increasingly interested in the projects' socioeconomic impacts to justify their expenditures. Indeed, the need to demonstrate sustained impacts is crucial in the international development environment where implementers compete for limited aid budgets (Roche 1999). As a funder of research *for* development, IDRC early on recognized the importance of understanding the development impact of ICTs alongside the concern for access and readiness. Consequently, there was an effort to try to evaluate the impact of ICT4D initiatives (that is, impact evaluation or impact assessment).

Impact evaluation is the "systematic analysis of the lasting of significant changes – positive or negative, intended or not – in people's lives brought about by a given action or series of actions" (Roche 1999, 302). It seeks to establish a causal relationship between a program and a development result of interest (Chong 2011). Impact assessment evaluative research can help answer questions such as: what are the social and economic impacts of ICTs on the lives of beneficiaries? To what extent did a new e-government service improve the lives of people in a particular village? How has the introduction of mobile phones changed the economic opportunities of micro-enterprises in rural Kenya?

IDRC's work on impact resulted in a history of supporting *evaluative research* that attempts to uncover the value of an ICT4D intervention, both to inform the field and to feed into policy processes. This work straddles the fuzzy boundary between evaluation and research. Some argue that there is a clear distinction. Evaluation judges the merit, worth or value of something; social science research is value free – it draws factual and not evaluative conclusions (Scriven 1991). In practice, however, this can be a distinction without a difference. This is particularly true when engaging in research *for* development, as research findings are used to feed policy and practice recommendations that must be made and weighed against the perceived value of other potential activities. While recognizing the larger debates within the field on impact evaluation, for the purposes of this chapter, we consider evaluative research with the purpose of assessing ICT4D impact as equivalent to impact evaluation.

Perhaps the most well-known methodology for impact evaluation is randomized control trials (RCTs). An RCT is a randomized experiment where members of treatment and control groups are assigned to the groups randomly, ensuring the same characteristics in the two groups. The experiments "make it possible to vary one factor at a time and therefore provide 'internally' valid estimates of the causal effect" (Banerjee and Duflo 2009). Influential groups, such as economists at the MIT Poverty Action Lab, argue that RCTs are the "gold standard" in development (Banerjee 2007). A recent meta-review of RCTs in ICT4D projects (Chong 2011) illustrates the usefulness of RCTs in assessing impact and deepening our understanding of the average effect of the intervention.

There is, however, considerable debate over the primacy and applicability of RCTs in development (Prowse 2007; Banerjee and Duflo 2009). While RCTs have the benefits of high internal validity, they are necessarily narrow in scope, with low levels of external validity (generalizability) (Cartwright 2007). Prowse (2007) highlights four types of challenges to the use of RCTs in the real and complex world of international development:

1. Scale and reach (e.g., limited applicability of RCTs, generally applicable at micro-level, but not the macro level)
2. Technical concerns (e.g., baseline data may not be available; short time horizons of donors)
3. Ethical issues (e.g., is it ethical to withhold an intervention that may save lives?)
4. Political dimensions (e.g., a focus on efficiency/effectiveness ignores the political realities on the ground that may render the evaluation pointless)

The ICT4D context also raises challenges for the implementation of RCTs, such as the changing contexts of implementation (e.g., the continued diffusion of ICTs), changing technologies during the course of a study, ICTs cutting across and impacting a variety of domains, the link between technology and expected impacts often being indirect and thus harder to measure (Souter 2008). Finally, it is worth mentioning that RCTs are not applicable in a situation where there is not a well-established model to assess; work must first be done to develop rather than test (Patton 2011). Note that this situation applies when one is attempting to scale-up a "proven" model.

This is not to argue that impact evaluation is inappropriate in a development context, merely that there are challenges and that innovative approaches to studying impact assessment may be needed. As stated, the IDRC evaluation approach posits that there is no evaluation approach or methodology that is more appropriate, rigorous or influential than another; none is inherently better than another. Rather, the appropriate methodology (or methodologies) depends on the intended purpose of the evaluation, the priority questions to be answered and the context in which it is being conducted. The rest of this section details two research initiatives that have experimented with ICT4D impact assessment frameworks.

Impact assessment frameworks

IDRC worked in the ICT4D field well before it was labeled ICT4D. By 1992, IDRC's Information Sciences Division had supported over five hundred information projects in developing countries based on the supposition that information is a critical development resource. However, the information community (and the burgeoning ICT4D community) had little understanding of how to measure the extent to which information activities impacted social and economic development.

Consequently, in the early 1990s, IDRC supported research that sought to establish methodologies and indicators to assess such impacts. This happened in a context where a majority of impact studies were done in the North with generally quantitative methods and a narrow economic notion of impact. This project recognized the potential to expand the concept of impact into social, cultural, economic, political and environmental domains.

Figure 10.3. Conceptual framework for impact assessment: Interaction and externalities

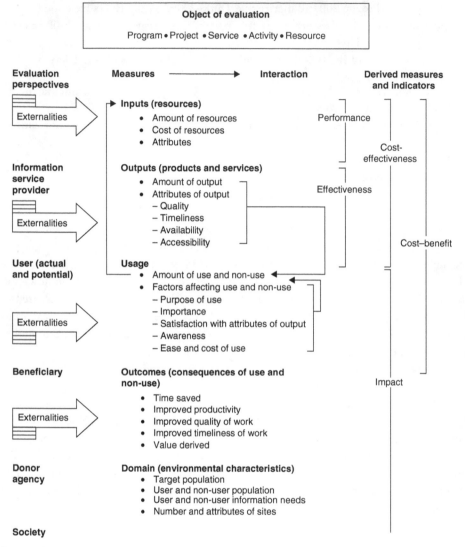

Source: Adapted from Menou (1993).

They developed a generic impact assessment framework that allowed for a variety of objects of evaluation (e.g., ICT4D project, service and program) and evaluation perspectives (e.g., the beneficiary, the donor, the information service provider). (See Figure 10.3.)

The framework was subsequently tested through a set of case studies. Analyzing the cases, the researchers uncovered a series of important issues to consider (McConnell 1995, 20–21) when engaging in impact evaluation of ICTs – issues such as the following:

• The difficulty in forming a consensus on definitions of terms like information and impact.
• The importance of including stakeholders in the definition and selection of impact indicators.

- The critical importance of defining and describing the context of both information user and provider.
- Impact assessment as an ongoing process rather than a one-off event.
- Evaluations of impact having to address issues of causality.

This project illustrated early on that evaluating the impact of an ICT4D intervention in a comprehensive manner was not a simple venture. These lessons have informed IDRC's later work on impact evaluation as well as the fundamental concepts underpinning outcome mapping.

Fifteen years after the original work to develop an impact assessment methodology, the field had advanced considerably. Heeks and Molla (2009) pulled together a compendium of approaches to impact assessment for ICT4D projects, placing the approaches into six categories:

1. Generic frameworks that are usable for any development project (e.g., cost–benefit analysis)
2. Discipline-specific (e.g., Sen's capability approach [Sen 1999])
3. Issue-specific (e.g., gender)
4. Application-specific (e.g., telecenters [Hudson 1999])
5. Method-specific (e.g., participatory)
6. Sector-specific (e.g., health)

This diversity illustrates how the number of impact assessment frameworks and approaches has multiplied from the relative lack of frameworks in the early 1990s. This diversity also highlights the multitude of relevant aspects that have to be considered when engaging in impact evaluation. First and foremost, however, one needs to be clear on what the purpose of the evaluation is, as this can help one navigate the diversity of impact assessment tools.

Assessing the impact of public access to ICTs

The second impact evaluation research initiative is the Global Impact Study. This project, supported by IDRC and the Bill and Melinda Gates Foundation (BMGF), is a five-year, multi-country study of public access to ICTs. The Global Impact Study has three main research questions:

1. What are the social, economic and political impacts of public access to ICT?
2. What is the magnitude of these impacts and how can we measure them?
3. What is the relationship between costs and benefits of providing and using public access to ICTs?

Consistent with the earlier findings from Menou's (1993) and McConnell's (1995) work on ICT4D impact evaluation, it was recognized that there are neither simple answers nor straightforward approaches to answer these questions. The first six months of the project involved a group of research experts collaboratively developing a research design. This process included, first and foremost, the development of shared terminology and the scope of the project. In particular, they had to deal with the distinct challenge of trying to determine the difference between the impacts of *public access* to ICTs and those of *access* to ICTs. In other words, what, if anything, does accessing ICTs in a public venue add to the use of ICT experience and how might that alter the impact of the experience? Researchers François Bar and Mike Best described the difference as follows: "To the extent public use differs from private use, we need to understand what the differences are and articulate the mechanisms through which they produce impact. For example, does staff assistance (or infomediaries) in a public venue allow job seekers to be more successful in securing employment than if they searched alone? Do collective use practices emerge in public venues with impact different from that of private individual use?" (Bar and Best 2008, iii).

To tackle this question, the study drew from a variety of sources beginning with a literature review that examined past research on issues around the impact of public access to ICTs (Sey and Fellows 2009) as well as the Heeks and Molla (2009) impact assessment compendium. The researchers found there were few pieces of research that attempted to assess the impact of the public access to ICTs. So it was realized early on that creating a research hypothesis prior to any field work would be presumptuous at best. Consequently, the project began with an information ecology mapping exercise that deepened their understanding of how people access and information at a public access venue (Beresnevičiūtė et al. 2009; Hinostroza et al. 2009; Raihan et al. 2009).

From these sources, the researchers generated a general hypothesis that there is a relationship between six factors (see Table 10.2) and the impact of public access to ICTs. Each of these six factors represents sub-hypotheses of different mechanisms that generate or modify the impacts of public access to ICTs. Their general hypothesis also accepts the realization, as in the Menou impact of information on development framework, that access and use of information can bring positive and negative impacts on a variety of dimensions of people's lives. Consequently, the study examines six "development domains" of impact areas: health, governance, communication and leisure, employment and income, education, and culture and language. The study is also open to finding impacts that fall outside of these domains.

To investigate these questions and test these hypotheses, the study includes in-depth studies of public access to ICTs in telecenters, cyber cafés and libraries; surveys of venue operators, users and non-users; and an inventory of public access venues in developing countries. Each of these in-depth studies focused on a specific topic including intermediaries, collaborative sharing, mobile phones and public access and cost–benefits.[10] Through these methods, the researchers hope to uncover a variety of types of findings including the impact mechanisms (how public access to ICT has an impact), the direct and indirect impacts themselves and, finally, their reach and magnitude. (See Figure 10.4 for a diagram of the research design.)

The Global Impact Study is scheduled to analyze all data and produce findings by the end of 2012. These results will draw from various in-depth studies that comprise

Table 10.2. Impact factors with example questions

Impact factor	Example questions
Reach	What are the mechanisms by which public access ICT services are accessed and used directly and indirectly? How does this translate into impacts?
Use	What different types of uses occur at public access ICT venues (e.g., individual or collective uses, instrumental or not, etc.)? What is the impact of different types of usage?
Physical design and location	How does the physical design/architecture and location of public access ICT venues affect their accessibility, use, long-term sustainability and impacts?
Venue services and operations	How does the design of public access ICT services and operations affect their accessibility, use, long-term sustainability and impacts?
Information ecologies	What is the sociocultural context of public access ICT provision and use? How does this explain usage patterns and associated impacts?
Policy and regulatory context	How do policy and regulatory environments affect the provision, design, use and impact of public access ICTs?

Source: http://www.globalimpactstudy.org/researchdesign/research-problem/ (accessed 8 July 2012).

the larger study. This will be followed by a final phase of integration and analysis, contributing to drawing some larger conclusions. It is anticipated that this process will be difficult given the variety of hypotheses that are being tested and refined within the diverse contexts of the different studies.

Proving impact is clearly an important endeavor in the ICT4D sector as it can justify the expenditure of limited resources and, if translated into informed decisions, can lead to enhanced efficiency and efficacy of development activities. However, it is not a straightforward venture, particularly in light of the fact (discussed in the OM section) that development research is a complex process occurring in open and dynamic systems. This complexity limits the applicability of traditional methods (such as RCTs) that attempt to directly infer cause and effect in the development research context. Consequently, it is no surprise that projects attempting to engage in impact assessment have met a multiplicity of challenges. These challenges have resulted in diverse methodological innovations to try and crack this nut. This diversity, combined with the various perspectives of the different stakeholders, highlights the necessity of getting through the difficult process of developing a shared understanding of the concepts, assumptions and purpose underlying the impact study itself. This understanding can help the researchers select from among the many approaches to impact assessment. Finally, if we want to truly understand impacts, we have to expand the scope of the impact assessment beyond the anticipated positive uses and benefits of technologies to the unintended, but sometimes predictable, uses and outcomes.

Figure 10.4. Global impact study research design

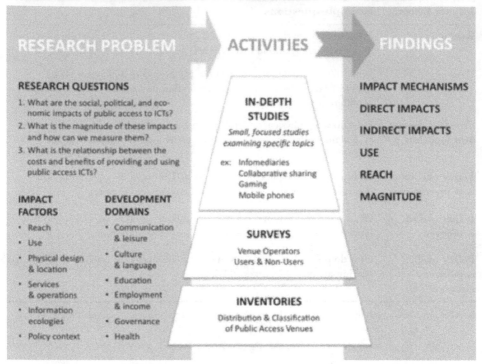

Source: www.globalimpactstudy.org/researchdesign/ (accessed 8 November 2012).

Supporting and Strengthening Evaluation Use and Capacities by ICT4D Researchers and Practitioners

IDRC's use-oriented approach is premised on utility guiding all aspects of an evaluation, from the early design stage through to facilitating the use of the findings that emerge. The focus on use revolves around "how real people in the real world apply evaluation findings and experience the evaluation process" (Patton 2008, 37). Applying utilization-focused evaluation (UFE) – or any other approach, for that matter – to a specific situation benefits greatly from the presence of relevant exemplars, often derived from a similar discipline.

UFE is often mistakenly perceived to be a specific methodology. In fact, it is an approach to situate and focus on the intent of an evaluation. This is an important distinction to make as projects can follow a UFE approach and end up using very different methodologies and methods to carry out the different evaluation activities. The UFE approach refrains from selecting a particular methodology until there is a clear sense of what the primary intended uses are for the primary intended user(s). The centrality of "use" is what binds these projects – specifically, the way in which all decisions and activities are shaped by the users for the uses that have been discussed.

This section presents interim lessons and findings from the Developing Evaluation Capacity in ICT4D (DECI) project, a learning-focused research project on UFE being used in five different ICT4D research projects in Asia. DECI supported and strengthened evaluative thinking and practice within and across these projects. By exposing local evaluators to UFE and by providing them with an opportunity to give technical assistance to the projects, DECI helped to strengthen innovative evaluation leadership in Asia. Moreover, DECI itself is a research project that is systematically analyzing, learning and documenting lessons on the application of UFE within ICT4D research projects.[11]

The DECI project was born out of an expressed demand from IDRC grantees for dedicated support that strengthens their capacity to design, implement and facilitate UFE-oriented evaluation studies. There is considerable variation across the five research projects. While each of them adopted a UFE approach, the primary intended users, primary intended uses, study design, evaluation questions, methodology and analysis differed significantly. There is also significant variation in thematic focus and structure among the projects. The unifying aspects of DECI include the fact that they each focus on ICT4D research, follow the UFE approach and own the evaluation process. Analysis across the studies is presented in the UFE primer that has been developed by the DECI project. Figure 10.5 illustrates the engagement between DECI and the different projects. The figure shows some differences in the projects such as where the evaluator was situated relative to the project (an internal evaluator embedded as a project team member or as an external evaluator hired by the project) and the pairing of UFE mentors and the projects (some projects working with one and others where it made sense to have them pair up). Each of the five projects involved in DECI is described briefly in Table 10.3.

As part of building evaluation capacities within ICT4D research projects, DECI also focuses on strengthening evaluative thinking among the project partners, as well as among the regional evaluation mentors. According to IDRC's Evaluation Unit, evaluative thinking must go beyond the conduct and dissemination of formal evaluation studies. DECI is designed to provide deliberate points of reflection, mechanisms to capture and analyze these reflections, and dedicated support and mentorship to help respond to questions and to learn alongside the different projects as they delved deeper into a UFE experience.

Reflections to date from DECI

Patton's 2008 *Utilization-Focused Evaluation* provides rich context for the development of UFE, a range of real world examples and a set of 12 steps to follow (see Table 10.4). These materials were used to develop a UFE curriculum to help familiarize the regional evaluators (mentors) and members of the ICT4D research projects with the basics of UFE. These steps of UFE also served as a helpful guide for DECI to work through UFE in practice.

Given that each of the five projects included in DECI has its own evaluation users, uses and questions, this discussion will focus on reflections related to the structures, processes and practices within DECI. The findings presented on the following pages have been gleaned from the UFE DECI Primer (Ramírez and Brodhead 2013).

Figure 10.5. Visual representation of how DECI supports IDRC ICT4D research projects

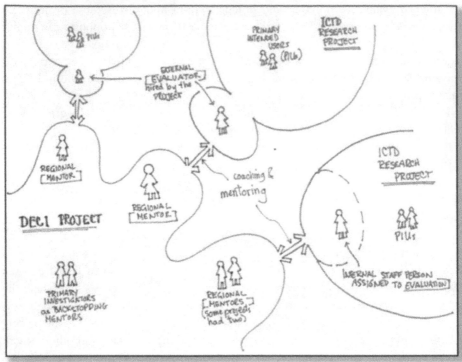

Source: Ramírez and Brodhead (2013).

These have been divided according to findings related to sensitization to UFE and selection of primary intended users.

Sensitization to UFE

Analysis across each of the five projects indicates the critical importance of the early steps in the UFE approach. Specifically, this is related to everyone in the evaluation process gaining a clear understanding of certain central terms, as well as ensuring adequate measures are taken to establish a solid foundation in adopting a use-oriented approach. Findings from the DREAM-IT project indicate that the word "evaluation" created stress for many among the project team because they felt this would resemble an audit. Engagement with different members of the DECI team throughout the project helped them realize that evaluation had other connotations and could benefit DREAM-IT through focused learning. Similarly, the staff of SIRCA had initial expectations that the entire evaluation process would be akin to an audit, with the evaluator playing the role of an auditor who summarizes and prepares the findings largely in isolation from the project team. Over time, SIRCA, DREAM-IT and the other three projects underwent different sensitization activities to build the "UFE mindset" upon which to build and learn. In this case, a UFE mindset can be thought of as a realization that the primary intended users

Table 10.3. Description of projects included in DECI

Project	Description
LIRNE*asia*	LIRNE*asia* was inaugurated in 2005 as a think tank to conduct policy and regulation research on ICT and related infrastructure development in 13 Asian countries. The focus of the evaluation is "Communications Policy Research South" (CPRsouth), a capacity building effort that holds an annual conference in the region (http://lirneasia.net/capacity-building/cprsouth/). Report: http://idl-bnc.idrc.ca/dspace/bitstream/10625/48141/1/IDL-48141.pdf.
PANACeA	Since August 2007, Pan Asian Collaboration for Evidence-based eHealth Adoption and Application (PANACeA) has enabled a network of health researchers and institutions to conduct collaborative research on eHealth applications in the Asian context (http://panacea-ehealth.net/). Report: http://idl-bnc.idrc.ca/dspace/bitstream/10625/48142/1/IDL-48142.pdf.
ISIF	The Information Society Innovation Fund (ISIF) is a grants program aimed at stimulating creative solutions to ICT development needs in the Asia-Pacific region. ISIF places emphasis on the role of the Internet in social and economic development in the region, toward the effective development of the information society (http://www.isif.asia/). Report: http://idl-bnc.idrc.ca/dspace/bitstream/10625/48143/1/IDL-48143.pdf.
SIRCA	The "Strengthening Information Society Research Capacity" program (SIRCA) identifies future research leaders, particularly emerging researchers who are relatively new to ICTD and "Information." The researchers benefit from concerted capacity building and mentorship arrangements with established researchers and grant recipients. This grant focuses on social science research; in particular, the relationships between ICTs and information society (http://www.sirca.org.sg/). Report: http://idl-bnc.idrc.ca/dspace/bitstream/10625/46288/1/132777.pdf.
DREAM-IT	The DREAM-IT "Mega Mongolia" project is a country-wide research program on the interrelationships of policy, innovation and the socioeconomic effects of ICT. It provides competitive grants to the sub-projects in different sectors including education, health, governance and the environment (http://www.dreamit.mn/index.php). Report: http://idl-bnc.idrc.ca/dspace/bitstream/10625/46700/1/133180.pdf.

Note: All reports accessed 29 April 2012.

can choose how the evaluation will be designed, implemented and used. Thus, it can benefit them rather than being just an accountability mechanism.

Selection of primary intended users

As the name implies, selecting the primary intended user(s) is a vital aspect that shapes the rest of the evaluation. Beyond the selection process itself, there is also an accompanying process of sensitizing all the stakeholders who may be the primary intended users (PIUs)

Table 10.4. The 12 steps of utilization-focused evaluation

Utilization-focused evaluation steps	
1. Program/organizational readiness assessment	7. Evaluation design
2. Evaluator readiness and capability assessment	8. Simulation of use
3. Identification of primary intended users	9. Data collection
4. Situational analysis	10. Data analysis
5. Identification of primary intended uses	11. Facilitation of use
6. Focusing the evaluation	12. Meta-evaluation

Source: Patton (2008).

about the type of commitment and responsibility that comes with the label of PIU. The level of commitment needed by the PIU is important for the evaluator to keep in mind, for the potential PIUs to be aware of and for the different participants in the evaluation process to accept.

The selection process played out differently in the five cases, with significant implications. For example, selecting the PIU for LIRNE*asia* proved to be a critical decision in ensuring the findings would be used. In this case, the PIU was also the CEO for the organization, who participated throughout the UFE process. For PANACeA, the process of selecting a PIU generated some challenges. In this case, the PIUs consisted of 23 individuals – all the members of the multiregional research network. These 23 PIUs were based in seven different countries and had varying roles within the network. The PANACeA network is one that supports an ethos of egalitarianism; this is represented in the decision to include all members as PIUs. The opinions of PIUs and their involvement in the PANACeA UFE study strengthened the sense of collective ownership and brought richness to the evaluation issues and findings; however, the large number also caused some delays and communication challenges (Sajwani et al. 2011).

These are different reflections on how an ICT4D research project facilitating a UFE approach can unfold. Additional lessons continue to emerge as the findings from the studies are used by the PIUs. One example includes a comment from the leadership at LIRNE*asia*. He gained a far greater value from the UFE study of LIRNE*asia* than previous external evaluations and could find no reason why external evaluations would have more credibility with donors (Ramírez and Brodhead 2013). The documentation efforts within the project – which included interviews with all of the different actors – are being shared through a number of different communication channels. As a project premised on use, the intention of DECI is to communicate the findings of the project to interested audiences within the ICT4D research, evaluation research and other development research communities. This includes, but is not limited to, the primer that has already captured significant reflections and lessons to date.

IDRC and DECI

In the case of DECI, IDRC took a deliberate stance that it should not be included within the primary user group. According to Watson (2005), the effectiveness of evaluations increases relative to the degree of ownership felt by individuals and organizations. However, often the default users of donor-supported project evaluations are the donors themselves. As a result, "evaluation is often something that is *done to* programs by funders who hire external evaluators [...] many evaluations fail to yield information that is of immediate, practical value to programs, including information about how the program could be spread to new settings" (P/PV 2011).[12] As a result, the motivation to learn from project experiences and to use the evaluation findings to make improvements can be limited due to a fear of being policed (Horton 1999). These considerations informed IDRC's decision to hand over ownership of the entire evaluation process to grantees. The close interactions between IDRC program staff and recipients, the complex situations in which the projects unfold, combined with the desire to support evaluation findings that are useful for the researchers in future endeavors, contributed collectively to the decision that this evaluation activity would replace any other evaluation-related activity for the purposes of reporting to IDRC.

With respect to IDRC involvement in DECI, the experience with DECI was one that afforded an opportunity to learn alongside our research partners, as well as evaluators, to strengthen our understanding of UFE in theory and in practice. Some of our reflections to date include the following:

- Mind shift: It was clear that consistently coming back to the users and uses of an evaluation study is something that involves time and requires a mind shift for the PIUs themselves, as well as the others involved in the evaluation process.
- Value of engagement: Once the mind shift has taken place and different users and other respondents are engaged, the value of this engagement speaks for itself. For instance, the SIRCA and PANACeA projects enjoyed a 96 percent and 95 percent response rate respectively to questionnaires.
- Requisite skills: There can be a tendency to assume that UFE as an approach requires specialist expertise from a specific domain. The notions underpinning UFE are not esoteric or overly cumbersome; however, to follow a UFE approach from beginning to end, there are some requisite skills in evaluative thinking that are required.
- Exemplars: The application of a UFE approach to actual projects and case studies that unfold in the same or similar field of study can greatly enhance engagement and uptake of the concepts and their effective use.
- Power dynamics: When a granting agency takes deliberate actions to ensure the grant recipients own the evaluation process and outcomes that are being commissioned, there is a need to recognize the underlying power dynamics and take concerted measures to clarify roles. This involves trust and transparency between the granting agency and the grant recipients.

The flexibility and responsiveness demonstrated by the different participants in the DECI project challenges assumptions that there is a single "right" way of supporting development research evaluation studies. The learning-by-doing process and the mentorship component demonstrate that UFE is best understood by its practice and the iterative learning to which it contributes.

Moreover, the realization that the UFE evaluator is a facilitator and not the final major decision maker (that would be the primary intended users) reinforces the fact that the value of the evaluation will be judged on the basis of actual use. As a granting agency, those involved from IDRC have learned a great deal about supporting and strengthening the use of evaluation findings for ICT4D research projects.

Conclusion

This chapter provides examples from experiments in evaluating ICT4D research projects over the last two decades: outcome mapping, gender evaluation methodology, impact evaluation and utilization-focused evaluation. The combined effect of research partners' commitment to innovation and learning, IDRC's commitment to support research on evaluation and the willingness of IDRC staff to relinquish ownership of evaluations in the interest of learning has contributed to how these innovations have unfolded.

Drawing from these experiences, a few key lessons emerge. First, in ICT4D evaluation, there is not, nor can there be, one "best" way to do evaluation. The choice of evaluation approach, methodology and design must fit the specific purpose and context. Second, the ICT4D field demands and deserves an approach to evaluation that does not oversimplify the complexity of the development problems and contexts in which we work. Third, determining who the user(s) is and the use(s) of an evaluation is an important, power- and value-laden exercise with implications that ripple throughout the evaluation process. Evaluation use occurs neither naturally nor effortlessly. It requires intentionality and careful attention and reaction to emergence. It needs committed participants and skilled evaluators. Finally, to support innovative and influential ICT4D development research, we have to challenge traditional views and change our mindset about evaluation. In many development circles, evaluation has a negative connotation – it is the mechanism of upward accountability, generally from grant recipients toward donors. We have to promote and support evaluation studies and deep reflective practice that benefit those actually implementing the work, not only those funding it. Handing over the evaluation agenda to the implementers implies that donors must give up the power that comes with control over evaluation. This is neither simple nor straightforward, but it is worth it.

Notes

1 We sincerely appreciate the work of all IDRC-supported researchers who have designed and implemented insightful – and, at times, innovative – evaluation studies in the field of ICT4D research. The richness and quality of their inquiry and reflection form the backbone of this chapter. These evaluation lessons, as well as an overall emphasis on learning-oriented evaluation practice, have contributed significantly to the trajectory and focus of IDRC's ICT4D program. We would also like to thank Jennifer Vincent for her background research and Katie Bryant for her editorial inputs to the chapter.
2 See www.outcomemapping.ca. For the reflections of Dwayne Bailey – a researcher in the First Mile, First Inch project – on his introduction to outcome mapping in 2004, please see his blog at http://translate.org.za/blogs/old/dwayne/archives/2004/05/index.html (accessed 25 April 2012).

3 Boundary partners are individuals, groups and organizations with whom the program interacts directly to effect change and with whom the program can anticipate some opportunities for influence (Earl et al. 2001).

4 An outcome challenge is a statement of the ideal changes in the behaviors, relationships, activities and/or actions of a boundary partner (Earl et al. 2001).

5 Progress markers are a set of graduated indicators of changed behaviors for a boundary partner that focuses on depth or quality of change (Earl et al. 2001).

6 For a full elaboration of this case, see Ambrose et al. (2010).

7 The GEM practitioners' network can be found at http://www.genderevaluation.net.

8 GEM website: http://www.apcwomen.org/gem/?q=about (accessed 8 July 2012). Other GEM resources can be found at http://idl-bnc.idrc.ca/dspace/handle/10625/47201/browse?type=title&submit_browse=Titles (accessed 10 September 2012).

9 The OMg tool is available at http://www.genderedom.net/Login/php (accessed 30 April 2012).

10 For details, see http://www.globalimpactstudy.org/researchdesigns/research-activities/ (accessed 10 September 2012).

11 A primer has been developed to share the experiences from DECI with evaluation practitioners interested in following a UFE approach in general, with specific examples drawn from ICT4D (Ramírez and Brodhead 2013).

12 Emphasis in the original.

References

Alkin, M. C. and C. A. Christie. 2004. "An Evaluation Theory Tree." In *Evaluation Roots: Tracing Theorists' Views and Influences*, edited by M. C. Alkin, 12–65. London: Sage Publications.

Ambrose, K. et al. 2010. *Outcome Mapping on the Move: Using ICTs to Assess Changes in Behaviour Towards ICTs*. Ottawa: IDRC. Online: http://idl-bnc.idrc.ca/dspace/handle/10625/45619 (accessed 30 June 2012).

APC (Association for Progressive Communications). 2005. *Gender Evaluation Methodology for Internet and ICTs: A Learning Tool for Change and Empowerment*. Melville: APC. Online: http://www.genderevaluation.net/sites/default/files/sites/dev.genderevaluation.net/files/GEMEnglish_0.pdf (accessed 13 May 2012).

Baker, A. and B. Bruner. 2006. *Evaluation Capacity and Evaluative Thinking in Organizations* 60. Cambridge, MA: Bruner Foundation.

Banerjee, A. V. 2007. *Making Aid Work*. Cambridge, MA: MIT Press.

Banerjee, A. V. and E. Duflo. 2009. "The Experimental Approach to Development Economics." *Annual Review of Economics* 1, no. 1: 151–78.

Bar, F. and M. Best, M. 2008. "Assessing the Impact of Public Access to ICTs." *Information Technologies and International Development* 4, no. 3: iii–iv.

Beresnevičiūtė, V. 2009. "Using an Information Ecology Approach to Identify Research Areas: Findings from Lithuania." Global Impact Study Information Ecology Report Series, S4ID, Vilnius, Lithuania. Online: http://library.globalimpactstudy.org/doc/using-information-ecology-approach-identify-research-areas-findings-lithuania (accessed 20 April 2012).

Cartwright, N. 2007. "Are RCTs the Gold Standard?" *BioSocieties* 7, no. 2: 11–20.

Chong, A., ed. 2011. *Development Connections: Unveiling the Impact of New Information Technologies*. New York: Palgrave Macmillan.

Cockburn, C. 1985. *Machinery of Dominance: Women, Men and Technical Know-How*. London: Pluto Press.

Earl, S. et al. 2001. *Outcome Mapping: Building Learning and Reflection into Development Programs*. Ottawa: IDRC.

Heeks, R. and A. Molla. 2009. *Compendium on Impact Assessment of ICT-for-Development Projects*. Ottawa: IDRC. Online: http://idl-bnc.idrc.ca/dspace/handle/10625/45567 (accessed 2 April 2012).

Hinostroza, J. et al. 2009. "Using an Information Ecology Approach to Identify Research Areas: Findings from Chile." Global Impact Study Information Ecology Report Series, Universidad de la Frontera Instituto de Informática Educativa, Temuco, Chile. Online: http://library.globalimpactstudy.org/doc/using-information-ecology-approach-identify-research-areas-findings-chile (accessed 3 April 2012).

Horton, D. 1999. "Building Capacity in Planning, Monitoring and Evaluation: Lessons from the Field." *Knowledge, Technology & Policy* 11, no. 4: 152–88.

Hudson, H. 1999. "Designing Research for Telecentre Evaluation." *Telecentre Evaluation: A Global Perspective*, edited by R. Gómez and P. Hunt, 149–64. Ottawa: IDRC.

IDRC. 2010. *IDRC Evaluation Strategy, 2010–2015*. Ottawa: IDRC. Online: http://web.idrc.ca/en/ev-157545-201-1-DO_TOPIC.html (accessed 29 April 2013).

Jones, H. and S. Hearn. 2009. "Outcome Mapping: A Realistic Alternative for Planning, Monitoring and Evaluation." ODI Background Notes Series, Overseas Development Institute, London. Online: http://www.odi.org.uk/resources/details.asp?id=4118&title=outcome-mapping-realistic-planning-monitoring-evaluation (accessed 30 June 2012).

Kuga, T. A. 2011. *Gender Evaluation for Rural ICT for Development*. Melville: Association for Progressive Communications (APC). Online: http://idl-bnc.idrc.ca/dspace/handle/10625/46894 (accessed 3 April 2012).

McConnell, P., ed. 1995. *Making a Difference: Measuring the Impact of Information on Development*. Proceedings of a workshop in Ottawa, 10–12 July. Ottawa: IDRC.

Menou, M. J., ed. 1993. *Measuring the Impact of Information on Development*. Ottawa: IDRC. Online: http://publicwebsite.idrc.ca/EN/Resources/Publications/Pages/IDRCBookDetails.aspx?PublicationID=764 (accessed 29 April 2012).

Patton, M. Q. 2008. *Utilization-Focused Evaluation*, 4th edition. Thousand Oaks: Sage Publications.

_____. 2011. *Developmental Evaluation: Applying Complexity Concepts to Enhance Innovation and Use*. New York: Guilford Press.

P/PV (Public/Private Ventures). 2011. *Priorities for a New Decade: Making (More) Social Programs Work (Better)*. New York: P/PV.

Prowse, M. 2007. *Aid Effectiveness: The Role of Qualitative Research in Impact Evaluation*. London: Overseas Development Institute.

Raihan, A. et al. 2005. *Pallitathya Help Line: A Precursor to People's Call Center*. Dhaka: D.Net.

_____. 2009. "Using an Information Ecology Approach to Identify Research Areas: Findings from Bangladesh." Global Impact Study Information Ecology Report Series, D.Net, Dhaka. Online: http://library.globalimpactstudy.org/doc/using-information-ecology-approach-identify-research-areas-findings-bangladesh (accessed 3 July 2012).

Raihan, A. and M. Hasan. 2007. *Impact of ICT-Carried Livelihood Information on Rural Communities of Bangladesh*. D.Net final technical report. Ottawa: IDRC.

Ramírez, R. 2007. "Appreciating the Contribution of Broadband ICT with Rural and Remote Communities: Stepping Stones toward an Alternative Paradigm." *Information Society* 23, no. 2: 85–94.

Ramírez, R. and D. Brodhead. 2013 *Utilization-Focused Evaluation: A Primer for Evaluators*. Malaysia: Southbound Publishers.

Roche, C. 1999. *Impact Assessment for Development Agencies: Learning to Value Change*. Oxford: Oxfam. Online:http://policy-practice.oxfam.org.uk/publications/impact-assessment-for-development-agencies-learning-to-value-change-122808 (accessed 30 June 2012).

Sajwani, A. et al. 2011. *PANACeA Formative Network Evaluation Report*. Ottawa: IDRC.

Scriven, M. 1991. *Evaluation Thesaurus*, 4th edition. Newbury Park: Sage Publications.

Sen, A. 1999. *Development as Freedom*. Oxford: Oxford University Press.

Sey, A. and M. Fellows. 2009. "Literature Review on the Impact of Public Access to Information and Communication Technologies." CIS working paper no. 6, Technology & Social Change Group. Seattle: University of Washington. Online: http://www.globalimpactstudy.org/wp-content/uploads/2010/12/TASCHA_Public-Access-Review_2009.pdf (accessed 3 July 2012).

Smutylo, T. 2005. "Outcome Mapping: A Method for Tracking Behavioural Changes in Development Programs." ILAC (Institutional Learning and Change Initiative) brief 7, Maccarese, Italy.

Souter, D. 2008. "The Challenge of Assessing the Impact of Information and Communications on Development." Building Communication Opportunities (BCO) Alliance. Online: http://www.givewell.org/files/DWDA 2009/APC/BCO_FinalReport.pdf (accessed 29 June 2012).

Thompson, G. 1993. "Causality in Economics: Rhetorical Ethic or Positivist Empiric?" *Quality & Quantity* 27, no. 1: 47–71.

Wajcman, J. 1991. *Feminism Confronts Technology*. University Park: Penn State University Press.

Watson, D. 2005. "Monitoring and Evaluation of Capacity and Capacity Development." Discussion paper 58B. Maastricht: ECDPM. Online: http://www.ecdpm.org/dp58B (accessed 3 April 2012).

Chapter 11

CONCLUSIONS: A DECADE OF INNOVATION THAT MATTERS

Richard Fuchs and Laurent Elder

The aim of this book is to document and synthesize a special time and space in the business of international development. During the first decade of the new millennium, a major effort was made to assist the developing world to adopt information and communications technologies (ICTs) in their approaches to social and economic development. Canada's International Development Research Centre (IDRC) was a major actor in this endeavor.

As we enter the second decade of the twenty-first century, things have changed dramatically. The mobile phone has become a nearly ubiquitous device, especially in the developing world. With more than six billion mobile phone subscriber accounts[1] in the world, Millennium Development Goal 8f – to increase access to telephone signals by 2015 – has already been met, nearly five years early. Twitter and Facebook are understood to have had major impacts in the transition toward democracy in many parts of the world. The Internet has become an even more important backbone to social development.

None of this happened by accident. Decisions about new telecommunications policies created the environment in which greater competition and accelerated new technology adoption lowered costs, fostered innovation and broadened access to ICTs.

In Africa, for example, a continent with a population smaller than India's but with 53 national governments, this took new knowledge and new institutional capacity in each distinct jurisdiction. In Asia, the most rural continent that is now experiencing accelerated urbanization, it meant the extension of telephony and Internet services far beyond metropolitan area markets and the adoption of new technologies to solve old problems of access in education, healthcare and local government.

People don't know what they don't know. Without learning, producing and sharing new knowledge, the opportunity to "know" about the relevance of information and communications technologies to development could have been forestalled. Engaging developing-world universities, NGOs, national policy activists and others in research about ICTs in development was the special IDRC niche. The preceding chapters in this book provide a testament to some of what was done and much of what was learned in this process.

Avoiding Technological Colonialism

The body of work documented in the preceding chapters was important in helping to prevent a new type of technological colonialism from occurring. In almost every respect, the digital development solutions that worked in New York, London and Ottawa had little relevance to Maputo, Phnom Penh and Lima. Assumptions about bandwidth, connectivity and power generation – not to mention the availability of trained and knowledgeable technologists – are easy to make. If it worked "here," it should work "there." In almost every case, it doesn't!

In Uganda, the state-owned telecom did not realize that the manually operated switching station in Nakaseke, 90 minutes from the capital, had been non-functional for 10 years. The telephone lines had all been cut down during the liberation struggles. They had been "redeployed" by local farmers to wrap plantain on bicycles en route to local roadside markets. There was no electricity other than that produced by expensive petrol-fired generators. The local hospital was managing a major HIV/AIDS epidemic with no connections to the outside world other than via bicycle or lorry. Launching a multipurpose community telecenter in Nakaseke in 1998 – as IDRC did with UNESCO and the International Telecommunication Union (ITU) – presented very different challenges than could have been imagined in the developed world.

Chapter 1 describes how, in the capital (Kampala), an email to the colleague in the office next door had to travel to Oslo before being delivered with major cost and time implications. The few Internet and email signals transmitted from the capital had to be sent via expensive satellite transmission as there was no fiber connection to East Africa from the rest of the world. This is but one example of technological colonialism.

Ten years later, Uganda has among the most successful universal telecom policies and practices in the world. Important trials can now be implemented using mobile phones in rural healthcare delivery. The completion of the Eastern Africa Submarine Cable System (EASSy) to provide fiber connection to the rest of the world through Mombasa in Kenya reduces costs and dramatically increases productivity. With a new national Internet exchange point, email destined for the office next door now does not have to travel to Europe to be delivered.

It was Ugandans who made this happen. They influenced and changed policies, integrated ICTs into social and economic development and trained people in new technology skills. They listened to local research, learned from policies in adjoining countries and developed local solutions. Sissy Senono, born and raised in Nakaseke, walked barefoot to the local rural school as a young grade school student. Her headmaster's office was a thatched-roof hut. Ten years later, she has a university degree in ICTs from Makerere University.[2]

Without the investment in local people and local tools to address development problems, technology solutions from the "mature" markets could easily have been imposed. The distance education service from a "mature" market circumstance might have precluded the development of a more relevant local one. A decade later, the biggest open university does not originate in the developed world. Rather, with over four million online learners and a multiplicity of campuses, the Indira Gandhi National Open University has grown to be the largest of its kind in the world.[3]

Had systems from the North been applied to local healthcare solutions, the mobile phone would not be the foundation for health communications that it has become in places as far flung as the Philippines and South Africa. The exponential growth of mobile telephony in the last decade began in the developing world where most people will never have a landline. Throughout the chapters of this book, the introduction of the mobile phone into local economic development, healthcare, local government and distance learning, among others, is a major theme emerging from the research supported by IDRC. This response to a local advantage helped prevent the type of digital colonialism that might have arisen had local skills and capacities not been developed.

"Making" the Market

Almost all the outcomes documented in the preceding chapters occurred in "pre-market" circumstances. Where consumer, health or education ICT services existed, they were premium priced, elite-based and unrelated to social and economic development policy and practice. As stated in Chapter 1, IDRC and its partners paved the way for governments and other donors to commit resources, greatly increasing the spread of ICTs in less developed regions of the world as a result. It also spurred a demand for ICT services that, in many cases, could then be taken up by the private sector.

In a very real respect, the work of IDRC-supported researchers in this area helped raise awareness about the importance of ICTs well before any broad market solutions were considered, much less developed. Also, as is so often the case, many who participated in the projects described in the preceding chapters came to have increasing influence in the formation of national policies affecting social and economic development. This helped to accelerate eventual, sustainable market solutions.

One case from Asia is especially relevant. Dr Onno Purbo had been an Internet activist in his home country of Indonesia for many years. During a sabbatical with IDRC in Ottawa where he translated his numerous online "how to" connectivity books into English, he was invited to give a presentation at the Indonesian embassy. His presentation was covered by Indonesian press and it created quite a stir back home for policy change. The new national government in Jakarta had promised 100 new policies in 100 days. Easier said than done! Dr Purbo's presentation gave them several ideas to consider.

Once home, he was invited to meet the recently elected new president, Susilo Bambang Yudhoyono. One of the 100 new presidential policies that was subsequently announced was Dr Purbo's recommendation to deregulate the 2.4 MHz spectrum,[4] essentially liberating "last mile" Internet access from telecom regulation and rent-taking. The consequence was an explosion of local Internet points of presence and a new local market for Internet services was "made." Many new local entrepreneurs established local ISPs to provide the new services at affordable cost. Dr Purbo[5] participated in ICT for Development projects beyond Indonesia. He became part of the "wireless road show" that visited Africa and the Middle East and also participated in IDRC's major site at the World Summit on the Information Society exhibition space in Geneva (2003) and Tunis (2005).

In almost every country where IDRC's ICT for Development programming operated, it helped build awareness of the need for certain things to be done and often invested in applied research to help rationalize their adoption. Internet exchange points (IXPs) in Africa is another clear illustration of this. Something needed to be done so email traffic originating in Africa could be transmitted via national Internet networks rather than being routed through North American or European IXPs. As was indicated clearly in Chapter 1, IDRC's ICT4D programming continued to recognize that connectivity was not only related to technical and cost challenges, but also to policy and regulation.

AfriSPA, with support from IDRC, developed technical guidelines for establishing IXPs that were applied in six countries – Nigeria, Tanzania, Uganda, Mozambique, Ghana and Kenya. These IXPs made it possible for local Internet traffic between ISPs to be routed within a country, bypassing the need for an upstream service that was likely outside the country or even the continent.

The research IDRC supported helped raise awareness about the need for mission-critical innovations to support development. It supported researchers in developing evidence-based mechanisms to bring about these innovations (as in the case of AfriSPA) and thereby contributed to "making" the market for greater thresholds of ICT use and eventual market development.

In its early stages, the ICT4D program at IDRC was active in helping to foster the start-up of community based telecenters. Working closely with other agencies such as UNESCO and ITU, IDRC provided the research framework to try to help local organizations document and learn from these early experiences. However, once local awareness, skills and entrepreneurship were animated, IDRC largely withdrew from direct participation in these projects. As was shown in Chapter 1, IDRC left this space but in a developmental way. It helped to ensure that an international entity, the Telecentre. org Foundation – funded by Microsoft and IDRC and with direct participation and ownership from telecenter networks all over the world – existed to help share knowledge and address global problems such as training and certification in this sector.

As evidenced in the foregoing chapters, the IDRC approach was to engage local researchers and institutions in technology innovations for development problems in pre-market circumstances. Whether with telecenters, WiFi trials or using mobiles as market intermediaries in agriculture and fisheries, local entrepreneurs and markets could begin to provide the services on a sustainable basis as their skills, experience and technologies became more sophisticated.

Capacity Development

Capacity development is another common theme that runs through many of the outcomes identified in the contributions to this book. In building the capacity of local researchers and research institutions to participate in ICT for development, research and practice was essential to the work described in the preceding chapters. Whether it was the award-winning local government innovation of eFez in Morocco, the introduction of

ICTs into primary healthcare in the Philippines or testing the field use of mobile phones in agricultural markets in West Africa, the knowledge, skills and context for applied research in these areas was scarce prior to IDRC's involvement.

While IDRC responded to many ideas brought to its attention, it also served as a convener and networker to link applied researchers so they could learn from and contribute to one another's knowledge and capacity. As shown in Chapter 2, IDRC has supported RIA (Research ICT Africa), LIRNE*asia* and the DIRSI networks over several generations of programming. When IDRC's funding support for these networks started around 2002, it was difficult to find researchers interested or with the competencies in this subject outside of a very few dedicated researchers and activists. Indeed, at the onset, this "specialization" was much more of a vocation for these researchers who had "day jobs" as academics in political science, sociology, engineering and other disciplines.

A decade later, these networks have helped build the research skill sets of hundreds of policy researchers in most countries in the developing world. These policy researchers played an important role in shaping the face of access in the global south. When African national telecom policymakers were all meeting in Tunis at the World Summit on the Information Society in 2005, the results from RIA research became a very hot topic for consideration. Some countries were making lots of progress. Others weren't. The "laggards" were politely embarrassed that they fared so poorly in relation to their neighbors in more progressive jurisdictions. This fact alone accelerated the adoption of new, more developmental policies that affected the cost, availability and reliability of both mobile telephony and Internet access. As mentioned in Chapter 2, however, there were real and important policy outcomes from the research:

> The quality and scope of the research carried out by the three networks not only informed and supported policies and regulation benefitting millions in developing countries, but also built capacity among talented young researchers in the developing world. This new generation of policy entrepreneurs now has the tools and the skills to continue to support the important and valuable work of their national ICT policy and regulatory bodies from within each country.

Before becoming minister of science and technology in Mozambique, Dr Venancio S. Massingue was the head of the Faculty of Engineering at Eduardo Mondlane University in Maputo. He had previously been the chairman of Mozambique's national Acacia Committee that oversaw IDRC's early project developments involving policy research and telecenter development in his country.

Dr Massingue maintained an active brief on ICTs and remained interested in new projects that might be of benefit. Mozambique was one of the countries where there were important innovations in the application of ICTs in healthcare, as Chapter 7 illustrates:

> A flagship project for the Mozambican OASIS node (M-OASIS) was a registration system for hospital deaths (SIS-ROH). Originally designed and deployed for the central hospital in Maputo, the registration system has been approved for deployment in 14 other hospitals. The system produced the first systematic data collected

routinely in hospitals and allows deaths to be coded using the international ICD-10 standard. Data collected in SIS-ROH are being used to improve the monitoring of morbidity, mortality and prevalence of disease.

Without the early involvement of Dr Massingue in ICT4D applied research in southern Africa and his active support of the sector in his country, the local capacity to design and deliver a project like M-OASIS would have been very hard to find.

As the discussion of outcome mapping in Chapter 10 indicates, the particular approach to understanding outcomes relates directly to the development of new capacities in people, institutions and, over time, societies. Aid agencies are often preoccupied with attribution. The likelihood that a modestly financed research-for-development project will change gross domestic product, employment ratios, or other macroeconomic or social markers is very slight. A more modest approach is to specify and seek changes in the behavior of people and organizations to do smarter, more effective things, ideally at reduced cost. IDRC's programming in ICT4D was rooted squarely in this approach. The few examples cited here and the many more noted in the preceding chapters speak to this clearly and abundantly.

Partners, not Projects

As is commonly referenced in this book, support was given to partners, not projects. The approach within IDRC's ICT4D program was to build the capacity of partners over extended periods of time. This approach provided a framework in which small groups of researchers could grow to become major international knowledge networks dealing with important development issues.

Almost every chapter in this volume describes a major international knowledge network that started small and grew over several generations of social investment. For example, the local language processing network, Pan Localization (discussed in Chapter 4), began as a response to a small grants competitive call for proposals in 2002. It has since grown from one Asian country to nine and from one language to fourteen, making it the most important network on localization in the world. More recently, the skills developed through this approach have migrated to stimulate a similar network focused on indigenous language processing in Africa.

Earlier in this chapter and in Chapter 2, we have referred to the dramatic and successful growth of the Research ICT Africa (RIA) network. In Chapter 7, the work of the PANACeA network is described. Starting small, but growing quickly, this network of researchers is focusing on research in support of eHealth innovations, especially in Asia. As the cost of live, in situ learning increases faster than the incomes of many in the developing world, IDRC has provided support to another group of partners involved with open universities and distance learning in the formation of PANdora. The work of the network is described in Chapter 8. This serves to reinforce the approach of supporting "partners, not projects" within this field. Of course, single purpose, one-off projects can also be useful. Many of the longer term networks supported by IDRC began this way and grew into much more substantial undertakings. Others had a much shorter life as they did not generate sufficient local and regional interest to attract scholars and researchers.

The approach to supporting long-term partnerships with developing world researchers saves time in the ramping up and winding down of projects and interorganizational relationships. Over the last decade, the ICT4D programming at IDRC was reliably there. While it began modestly and grew to significant proportions in the last decade, it was able to be an effective incubator for many new ideas and innovations in how ICTs can contribute to efficiency, transparency and productivity in development policy and practice.

How to Fund Research that Makes a Difference

As seen in the conclusion – and the book as a whole – IDRC's approach to supporting ICT4D research projects was likely as important as the funding it provided. Much of this relates to IDRC's mandate which, as stated in earlier sections, centers on research *for* development, rather than research *on* development. If the result of IDRC's support was a book that gathered dust on a shelf, we wouldn't be doing our job very well. IDRC's ICT4D program took a series of strategic decisions to help ensure that the research it supported made a positive difference to people's lives in developing countries. Those choices were taken in a context where tensions arose between, for instance, supporting more applied research on implementing ICT4D interventions vs. observing their socioeconomic impact, building local research capacity vs. simply working with Northern-based academics to produce academic journal articles and investing in applied or policy focused questions rather than more broadly academic ones. What follows is a more in-depth discussion on IDRC's approach in navigating those tensions to shed light on lessons that might be of use to others supporting research in this area.

How does one assess the feasibility or impact of a telecenter when telecenters don't exist? How do you assess the potential of computers in schools if no computers are present? How can you gauge the usefulness and cost-effectiveness of a mobile health information application when it's an idea on paper? The answer, for IDRC's ICT4D program, was, most often, to support applied or action research. Many of these research projects took the form of demonstration or pilot projects such as school networking, telecenters, telemedicine, e-government, community wireless setups and ISPs. As we've seen, these pilots yielded important benefits from building much needed local human resource capacity to demonstrating that an idea could work. They also, however, sometimes left communities with underfunded and unsustainable interventions. Moreover, these interventions didn't always offer empirically sound answers to the most pressing stakeholder questions: how do these interventions make a measurable difference to the communities that are meant to benefit from them?

Pilot studies were useful for answering questions related to technical feasibility, resource requirements or user access, adoption and usage. The development outcomes were also the ones you would generally expect: communities had greater access to technology, information and developed ICT skills. However, early demonstration projects weren't as effective in measuring what is often referred to as "downstream impacts" and questions such as: have these interventions lead to measurable improvements in livelihoods, empowerment, learning or health?

Supporting Research through Networks

In light of these challenges, IDRC chose to allocate many of its grants through research networks. Networks seemingly balanced opportunities to support technical innovations and policy outcomes while offering means to build research capacity and develop comparative and cross-case analysis platforms. Research networks, which generally supported a number of specific research institutions to conduct research in particular countries or regions, were also assumed to have certain advantages, especially when compared to supporting stand-alone projects or competitive calls. Exploring development questions that are relatively new was facilitated by networking with peers and was also deemed an important facet of building the capacities of Southern-based researchers to address these new issues. Additionally, the connections made, skills developed and research produced were expected to be sustained beyond the period of IDRC's support. An independent evaluation of research networks commissioned by IDRC, confirmed many of these assumptions about networks as a programming modality (Real and Wilson-Grau 2008). The evaluation suggested that research networks were successful at the following:

- Fostering knowledge sharing
- Enabling more scope for research activities
- Ensuring capacity building
- Developing resilience and risk mitigation through peer support and mentoring
- Facilitating changes in policies and practices

This book describes the principal networks that were formed: Research ICT Africa, DIRSI, LIRNE*asia*, PANACeA, Pan Localization, ANLoc, PANdora, OpenNet Asia, Privacy in Asia, OpenAir, OASIS, RED GEALC, LOGin, to name but a few. External reviews confirm these networks, comprising hundreds of researchers in several dozen developing countries, achieved outcomes related to generating useful knowledge, building research capacity and influencing policies. However, reviews also found that there was significant variance in the extent to which networks achieved these outcomes.

First, evaluations suggested that improvements could be made to the quality of research outputs, particularly those meant for the academic field. Research results were, at times, finding their way into global and local policy processes, but they were infrequently published in peer reviewed journals. As a result, IDRC developed a mix of strategies to improve upon this by developing peer mentorship arrangements between established experts in the field and emerging scholars. Research networks also took on more competitive approaches to identifying partners to conduct and form the network. Also, a program entitled SIRCA (Strengthening ICT Research Capacity Alliance), managed through Nanyang Technological University in Singapore, took on this task as well.

Second, although there were numerous instances of ICT4D research networks having contributed to policy reforms, these tended to be concentrated amongst a smaller subset of networks, mainly those focused on telecommunications policy reform. Evaluations pointed to a lack of support for research to policy or research uptake strategies within projects as one potential reason for this. To address this issue, IDRC brought in more systematic integration of budgets and strategies for research uptake activities within networks and created peer support activities that ensured partners were well versed in communications for policy influence could train others who were newer to the field.

Competitive Grants: Seeding Innovation?

Although IDRC's ICT4D program supported most of its research through networks, it also supported ICT4D activities through more traditional competitive granting calls as well. Competitive processes were used to support small grants to help identify new issues and partners and potentially solve more targeted development problems. Generally, they were used to seed technical innovations in ICT4D. Amongst the most important competitions were the Pan R&D grants program – which later became the Information Society Innovation Fund (ISIF), managed by the Asia Pacific Network Information Centre – and FRIDA – the Regional Fund for Digital Innovation in Latin America and the Caribbean, managed by the Latin America and Caribbean Internet Addresses Registry (LACNIC). These competitions comprised a small slice of IDRC's ICT4D program resources but, nevertheless, were useful in meeting certain objectives. The Pan R&D grants program, for instance, never formally had the intention to build the research field, influence policy or build research capacities and, true to their intent, they achieved little with respect to those goals. They were, above anything else, meant to seed innovation. Innovation is, however, quite difficult to measure. IDRC's ICT4D program has often grappled with challenge of demonstrating the extent to which competitive awards spurred innovation or made a difference from a local development perspective. Documenting international awards and recognition, as well as a few cases of applications going to scale, was a start, but there is still more that needs to be done.

IDRC's ICT4D program also developed and supported another competitive awards process, SIRCA, which is focused on building social science research skills. We have much clearer evidence of SIRCA's achievements in building research capacity due to the fact that it has built mentoring and monitoring into their activities. Emerging ICT4D scholars supported through this process published in peer reviewed journals and advanced in their academic careers. However, much like the innovation awards, SIRCA has limited outcomes in the area of policy or practice reforms.

Questions still remain for IDRC on the appropriate mix of modalities one should use to meet the myriad goals a development research funder sets out for itself: producing research that gets published in the highest ranking journals, developing evidence that leads to policy reforms or improved technological practices and building Southern research capacities. Unfortunately, these goals generally can't all be achieved using one approach. Nevertheless, for IDRC's ICT4D program, supporting research through networks helped achieve the best balance of results.

A New Era of ICT4D

ICTs in development catapulted onto the international development agenda at the onset of the new millennium. The G8 DotForce, the UNICT Task Force and two episodes of World Summits on the Information Society were institutional trampolines that ushered ICT and development in like a lion. Even more quickly it went out like a lamb. By the time the Arab Spring had erupted onto the world stage 8 years later with Facebook and Twitter figuring prominently in citizen mobilization and participation, ICTs were no longer central to development policy debates. The reality is that there is often a lag between donor priorities and the situation on the ground. ICTs have, essentially, been mainstreamed in developing countries. Many emerging economies have dedicated government budgets for ICT projects. Some are investing in their own massive ICT4D implementations, such as biometric ID systems in Argentina and India. The new forms of m-banking, eHealth and e-governance that have arisen in the global south are testament to the lasting effect that the policies, people and understanding of ICTs have secured. Moving forward, we can anticipate new innovations based on the near ubiquity of mobile telephony in the developing world.

But mobile telephony brings with it a new form of digital feudalism. The interoperability that characterized the first wave of digital adoption in the developed world – underpinned by the near ubiquity of a single DOS operating system – is nowhere to be found in the global south. The world of the mobile phone has formed into new digital, feudal enclaves among competing operating systems. Android, Apple, Windows, Blackberry and Nokia don't play easily with one another while their sponsors seek a "knock-out" punch that establishes a global standard for this or that version with digital serfdom the increasing result.

As we've shown in this book, digital technologies accelerate productivity and efficiency. Their impact in the developed world has been mixed. Critics point to a hollow new economy with a small number of high paying jobs at the top of the tech sector and very few in the low and middle. Much of that evolution stems from digital job migration from the global north to the global south. Is the developing world benefitting from this migration of digital jobs? What are the longer term consequences for the developing world of this kind of impact on their still developing economies and labor markets?

Just as worrisome, we can anticipate more invasive state surveillance of citizens and other related intrusions into people's lives and that of their communities. Governments may be late adopters but, now that they've figured it out, they could teach George Orwell a few tricks about life in a new digital world. The corporate world, as well, has learned to hone its marketing pitches based on what citizens do online. The classic "on the Internet, no one knows you're a dog" metaphor is long gone. Now, every key stroke online enters the world of metadata that those with the biggest budgets can use to shape how we live, buy and behave. Now on the Internet, everyone who wants to can know exactly what kind of dog we are.

The developing world need not be a repeat performance of what occurred in the postindustrial, mature economies of the North. Applied research for development in the global south can help guide the policy making process for a more beneficial, inclusive and sustainable future society and economy there.

There are many legacies to the important work chronicled in this volume. First are the hundreds of researchers who have come to incorporate ICTs and development as part of their professional specialization and competency. Equally important are the impressive number of research institutions – principally within universities and NGOs in the developing world – that have come to include ICT4D as a major theme for their work.

Perhaps most important are the actual changes in the progress of developing countries in which the work of IDRC's ICT4D partners made an observable and important contribution. Not many in the aid business get to see the actual changes they tried to bring to life and support. In the ICT4D field, we have. We continue to watch them grow and constructively affect people's lives. In the end, this is the real reward for the tremendous energy, dedication and imagination that helped the work described in the foregoing chapters succeed.

Notes

1 Figures taken from International Telecommunication Union (http://www.itu.int/ITU-D/ict/statistics/at_glance/keytelecom.html, accessed 1 June 2012).
2 For more on this, see R. Fuchs' "More Lemonade...!" at http://telecentreeurope.ning.com/profiles/blogs/more-lemonade-by-rich-fuchs (accessed 13 June 2012).
3 More detailed information provided at http://www.ignou.ac.in/ignou/aboutignou/profile/2 (accessed 2 June 2013).
4 For a more detailed description of this, see R. Fuchs' "It Is Liberated" at http://www.idrc.ca/EN/Resources/Publications/Pages/ArticleDetails.aspx?PublicationID=733 (accessed 1 June 2012).
5 Borrowing from theology, the author came to refer to Dr Purbo as a "Liberation Technologist"!

Reference

Real, M. J. and R. Wilson-Grau. 2008. *Formative Evaluation of PAN's Networking Approach.* Ottawa: Pan Asia Networking, IDRC.

Epilogue

INTO THE FUTURE: NEW OPPORTUNITIES AND THREATS IN A GLOBAL NETWORKED SOCIETY

Laurent Elder

As we've seen in the previous chapter and the book as a whole, information and communications technologies (ICTs) continue to transform developing countries by increasing people's access to services as well as stimulating economic growth. For example, Chapter 5 illustrated how mobile phones have greatly expanded opportunities for those living at the "bottom of the pyramid" (BOP) in developing countries. The chapter also shows that the positive social impacts of ICTs seem particularly strong in poverty-stricken contexts. Furthermore, the societal transformations linked to the accelerating pace of technological change suggest that the changes we will see in emerging network societies in the global south over the next 10 years will have even greater impacts than those of the previous decade.

ICTs have transformed the landscape of developing countries and opened up new opportunities for advancing human development. The increasing presence of these technologies is shifting developing countries toward a more highly networked society, where social structures and activities evolve around networks through ICTs. Almost 6 billion people use mobile phones. This includes much of the world's poorest, including nearly ninety percent of the poorest populations of Brazil, India, China and South Africa. Nearly two billion people access the Internet, most of them living in developing or emerging economies. Popular and continually evolving applications, often in the form of social media, are driving demand. This historic increase in access to the Internet and mobile phones opens up a series of unique and potentially transformative development opportunities.

"Open development," for instance, represents an emerging set of models to catalyze positive change (Smith et al. 2010). Chapter 3 on intellectual property rights (IPRs) described how openness is influencing the way people access knowledge and creating new business opportunities. Openness is also alluded to in the governance chapter as a significant aspect of transparency and accessibility issues that are important to the field of international development. New opportunities abound for openness to transform entire sectors of society:

- Open government advocates for more transparent, accessible and responsive government. This can be made possible through the release of government data on health, education, procurement or transport – to name just a few – in a digital format that allows citizens to use and reuse the data and create opportunities for both governments and citizens.

- Open learning initiatives where educational resources are freely shared on the Internet could improve access to and quality of educational resources and learning. MIT's Open CourseWare, which has been accessed over one hundred million times around the world, is perhaps the best-known illustration of this.
- Open business models could enable entrepreneurs to generate revenue through free and openly licensed content on the Web. A well-known example is *tecno brega* in Belém, Brazil, where artists forego traditional copyright and willingly share their creations with informal street vendors to market and distribute their music. Significant revenues, however, are realized through paid events, such as highly popular dance parties that bring in millions of dollars.
- Open science encourages transparency in experimental methodology, observation and collection of data. It is also concerned with the public availability and reusability of scientific data, the public accessibility and transparency of scientific communication and the use of web-based tools to facilitate scientific collaboration.

Another key opportunity relates to the mobile revolution that has already been described in the various chapters of this book. Research supported by the International Development Research Centre's (IDRC's) "Information and Communications Technologies for Development" (ICT4D) program confirms that mobiles play an important role in enhancing the lives of the poor, whether the mobiles are used to access banking services (m-banking) or learning materials (m-learning). More recent collaborative mobile applications illustrate their value as tools that enable more participatory action around development issues. In Accra, Ghana, for example, taxi drivers' mobiles were coupled with CO_2 sensing devices that map air quality in real time on the Internet.

Many researchers and journalists also point to how blogging, Facebook and Twitter helped people express their views, organize and communicate during the recent events in Egypt and Tunisia. Other innovative applications have also contributed to new ways of getting things done. Ushahidi, a tool that can deliver crisis information, was initially developed to map reports of violence in Kenya after the 2008 post-election fallout. It allows anyone to gather distributed mobile data and visualize it on a map or timeline, which essentially translates technical information into a form that anyone can understand. This open source platform has been adopted and deployed over 12,000 times across the world for a wide variety of problems.

Challenges in an Increasingly Networked World

Although changes brought on by a networked society can open up opportunities for development, they might also lead to certain development problems. For instance, if "going digital" is increasingly the norm to access social services or to gain competitive advantage, those without access will be further excluded from such benefits. In many developing countries, women are underrepresented in the production and consumption of digital products. Moreover, power, gendered and social relationships within societies are often replicated and reflected in the virtual world, which could create new forms of exclusion. The open source community, for instance, has been perceived as being male dominated.

The Internet greatly reduces the transaction costs for digital copying and also allows for infinite reproduction. As a consequence, certain industries (especially creative ones like music, publishing or movies) are dramatically changing through widespread piracy or the creation of new business models. The socioeconomic ramifications of these transformations are still unclear. Are there more or fewer opportunities for innovation, employment and revenue generation in these industries as a result of the growth of digital media? Are there new forms of exploitation and who suffers from it?

As described in Chapter 3, intellectual property laws are crucial to this evolving environment. They determine who uses and controls the most important assets of networked societies: technology and knowledge. The traditional assumption has been that greater IP protection yields greater development. In reality, these relationships have become increasingly complex in networked economies. Google, Apple and eBay derive much of their value from flexibilities in IP laws. As a result, the "fair-use economy" in the United States, which depends on the limitations to copyright protection, is estimated to be worth US$4.7 trillion. Similar trends affect the developing world. Nevertheless, international IP agreements have been slow to respond to these trends.

Moreover, as discussed in Chapter 9 on governance, ICTs can be perceived as a liberating force. However, some point to the fact that authoritarian states are exploiting the benefits of technology to consolidate their positions of power. Censorship is rampant in cyberspace and extends far beyond "the great firewall of China". Following protests in 2009, the Iranian government was able to capture data from mobiles and social media to crack down on protesters. And, during the recent Tunisian protests, the Tunisian government allegedly created fake Facebook, Twitter and Gmail sites so that unwitting protesters would log on to their government-controlled imitations.

Related to this, the greater prevalence of social media, video surveillance, biometric identity scanners or radio frequency identification (RFID) tags leads to growing concerns about the enhanced surveillance capabilities of the state or corporations. This is especially troubling in an age where computers are able to permanently store records of virtually everything. The worry is that information could be used for illegal purposes or to curtail rights and freedoms generally associated with privacy. India provides a telling example, where the government in 2011 proposed a biometric digital process for its 15th census. The use of ID schemes in other countries reveals a history of abuse, including genocide and lesser forms of discrimination and oppression. India, with its history of ethnic and religious violence, could share the same fate if it proceeds without precautions.

IDRC's Role in this Agenda: Information and Networks Program

In sum, the various chapters identified a number of trends that were deemed important for the future role of ICTs in development. One of the most notable themes is the explosive growth of mobiles, which continues to make digital access less challenging and, as a result, opens up new forms of access to information and ways for people to collaborate. Phenomena such as free access to research results and educational or government resources, online crowd sourcing and Ushahidi have, in a few years, gone from being largely irrelevant to having a demonstrable impact on development. Nevertheless, although much of the research highlighted in this book has illustrated the empowering potential of ICTs, evidence from other IDRC-supported projects (for example, the Open Net Initiative) suggests that the growing prevalence of ICTs is facilitating the curtailment of individual rights to freedom of expression, privacy and collective action in the developing world. The Gender Research for African Community Empowerment (GRACE) network expressed concern about the extent to which women who are marginalized are able to productively take part in emerging networked societies. The most recent external evaluations of IDRC's ICT4D programs also suggested that, because of the increasing importance of networked technologies in all facets of society, it will be essential to take an integrated interdisciplinary approach to study the increasing role of information networks in development and their impact on socioeconomic inclusion. ICTs have created new ways of knowing and experiencing the world – new power asymmetries. As a result, new epistemologies and innovative methodologies are required to understand how these shifts contribute to trends and tipping points, possibly even changes in power relationships.

In light of the above, IDRC will continue to play a critical role in contributing to the field of ICTs through mainstreamed ICT research in health, agriculture, state accountability and legitimacy, climate change and economics. Yet, the recent external evaluations also indicated that important emerging networked society policy issues – such as digital openness, privacy, censorship and intellectual property rights – have increasingly significant implications across programming areas and merit a consolidated research approach. Consequently, to respond to the evaluations' recommendation, IDRC developed a networked society program –Information and Networks (I&N) – that supports critical Southern perspectives to better understand and catalyze inclusive and beneficial uses of open and networked platforms enabled by the Internet and mobiles.

The program focuses on three principal areas: (i) the enhanced quality of openness that networked technologies enable; (ii) the protection of citizens', consumers' and prosumers' rights; and (iii) the inclusion of marginalized communities in the benefits of information networks.

The enhanced quality of openness

The emergence of the networked society is particularly powerful because it has played a role in reducing the transaction costs of knowledge creation, communication and distribution. Knowledge, a key input to human development processes, has traditionally been a high-cost product, particularly for the majority of those in the developing world (Benkler 2006). However, digital information can now be accessed, produced, used, reused and shared around the world at little cost. In addition, new ways of organizing and producing are emerging (Benkler 2006; Shirky 2008). For instance, "Commons-based" production methods describe collaborative efforts, such as free and open source software and Wikipedia, which are based on the sharing of information. These collaborative processes have spread significantly in the realms of the creative economy, science, government and learning (Lemos and Mizukami 2008). Finally, the increased ability to communicate also enables new forms of collective action toward a common goal. An Ushahidi implementation in Mexico, *Cuidamos el Voto*, enabled citizens to report incidences of fraud in the electoral process that resulted in 335 official investigations (Ramey 2009). Also, social media like Facebook and Twitter may make it easier to act collectively and affect social change, as the recent events in the Middle East appear to indicate.

IDRC's programmatic position on openness touches on two aspects. First, it is the content available on information networks. Second, it is the means that people use to connect, share, organize and produce on information networks. Although, as we have discussed above, the quantity of openness has increased over the past few decades, the goal will be to enhance the quality of openness and how information's quality can be enhanced to ensure it achieves its development outcomes.

Examples of potential research questions for this area could include: what are effective mechanisms for the collaborative production of open educational resources in the global south? How are creative entrepreneurs in developing regions making use of open business models to create vibrant, dynamic and knowledge-intensive services and industries? How can open access to research findings and data enhance the production, uptake and quality of research outputs? What types of ICT-enabled models could best support innovative ways of collecting data and what are the effects on research quality, ethics and impact?

The protection of citizens', consumers' and prosumers' rights

A number of human rights have been identified as closely linked to the Internet. These rights include freedom of expression; the right to information, data protection, and privacy; and freedom of association. Although the expansion of networked societies can help promote citizens', consumers' and prosumers' rights, as well as expand their capabilities and freedoms, these same technologies can also be used to curtail them. For example, the potential of networked technologies to support freedom of expression and association is debatable (Deibert et al. 2010). The recent events in Egypt and Tunisia speak to the potential of networked technologies to facilitate collective action to bring about social change (Shirky 2011). Yet, others question the role social media has in stimulating effective collective action (Morozov 2011). For the latter, the expansion of networked societies can also restrict these rights – in particular, through the chilling effects of ubiquitous surveillance. For example, authoritarian states can exploit the benefits of technology to consolidate their positions of power.

In addition to these issues, an expanding networked society also highlights the need to have an appropriate IPR regime. Copyrights and patents are generally considered important policy tools to boost access to information, creativity and innovation. However, the expansion of strong IPRs in the developing world, which has emerged in response to rampant piracy, potentially threatens entrepreneurial innovation and the ability to access knowledge for learning and creativity (Karaganis 2011; Kenny 2011).

Examples of potential research questions for this area could include: what is the right balance among the IPRs of creators, distributors and consumers in networked societies?

Which data protection regulations help or hinder the protection of privacy? How are digital technologies being used in developing countries to expand pluralism and freedom?

The inclusion of marginalized communities in the benefits of information networks

Although there are many benefits emerging from the expansion of information networks, these benefits are not equitably distributed, particularly in the developing world. For instance, marginalized communities and groups are often excluded from these benefits based on a variety of factors, including their socioeconomic position, gender and education. A study in Bangalore illustrates this point as the government's digitization of land records led to a land capture by rich and empowered Indians; India's elites took advantage of the open data instead of the members of the poor and disempowered groups for which the opening of the data had been intended (Benjamin et al. 2007). This example demonstrates that networked societies might actually exacerbate exclusion and reinforce existing power asymmetries as opposed to eradicating them as the initial purveyors of these applications often assume (Gurumurthy 2009).

To determine ways of addressing this issue, IDRC's I&N program will seek to improve the possibilities of marginalized communities' economic and social participation by investigating issues of socioeconomic integration, creativity, entrepreneurship and their relationship to emerging networked societies. Currently, the vast majority of new connections to mobiles and the Internet occur among the urban poor, a trend that is projected to continue. Therefore, the frontier of socioeconomic exclusion and inclusion in emerging networked societies is in urban spaces (Qiu 2009). In Rio, Beijing, Delhi and Cairo, many disadvantaged groups move from exclusion to inclusion or from vulnerability to resilience and digital technologies (particularly mobiles) are playing an increasing role in this movement. Studying the phenomenon of moving from unconnected to connected in urban spaces may be the best way to catalyze inclusive networked societies. As the poor and marginalized in various urban settings develop innovative ways to access and use technologies, they can be documented and replicated elsewhere. For example, prepaid mobile phone subscriptions were essentially an innovation developed to meet the needs of poorer consumers who did not have regular monthly incomes. Yet this innovation is one of the main reasons mobiles are now ubiquitous.

Examples of potential research questions in this area include: how are the urban poor using ICTs to improve their situation? In what contexts are the urban poor benefitting or not from these tools? What policies or regulations would be most apt to facilitate the urban poor's sharing in the benefits of ICTs in learning, entrepreneurial activities and civic empowerment?

References

Benjamin, S. et al. 2007. "Bhoomi: 'E-Governance' or an Anti-politics Machine Necessary to Globalize Bangalore?" CASUM-m working paper. Online: http://casumm.files.wordpress. com/2008/09/bhoomi-e-governance.pdf (accessed 23 July 2013).

Benkler, Y. 2006. *The Wealth of Networks: How Social Production Transforms Markets and Freedom.* New Haven: Yale University Press.

Deibert, R., ed. 2010. *Access Controlled: The Shaping of Power, Rights, and Rule in Cyberspace.* Cambridge, MA: MIT Press.

Gurumurthy, A. 2009. *Social Enterprise to Mobiles – The Curious Case of a Propped Up ICTD Theory.* Publius Project at the Berkman Center for Internet & Society. Cambridge, MA: Harvard University. Online: http://publius.cc/social_enterprise_mobiles_%E2%80%93_curious_case_propped_ictd_theory/091709 (accessed 29 July 2013).

Karaganis, J., ed. 2011. *Media Piracy in Emerging Economies.* New York: Social Science Research Council.

Kenny, C. 2011. "Mickey Mouse, Villain: How Copyrights for US Cartoons are Holding the Developing World Hostage." *Foreign Policy* (March/April 2011) Online: http://www.foreignpolicy.com/articles/2011/02/22/mickey_mouse_villain (accessed 23 July 2013).

Lemos, R. and P. N. Mizukami. 2008. "From Free Software to Free Culture: The Emergence of Open Business." Fundaçao Getulio Vargas. Online: http://bibliotecadigital.fgv.br/dspace/handle/10438/2674 (accessed 25 July 2013).

Morozov, E. 2011. *The Net Delusion: How Not to Liberate the World.* London: Allen Lane.

Qiu, J. L. 2009. "Life and Death in the Chinese Informational City: The Challenges of Working-Class ICTs and the Information Have-Less." In *Living the Information Society in Asia,* edited by E. Alampay. Ottawa: IDRC. Online: http://www.idrc.ca/openebooks/453-6/ (accessed 23 July 2013).

Ramey, C. 2009. "Mexicans Report Votes (and Non-votes) with SMS." MobileActive.org. Online: http://mobileactive.org/mexicans-report-votes-and-nonvotes-sms (accessed 1 August 2013).

Shirky, C. 2008. *Here Comes Everybody: The Power of Organizing without Organizations.* New York: Penguin Press.

_____. 2011. "The Political Power of Social Media." *Foreign Affairs* (January/February). Online: http://www.foreignaffairs.com/articles/67038/clay-shirky/the-political-power-of-social-media (accessed 24 July 2013).

Smith, M. et al. 2010. "Open Development: A New Theory for ICT4D." *Information Technologies and International Development* 7, no. 1: iii–ix.

AUTHOR BIOGRAPHIES

Editors

Laurent Elder was the program leader of IDRC's Pan Asia program and now leads IDRC's Information and Networks program studying the impacts of emerging networked societies in the developing world, including how the Internet or mobile phones help foster development outcomes in learning, governance, entrepreneurship and science. He is co-author of various articles on the relationship between information and communications technologies (ICTs) and development, such as "Open Development: A New Theory of ICT4D" in *Information Technology & International Development*; "Past, Present and Future: Experiences and Lessons from Telehealth Projects" in *Open Medicine*; and "Mobile Phones and Development: An Analysis of IDRC-Supported Projects" in *EJISDC*.

Heloise Emdon was the program leader of two IDRC programs: Acacia – ICTs for Development (Africa) and Innovation for Inclusive Development (global). Heloise has over two decades of experience in ICTs and communications for social and economic development. She began her career in cooperative scientific programs at CSIR in South Africa and worked for a decade as a journalist before joining the Development Bank of Southern Africa in 1990 and IDRC in 2002. She has contributed to *Long-Term Solutions for a Short-Term World: Canada and Research Development*, edited by R. Harpelle and B. Muirhead (2011) and *Open Development: A New Theory for ICT4D* (2011). Her blog on ICTs for development can be found at http://mayafrica.wordpress.com/.

Richard Fuchs, guest editor, has worked on ICTs and development for over twenty-five years and was IDRC's first director of Information and Communications Technologies for Development, 2001–2006. During his tenure, ICT4D programming grew with major new externally funded initiatives. His consultancy, Futureworks Consulting Inc., won Canada's Export Excellence Award in 2001, principally for his work with telecenters in Africa and Asia. In 2011, he received the Lifetime Achievement Award for his work. His recent publications include *The New Digital Divergence* and "So *Few Lessons Learned: Quality Assurance in Training for the Global Telecentre Movement*.

Ben Petrazzini was the program leader of IDRC's Connectivity and Equity in the Americas program, a senior policy advisor for the International Telecommunication Union, and its representative to the United Nations. He holds a doctorate in communications from the University of California, San Diego, was assistant professor at the Hong Kong University of Science and Technology, was an advisor to the National Congress of Argentina and taught at the National University of Buenos Aires. He has published extensively on issues related ICTs in developing countries and is currently a member of IDRC's Supporting Inclusive Growth program.

Contributors

Sara Bannerman is an assistant professor at McMaster University, conducting research in the areas of intellectual property and communications. She worked with the Acacia and Pan Asia Networking (PAN) programs in summer 2007.

Katie Bryant-Moetele is a doctoral student in McGill University's Department of Integrated Studies in Education, focusing on university students and faculty members' writing practices, specifically in a southern African context. She has been coordinator of Carleton University's Writing Centre, an intern at IDRC, a lecturer at Carleton University and the University of Botswana and currently works as a consultant with the Botswana–University of Pennsylvania partnership, researching medical students' writing practices.

Alioune Camara was a senior program officer working from IDRC's West Africa regional office. With over seventeen years of experience, he managed research on ICTs for economic and social development in the West Africa. His areas of expertise include ICTs for good governance and the integration of ICTs into African schools and in the informal sector of the economy and society. His educational background is in international public law and information sciences.

Florencio Ceballos is an expert on citizen participation and ICTs as tools for development of poor and marginalized communities. His focus now is on how technology helps communities to redefine the quality and accountability of governance and states. Before joining IDRC in 2005, he was director of research at Ekhos I+C Consultants, bringing ICT-based development opportunities to marginalized communities. Ceballos is a doctoral candidate in political sociology at École des Hautes Études en Sciences Sociales, Paris.

Jeremy de Beer is a law professor at the University of Ottawa, specializing in technology innovation, intellectual property and international development. He teaches, among other things, courses on global intellectual property policy and social justice, and intellectual property and sustainable development. His recent publications include *Access to Knowledge in Africa: The Role of Copyright* and *Implementing the World Intellectual Property Organization's Development Agenda*.

Kathleen Diga has worked as a research officer with IDRC's Acacia ICT4D Africa program based in Nairobi and Johannesburg. She is currently a research project manager at the University of KwaZulu-Natal, Durban, South Africa. She is also a doctoral candidate in the Institute for Social Development at the University of the Western Cape, South Africa, undertaking research in the area of poverty and ICT4D.

Sarah Earl worked with IDRC's Evaluation Unit for 12 years. While at IDRC, she was a co-creator of outcome mapping and worked very closely with ICT4D programs and projects. She champions evaluation for development and supports people to use evaluation to improve their effectiveness. She holds master's degrees in European- and Russian-area studies from Carleton University in Ottawa, and in Russian history from the University of Toronto.

Tara Fischer works as the advocacy and communications coordinator for a Canadian NGO, encouraging federal public policy solutions to national and international human rights issues. She was the 2010 summer student for IDRC's Pan and Acacia programs and worked on municipal public policy issues in Ottawa. She holds a bachelor's degree in international development from the University of Guelph and a master's degree in social work from Carleton University.

Khaled Fourati is a senior program officer at IDRC. His areas of expertise are southern Africa, ICT4D, intellectual property rights and access to knowledge, telecom policy and regulation, national research and education networking and open access. He has also worked on research related to trade, employment and competitiveness. He holds an MBA in finance and computer information systems and a master's degree in international affairs.

Dominique Garro-Strauss is a program management officer at IDRC, currently in the area of social and economic policy and with previous experience in the Global Health Policy and ICT4D programs. Prior to joining IDRC, she worked at several international organizations and NGOs headquartered in Paris. She holds a master's degree in international affairs with a specialization in development from the Institut d'Études Politiques de Paris.

Raymond Hyma is a research communication advisor for migration and resettlement issues at York University. He formerly served as a program management officer with the Information and Communications Technologies for Development (ICT4D) and Science and Innovation programs at IDRC. Raymond holds a master's degree in international relations from Universidad del Salvador (Argentina) and a bachelor's degree in political science, Latin American studies, from Simon Fraser University.

Maria Ng served as an IDRC staff member from March 1976 to July 2012. She was a specialist program officer in ICTs in IDRC's Pan Asia Networking and Information and Networks programs. She holds master's degrees in information sciences and in education. She is currently continuing her commitment to the field of Asian development by engaging in local and regional advisory services.

Ahmed T. Rashid is a program management officer at IDRC, interested in social, economic and political dimensions of development. He has written on issues of political democracy and decentralization, the role of NGOs and business in development, and the use of ICTs for development (ICT4D). He holds a master's degree in sociology from McMaster University.

Alicia Richero was based in Montevideo, Uruguay as senior program officer in the area of ICT4D in the IDRC Latin America and the Caribbean Regional Office until August 2009. Currently retired, Alicia Richero is an independent consultant on ICTs and education, gender and social impacts of the use of technologies. She also mentors several research works of awardees in ICT projects and works as a Spanish/English translator, reviewer and editor.

Chaitali Sinha is a senior program officer at IDRC with experience in research on social systems in developing countries, particularly with respect to global health. This includes examining how health information systems can be designed and implemented to strengthen governance and contribute to more equitable health systems. She holds a master's degree in international affairs, a bachelor's degree in management information systems and is currently taking graduate courses in global health.

Matthew L. Smith is a senior program officer at IDRC. Smith oversees research on how information networks can be used to promote open, inclusive and rights-based information societies in the South. He has published on open development, ICT4D and information systems research, among other topics. Smith holds a doctorate in information systems from the London School of Economics (LSE) and master's degrees in development studies (LSE) and artificial intelligence (University of Edinburgh).

Frank Tulus, a senior program officer, joined IDRC in 1998 and has more than ten years of experience in the ICT4D sector in Asia and Africa. He currently oversees research on the impact of technology on society and how its innovative use can lead to a more inclusive knowledge society. He holds a bachelor's degree in sociology and psychology from the University of Ottawa and a master's degree in collaborative international development studies from the University of Guelph.

Ahmed T. Rashid is a program management officer at IDRC interested in social, economic and political dimensions of development. He has written on issues of political democracy and decentralization, the role of NGOs and business in development, and the use of information and communications technologies for development (ICT4D). He holds a master's degree in sociology from McMaster University.

John-Harmen Valk worked as a summer intern with IDRC's Acacia and Pan Asia Networking (PAN) program initiatives. He is a doctoral candidate in the School of International Relations at the University of St Andrews, Scotland, undertaking research in the area of international political theory.

Printed in the USA
CPSIA information can be obtained
at www.ICGtesting.com
JSHW021436221024
72172JS00002B/17

9 781783 082537